The s

A factfile ...ng renewal policies i...

Second e...

Kerry Revell a...

The POLICY
PRESS

First published in Great Britain in November 2000 by

The Policy Press
34 Tyndall's Park Road
Bristol BS8 1PY
UK

Tel no +44 (0)117 954 6800
Fax no +44 (0)117 973 7308
E-mail tpp@bristol.ac.uk
www.policypress.org.uk

Published for the Joseph Rowntree Foundation by The Policy Press

ISBN 1 86134 228 4

Kerry Revell is Research Assistant, and **Philip Leather** is Professor of Housing and Urban Renewal, both at the Centre for Urban and Regional Studies, University of Birmingham.

The **Joseph Rowntree Foundation** has supported this project as part of its programme of research and innovative development projects, which it hopes will be of value to policy makers, practitioners and service users. The facts presented and views expressed in this report are, however, those of the authors and not necessarily those of the Foundation.

Cover design by Qube Design Associates, Bristol
Printed in Great Britain by Hobbs the Printers Ltd, Southampton

Contents

List of tables, figures and maps

Tables

Figures

Maps

Acknowledgements

A large number of people and organisations have provided assistance with data used in the preparation of this report. Anne Kirkham and Terry McIntyre from the Department of the Environment in England provided access to data on housing conditions, renewal areas and group repair. We are also grateful to Ian Parker and Peter Shibbs for providing data on grant activity in England. Brendon Hilbourne, and Ed Swires-Hennessy at the Welsh Office, Katrina Lloyd at the Northern Ireland Housing Executive, and Jennifer Waterton and Robert Spratt at Scottish Homes were also extremely helpful in providing access to house condition survey data and information on progress with grants, demolitions and other indicators including much unpublished material.

Much of the information on local levels of demolitions, grant provision, and investment in the public and housing association sectors comes from official sources such as *Local Housing Statistics* and *Housing and Construction Statistics* published by HMSO and we gratefully acknowledge the value of these sources.

Many tables, figures and maps in this report make use of data from the 1996 English, 1996 Scottish, 1996 Northern Ireland, and 1993 and 1998 Welsh House Condition Surveys. Data for England, Scotland, and Northern Ireland was mainly produced by the authors from original survey data supplied by the Department of the Environment, Scottish Homes, and the Northern Ireland Housing Executive. Much of the data has not been previously published, but in a small number of instances, there are small differences between the figures in this report and those in the published survey reports which arise from differences in the bases which tables use, adjustments to weightings, the treatment of missing values, or rounding. Responsibility for the figures in this report lies with the authors and not with the organisations which provided access to the survey data.

Foreword

Although problems of homelessness rightly attract our attention because those affected need immediate help, the condition of a significant proportion of the UK housing stock is also an important problem which is all too often overlooked. Living in sub-standard housing is not just a miserable experience for those affected – there is increasing evidence of links between poor housing and poor health, especially for children and older or disabled people who spend more time than average in their homes. Poor conditions can also mean danger – from faulty wiring or steep stairs – or social stigma – especially for children – with all the related effects. Poor housing can also inhibit attempts to regenerate an area economically and socially. Sub-standard conditions thus deserve a high priority in our attempts to tackle housing and broader social and economic problems.

The nature of house condition problems varies across the UK. In Scotland, the national House Condition Survey has identified dampness as a key issue. Scotland's legacy of tenement housing also brings with it particular challenges when it comes to persuading a multiplicity of owners to get together to repair common elements such as roofs. In Northern Ireland, as in Scotland, some of the worst conditions are found in remote rural dwellings without access to modern services and amenities. Rural housing problems are also found in Wales, but the immense task of regenerating housing in the Valleys also exists, much of it presenting a structural challenge and often being in the ownership of older people on very low incomes. In England, the sheer scale of the task of renovating the pre-1919 terraced stock in the centres of the larger cities and towns in former mining areas can seem daunting. In some areas, an underlying lack of demand is leading to high levels of vacancy which in turn leads to a rapid deterioration in physical conditions. Concerns about some of the interwar stock, and even some postwar dwellings, are also emerging throughout the UK.

The Joseph Rowntree Foundation concerns itself with a wide range of housing and social problems and has identified poor housing conditions and housing renewal policies as one of its priorities. It recently published the report *Crumbling castles? Helping owners to repair and maintain their homes* (Leather, 2000) which set out the findings of a programme of research on housing renewal and set out the framework for a wide-ranging review of policy in this area. To provide a background to this work and to produce a consistent picture of problems and policies across the UK as a basis for debate on appropriate policy solutions, the Foundation also supported the preparation of this report, which is a comprehensive update of an earlier edition, published in 1997. It is disappointing to report that there is little overall evidence of an improvement in housing conditions over the intervening period, which makes it all the more important to develop effective policies which will make a real impact on the problems.

This report concerns itself with house conditions in all tenures. It draws together data from the four national house condition surveys and a wealth of other sources and aims to present a historical perspective on both the problems and the policies. It includes a great deal of local data which local authorities, housing associations and other organisations will find useful in comparing their problems and policy responses with other areas. Given the growing importance of private investment in dealing with sub-standard housing, the report also devotes attention to the work which people fund for themselves and the contribution which this makes to tackling poor housing problems.

The state of UK housing is essential reading to all those with an interest in or concern about the condition of the nation's housing stock. At the beginning of the 21st century, we still have a great deal of housing which belongs to the century before last in terms of the conditions it provides to its occupants. I hope that the report will contribute to the urgent task of finding ways to increase investment to ensure that the housing stock of the 21st century is something we can be proud of.

Raymond Young
Chair of Overview Group, Joseph Rowntree Foundation
Research Programme on Poor Housing Conditions and
Housing Renewal in the Private Sector

Executive summary

Poor housing conditions in the UK

Although there have been frequent national surveys of housing conditions in England, Scotland, Wales and Northern Ireland, there is no overall source of information on poor housing conditions covering the whole of the UK nor any single source of data on measures to deal with these problems. This report aims to fill that gap and to raise awareness of housing condition problems across the UK. It updates the previous edition of *The state of UK housing* (Leather and Morrison, 1997) to take account of the 1996 round of national house condition surveys and including preliminary results from the 1998 Welsh survey.

The measurement of poor housing conditions is a difficult and complex task but the variety of definitions used in national surveys, differences in the way surveyors are briefed, and variations in how repair costs are estimated make comparisons between countries in the UK impossible. Further difficulties arise due to different timings of the House Condition Surveys. The data in this report cannot be used to definitavely argue that conditions are worse in any part of the UK than another.

Unfit dwellings or dwellings below the tolerable standard

In 1996, some 1,455,000 occupied dwellings in the UK were either unfit for human habitation or below the Scottish tolerable standard (BTS). This represented about 6% or one in 16 dwellings in the UK in 1996. The level of unfitness was highest in Wales where 8.5% of dwellings were unfit. The proportion of dwellings lacking one or more basic amenities follows a similar pattern with Wales again having the most severe problem.

Lack of facilities for food preparation is the main reason for unfitness in England, Wales and Northern Ireland, whereas the main reason for BTS in Scotland is dampness.

Disrepair

Problems of disrepair are more widespread than unfitness, with almost one in a third dwellings in England having urgent repair costs of more than £1,000 in 1996. In Scotland, the proportion of dwellings with repair costs over £3,000 was nearly 30%. In Northern Ireland, 14% of dwellings had repair costs over £3,000. In Wales 23% of dwellings had repair costs over £1,000 and 4% had costs in excess of £5,000. Differences in repair standards preclude any comparisons between countries.

The pattern of unfitness/BTS

Unfitness is by no means evenly distributed. Areas with high levels of unfitness included large parts of rural Wales and Scotland, and rural or industrial districts in the North of England, particularly in the North West (Blackburn, Hyndburn, Allerdale, St Helens, Burnley, Wirral Liverpool), and a group of cities or industrial areas in the Midlands. Very few areas in the South had high unfitness levels. The area south of the Wash–Bristol Channel line stands out clearly as an area with below average unfitness levels compared with Wales and the north of England.

In Scotland, the problem of poor conditions in rural areas is prominent, with Eilean Siar (previously the Western Isles) the most significant with 26% of privately-owned stock being BTS. Argyll and Bute, Orkney and Inverclyde have over 10%of their privately-owned stock below standard. Glasgow also shows a very high level of private sector dwellings BTS (7.5%) but the equivalent figure for Edinburgh is much lower (3%). The proportion of dwellings which were unfit was similar in urban and rural areas in England and Wales, but in Scotland and Northern Ireland levels of rural unfitness/BTS were markedly higher.

Trends in house condition

Trends in house condition are difficult to assess because of differences in the interpretation of standards and changes in the definition of house condition indicators between surveys. The number of dwellings lacking one or more basic amenities has shown a clear and consistent decline over time, but trends in unfitness/BTS and disrepair are less clear, partly as a result of changes to standards. In England there was probably a reduction in unfitness and disrepair over the 1986-91 period as rising house prices encouraged owners to invest, but 1996 survey results show very little reduction in the rate of unfitness. In Northern Ireland and Scotland there was some improvement between 1991 and 1996, as there was in Wales between 1993 and 1998.

Housing conditions and the dwelling stock

Poor housing conditions are closely related to the age of the dwelling stock. The post-1964 stock has the lowest level of unfitness/BTS in all cases, and the proportion of dwellings in each age band which are unfit increases steadily with age before rising sharply for the pre-1919 stock. However, there are significant levels of unfitness in the interwar stock in Wales and Scotland.

In England, converted flats and terraced houses are the most likely types of dwellings to be unfit. In Wales, terraced houses also stand out as the most likely type of dwelling to be in poor condition. In Scotland, converted flats are the most likely to be in poor condition, although tenements also have relatively high repair costs. In Northern Ireland, converted flats are the most problematic, as well as detached dwellings in rural areas.

Dwellings in poor condition by tenure

Vacant dwellings are the most likely to be in poor condition, but in the occupied stock the private rented sector has the highest proportion of dwellings in poor condition throughout the UK. In the remaining stock, conditions vary, but the greater size of the owner-occupied stock means that in numerical terms the majority of occupied unfit dwellings are found in this sector.

People living in poor conditions

People on low incomes are more likely to live in poor housing conditions. In England for example, more than one in 10,000 with an income of less than £4,000 per annum lived in unfit dwellings compared with only one in 24 of those with an income of £24,000 or more. At least three quarters of those living in unfit housing or housing in serious disrepair had incomes below £12,000 in 1996. However, there is still a minority of more affluent households living in poor conditions, especially in England.

The types of household which experience poor conditions are very similar throughout the UK. Older people, and younger people just starting their housing careers, are the groups most likely to live in poor conditions, with middle-aged people generally better housed. Within older age groups the tendency to live in poor conditions becomes greater as age increases, particularly after 80 years old. In England the proportion of households living in unfit housing rises from 4.3% for households headed by a person aged between 60 and 64 to 10.3% for households headed by a person aged 85 or more.

Households headed by women are more likely to experience unfit housing conditions in all age bands, with the highest proportion in the 30-44 age group. Data on ethnic origin and poor housing conditions is only available for England and Scotland. In both countries households with a head from a minority ethnic community were generally more likely to live in poor conditions than those from the white community.

Tackling poor housing conditions

Clearance

The level of demolition has declined sharply from more than 80,000 dwellings per annum in the early 1970s to 4,200 in 1992, and to only just over 1,000 in 1997, an annual replacement rate of less than one in every 23,000 dwellings. The present level of clearance is widely regarded by professionals as too low but with a high proportion of older houses in individual ownership it is both difficult and expensive to implement clearance programmes. Any sustained recovery in demolition levels would require the provision of additional capital resources.

Grants to owners

Provision of capital grants to assist home owners with improvement, repair and adaptation to their homes reached a peak in the 1982-84 period when almost 300,000 grants per annum were provided across the UK. In England, provision has subsequently fallen to only about 60,000 per annum in the early 1990s, but the most recent figures show that the number of grants has dropped further, to 35,000, in 1997. In Wales the decline from the mid-1980s has been less pronounced. In Scotland provision has also fallen from the 60,000 grants provided in 1984 to a steady level of 20,000 per annum until 1995, but has since decreased steadily since then to about 13,000 in 1998. In Northern Ireland there was a high level of grant provision throughout the 1980s but in the 1990s this fell to around 7,000 per annum. Currently the number of grants is only about one third of the early 1980s level.

Setting these levels of provision against the size of the housing stock reveals that until the late 1980s investment levels in Northern Ireland generally exceeded those elsewhere in the UK. After a slow start, the number of grants in Scotland per 1,000 privately owned dwellings increased rapidly in the late 1970s and has generally remained above the level in England or Wales. Grant provision in Wales has exceeded that in England and in the late 1980s became comparable with Scotland and Northern Ireland. In England, provision has remained consistently the lowest. As a result Glasgow, Belfast and Cardiff have received far higher levels of investment than many comparable cities in England.

Authorities with the highest rates of grant provision overall are predominantly Welsh including both urban and rural districts. In England the majority of authorities with high levels of provision are rural and few large urban authorities have given a large number of grants relative to the size of their stock. Data for Scotland at local authority level is not available for

an extended period, but, in recent years, rural areas in north Scotland such as Eilean Siar, Orkney and Shetland provided the highest number of grants per 1,000 dwellings, followed by some of the larger cities such as Aberdeen, Glasgow and Dundee.

Dealing with adaptations

In 1996, total grant provision for equipment and adaptations in the UK through disabled facilities grants, minor works assistance, and improvement grants amounted to £109 million. Spending fell in real terms in the early 1990s, but in 1994 rose again to an all-time high. Other sources of spending on equipment and adaptations include social services (an estimated £75 million in 1994/95) and capital and revenue spending by local authorities and housing associations on their own stock (£126 million). There is no spatial pattern to the distribution of authorities active in the provision of disabled facilities grants.

The size of grants provided

There is a perception that grant levels have risen sharply since the introduction of the new system in 1990. In real terms, however, the increase has been less dramatic, at least in England. Average grant values rose from about £4,000 in 1979 (at 1993/94 prices) to almost £8,000 in the mid-1980s, peaking at about £10,000 in 1994 under the new system. Since 1994 the average grant value has fallen to £8,500 in 1997. In Wales, however, the average increased more rapidly after 1990 to £18,000 in 1994, but as in England this average value has fallen in 1997 to £4,500. In Scotland, where the old system remained in place, grant values have also increased but more steadily, rising from about £3,500 in 1979 to £7,500 in 1990. In Scotland the average grant value reduced considerably in 1997 to £5,000. In part, the initial increases in average grant levels under the new system were due to the higher effective grant percentages paid under the new system in England and Wales. On average, renovation grants covered 88% of the total costs of grant-aided work in 1996/97, with disabled facilities grants covering an average of 93%. Some 60% of renovation grants and 80% of disabled facilities grants covered 100% of the cost of works in 1996/97.

Grant recipients

There has been no ongoing monitoring of the characteristics of grant recipients. A study carried out for the Department of the Environment in the early 1990s showed 48% of renovation grant approvals were awarded to people aged over 60. This was a much higher proportion than under the pre-1990 system. In addition 75% of disabled facilities grant approvals were awarded to those aged 60 or more. As a result of the test of resources, grants were closely targeted on those with low incomes. In total, 60% of those who had grants approved were in receipt of some form of state benefit. In terms of tenure, private landlords have fared badly under the new system compared with their position under the old system.

Area renewal

Local authorities can declare special areas on which they will focus their housing renewal activities. In England and Wales, some 104 renewal areas had been declared by March 1995. In the next three years another 30 new renewal areas were declared in England, but in Wales the number of renewal areas increased only slightly. In total, some 160,000 dwellings were included in renewal areas in England (an extra 34,000 dwellings since 1995), an average of just under 1,400 per area. In England, renewal areas are predominantly located in the North (64%) and the Midlands (25%). The North West has 38% of the declared renewal areas. Overall public expenditure on renovation in renewal areas in England was about £88.9 million in 1996/97. Some 57% of investment came from local authority sources, 27% from housing associations (including Housing Association Grants [HAG] and Local Authority Housing Association Grants [LAHAG]), and 16% from private sources. In recent years grant aid has been the largest component of renewal area investment, accounting for 36% in 1997/98, although in the previous three financial years this had accounted for 50% of the investment. Some 24% of spending took the form of group repair, spending on the environment in renewal areas accounted for 16%, followed by demolitions which accounts for only 8%. Grants and group repair consume the majority of investment in renewal area (60%),

The mechanism for area-based renewal in Scotland has remained the Housing Action Area (HAA). By the end of 1996, just under 1,700 HAAs had been declared. New declarations remained at close to 100 per annum until 1991 after which there was a steep decline in activity. HAAs in Scotland typically contain far fewer dwellings than those in England and Wales. Housing associations have been the dominant force for improvement, but their contribution was at its greatest in the early 1980s. In the early 1990s, grant take up by individual owner-occupiers, as in England and Wales, has become more dominant.

Area improvement has never been a dominant element of renewal programmes in the UK, except in a small number of local areas where these policies have been pursued more intensively. Grants in General Improvement Areas [GIAs], HAAs or renewal areas rarely exceeded 15% of all grants given (1989). However, the abolition of mandatory renovation grants in 1996 in England, Wales and Northern Ireland may increase the proportion of investment in renewal areas.

Improving the local authority stock

Substantial house condition problems are found in the local authority sector. The majority of poor condition local authority dwellings were constructed after 1945. In addition to the need for improvements to amenities and repairs in the traditionally-built housing stock, there are substantial problems of repair in the non-traditional stock, especially in Scotland. Renovation levels reached a maximum in the late 1980s when many local authorities made use of accumulated capital receipts to improve the condition of their stock. The number of local authority dwellings renovated overtook the number of private sector dwellings renovated in 1978, and since 1994 local authority renovation has run at almost five times the level of private sector renovation. The exception to this picture is Wales, where local authority renovation has generally been much lower than the level of grant provision to the private sector. Activity levels have generally been highest in the South East and the South West of England and in parts of the Midlands. It is notable that the majority of metropolitan districts with large public sector stocks have not been able to achieve as much renovation relative to the size of their stock as smaller districts.

The role of housing associations

In England, there was a rapid increase in the level of renovations by housing associations as a result of the introduction of HAG in 1975. The level of renovation activity fluctuated between 10,000 and 20,000 throughout the 1980s before falling to below 6,000 per annum for most of the 1990s, although some recovery has been experienced since 1995 to around 10,000. The decline was partly attributed to the new arrangements for funding housing associations introduced by the 1988 Housing Act. Lower levels of HAG and the requirement that associations should bear any cost over-runs in full have made rehabilitation much less attractive than new-build schemes. A similar decline occurred in the remainder of the UK.

In the past, the majority of housing association renovation work has been undertaken on dwellings purchased from private sector owners, so this activity has made an important contribution to the alleviation of poor housing conditions in the private sector. Housing association renovations have been heavily concentrated in urban areas with a high proportion of private sector housing in poor condition, including London and the larger metropolitan areas or cities.

Renovation's share of public expenditure

Renovation took an increasing share of public expenditure during the 1980s while new building declined. Expenditure on local authority renovation has taken the main share of spending throughout the 1979-97 period, accounting for over half of all renovation expenditure in most years. Private sector renovation spending only approached spending on the local authority stock in the early 1980s during the repair grants boom. Investment in renovation by housing associations has remained consistently below both other programmes. Only reductions in unit costs since 1990 have sustained the volume of local authority renovation output.

Private investment in housing renovation

In addition to public expenditure on renovation, individual households invest a substantial amount of their own resources – over £30 billion in England in 1991. Relatively little is known about this investment. In real terms there was a fall in spending by households in repair and maintenance between 1986 and 1988, followed by an increase in spending between 1989 and 1991 when the average across all households exceeded £400. In subsequent years the total fell back to only £336 in 1994, increasing since to £354 (1996/ 97).

As might be expected, homeowners spend more than those in other tenures on repair, maintenance and decoration. Expenditure in 1994 was greatest among the 30-49 and 50-64 age groups and least among those under 30 and over 75. Among homeowners, spending was highest in Wales, the North East, London and Eastern, and lowest in the South West, Yorkshire and Humberside, the East Midlands, North West and the West Midlands. This may be related to the age profile of the dwelling stock. Expenditure increased with income both for households as a whole and for homeowners, but the proportion of total income devoted to these items decreased as income rose.

The future

The abolition of mandatory renovation grants in England and Wales through the 1996 Housing Grants, Construction and Regeneration Act relieved the worst pressures on local authority private sector renovation budgets, and the forthcoming introduction of a single capital pot for housing may lead to a further reduction in public spending on private sector renewal if hard-pressed local authorities cut back on grant provision. In the absence of new measures to encourage private spending and make it more effective, there is a strong prospect that housing conditions for low-income homeowners and those in the private rented sector may deteriorate in the medium and long term. The Foundations report proposes a new framework for private sector housing renewal policy which aims to make better use of the current resources and to draw in more private spending.

Introduction

The aim of this report is to provide a comprehensive overview of poor housing conditions in the UK and to examine progress in dealing with these problems. Although there have been frequent national surveys of housing conditions in England, Scotland, Wales and Northern Ireland, there is no overall source of information on poor housing conditions covering the whole of the UK, nor any single source of data on measures to deal with these problems. This report is intended, as far as data sources permit, to fill that gap. Wherever possible, the report presents a UK-wide picture, although in a few cases data for one part of the UK, usually Northern Ireland, is not available.

This is the second edition of the report. For this new edition, the report has been comprehensively revised to incorporate the results of the 1996 round of national house condition surveys (1998 in Wales) and to update the sections on progress in dealing with poor conditions by the addition of the most recent data available. Additional material energy conservation has been incorporated. As before this edition makes heavy use of graphs and charts but there is also an extensive section of detailed tables providing supporting and background information. As before, the report also includes a selection of indicators relating to individual local authorities.

Extensive reference is made in the tables, maps and figures to the four national house condition surveys. Information has been obtained from the published reports of the surveys (see References and sources), from special tabulations produced by the Welsh Office from the 1998 Welsh House Condition Survey (WHCS), and from direct analysis of the 1996 English House Condition Survey (EHCS), Scottish House Condition Survey (SHCS) and Northern Ireland House Condition Survey (NIHCS). The relevant source is indicated in each instance.

Local data is based on districts in existence at 31 March 1999.

2

Measuring poor housing conditions

The measurement of poor housing conditions is a difficult and complex task and comparisons between countries within the UK are made more problematic by differences in the definitions used. Some definitional variations stem from differences in national legislation on housing standards within the UK, but others stem from variations in the methodologies of the national house condition surveys.

In this report, three main aspects of poor housing conditions are distinguished.

Unfit for human habitation or below tolerable standard

Fitness for human habitation is an important statutory concept which applies in England, Wales and Northern Ireland. In Scotland, the minimum standard is the tolerable standard. The fitness standard plays an important role in determining whether a local authority is obliged to take action to deal with poor conditions. In England and Wales, between 1990 and 1996, it also determined whether property owners were entitled to mandatory grant aid to deal with poor housing conditions (1992-96 in Northern Ireland). It is likely to continue to be an important determinant of grant priorities in the future. The definition of unfitness remained unchanged from 1957 to 1990 when a new definition was set out in the 1989 Local Government and Housing Act and subsequent circulars and codes of guidance (the equivalent order in Northern Ireland came into effect in 1992). The information in this report on unfitness relates to the new standard. The determination of whether an individual property is unfit or not is a matter for skilled judgement rather than precise measurement and one of the key problems in comparing housing conditions is

to obtain consistency in the interpretation of this standard by different surveyors. The tolerable standard, which in its current format is set out in the 1987 Housing (Scotland) Act, fulfils a similar role in Scotland. Table 2.1 sets out the components of the two standards for comparison. The changes to the fitness standard introduced in the rest of the UK in 1990 and 1992 brought the two standards more closely into line but some differences remain. Most significantly, the tolerable standard excludes reference to serious disrepair and does not specifically require exclusive use of a suitably located wash hand basin and a bath or shower. There are also differences in relation to dampness (the tolerable standard makes no link between dampness and the health of the occupants). As a result, the tolerable standard is now less stringent than the fitness standard applied throughout the remainder of the UK.

Lacking or sharing amenities

The absence of certain basic amenities such as a WC, a sink, a wash hand basin, a bath or shower, and supplies of hot and cold water have been important measures of poor conditions which have also had statutory importance as the basis for determining entitlement to grant aid in some cases. The presence or absence of amenities is more easily determined than unfitness but even here there are differences in definition between surveys. Some refer to the availability of an *indoor* WC or a *readily accessible* WC, while others find an outdoor WC acceptable. Some surveys also refer to the *exclusive use* of amenities by a single household while others appear to accept the sharing of amenities by more than one household. As a result of these differences, comparisons of amenity levels between surveys must be made with caution. Provision of amenities has become less important as an indicator of poor housing conditions in recent years as the number of dwellings which lack amenities has declined significantly.

Disrepair

There is no statutory definition of disrepair and a variety of definitions have been used in surveys. A common approach is to measure the costs of bringing a dwelling up to a particular standard – often that which would be required to qualify for a mortgage from a building society, or to meet the standard of work required after provision of grant aid. There are many problems in defining these standards with precision, and in measuring the costs of repair. Identifying the nature and the scale of house condition problems is the first stage. This involves what are often difficult judgements about the scale of repair, especially where the relevant building elements are inaccessible. Some surveys also attempt to identify problems which will emerge in the future, for example within the next 10 years, as well as existing deficiencies. After this, it is necessary to arrive at a decision about what needs doing to remedy a problem, including the crucial choice between repair and replacement. Finally, the derivation of repair costs from this information is also complex. The first problem is the source of detailed data on the prices of specific jobs. Costs based on public sector renovation contracts have been extensively used in the past but have the disadvantage that they are often below the costs that would be charged for small scale jobs in the private sector. The repair costs of specific elements may also fail to take into account overhead costs or the costs of dealing with consequential repairs. On the other hand, when costs are derived from a large number of separate elements it may also be that economies of scale would be achieved in practice. From this it can be seen that estimates of repair costs, while valuable in summing up the significance of disparate elements of disrepair, are perhaps best seen as relative rather than absolute. As a result of differences in the definitions used in the national house condition surveys it has proved impossible to find a consistent definition of disrepair for use throughout the UK, but the following are the most commonly used in this report:

- *Urgent repairs:* in England and Northern elements regarded as needing urgent action to remove threats to the health, safety, security and comfort of the occupants, or to prevent further rapid deterioration in the building. In Scotland, urgent repairs are repairs to external or common parts only which are necessary to maintain the building in a wind and watertight condition or to remove a threat to safety, health or security. These definitions are broadly similar, but in Scotland exclude internal repairs. In practice the average level of urgent repairs is significantly lower in Scotland and the definitions are not comparable. This measure is not available for Wales.
- *General repairs:* in England, Wales and Northern Ireland, this is all repairs needing action within five years, with replacement only if repair was impossible, more expensive than replacement, or would not last for the five year period. In Scotland the nearest equivalent is *any repairs* but this excludes items not currently needing repair but likely to do so within the next five years. Again these standards appear similar but crucial differences such as the exclusion of works needed within five years in Scotland make comparisons unsafe.
- *Comprehensive repairs:* in England all repairs together with the replacement of any elements judged to have less than 10 years' life. This measure is not available in Wales or Northern Ireland.

Other measures

Information on disrepair is less readily available in other European countries than in the UK, and indicators of house conditions such as the standard of heating insulation and the presence of central heating are more widely used. The age of the dwelling stock is also widely used as a proxy indicator for poor housing conditions, although the emergence of problems in the 1919-45 housing stock, and in postwar dwellings built with non-traditional methods or materials, makes this increasingly less valid.

Fuller information on the definitions used in the national house condition surveys can be found in the individual survey reports (see References and sources). The variety of definitions used makes accurate comparisons between countries in the

UK impossible. Some differences arise because of variations in legislation, but England, Wales and Northern Ireland operate within the same legal framework. In relation to measures of amenities and disrepair no obvious reason presents itself to justify differences in standards, or the absence of at least one common standard. There is now increasing cooperation between those responsible for the national house condition surveys and it is to be hoped that this will produce more consistency between countries in future surveys in order to eliminate or reduce definitional differences to a minimum.

Table 2.1: The standard of fitness for human habitation and the tolerable standard

The standard of fitness for human habitation in England, Wales, and Northern Ireland	The tolerable standard for Scotland
The fitness standard is defined in Section 83 of Schedule 9 to the 1989 Local Government and Housing Act and the 1992 Housing (Northern Ireland) Order. A dwelling house is fit for human habitation unless, in the opinion of the local housing authority, it fails to meet one or more of the following requirements and, by reason of that failure, is not reasonably suitable for occupation.	The tolerable standard is defined in Section 86(1) of the 1987 Housing (Scotland) Act.
Common elements	**Common elements**
The dwelling should: • be structurally stable • be free from dampness prejudicial to the health of the occupants • have satisfactory facilities for preparing and cooking food including a sink with a satisfactory supply of hot and cold water • have a sink provided with a satisfactory supply of both hot and cold water within the house • have an adequate piped supply of wholesome water • have adequate provision for lighting, heating and ventilation • have a suitably located WC exclusively for the use of the occupants • have an effective system for the drainage of foul, waste and surface water	The dwelling should: • be structurally stable • be substantially free from rising or penetrating damp • have satisfactory facilities for the cooking of food within the house • have an adequate piped supply of wholesome water within the house • have satisfactory provision for natural and • artificial lighting, for ventilation, and for heating • have a WC available for the exclusive use of the occupants of the house and suitably located within the house • have an effective system for the drainage and disposal of foul and surface water
Different elements	**Different elements**
• have a suitably located bath or shower and wash hand basin, each provided with a supply of hot and cold water • be free from serious disrepair	 • have satisfactory access to all external doors and outbuildings

Source: DoE (1996); Scottish Homes (1996)

Housing conditions in the UK

Unfit dwellings or dwellings below the tolerable standard

As Chapter 2 indicated, the standard of fitness for human habitation and the Scottish equivalent – the tolerable standard – are the most important indicators of poor housing conditions. The latest information available on unfitness relates to 1996 in England (DoE, 1998) and Northern Ireland (NIHE, 1998), and to 1993 in Wales (Welsh Office, 1994), or 1998 where data is avilable (Welsh Office, 1999). For Scotland data on dwellings below the tolerable standard (BTS) relates to 1996 (Scottish Homes, 1996).

Table 3.1 and Figure 3.1 show overall levels of unfitness/BTS (see Chapter 2) across the UK. It is emphasised that comparisons between areas cannot be made because of differences in the definitions of each indicator. In total, some 1,455,000 occupied dwellings were either unfit for human habitation or below the Scottish tolerable standard. This represented about 6% or one in 16 dwellings in the UK in 1996. Although we cannot be precise because of the differences in definitions it is likely that the problem of unfitness was most severe in Wales where 8.5% of dwellings were unfit. In Northern Ireland the problem of unfitness of vacant dwellings is more pronounced. As the tolerable standard used in Scotland does not include disrepair, this indicator cannot be compared with unfitness elsewhere in the UK.

Table 3.1: Housing conditions in the UK (1996)*

			Repair costs		
	Unfit	Lacking amenities	Urgent over £1,000	General over £3,000	Comprehensive over £5,000
England 1996					
Dwellings (000s)	1,251 (1,471)	207	5,973 (6,400)	3,709 (4,045)	4,473 (4,819)
Dwellings (%)	6.1 (7.2)	0.9	29.4 (31.5)	18.2 (19.9)	22.0 (23.7)
Northern Ireland 1996					
Dwellings (000s)	32 (44)	9 (18)	122 (140)	83 (98)	
Dwellings (%)	5.3 (7.3)	1.6 (2.9)	20.3 (23.3)	13.7 (16.2)	

	Unfit	Lacking amenities	Repair costs over £1,500
Wales 1993/98†			
Dwellings (000s)	98	42	230
Dwellings (%)	8.5	3.6	20.4

			Repair costs		
	BTS	Lacking amenities	Urgent over £1,000	Visible over £2,000	General over £3,000
Scotland 1996					
Dwellings (000s)	21	5	113	199	593
Dwellings (%)	1.0	0.2	5.3	9.4	28.0

* Figures in brackets include vacant dwellings; otherwise figures relate to occupied dwellings only. It is emphasised that figures are generally not comparable between countries because of differences in definitions, briefings, interpretation, repair costings, and survey methodology. See Chapter 2 for further details.
† For Wales, data on unfitness relates to 1998; data on disrepair relates to 1993.

Sources: 1996 EHCS, 1996 SHCS, 1996 NIHCS: analysis of data; 1993 and 1998 WHCS: preliminary tables

Figure 3.1: Housing conditions in the UK

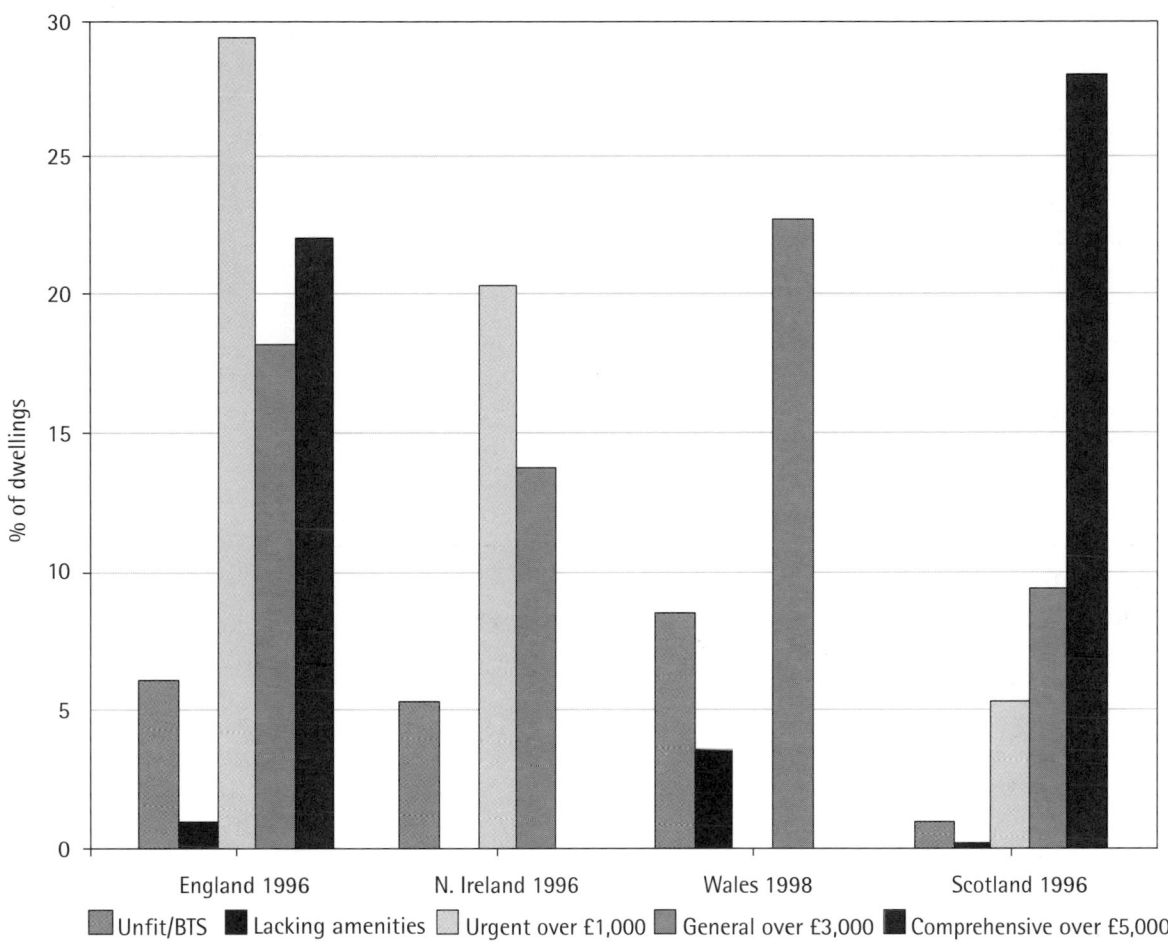

Table 3.2 shows the main reasons why dwellings were unfit or BTS. Dwellings in Wales failed the standard, on average, on just over three items, compared with just over two items in England and Northern Ireland, and 1.5 items in Scotland, but the distribution was very skewed, with 69% of unfit dwellings in England, for example, being unfit on only one item, and a further 18% unfit on two items. In 1996, more dwellings were unfit on one item alone than in 1991. In England, food preparation, disrepair, dampness and bath/shower/wash hand basin facilities were the main reasons why dwellings failed the fitness standard. In Wales, food preparation and disrepair were also major reasons for unfitness, with similar proportions to England. In Northern Ireland the same reasons were also prominent, but the proportions of dwellings failing on each was much higher, with 51% of unfit dwellings failing on the grounds of disrepair, for example,

compared with only 32% in England. In Scotland, differences between unfitness and the tolerable standard make comparisons difficult. Dampness (found in 33% of BTS dwellings) stands out above all others as the main reason for failing the tolerable standard in Scotland, although this is some improvement on the 1991 figure of 50%. However, Scotland does not have the same scale of problem with food preparation as is apparent in the other UK countries.

Table 3.2: Reasons for unfitness/BTS, UK (1996)

Reason	% of unfit/BTS dwellings			
	England	N Ireland	Wales	Scotland
Food preparation	38.1	55.9	37.8	12.0
Repair	31.7	50.7	28.8	na
Bath/shower/whb	21.6	46.9	21.2	na
Dampness	25.6	45.9	17.3	33.1
WC	8.9	35.4	23.0	9.4
Lighting	5.2	12.3	5.4	} 24.5
Ventilation	17.1	11.0	14.2	
Heating	7.7	17.7	7.1	
Stability	8.9	12.5	6.2	21.7
Drainage	7.1	20.2	3.1	8.6
Water supply	4.9	17.4	4.2	3.4
Water to sink	na	na	na	5.6
External access	na	na	na	9.6

Sources: 1996 EHCS, 1996 SHCS, 1996 NIHCS: analysis of data; 1999 WHCS: preliminary tables

Missing amenities

The proportion of dwellings lacking one or more basic amenities follows a similar pattern to unfitness (Table 3.1) with Wales having the most severe problems (3.6% of dwellings lacking one or more basic amenities), followed by Northern Ireland (1.6%) and then England (1.0%). In Scotland only 0.2% of dwellings lacked all five amenities but this excludes dwellings with an external WC.

Disrepair

Comparisons between the four components of the UK are impossible in relation to this indicator. In England, nearly one third of dwellings had urgent repair costs of over £1,000 in 1996. As these are works which need swift action in order to prevent further deterioration, this is a serious problem. Likewise around one in five dwellings had a general repair backlog of more than £3,000, and almost one in four had longer-term repair costs (incorporating some estimate of costs likely to arise in the next 10 years) of £5,000 or more.

In Northern Ireland around one in four dwellings had urgent repair costs in excess of £1,000 and

16% had general building repair costs of over £3,000. Information was not published on longer-term repair costs.

In Scotland 5.3% of dwellings had urgent repair costs of over £1,000 but this indicator is not comparable with that for England or Northern Ireland. The elements defined as urgent were more limited. A measure of visible repairs was also used in Scotland, covering all backlog repairs which surveyors could identify as present at the time of survey. On this indicator, 10% of Scottish dwellings faced costs of £2,000 or more.

In Wales, the repair cost standard used in 1998 was not comparable with those used elsewhere. Some 23% of dwellings had repair costs of more than £1,000.

Mean repair costs per dwelling

Figure 3.2 shows mean repair costs per dwelling for urgent, general and comprehensive repairs, and the costs of repairs to dwellings which were unfit or BTS (see also Table A3.1). Data in Figure 3.2 are for occupied dwellings. In England, the mean cost of urgent repairs (averaged across the whole stock) was just under £1,300. The average general repair cost was £1,900 and comprehensive repair costs averaged £3,400. As Table A3.1 shows the same costs for vacant dwellings were substantially greater. The final column in the chart shows the average general repair cost for unfit dwellings alone. This was over £5,000 for occupied unfit dwellings and nearly £11,000 for vacant unfits.

The distribution of repair costs on all indicators was highly skewed with most dwellings having nil or low costs and a smaller number having very high costs indeed. The median urgent repair cost for occupied dwellings in England for example is £397. 46% of dwellings had urgent repair costs of more than £500 and only 20% had urgent repair costs over £1,800.

Figure 3.2: Mean repair costs, UK

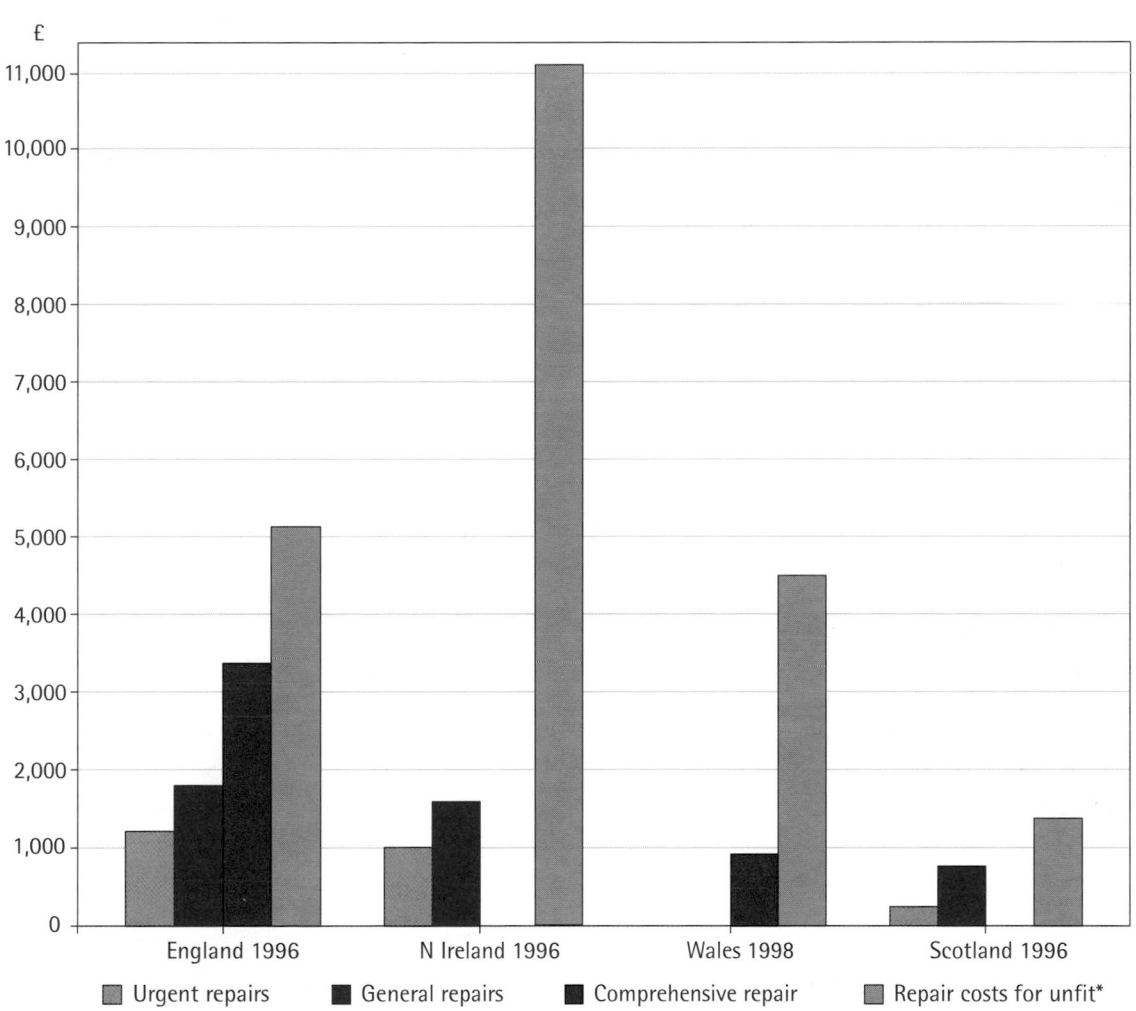

* Data for Northern Ireland is for all dwellings.

The pattern of unfitness in the private sector stock

Map 3.1 shows variations in the proportion of privately owned dwellings which were unfit in England at district level in 1998. Table 3.3 shows authorities in England and Wales with the highest levels of unfit private sector dwellings, and data for all authorities is shown in Appendix B. These estimates are based on 1998 HIP data provided by the DoE from returns made by local authorities. This data is often criticised because it is not derived from consistent sources, but the sample size of the EHCS does not provide data below regional level. In Wales, the 1998 House Condition Survey provides district level estimates of unfitness.

Areas with extremely high levels of unfitness in the private rented sector in England include a large group of rural or industrial districts in the North West of England, notably Blackburn with Darwen, Hynbdurn, Rossendale, Bolton, Allerdale, St Helens, Burnley and Wirral. Urbanised districts such as Middlesbrough; Liverpool; a group of cities or industrial areas in the Midlands including Stoke on Trent, Leicester, Birmingham, Walsall, Sandwell and Nottingham; in the South, Restormel, Swale and Peterborough; and a small number of London boroughs including Haringey, Hackney, Brent, Hammersmith and Fulham, and Camden.

There are relatively few areas anywhere in England and Wales with a very low proportion of unfit dwellings but the area south of the Wash–Bristol Channel line stands out clearly as an area with below average unfitness levels compared with Wales and the North of England.

Map 3.2 shows the distribution of dwellings BTS in Scotland in 1998. There are two sources of BTS estimates. The source used to construct the map below is from annual estimates made by the local authorities. National estimates elsewhere in this report are derived from the SHCS. These two sources give very different figures: the 1996 SHCS estimated that there were 27,000 BTS dwellings in Scotland, compared to an estimate of 84,000 obtained from the amalgamation of local authority estimates for that year. The true figure is likely to be somewhere in-between. Current research is underway into the methods used to produce the estimates.

Table 3.3: Authorities in England and Wales with the highest proportion of unfit private sector dwellings (1998)

Local authority	Unfit private sector dwellings (per 1,000)
Blackburn with Darwen	41.06
Hyndburn	31.94
Rossendale	29.48
Bolton	24.51
Allerdale	22.29
St Helens	22.12
Burnley	22.00
Stoke-on-Trent	21.99
Haringey	21.30
Restormel	20.84
Peterborough	20.68
Middlesbrough	20.54
Leicester	19.93
Birmingham	19.11
Wirral	18.77
Swale	18.48
Liverpool	17.85
Walsall	17.71
Erewash	17.35
Hackney	17.03
Sandwell	16.61
Hastings	16.56
Pendle	16.47
Preston	16.36
Nottingham	16.23
Brent	16.02
Hinckley and Bosworth	15.99
Tameside	15.94
Hammersmith and Fulham	15.74
Camden	15.68

Source: DoE estimates (1998) and WHCS preliminary tables (1999)

Map 3.1: Unfitness per 1,000 privately owned dwellings, England and Wales (1998)

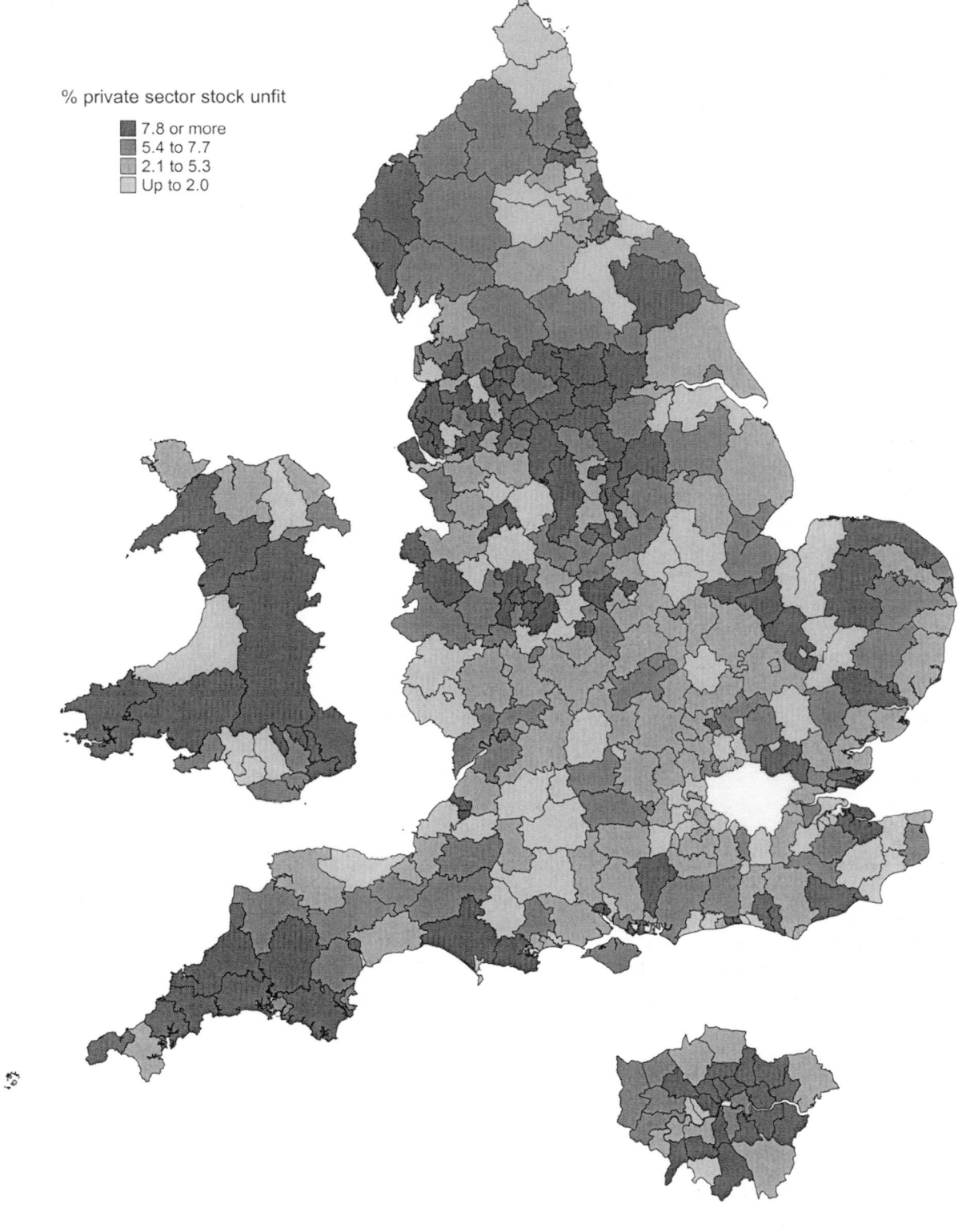

% private sector stock unfit

- 7.8 or more
- 5.4 to 7.7
- 2.1 to 5.3
- Up to 2.0

The problem of poor conditions in rural areas in Scotland (see below) is well illustrated by Map 3.2. Eilean Siar (previously Western Isles) has 26% of it privately owned stock BTS. Argyll and Bute, Orkney, and Inverclyde also have over 10%, and the Scottish Borders, Glasgow, Angus and Renfrewshire also have a high percentage (over 5%) of their privately owned stock BTS. Aberdeen and Edinburgh each have around 3% of their private stock BTS.

Map 3.2: Below tolerable standard per 1,000 privately owned dwellings, Scotland (1998)

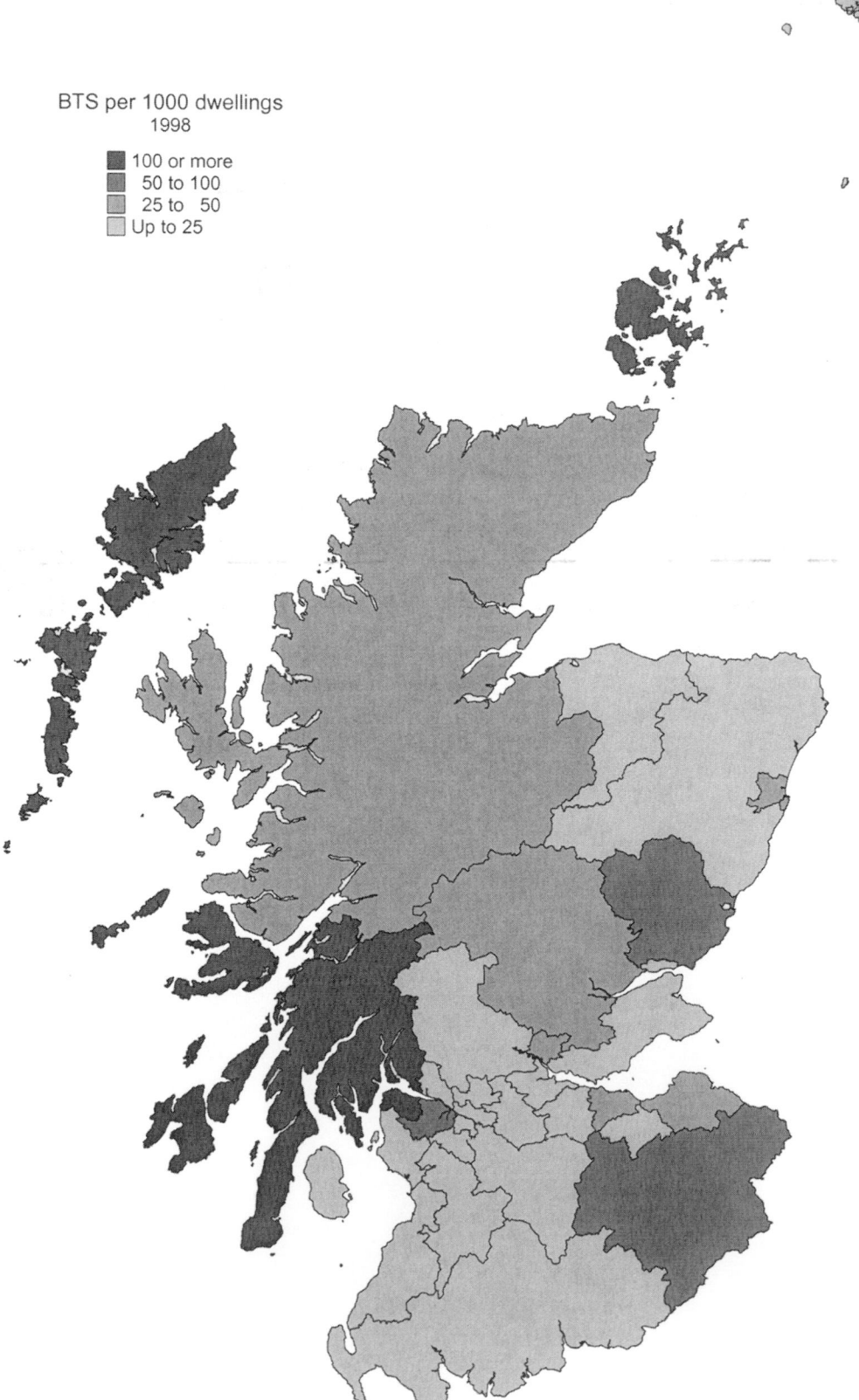

BTS per 1000 dwellings
1998

- 100 or more
- 50 to 100
- 25 to 50
- Up to 25

Contrasts between urban and rural areas

In England there are more unfit dwellings in urban areas. Northern Ireland and Scotland experience a contrasting pattern as a higher percentage of unfit dwellings are in rural areas. The problem of rural unfitness is more distinct in Northern Ireland where unfit dwellings are twice as likely to be found in rural as urban areas. In Wales the distinction between unfit urban and rural housing is not as clear (Appendix Table A3.2).

Figure 3.3: Unfit housing by urban/rural location, UK

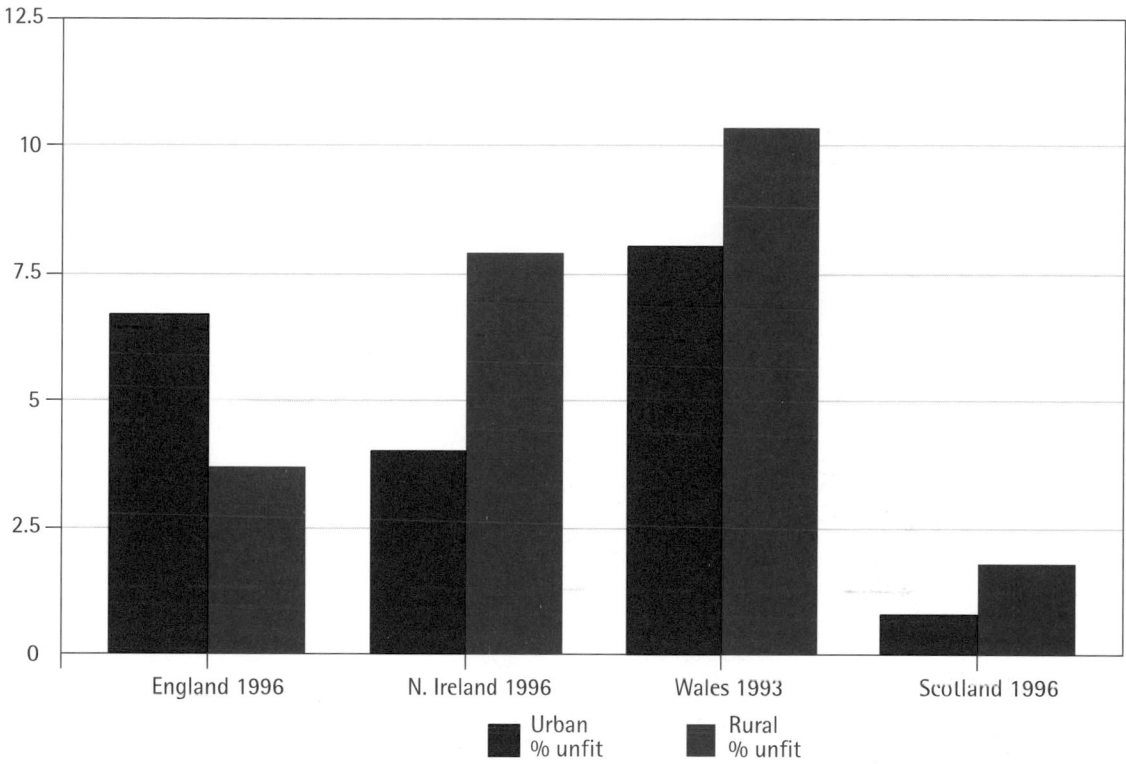

Trends in house condition

Trends in house condition are also difficult to assess because of differences in the interpretation of standards and changes in the definition of house condition indicators between surveys. In England, the number of dwellings lacking one or more basic amenities declined from almost three million in 1971 to only 207,000 in 1996. Trends in unfitness and disrepair are based on re-interpretations of the results of previous surveys. Between 1981 and 1986, unfitness was estimated to have fallen from 6.3% to 5.6% of the stock under the old pre-1989 standard, while disrepair fell from 6.5% to 5.9% (DoE, 1988). The change in the fitness standard in 1990 made further comparisons difficult but modelling of 1991 EHCS data suggested that levels of unfitness had fallen slightly since 1986 from 8.8% to 7.6%. The more recent survey in 1996 suggests that the rate of reduction in the number of unfit dwellings has slowed down, as the 1996 figure is 7.2%. For occupied dwellings the reduction in unfitness is greater with a fall of 1%. This indicates that differences in the condition of occupied and vacant dwellings in England have become more distinct.

In Wales, the proportion of dwellings lacking basic amenities fell sharply over the 1981-91 period, as in England. The level of unfitness also declined, from 8.8% to 7.2% under the old standard between 1981 and 1986, and from 19.5% to 13.3% under the new standard between 1986 and 1991. The recent 1998 survey illustrates a further sharp decline to 8.5% of the occupied stock unfit under the new standard. However the preliminary report stresses that the small sample size of the 1993 survey means that the change between the two surveys can only be regarded as approximate (Welsh Office, 1999).

In Northern Ireland, the proportion of dwellings lacking one or more basic amenities fell from 120,000 to 20,000 between 1974 and 1991. A figure for 1996 was not published. The level of unfitness also appears to have declined over this period. Under the new fitness standard, unfitness fell from about 11% to 9% between 1987 and 1991. This decreased over the following five years to 7.3%. It may be that in Northern Ireland, as in England, the level of unfitness has fallen to a basic 'hard core' level. The increase in disrepair identified in Northern Ireland between 1979 and 1984 has now been compensated for by a

continuous period of reduction since that point in time.

In Scotland comparisons over the same time-scale are not possible as the 1991 survey was the first to be carried out. Over the last five years the number of BTS dwellings in Scotland apparently fell sharply – from 4.7% to 1.0% in 1996 – but these figures are being re-examined to unravel the impact of change in definitions and interpretations by surveyors. The number of dwellings lacking amenities also decreased but not to the same extent.

Housing conditions and the dwelling stock

The quality of the initial construction of dwellings and the extent and effectiveness of subsequent repair and maintenance are the main influences on the condition of the majority of dwellings. Dwelling type and age are reasonable, although far from perfect, proxies for these factors. These basic influences on house condition are, in turn, subject to a large number of other important influences, such as the prevailing technologies and legislative controls at the point of construction, the resources available to social rented sector landlords at this stage, or to those seen as potential clients by a speculative builder, and subsequently the resources of those who own and/or occupy the dwellings and the extent to which they are prepared to invest in repair and maintenance.

In this chapter we first examine the age and type profile of the dwelling stock and the extent to which variations in condition are associated with these factors. We then move on to look at variations in condition by tenure. Although there are distinct variations in conditions by tenure and clear differences in the ways in which owners in different tenures approach the task of investment in their upkeep, variations in condition by tenure are obscured on the one hand by the large-scale tenure transfers of this century, firstly of dwellings built for private renting into the owner-occupied sector, secondly of dwellings from the council sector in to homeownership, and thirdly the more small-scale transfer of private rented and some owner-occupied dwellings into housing association ownership in specific, mainly inner-city locations.

Age of the stock

There are significant differences in the profile of dwellings by age in the UK. In England and Wales almost half the housing stock was built before 1944 with 23% and 33% respectively built before 1919 (Figure 4.1, Table A4.1). Scotland's housing stock is slightly newer on average but in Northern Ireland the stock is much more recent with only a third built before 1944, and nearly half of the stock (47%) built since 1965. The age of the stock has a significant impact on condition as the following sections will show.

Figure 4.1: Age of housing stock, UK

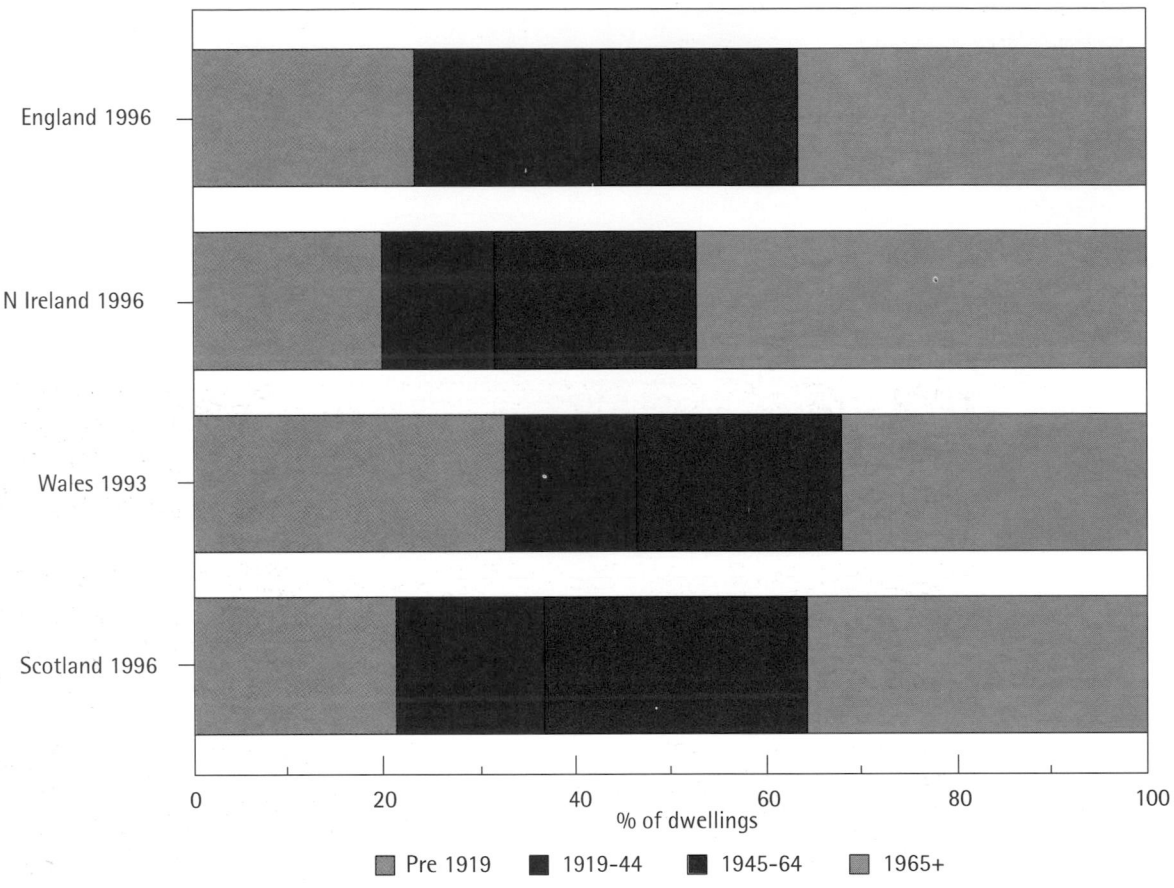

Dwelling type

The dwelling type profile also varies within the UK (Figure 4.2, Table A4.2). In England, semi-detached and terraced houses are the most common types of dwelling, each accounting for about 30% of the stock. About one fifth of dwellings are detached houses. Of the remaining 20% of dwellings, almost three quarters (15% of the total) are purpose-built flats, with the remainder being flats produced by conversion from other dwelling types. In Wales, terraced houses form over one third of the stock, with semi-detached houses accounting for 32%, and detached houses 24%. Only about 10% of dwellings in Wales are flats, the majority purpose-built.

In Scotland, the stock profile is substantially different. Only 62% of dwellings are houses. Terraced houses (24% of all dwellings) are the most common type, closely followed by semi-detached houses (21%) and detached houses (17%). Purpose-built flats (including both older tenements and more modern local authority flats) are by far the most common dwelling type (36%).

The Northern Ireland dwelling stock is more similar to that in England and Wales with relatively few flats (8%, of which the majority are purpose built). Terraced dwellings are the most common (37%), followed by detached houses (31%) and semi-detached houses (23%).

Figure 4.2: Type of dwelling stock, UK

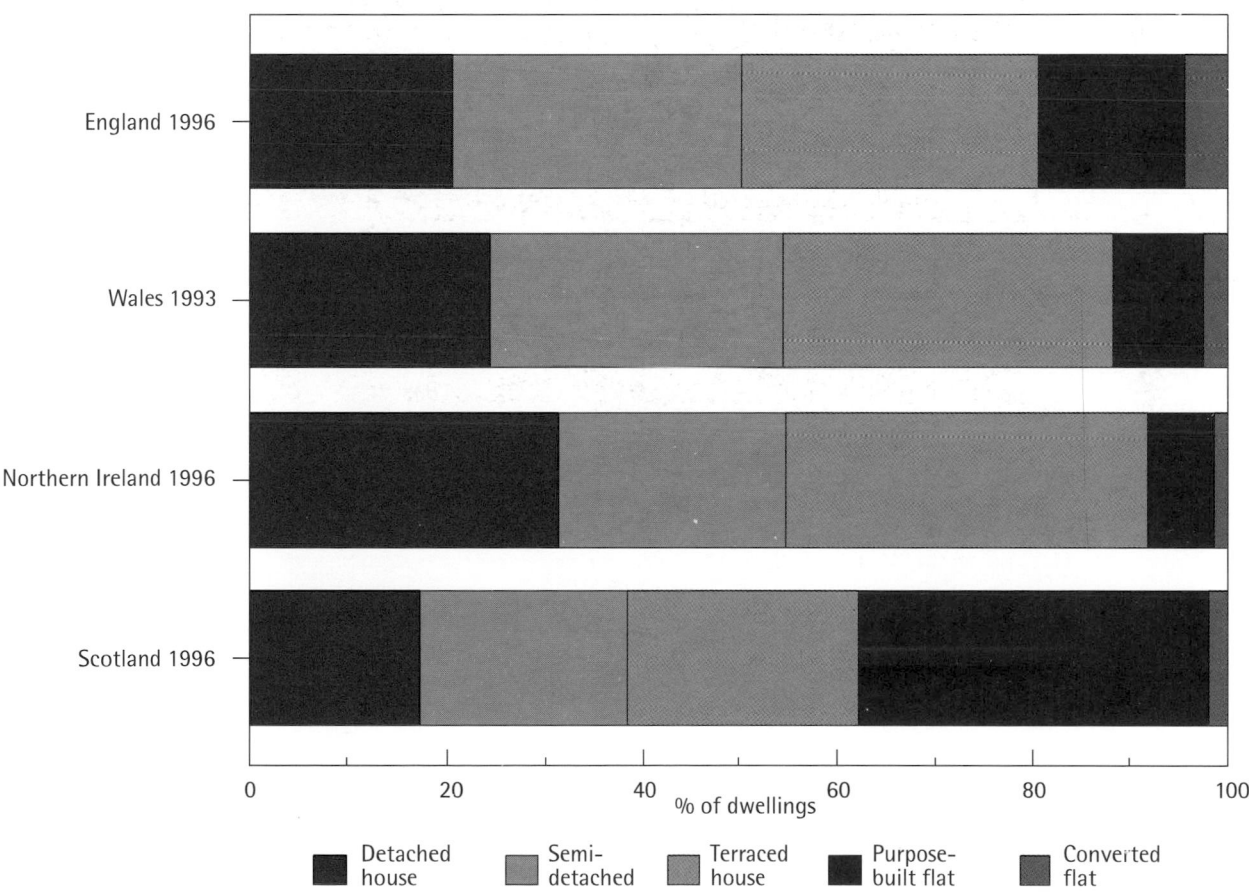

Age and type of dwelling

Figure 4.3 shows the composition of the housing stock in the UK by a number of key dwelling age/type categories. Appendix Table A4.3 shows detailed figures by country. Post-1945 dwellings make up more than half the stock, with semi-detached dwellings forming the largest group (17% of the stock), followed by detached houses (14%), terraced houses (13.5%) and purpose-built flats (12%). The only other significant groups are pre-1919 terraced houses which account for 12% of the stock, and interwar semi-detached houses which form 9%. Purpose-built and converted pre-1919 flats form only 4% of the total stock. Pre-1919 dwellings together with post-1945 purpose-built flats form only about a third of the stock overall but, as following sections will show, this is where the majority of house condition problems lie.

Figure 4.3: Components of housing stock by age and type, UK

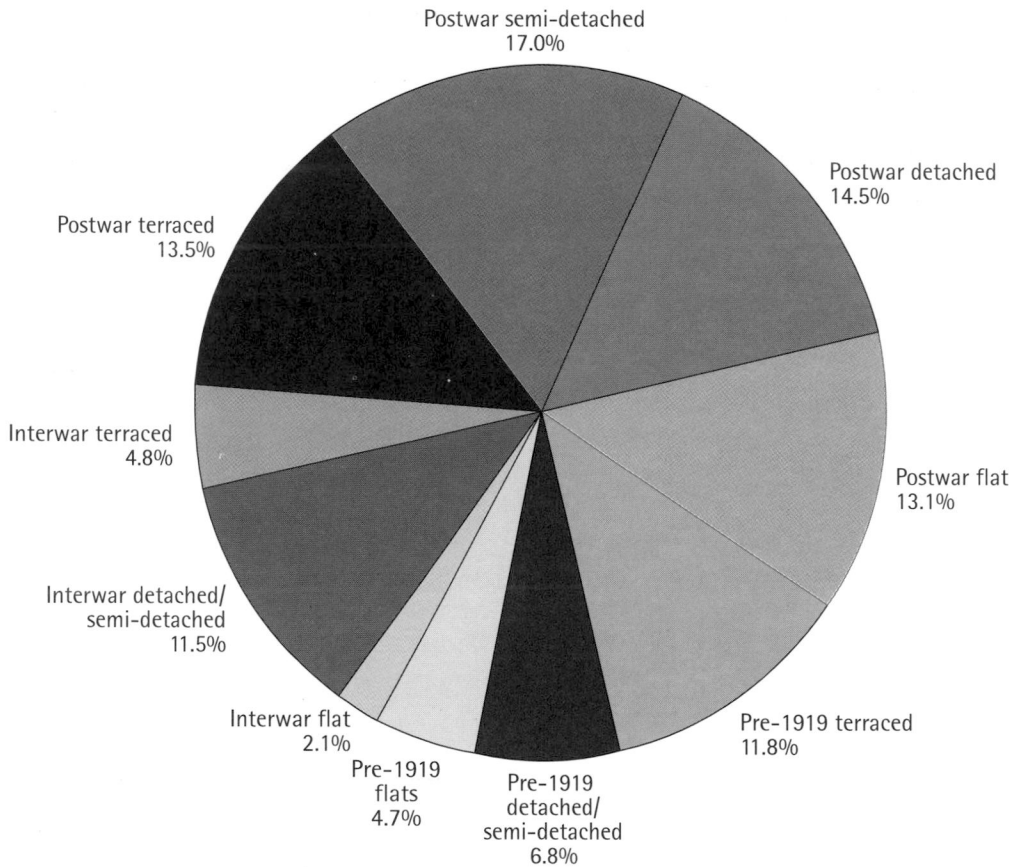

Postwar semi-detached
17.0%

Postwar detached
14.5%

Postwar terraced
13.5%

Postwar flat
13.1%

Interwar terraced
4.8%

Interwar detached/
semi-detached
11.5%

Pre-1919 terraced
11.8%

Interwar flat
2.1%

Pre-1919
flats
4.7%

Pre-1919
detached/
semi-detached
6.8%

The pattern of older private sector properties

Although older housing is found in all districts the greatest concentrations of privately-owned older housing are found in the North of England, Wales and parts of the South West (Map 4.1). Four areas stand out as having very high levels of older properties. These include a band across Cumbria and into the west of County Durham which is mainly rural but also includes old mining settlements (Allerdale, Eden, Teesdale and Wear Valley); a cluster of towns in north east Lancashire (Pendle, Burnley, Hyndburn, Rossendale and Blackburn); South Wales valleys (Rhondda Cynon Taff); and parts of inner London (Islington, Hackney, Hammersmith and Fulham, Camden, Kensington and Chelsea, Westminster). Table 4.1 shows those authorities with the highest proportion of pre-1919 stock and data for all authorities is shown in Appendix B.

Table 4.1: Authorities in England and Wales with the highest proportion of pre-1919 private sector dwellings (1986)

District	% private sector stock pre-1919
Islington	96.1
Hackney	88.5
Hammersmith	88.3
Rhondda	78.8
Camden	77.2
Kensington	76.9
Pendle	75.9
Hyndburn	70.2
Westminster	69.6
Lambeth	69.0
Wandsworth	68.7
Lewisham	68.4
Newham	68.3
Teesdale	68.0
Haringey	66.1
Eden	65.7
Burnley	65.2
Blackburn	63.8
Wear Valley	63.4
Waltham Forest	61.6
Rossendale	61.4
Allerdale	61.2
Cynon Valley	60.2
Barrow-in-Furness	59.2
South Shropshire	58.5
Craven	58.1
Manchester	56.8
Penwith	55.6
Brighton	55.4
Calderdale	55.2

Note: This table uses 1986 local authorities as more recent information is not available.
Source: DoE estimates and Welsh Office (1988)

Map 4.1: Percentage of pre–1919 privately owned dwellings England (1986) and Wales (1997)

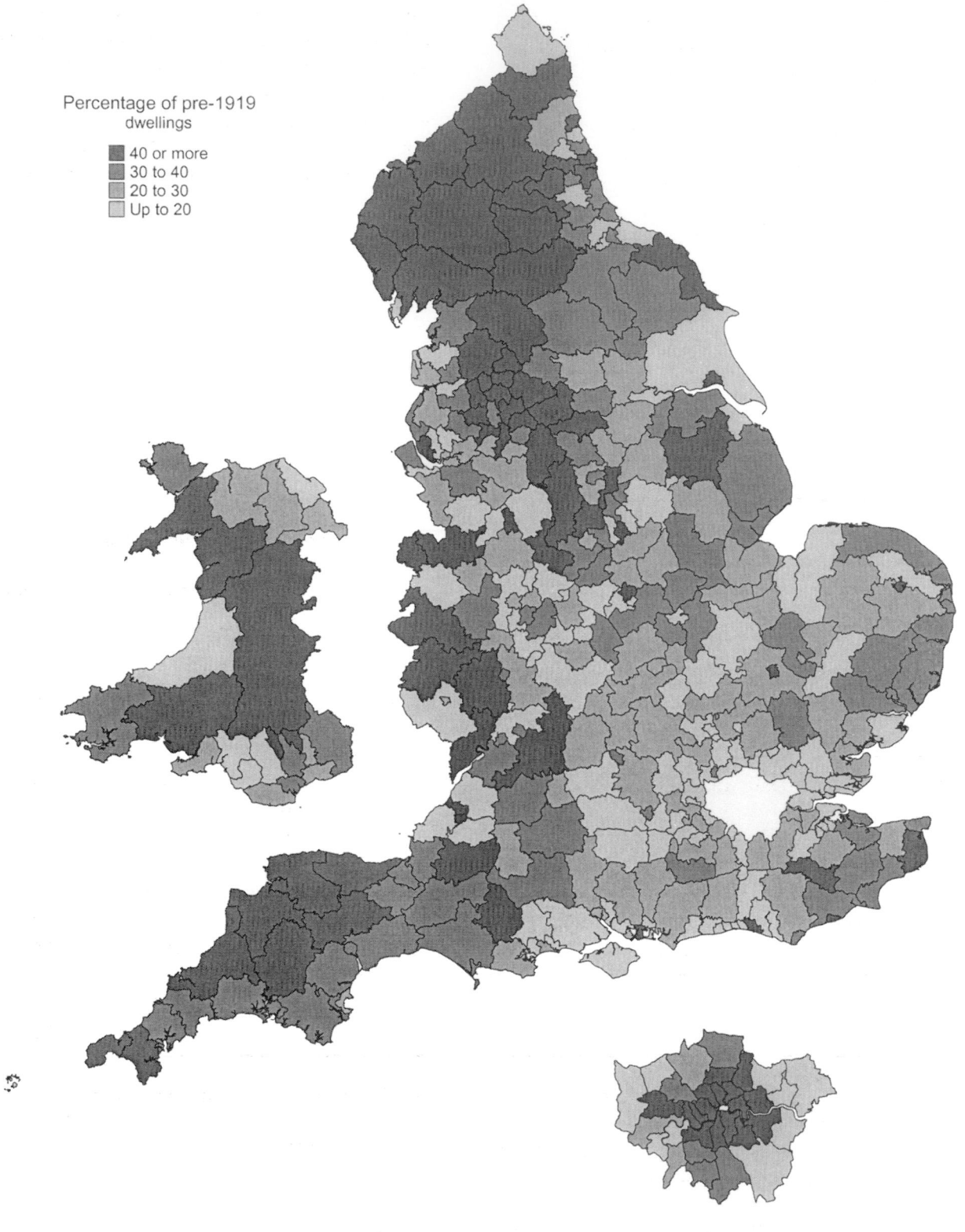

Percentage of pre-1919 dwellings

- 40 or more
- 30 to 40
- 20 to 30
- Up to 20

Dwellings in poor condition by age

Poor housing conditions are closely related to the age of the dwelling stock. Table 4.2 shows the proportion of dwellings in different age groups which are unfit, or in disrepair. Appendix Table A4.4 shows fuller details. It should again be noted that figures cannot be compared between countries. The post-1964 stock has the lowest level of unfitness/BTS in all cases, and the proportion of dwellings in each age band which are unfit increases steadily with age before rising sharply for the pre-1919 stock. However, there are significant levels of unfitness in the interwar stock in Wales and Northern Ireland.

In terms of disrepair the pre-1919 stock is again consistently most likely to be in the worst condition, with the proportion of dwellings in disrepair decreasing in the newer stock. The difference between newer and older dwellings is greatest in Northern Ireland where pre-1919 dwellings are 15 times as likely to be in poor repair as those built after 1964. In Scotland the same ratio is nearly seven, in Wales five, but in England only four, suggesting that disrepair in England has become more evenly spread across the stock.

Table 4.2: Dwellings in poor condition by age, UK (1996)

			% of dwellings in each age group			
			Pre-1919	**1919–44**	**1945–64**	**Post-1964**
England 1996	Unfit	All	15.1	9.7	5.1	2.2
		Occupied	12.5	8.4	4.2	2.0
	Disrepair*	All	54.8	40.4	28.8	13.3
		Occupied	54.4	37.6	27.2	12.9
Northern Ireland 1996	Unfit	All	20.6	12.1	5.4	1.4
		Occupied	14.0	9.0	4.4	1.0
	Disrepair*	All	46.9	35.1	22.2	10.9
		Occupied	38.8	30.6	19.5	10.2
Wales 1993/99†	Unfit	Occupied	15.0	9.1	7.7	2.7
	Disrepair‡	Occupied	33.8	23.4	18.2	6.8
Scotland 1996	BTS	Occupied	3.3	0.8	0.3	0.1
	Disrepair*	Occupied	14.4	6.4	2.8	1.3

* Dwellings with urgent repair costs over £1,000. Note, however, that comparisons cannot be made between countries on this indicator.
† For Wales, data on unfitness relates to 1998; data on disrepair relates to 1993.
‡ Dwellings with repair costs over £1,500.

Sources: 1996 EHCS, 1996 SHCS, 1996 NIHCS: analysis of data; 1994/1999 WHCS

Figures 4.4 and 4.5 (and Table A4.5) show how unfit/BTS dwellings and dwellings in disrepair are split between the four dwelling age groups (in contrast to Table 4.2 which showed the proportion of dwellings in each age group which were in poor condition). The figures do not take account of the overall number of poor condition dwellings, which is much greater in England because of its larger dwelling stock (see Table 3.1).

Not surprisingly, the majority of unfit/BTS dwellings were built before 1919. The proportion is highest in Scotland (73%) followed by Northern Ireland (56%). The proportion of unfit properties

that are newer has increased, especially in Wales and England. Unfitness in newer dwellings has increased proportionately since the change in the fitness standard introduced in England and Wales in 1990 and in Northern Ireland in 1992. Evidence from the 1996 EHCS shows that there was a significant reduction in the level of unfitness (as measured by the old standard) in the pre-1919 stock during this period offset by substantial increases in unfitness levels in the newer stock. This also applies to Northern Ireland, but not in Scotland and Wales where unfitness is continuing to increase in the older stock only. Nevertheless unfitness remains predominantly a problem of the pre-1919 stock.

Figure 4.4: Unfit/BTS dwellings by age, UK

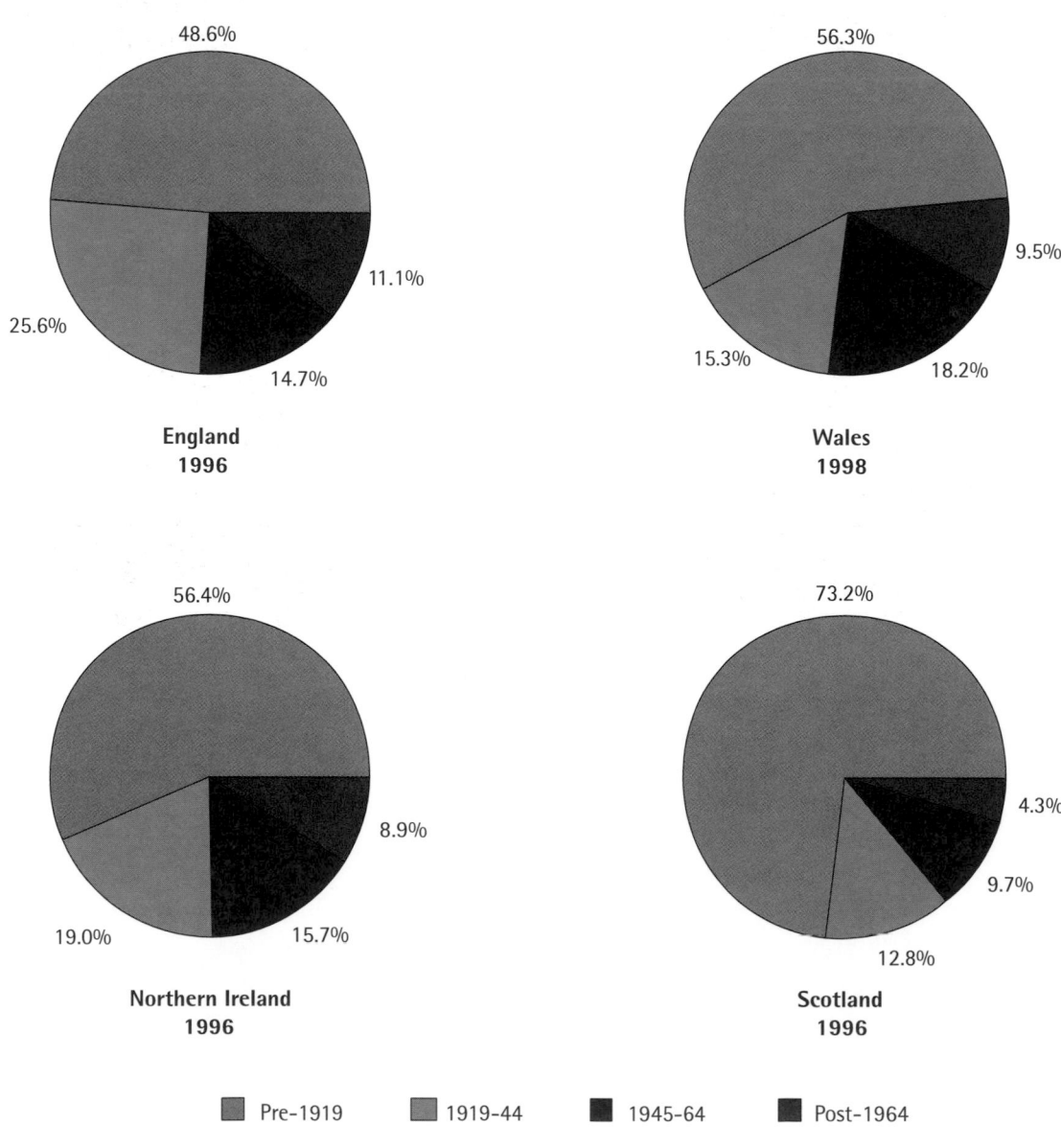

	England 1996	Wales 1998	Northern Ireland 1996	Scotland 1996

Pre-1919 ■ 1919-44 ■ 1945-64 ■ Post-1964 ■

The majority of disrepair is also consistently found in pre-1919 housing, despite differences in the standards used in each country. The share of disrepair accounted for by each age band declines steadily with age, except in Northern Ireland where the 1945-onwards stock accounts for a greater share than the interwar stock, but this is partly explained by the relatively low level of building between 1919 and 1945 in comparison with the postwar period. Houses lacking amenities were also predominantly built before 1919 but significant numbers date from the interwar period.

Figure 4.5: Dwellings in disrepair by age, UK

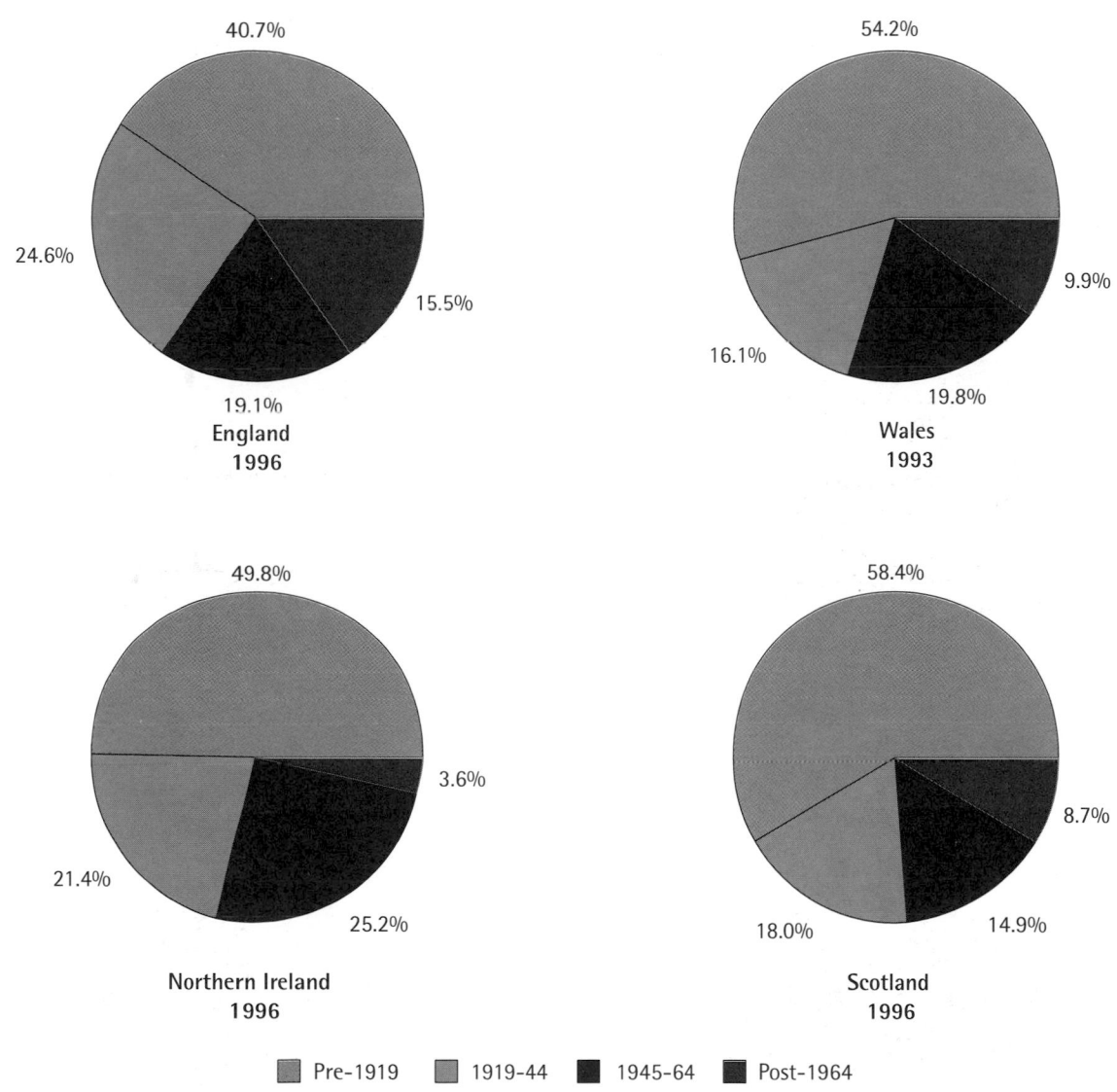

England 1996

Wales 1993

Northern Ireland 1996

Scotland 1996

Pre-1919   1919-44   1945-64   Post-1964

Dwellings in poor condition by type

Table 4.3 shows the proportion of dwellings of different types which are unfit, or in disrepair (Table A4.6 shows fuller details). Without placing too much emphasis on the actual proportions of dwellings in poor condition, which cannot be compared between countries, there are some interesting variations. In England, converted flats and terraced houses are the most likely types of dwellings to be unfit. Converted flats in particular and terraced houses, are also more likely to have higher repair costs. In Wales, terraced houses stand out as more likely to be in poor condition than any other dwelling type. In Scotland, converted flats are the most likely dwelling type to be in poor condition, although tenements also have relatively high repair costs. In Northern Ireland, detached houses are likely to both be unfit and have high repair costs. This is due to the high incidence of poor conditions on isolated dwellings in rural areas. Converted flats are also likely to be in poor condition in Northern Ireland.

Table 4.3: Dwellings in poor condition by type, UK (1996)

	% of dwellings in each type category					
	Terraced house	Semi-detached house	Detached house	Converted flat	Purpose-built flat	All types
England 1996						
Unfit	10.8	5.4	3.0	16.1	6.9	7.2
Disrepair*	39.0	29.5	25.3	50.8	22.4	31.5
Northern Ireland 1996						
Unfit	6.2	4.6	11.0	17.0	2.3	7.3
Disrepair*	20.1	17.2	33.7	31.1	10.2	23.3
Wales 1993/99						
Unfit†	11.4	6.8	6.1	9.5		8.5
Disrepair‡	37.4	18.8	13.0	9.8		20.4
Scotland 1996						
BTS	0.4	0.7	1.2	5.0	1.2	1.0
Disrepair*	3.1	4.1	8.3	14.9	5.6	5.3

Note: Figures for England, Scotland and Northern Ireland are for 1996, figures for Wales are for 1993/98. Data for Wales and Scotland are for occupied dwellings only. Comparisons cannot be made between countries.

* Dwellings with urgent repair costs over £1,000. Note, however, that comparisons cannot be made between countries on this indicator.
† For Wales, data on unfitness relates to 1998; data on disrepair relates to 1993.
‡ Dwellings with repair costs over £1,500.

Sources: DoE (1998); Scottish Homes (1997); NIHE (1997); Welsh Office (1994, 1999)

Figure 4.6 (Table A4.7) shows the proportion of unfit or BTS dwellings accounted for by each dwelling type by country. The proportions shown in Table 4.3 are significantly modified as a result of differences in the size of the stock of dwellings of each type. In England, terraced houses account for over 45% of all unfit dwellings and semi-detached houses a further 22%. Only one in 10 unfit dwellings is a converted flat. As in England, the majority of Welsh unfit dwellings are found in terraced housing. In Scotland, purpose-built flats, and particularly tenements, are the most frequent sub-standard dwelling type (45.8% of all BTS dwellings), followed by detached houses (21.5%).

This dwelling type dominates the picture in Northern Ireland, where over 45% of all unfit dwellings are detached houses, with a further 32% being terraced houses. The picture in relation to disrepair is similar.

Some of the differences in condition between the different dwelling stock types are accounted for by their age. Older dwellings are generally in poorer condition and where different countries have different age distributions by dwelling type this will account for some of the differences in condition.

Figure 4.6: Unfit/BTS dwellings by type, UK

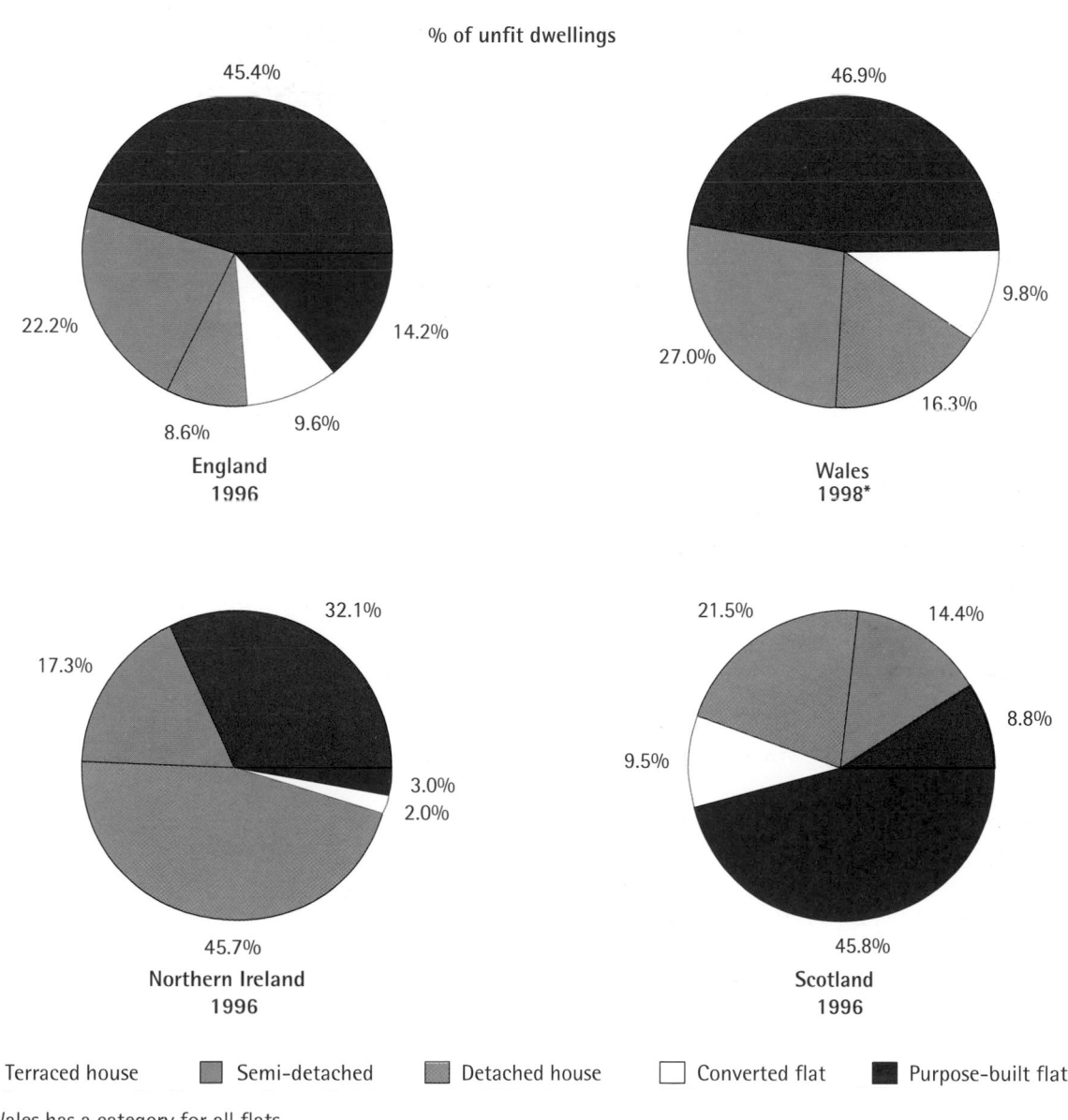

% of unfit dwellings

England 1996

Wales 1998*

Northern Ireland 1996

Scotland 1996

■ Terraced house ■ Semi-detached ■ Detached house □ Converted flat ■ Purpose-built flat

* Wales has a category for all flats

Figure 4.7 (Table A4.8) shows the distribution of unfit/BTS dwellings by a range of dwelling type/ age categories. This can be compared with Figure 4.3 which shows the proportions of the dwelling stock as a whole in each category. Pre-1919 terraced dwellings are more than twice as likely to be unfit as their frequency in the dwelling stock as a whole would suggest.

Figure 4.7: Unfit/BTS dwellings by age and type, UK (1993/96)

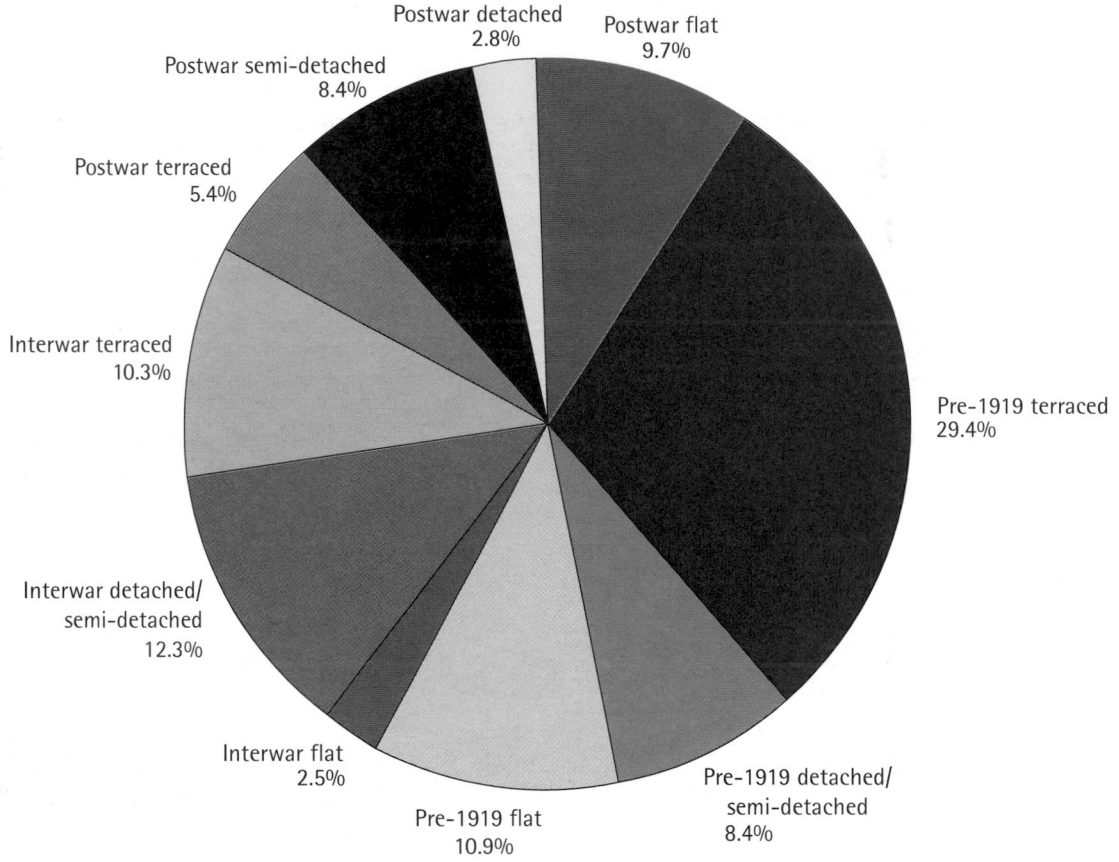

Postwar detached 2.8%

Postwar flat 9.7%

Postwar semi-detached 8.4%

Postwar terraced 5.4%

Interwar terraced 10.3%

Interwar detached/ semi-detached 12.3%

Interwar flat 2.5%

Pre-1919 flat 10.9%

Pre-1919 detached/ semi-detached 8.4%

Pre-1919 terraced 29.4%

Tenure

Owner-occupation is the majority tenure throughout the UK but it is highest in Wales (71% of households), similar in Northern Ireland (70%) and England (67%), and a little lower in Scotland (60%) (Figure 4.8, Table A4.9). A total of 16% of dwellings in England are rented from local authorities; England has the largest proportion of dwellings that are privately rented (11%). In Northern Ireland, the proportion of housing rented from the public sector (exclusively the NIHE) is higher (23%) and the private rented and housing association sectors are very small (4% and 3% respectively). In Scotland there is a much larger proportion of dwellings rented from public sector landlords (28%) than in the remainder of the UK, with relatively little private renting (7%).

Figure 4.8: Tenure of dwellings in the UK (1996)

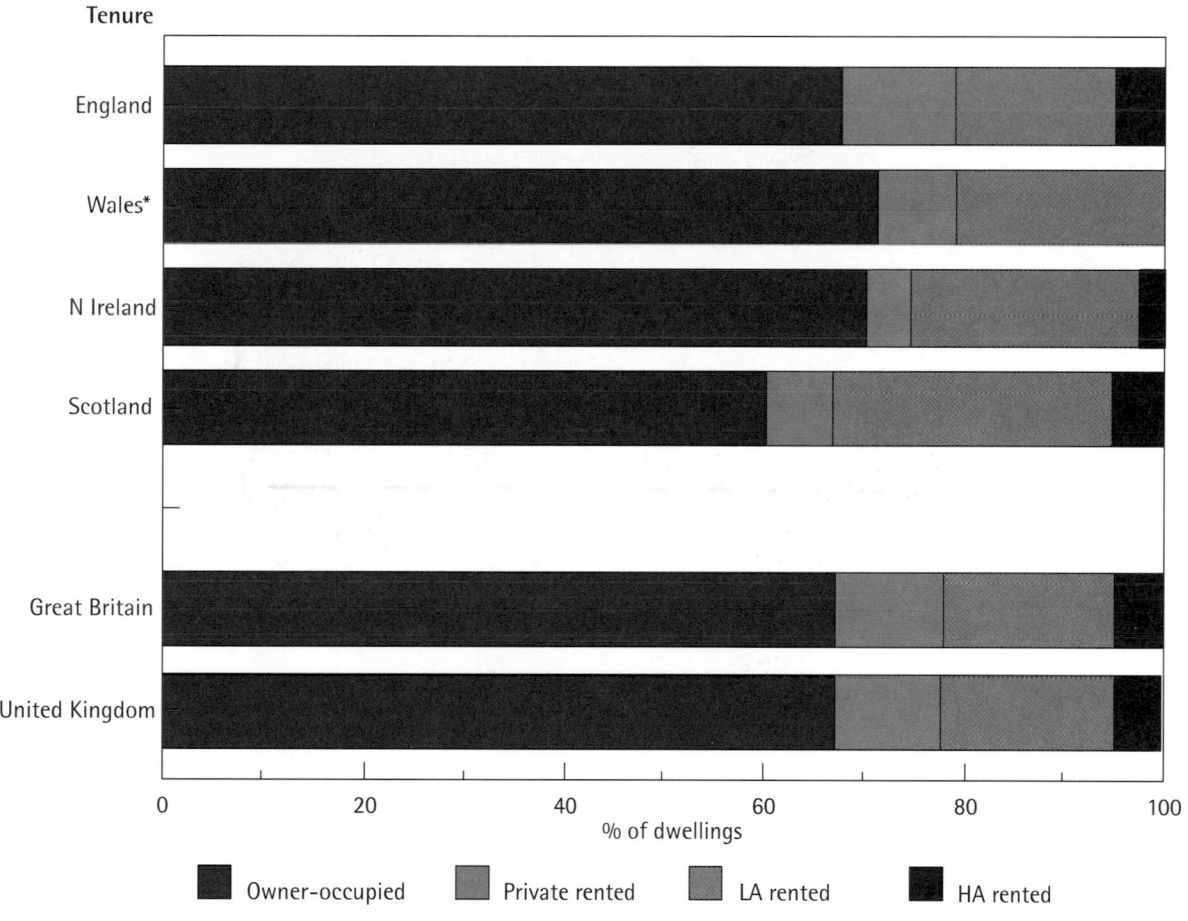

* Wales has a category for all social housing

Tenure and age of dwelling

Figure 4.9 shows the breakdown of dwellings in each tenure by age in 1996 for Britain as a whole. Table A4.10 provides fuller details. In total, over a third of all dwellings date from after 1964, with the remainder split evenly between the other three age bands. Dwellings owned outright are split more evenly across age groups, with slightly more in the post-1964 age group. Similarly dwellings bought with a mortgage are more likely to have been built after 1964. The local authority sector reflects the history of this form of provision with only 3% of dwellings dating from before 1919 and over three quarters built since 1945. The housing association sector reflects a more complex development with 17% of dwellings dating from before 1919 (a mix of dwellings built by the 19th-century associations and dwellings acquired more recently from private owners). Relatively few housing association dwellings date from the 1919-64 period, but nearly two thirds have been built since 1964, reflecting the active housing association new-build programme since the 1960s. The private rented sector is characterised by older dwellings, with 42% built before 1919, and half this amount (24%) dating from after 1964.

Figure 4.9: Age of dwelling by tenure, UK (1996)

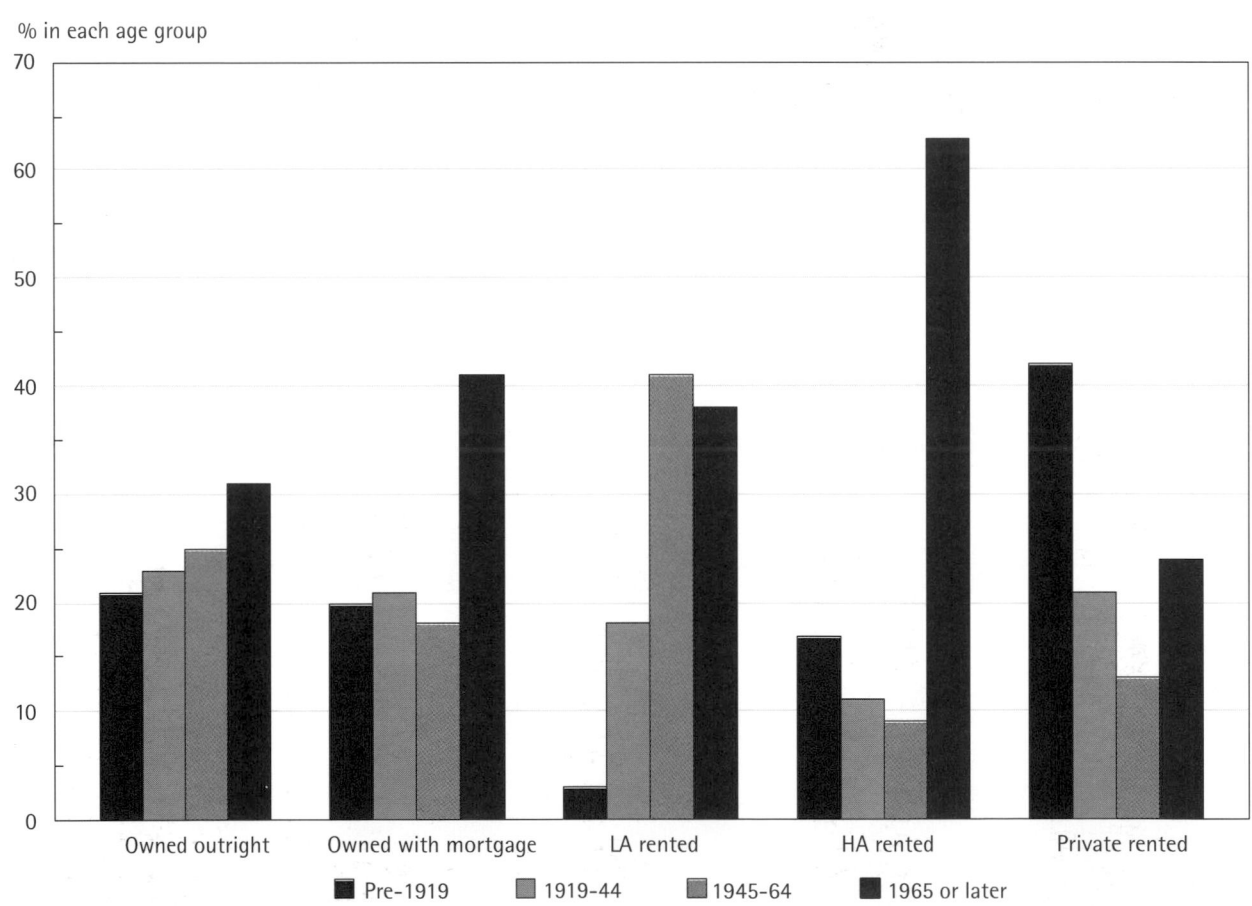

Tenure and dwelling type

Figure 4.10 shows the breakdown of dwellings in each tenure by type in 1996 for the UK as a whole. Table A4.11 provides detailed figures. Overall, semi-detached and terraced dwellings were the most common (accounting for about 32% and 27% of the stock respectively in 1996), followed by detached houses (21%), purpose-built flats (15%) and converted flats (5%). In the stock which is owned outright, detached and semi-detached houses are strongly over-represented (33% and 37% respectively). The other dwelling types, especially purpose-built flats, are under-represented, the latter reflecting the predominance of local authority ownership of this type of dwelling. Owners still buying with a mortgage are more likely to live in terraced or semi-detached houses, but again less likely to occupy a flat. Detached houses are a rarity in the local authority and housing association sectors, where terraced houses or purpose-built flats are most likely. Despite over 15 years of sales under the Right to Buy legislation, 60% of local authority dwellings and 39% of housing association dwellings are houses. Nevertheless, purpose-built flats are strongly over-represented in these sectors. In the private rented sector, the most notable feature is the concentration of converted flats (24%, compared to only 5% in the stock as a whole). Otherwise, terraced houses and purpose-built flats are found in this sector in about the same proportions as for the stock as a whole while detached and semi-detached houses are less common.

Figure 4.10: Dwelling type by tenure, UK (1996)

% in group by tenure

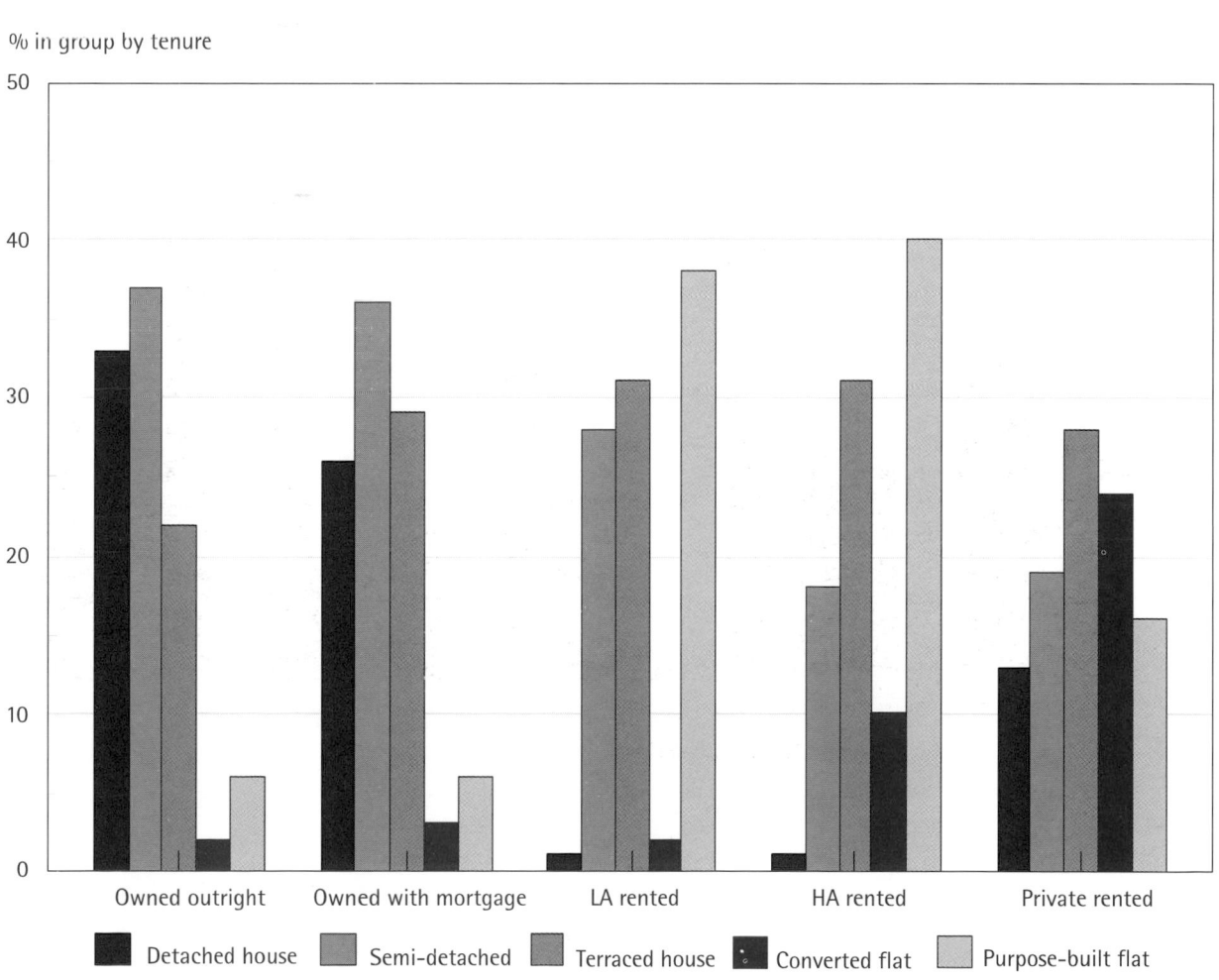

Dwellings in poor condition by tenure

There are distinct variations in housing conditions by tenure (Table 4.4, Table A4.12), although these can be masked by transfers between tenures. Vacant dwellings are the most likely to be in poor condition, but in the occupied stock the private rented sector has the highest proportion of dwellings in poor condition. In the remaining occupied stock the private rented sector is much more likely to be in poor condition throughout the UK. Owner-occupied dwellings are more likely to be in poor condition than the social rented sectors in Northern Ireland, this is also the case in England and Wales, although the difference is not as distinct. In Scotland the remaining tenures have generally similar proportions of dwellings BTS or in disrepair.

The much larger owner-occupied stock means that in numerical terms the majority of occupied unfit dwellings are found in the owner-occupied sector (Figure 4.11, Table A4.13). This concentration is greatest in Northern Ireland (71% of all unfit dwellings owner-occupied). Scotland has a higher proportion of private rented sector stock BTS. The housing association sector has significantly fewer unfit/BTS dwellings because of its small size. The picture in relation to disrepair is very similar, most disrepair is found in owner-occupied dwellings. Scotland is quite distinctive as nearly a third of its local authority rented dwellings are in need of repair.

Table 4.4: Dwellings in poor condition by tenure, UK (1996)

	% dwellings in each tenure group			
	Owner–occupied	Privately rented	LA rented	HA rented
England 1996				
Unfit	5.4	15.1	6.8	3.9
Disrepair*	29.3	53.9	28.0	13.8
Northern Ireland 1996				
Unfit	6.8	16.7	2.4	2.0
Disrepair*	25.7	41.9	11.1	3.4
Wales 1993/99				
Unfit†	7.6	18.4	8.2	
Disrepair‡	19.9	34.3	18.7	8.4
Scotland 1996				
BTS	0.9	4.1	0.5	0.2
Disrepair*	5.2	16.7	3.3	1.2

* Dwellings with urgent repair costs over £1,000. Note, however, that comparisons cannot be made between countries on this indicator.
† For Wales, data on unfitness relates to 1998; data on disrepair relates to 1993.
‡ Dwellings with repair costs over £1,500.

Sources: DoE (1998); Scottish Homes (1997); NIHE (1997); Welsh Office (1994, 1999)

Figure 4.11: Unfit dwellings by tenure, UK

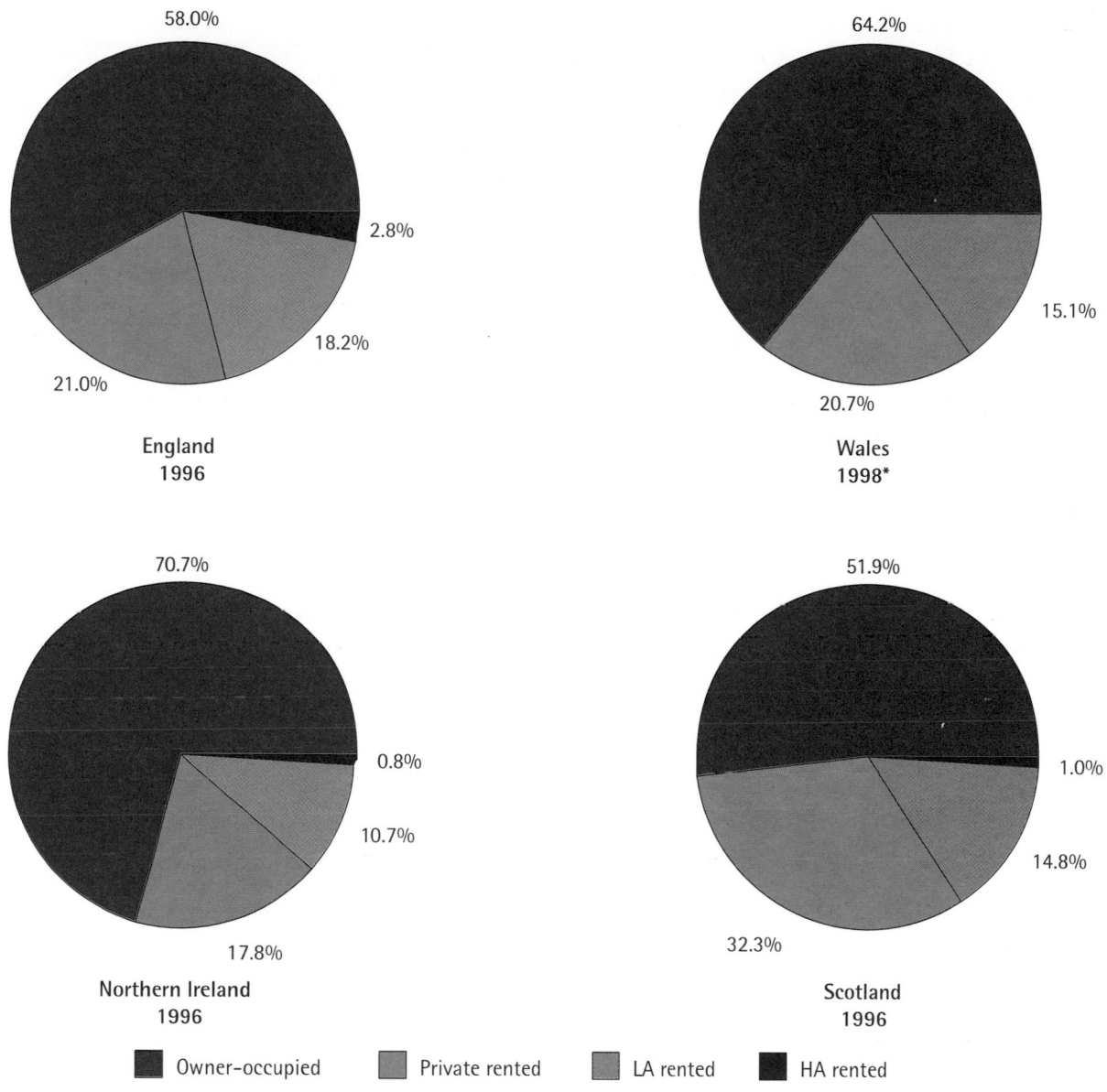

58.0%

2.8%

18.2%

21.0%

England
1996

64.2%

15.1%

20.7%

Wales
1998*

70.7%

0.8%

10.7%

17.8%

Northern Ireland
1996

51.9%

1.0%

14.8%

32.3%

Scotland
1996

■ Owner-occupied　　■ Private rented　　■ LA rented　　■ HA rented

* Wales has category for all social housing

An overview of dwellings in poor condition

Figures 4.12-4.15 combine information on tenure and age of the dwelling stock in each country to provide a profile of unfit/BTS dwellings (see also Table A4.14). In England the pre-1919 owner-occupied stock forms the largest single group of unfit dwellings, comprising more than 369,000

properties. There are a further 201,000 unfit inter-war owner-occupied dwellings. Pre-1919 privately rented dwellings make up another substantial group of poor condition properties (14% or 179,000). The next largest group of unfit dwellings is the post-1945 owner-occupied stock (11.3% or 144,000 dwellings). Together these dwellings make up about two thirds of the poor condition stock.

Figure 4.12: Unfit dwellings by age and tenure, England (1996)

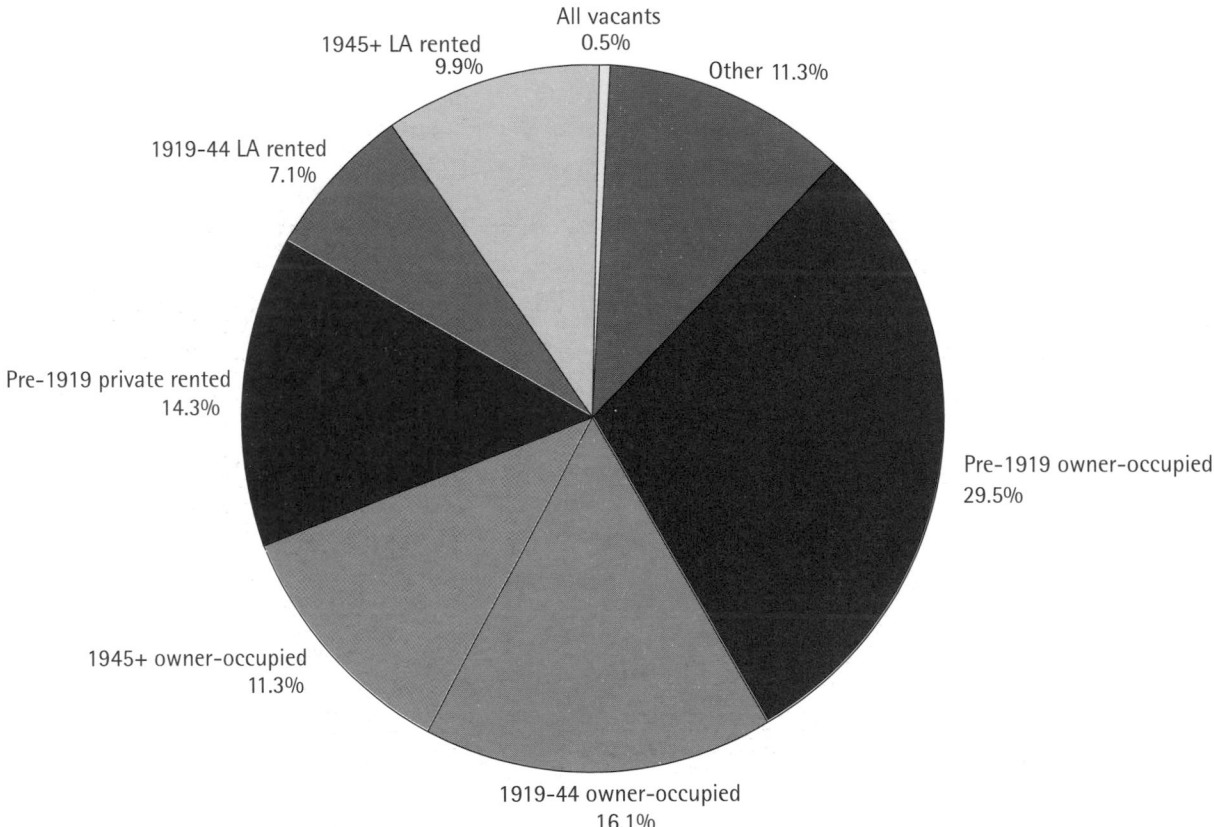

All vacants 0.5%
1945+ LA rented 9.9%
Other 11.3%
1919-44 LA rented 7.1%
Pre-1919 private rented 14.3%
Pre-1919 owner-occupied 29.5%
1945+ owner-occupied 11.3%
1919-44 owner-occupied 16.1%

In Wales, unfitness is more concentrated in pre-1919 owner-occupied dwellings (42% of all unfit dwellings), with postwar local authority dwellings, and postwar owner-occupied dwellings forming the next largest groups of unfit dwellings (15% and 13% respectively), closely followed by pre-1919 private rented accommodation (see Figure 4.13). In Scotland, pre-1919 owner-occupied dwellings also form the largest BTS group (41%),

followed by pre-1919 privately rented stock (Figure 4.14). In Northern Ireland, 30% of the unfit stock is pre-1919 owner-occupied. The next largest category is the vacant owner-occupied stock of all ages (20%), and again the pre-1919 privately rented stock is one of the categories with the highest percentage of unfit dwellings (Figure 4.15). (Table A4.15 shows the age and tenure breakdown of dwellings in disrepair.)

Figure 4.13: Unfit dwellings by age and tenure, Wales (1999)

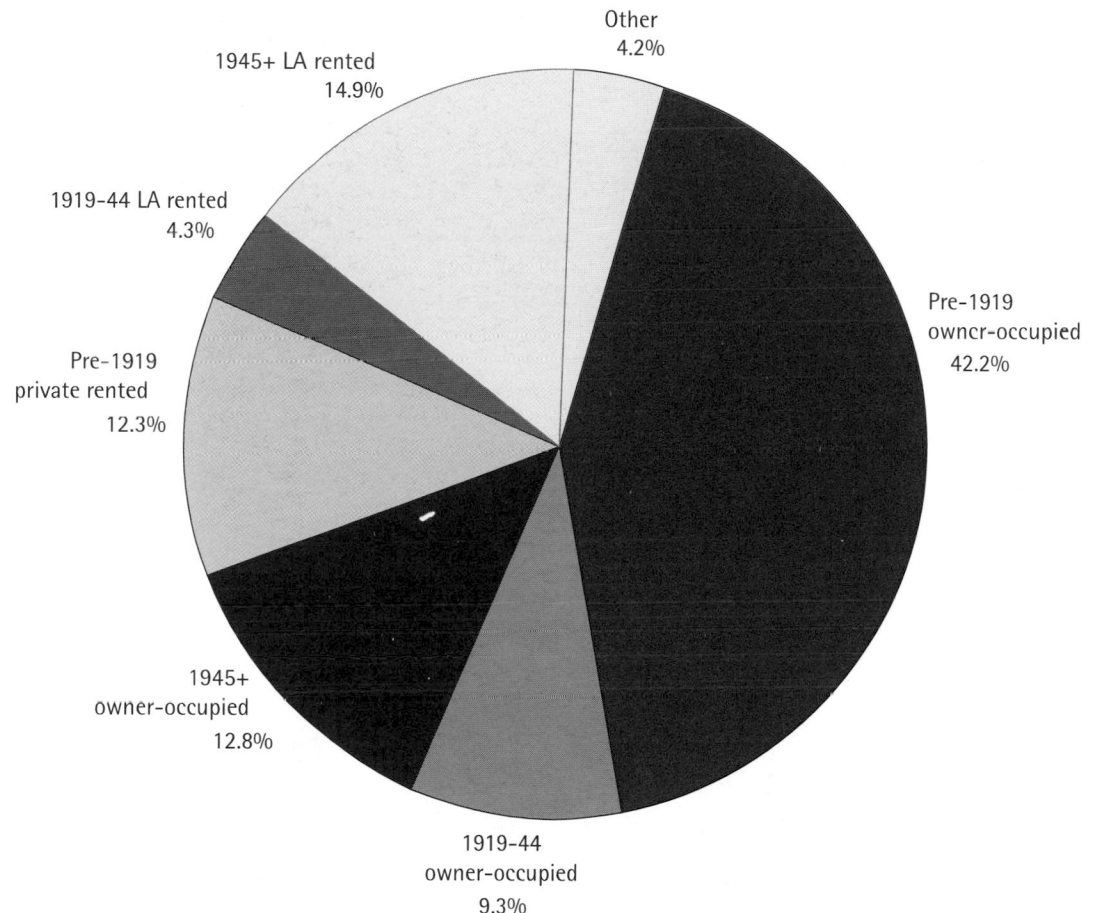

Figure 4.14: BTS dwellings by age and tenure, Scotland (1996)

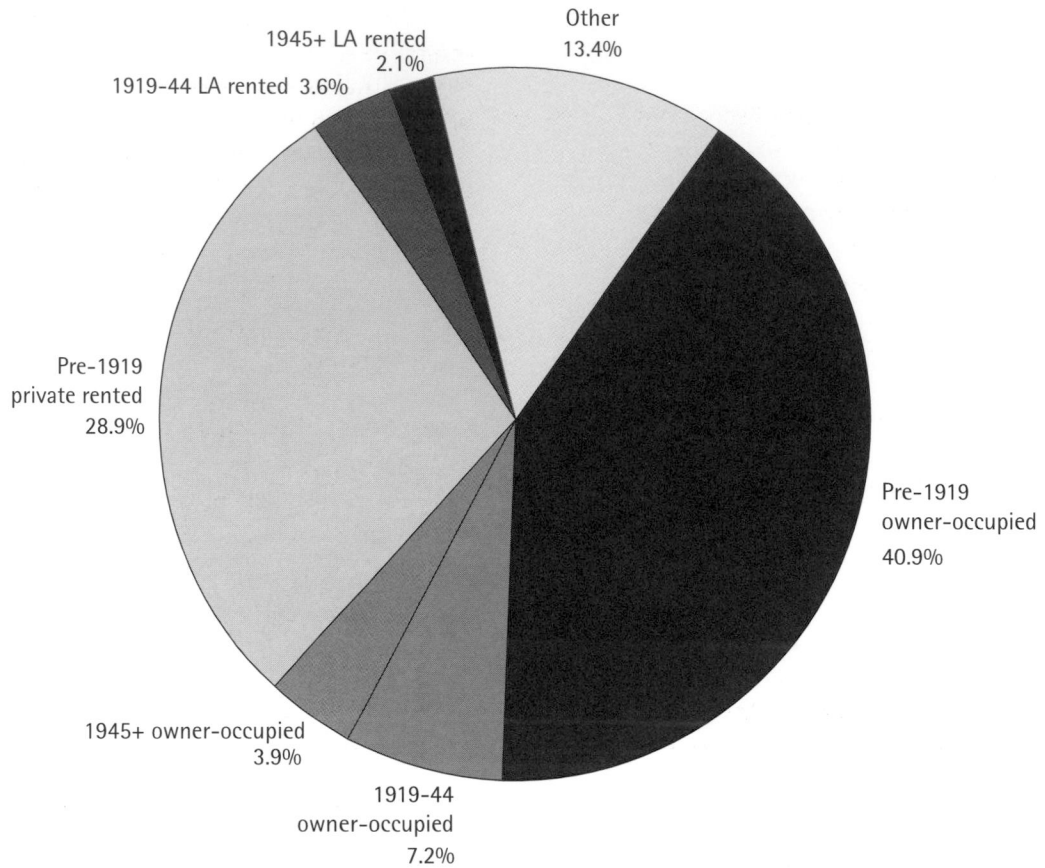

1945+ LA rented 2.1%

1919-44 LA rented 3.6%

Other 13.4%

Pre-1919 private rented 28.9%

Pre-1919 owner-occupied 40.9%

1945+ owner-occupied 3.9%

1919-44 owner-occupied 7.2%

Figure 4.15: Unfit dwellings by age and tenure, Northern Ireland (1996)

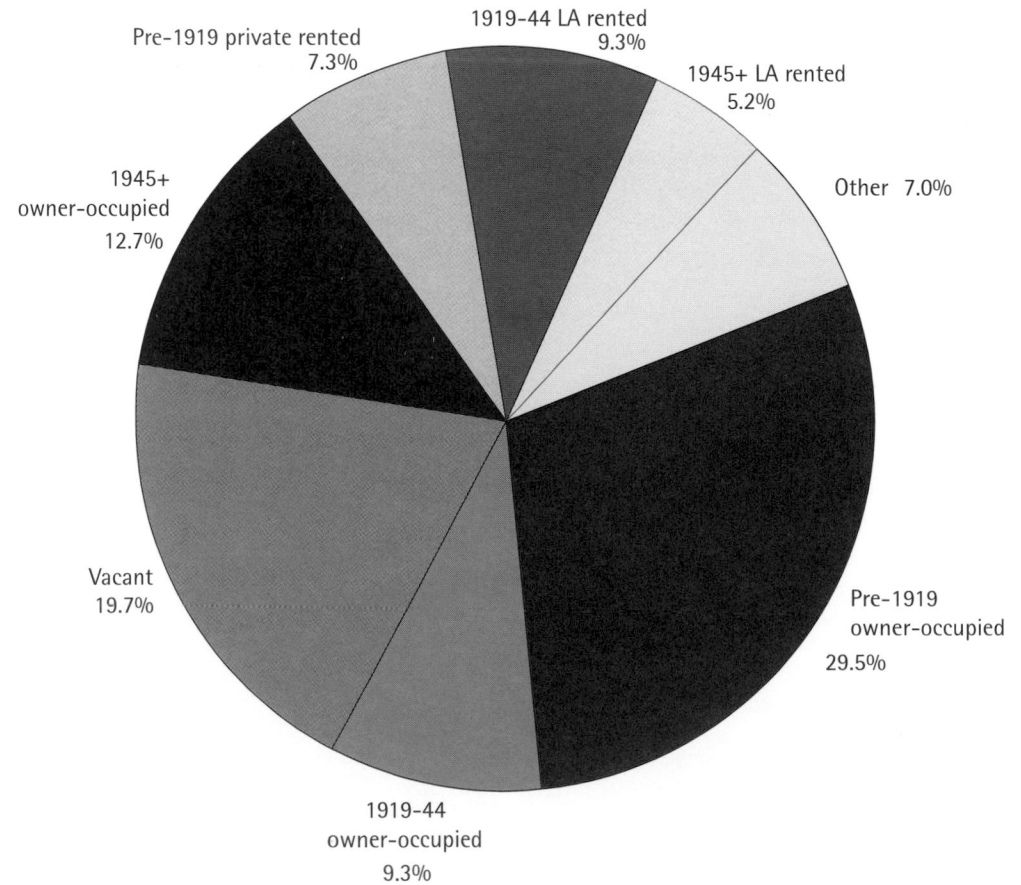

Pre-1919 private rented 7.3%

1919-44 LA rented 9.3%

1945+ LA rented 5.2%

1945+ owner-occupied 12.7%

Other 7.0%

Vacant 19.7%

Pre-1919 owner-occupied 29.5%

1919-44 owner-occupied 9.3%

Energy efficiency

Heating

A large majority of dwellings have central heating (Table 4.5). In each country over 80% of dwellings have some form of central heating. In each case only a very small percentage of dwellings rely on portable forms of heating. Data for England and Scotland distinguishes the extent of central heating, showing that most central heating systems are fully fitted.

The distribution of central heating varies with tenure. Figure 4.16 (and Table A4.16) shows the percentage of dwellings in the UK which have some form of central heating by tenure. Owner-occupied dwellings are most likely to have central heating. Little change has occurred in this tenure over the last five years, although the provision of central heating has increased in other tenures. The private rented sector is still least likely to be provided with this amenity, but this sector has experienced a substantial increase since 1991. Scotland in particular has been subject to substantial improvement in terms of central heating provision, especially in the housing association stock. In Wales the private rented sector has also improved in terms of provision of central heating.

Scottish data gives a breakdown of the dwellings without any heating facilities. These tend to be in older properties which are owner-occupied, a high proportion being tenements.

Table 4.5: Type of heating by country, UK (1996)

	Central heating		Fixed appliances		Portable/other	
	Full	**Part**	**Full**	**Part**	**Full**	**Part**
England	67.7	16.4	1.0	13.7	0.1	1.1
Scotland	73.4	13.8	10.5		2.2	
Northern Ireland	86.9		11.6		1.4	
Wales	89.0		9		2	

Note: Full heating is where 70–100% of the rooms are covered, anything less equals part.
Source: DoE (1998), NIHE (1998), Scottish Homes (1996), Welsh Office (1998)

Figure 4.16: Central heating by tenure

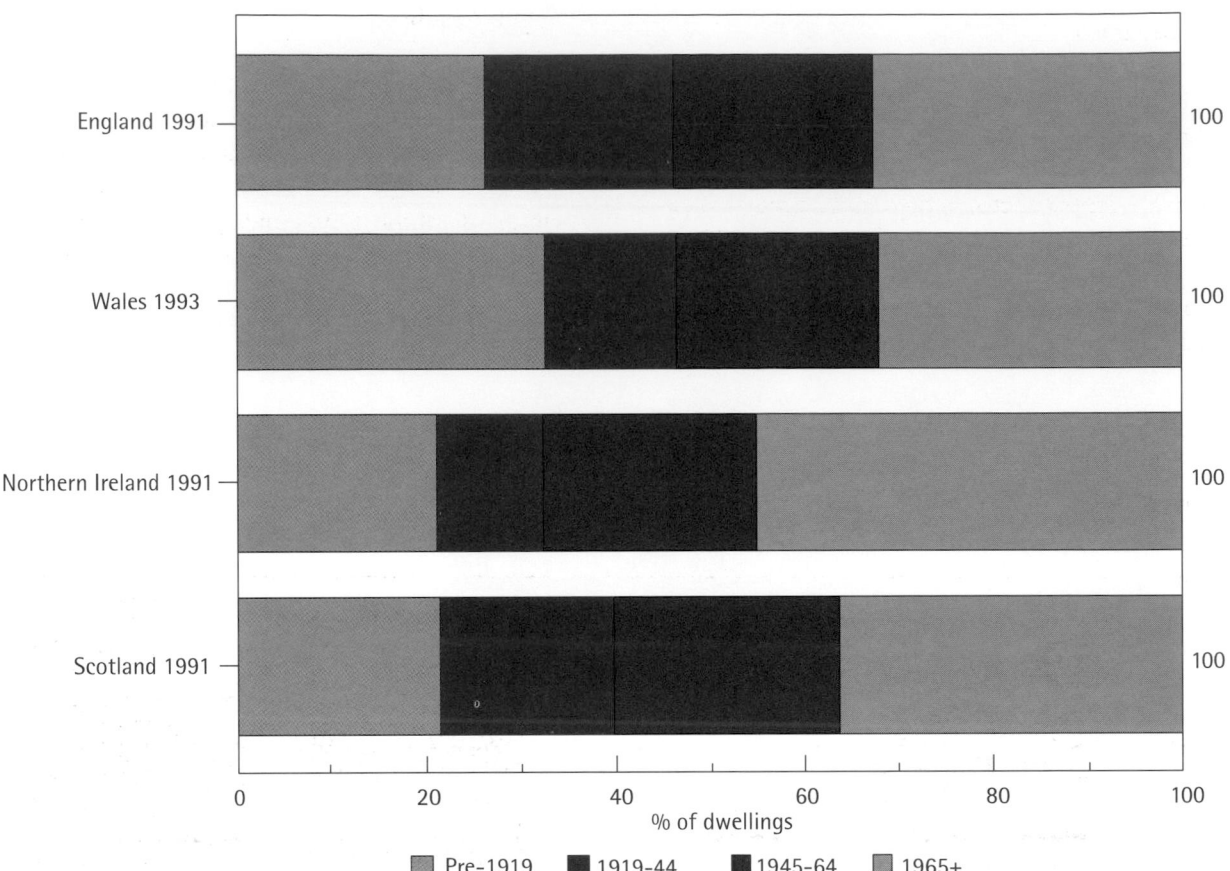

Thermal insulation

Loft insulation

The pattern of loft insulation is very similar for England, Scotland and Northern Ireland as Figure 4.17 shows (Table A4.17 for more details). The private rented sector is the tenure group that is least likely to have insulated lofts (about 70%), followed by the owner-occupied sector. A very high percentage of local authority and housing association dwellings has loft insulation. Data on insulation by tenure was not available for Wales, but, overall, 81% of households in Wales have insultaed lofts.

The effectiveness of insulation depends on its quality and thickness. In Scotland, although 80% of all dwellings have loft insulation, only 12% of these dwellings have loft insulation to the standards of the 1991 Building Regulations (Figure 4.18 and Table A4.18). Building regulations for loft insulation have gradually increased from 25mm in 1964 to 150mm by 1991.

Figure 4.17: Incidence of loft insulation by tenure, England, Scotland and Northern Ireland (1996)

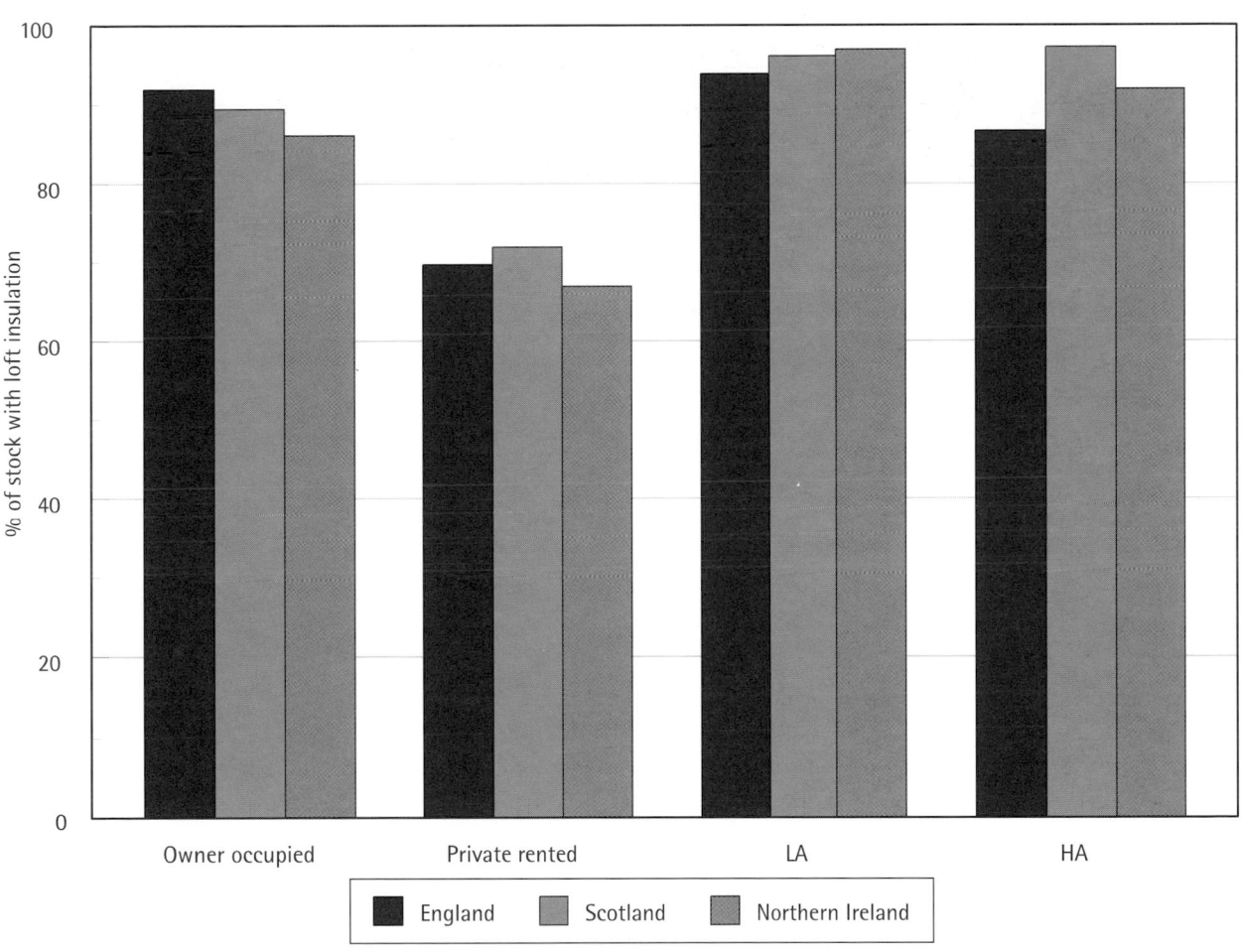

Figure 4.18: Depth of loft insulation, England, Scotland and Northern Ireland (1996)

% of stock

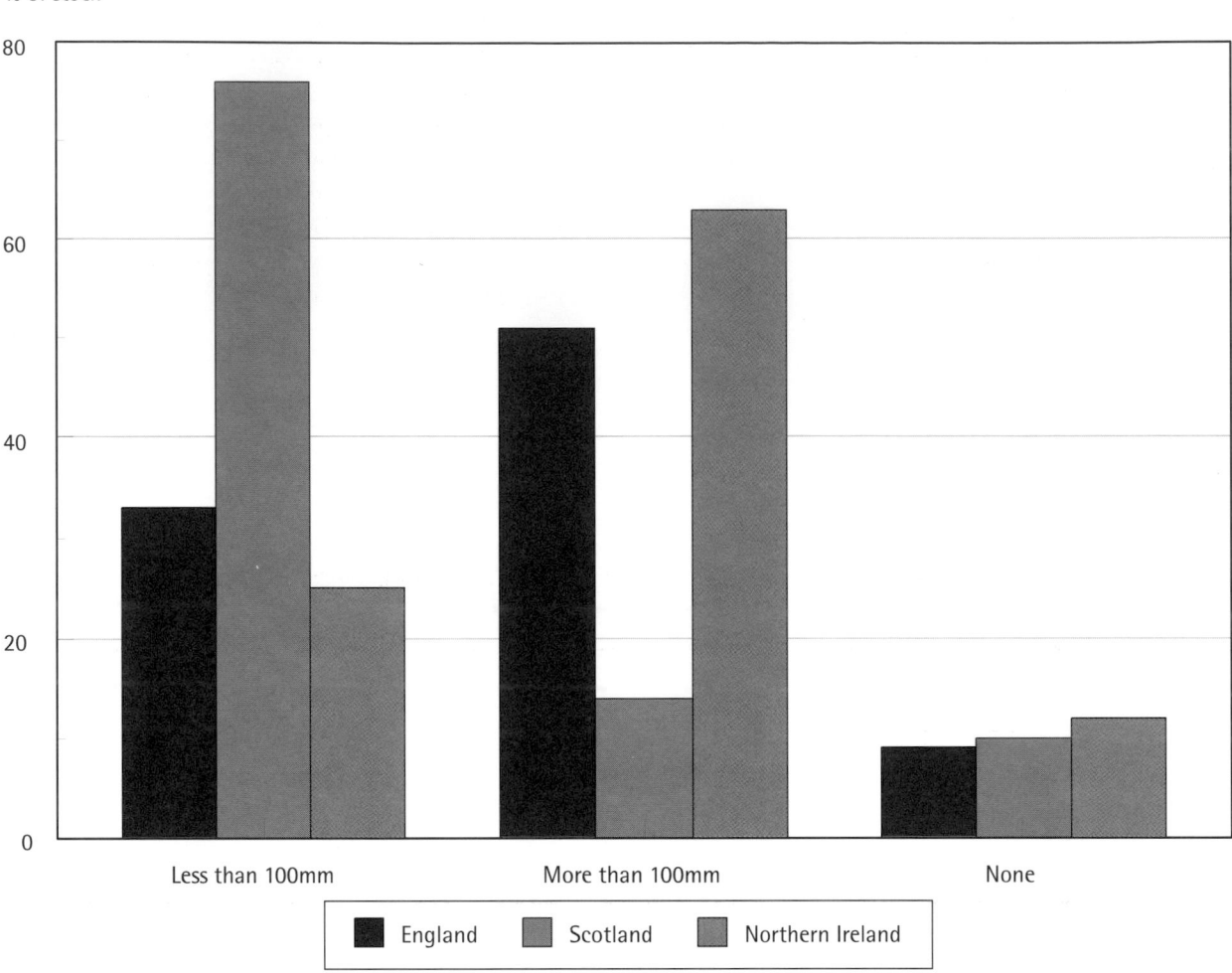

Hot water cylinder insulation

The house condition surveys also collect information on the presence of insulated hot water cylinders. In Scotland a large percentage (92%) of the dwellings with hot water storage tanks have these insulated. The equivalent figures are 89% in Wales, and in Northern Ireland and England 85%.

Insulation for hot water cylinders can take the form of either a jacket or a foam coating. The foam coating is a more efficient insulator, but only a quarter of cylinders in England, and 13% in Northern Ireland have this coating.

A breakdown of hot water tank insulation by tenure is available for England and Northern Ireland. Table 4.6 shows that high proportions of dwellings with hot water cylinders have some form of cylinder insulation. In England 94% of owner-occupiers have cylinder insulation compared to 81% of private rented dwelling. Similarly, in Northern Ireland it is the private rented sector that is less likely to have any insulation. Housing associations have a high percentage of their dwellings insulated in this way in England and Northern Ireland.

Table 4.6: Percentage of dwellings with cylinders that have them insulated in each tenure, England and Northern Ireland (1996)

	England	Northern Ireland
Owner-occupied	94.0	82.9
Private rented	81.0	76.3
Local authority	88.0	93.0
Housing association	90.0	96.7

Source: DoE (1998), NIHE (1998)

Double glazing

Figure 4.19 shows that Scotland and Wales have more dwellings with full double glazing than England and Northern Ireland. A large proportion of dwellings do not have any double glazing, especially in Northern Ireland (60% of all dwellings). Welsh figures do not distinguish between full- and part-glazed.

Table 4.7 below shows that owner-occupied dwellings are more likely to have double glazing in England and Northern Ireland (data for Scotland and Wales not available). In England this is more likely to be partial double glazing whereas Northern Ireland dwellings are more likely to be fully double glazed. In England the remaining three tenures have over three quarters of dwellings without any form of double glazing.

Figure 4.19: Incidence of double glazing, UK (1996)

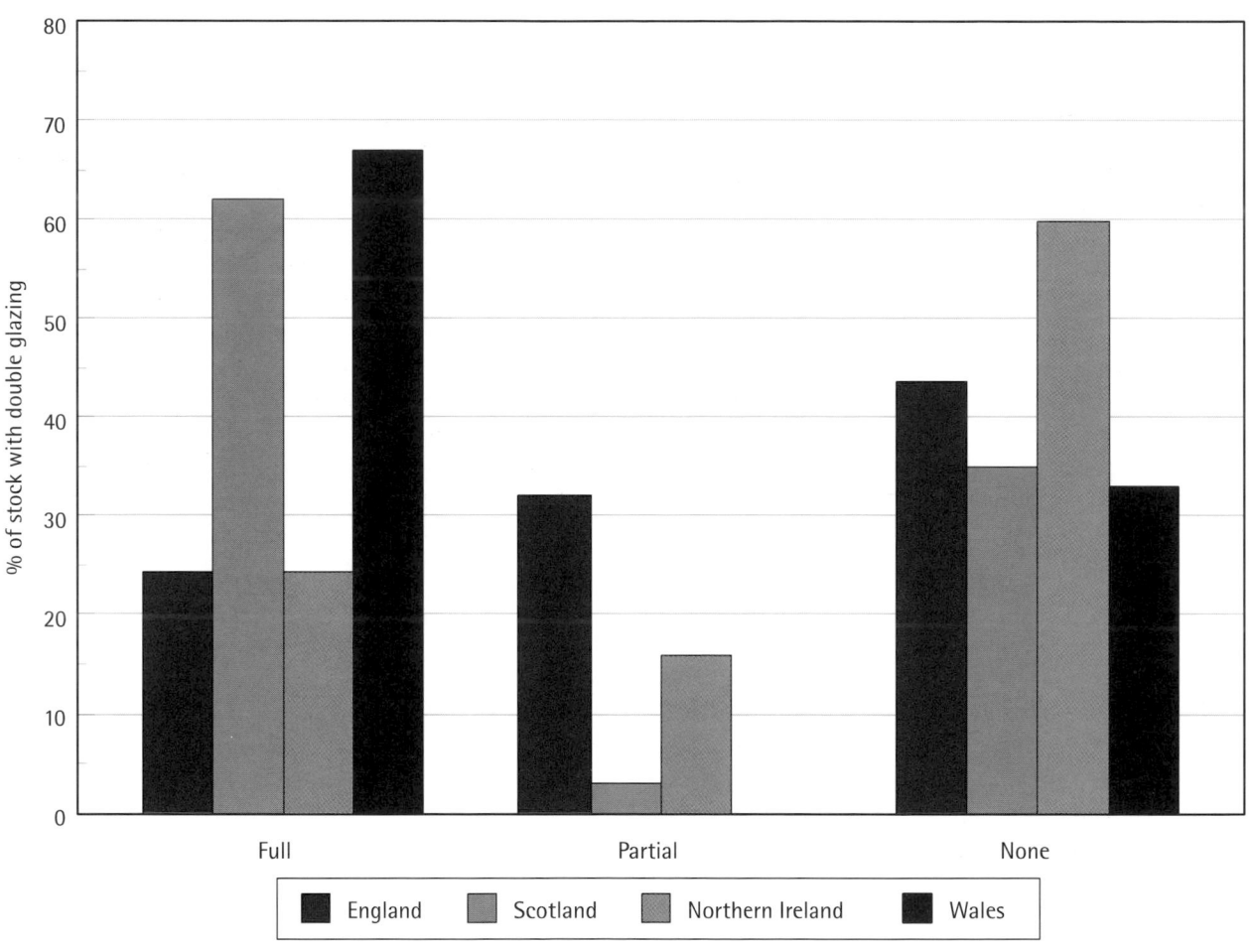

Table 4.7: Extent of double glazing by tenure, England and Northern Ireland (1996)

	England			Northern Ireland		
	Full	Partial	None	Full	Partial	None
Owner-occupied	30.6	42.5	26.9	33.7	21.8	44.5
Private rented	6.8	14.1	79.1	15.0	12.4	72.6
Local authority	12.8	8.3	78.9	2.3	2.0	95.7
Housing association	12.7	9.3	78.0	42.9	3.7	53.4
All dwellings	24.4	32.0	43.6	24.3	15.9	59.8

Source: DoE (1998), NIHE (1998)

Energy efficiency

The Standard Assessment Procedure (SAP) rating was introduced by the government to provide a common measurement of the energy efficiency of a dwelling unit on a standard heating regime. The SAP rating takes account of both heat loss from the dwelling and of the efficiency of heating systems, and price of fuel for heating. Ratings range from 1 (highly inefficient performance) to 100 (highly efficient performance). The average energy efficiency rating in England is just over 35, and in Northern Ireland this figure is 41. In Northern Ireland around 13% of dwellings have a poor energy rating falling below 20, compared to 15% in England.

Data on the alternative National Home Energy Rating (NHER) scores is available from the 1996 SHCS. The mean NHER in Scotland is 4.1 which translates to a SAP rating of 43. About 17% of Scottish dwellings have a poor SAP rating.

There are significant variations in the energy efficiency of dwellings depending on tenure, type and age. In England and Scotland data on SAP rating by tenure (Table 4.8) show that in all tenures, there is a concentration of neither poorly nor well-insulated dwellings. The worst tenure is the private rented sector, particularly in England where nearly half of the stock were rated as poor.

Age of dwelling also has an impact upon energy efficiency. Figure 4.20 and 4.21 (Table A4.20 for more detail) show that in England and Northern Ireland dwellings with a very low rating are predominantly older pre-1919 houses (over a third in Northern Ireland). A similar breakdown was not available for Scotland, but Table 4.9 below shows mean NHER scores by dwelling age. An average of about three quarters of each age band have moderate energy ratings, but older, pre-1919 housing has the highest percentage of dwellings in the poor band.

Table 4.8: SAP/NHER rating by tenure, England and Scotland (1996)

	Owner-occupied	Private rented	LA	HA
England				
Poor	10.5	42.6	17.8	18.1
Moderate	85.6	53.6	78.6	76.8
Good	3.9	3.7	4.5	5.2
Scotland				
Poor	14.0	31.0	20.0	13.0
Moderate	81.0	62.0	73.0	66.0
Good	6.0	7.0	7.0	21.0

Source: DoE (1998), Scottish Homes (1996)

Table 4.9: Mean NHER by dwelling age, Scotland (1996)

	Pre 1919	1919–44	1945–64	1965–82	Post–1982	All dwellings
Poor	21	13	19	17	6	17
Moderate	71	82	76	79	75	76
Good	8	5	5	4	19	7

Source: Scottish Homes (1996)

People living in poor conditions

Social surveys linked to the national house condition surveys provide information on the characteristics of people living in poor conditions. It was argued in the previous chapter that characteristics such as dwelling age or type were factors which, directly or indirectly, influenced dwelling condition. Household characteristics such as income, economic status, length of residence, age of household head and household composition are also strongly associated with housing conditions, but the relationship between these factors and physical conditions is often complex. Some characteristics may, to some extent, be contributory causes of poor conditions, for example low income making it difficult for an owner to afford to carry out repairs. Others, such as age of household head, have no obvious direct impact on condition but may be associated with variations in income, for example the lower resources associated with retirement. Others, for example length of residence, may be associated with attitudes to repair and maintenance which may, in turn, influence investment levels. But often, cause and effect are difficult to disentangle, as low-income households living in poor condition housing may have chosen this housing because its poor condition made it cheap to buy or rent.

Income

People on low incomes are generally more likely than those with higher levels of resources to live in poor housing conditions (Figures 5.1-5.4, Table A5.1). In England for example, around one in 10 households with an income of less than £4,000 per annum lived in unfit dwellings compared with only one in 25 of those with an income of £24,000 or more. In Scotland the same pattern applies in relation to BTS dwellings but there is less differentiation by income group in relation to disrepair. As Table A5.2 shows, most of those living in poor conditions have low incomes. In Scotland and Wales at least three quarters of those living in unfit housing or housing in serious disrepair had incomes below £12,000 in 1996, and just over 50% in England and Northern Ireland. Nevertheless, this still leaves a minority of more affluent households living in poor conditions. This phenomenon is more common in England, where in 1991 almost 100,000 households with incomes of £20,000 per annum or more lived in unfit dwellings. This figure had more than doubled to 211,000 households in 1996.

Figure 5.1: Households living in poor conditions by income group, England (1996)

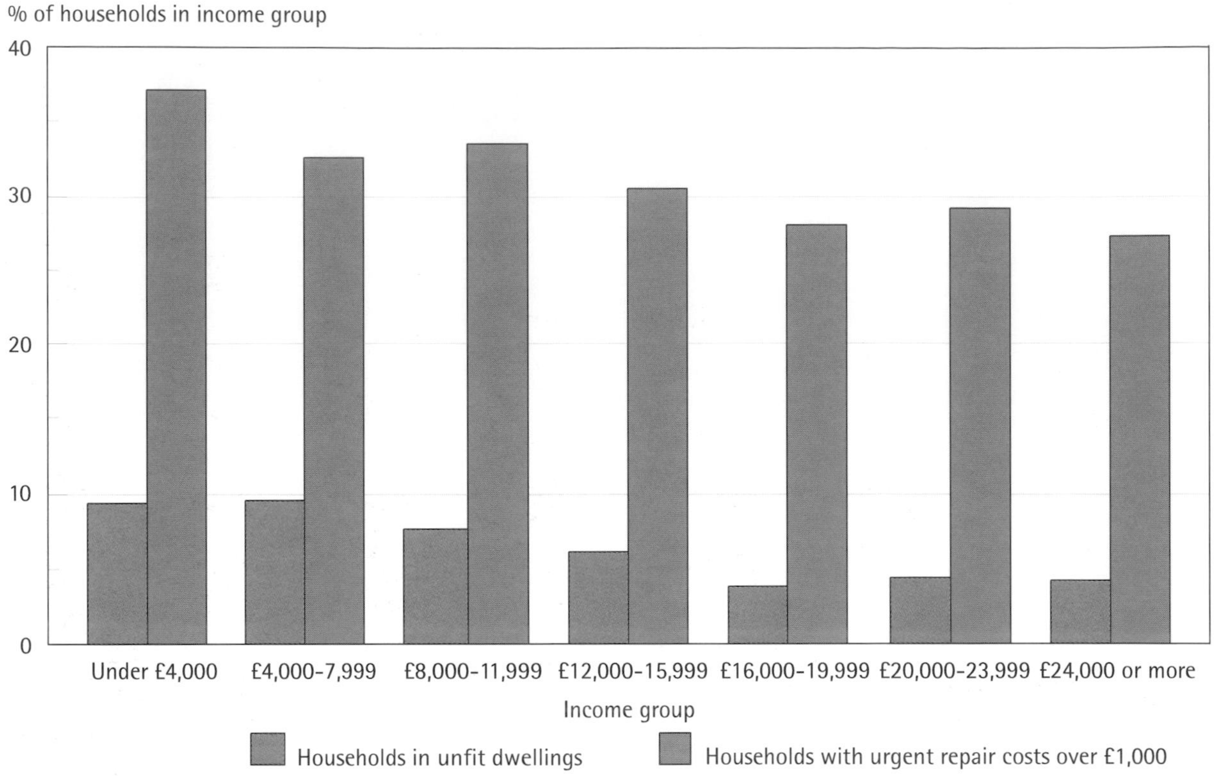

% of households in income group

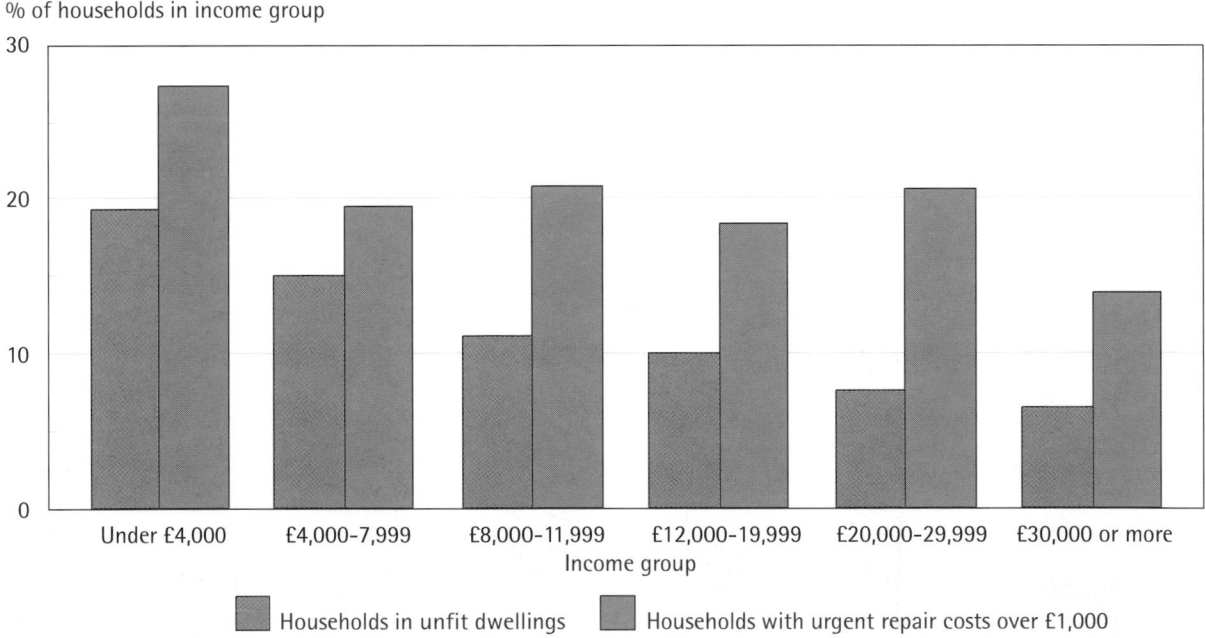

Income group

Households in unfit dwellings   Households with urgent repair costs over £1,000

Figure 5.2: Households living in poor conditions by income group, Wales (1993)

% of households in income group

Income group

Households in unfit dwellings   Households with urgent repair costs over £1,000

Figure 5.3: Households living in poor conditions by income group, Scotland (1996)

% of households in income group

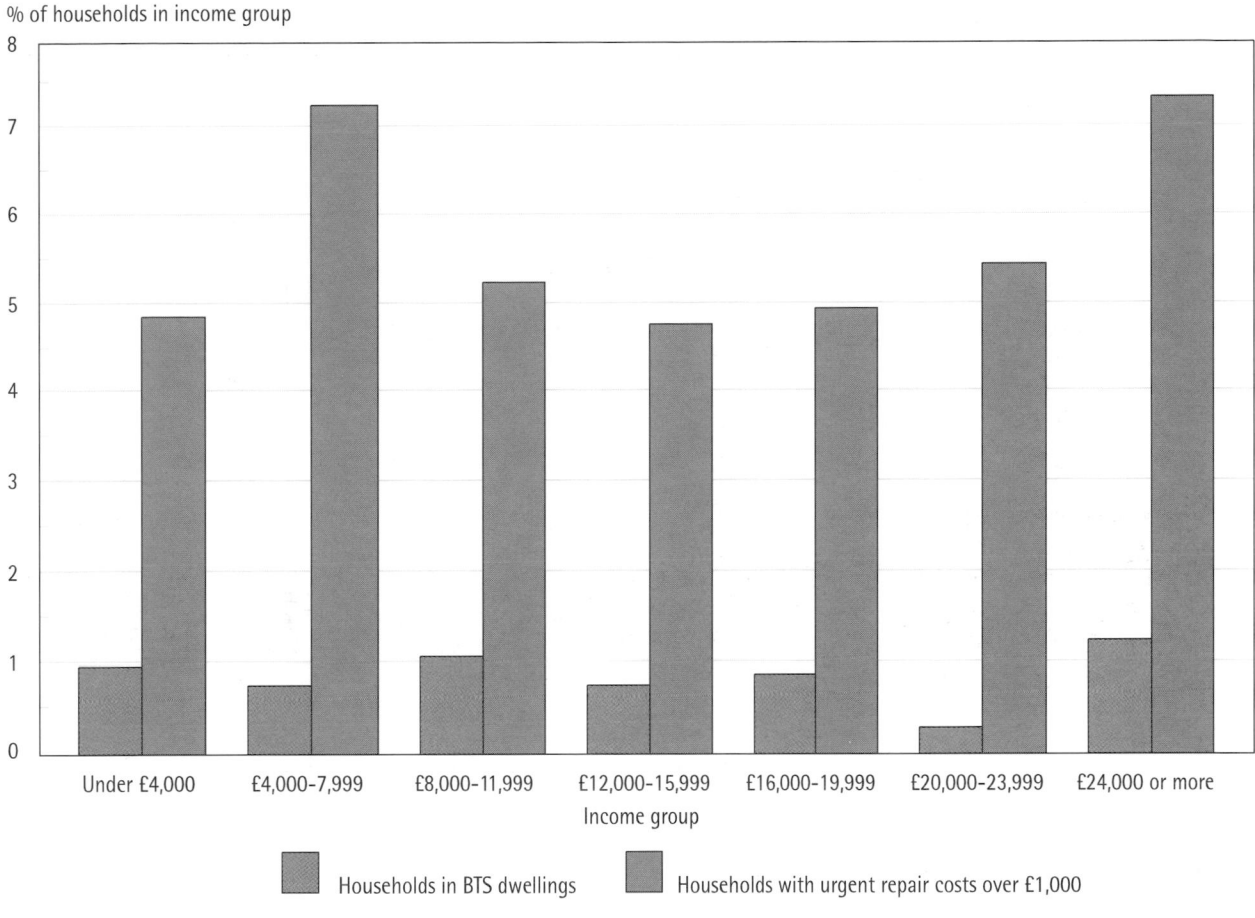

Income group

Households in BTS dwellings   Households with urgent repair costs over £1,000

Figure 5.4: Households living in poor conditions by income group, Northern Ireland (1996)

% of households in income group

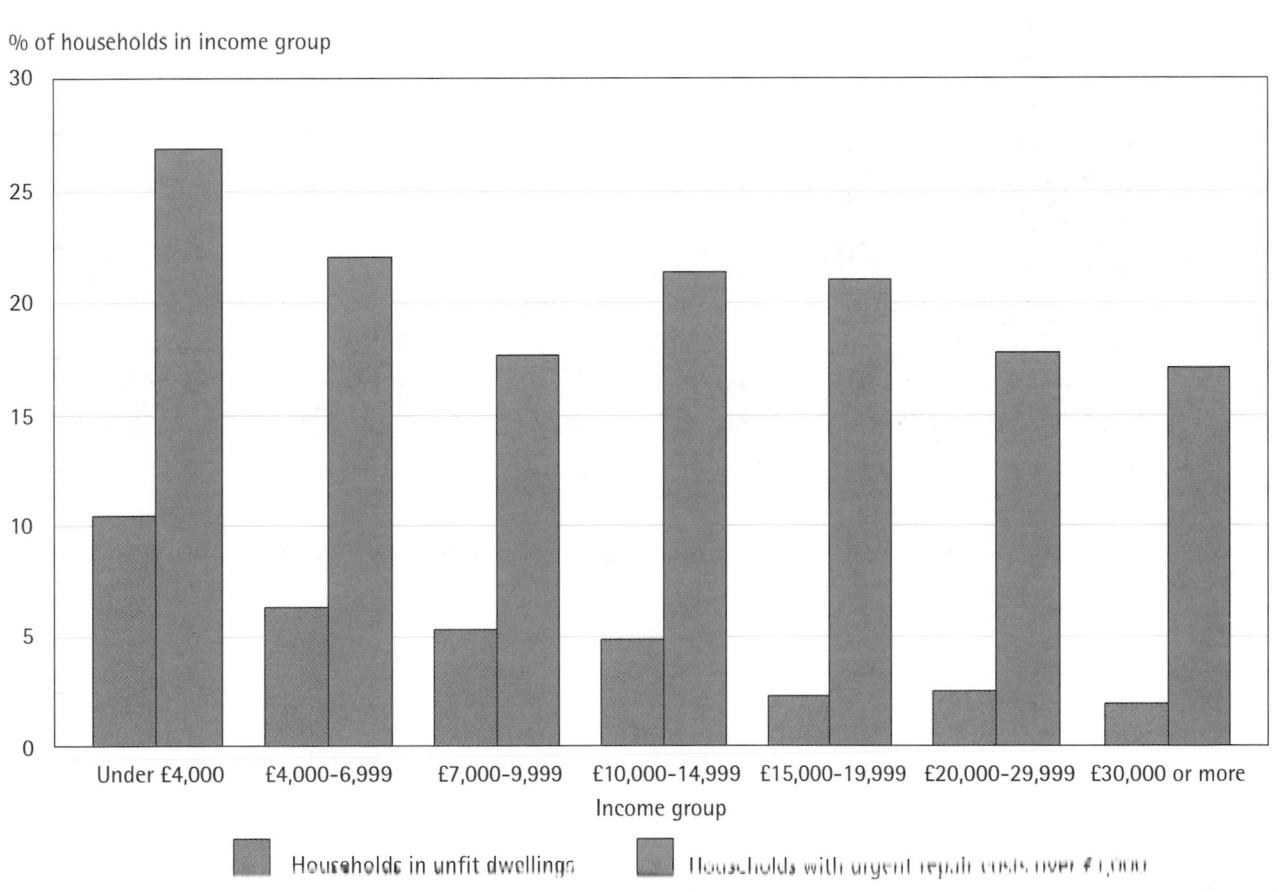

Income group

Households in unfit dwellings   Households with urgent repair costs over £1,000

Employment status

In England, households where the head is unemployed are more likely to live in poor conditions than other groups (Figure 5.5, Table A5.3). Almost 12% of unemployed households live in unfit housing compared with only 7% of all households. Households where the head is working are the least likely to live in poor conditions, while retired household heads fall in between.

The pattern in Scotland is broadly similar but the differences in the housing conditions between employment status groups are smaller (Figure 5.6, Table A5.3). In Northern Ireland the picture is different with retired households still the most likely to live in poor condition property, followed by those who are unemployed (Figure 5.7, Table A5.3). Recent data for Wales is not available, but in 1986 the position was similar to that in Northern Ireland. This may be accounted for by the high proportion of older people living in poor condition housing in rural areas and in the Welsh valleys.

Figure 5.5: Households living in poor conditions by employment status, England (1996)

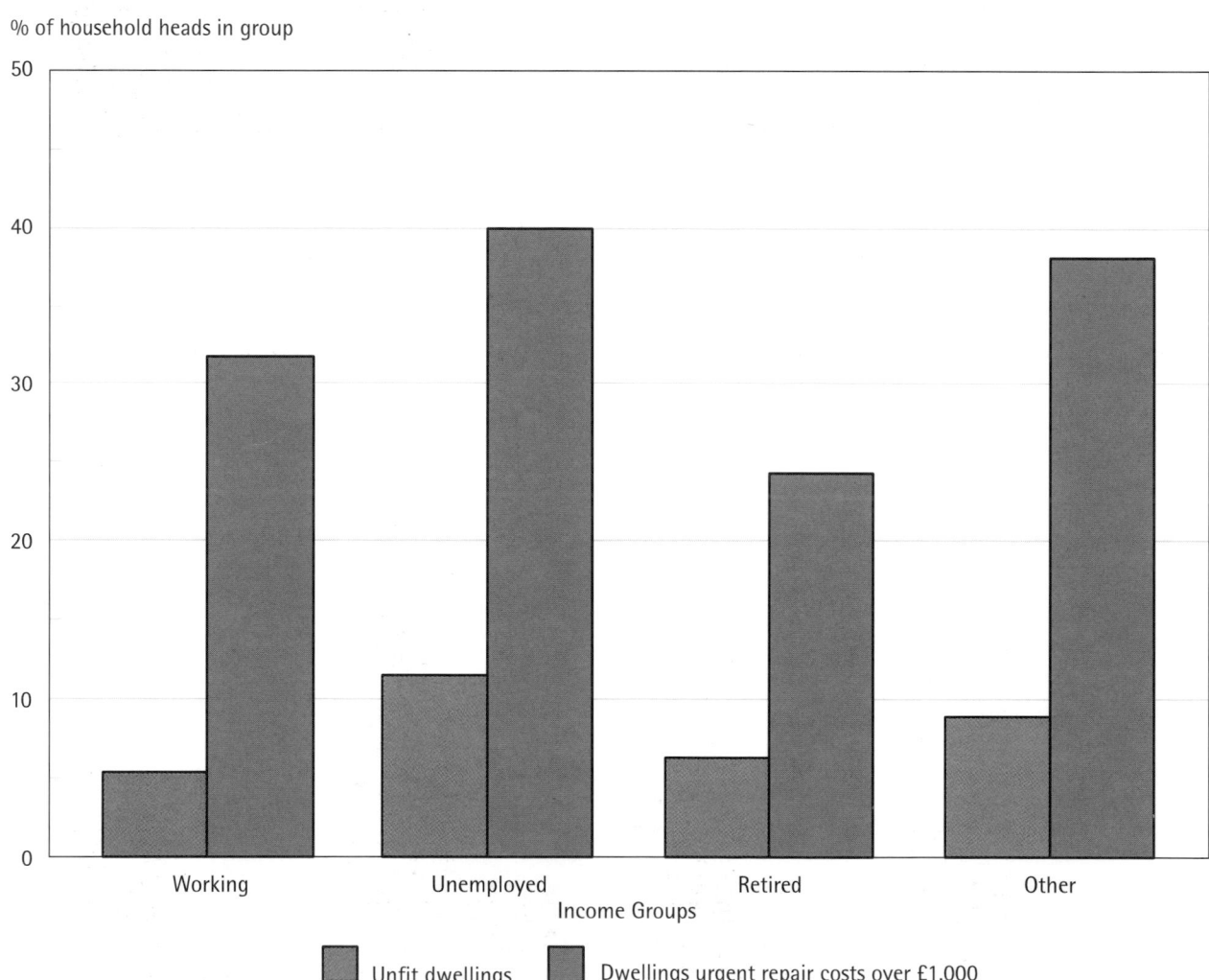

% of household heads in group

Income Groups

■ Unfit dwellings　■ Dwellings urgent repair costs over £1.000

Figure 5.6: Households living in poor conditions by employment status, Scotland (1996)

% of households in income groups

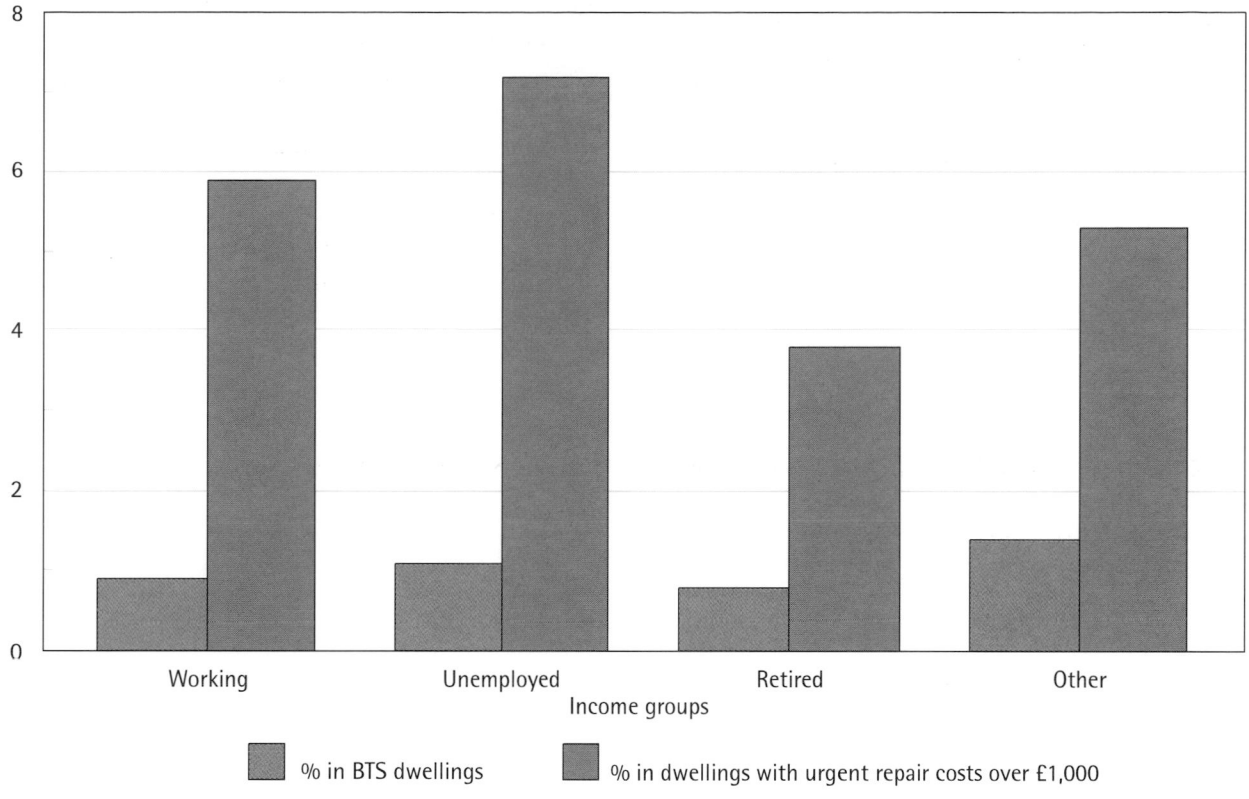

Figure 5.7: Households living in poor conditions by employment status, Northern Ireland (1996)

% of households in group

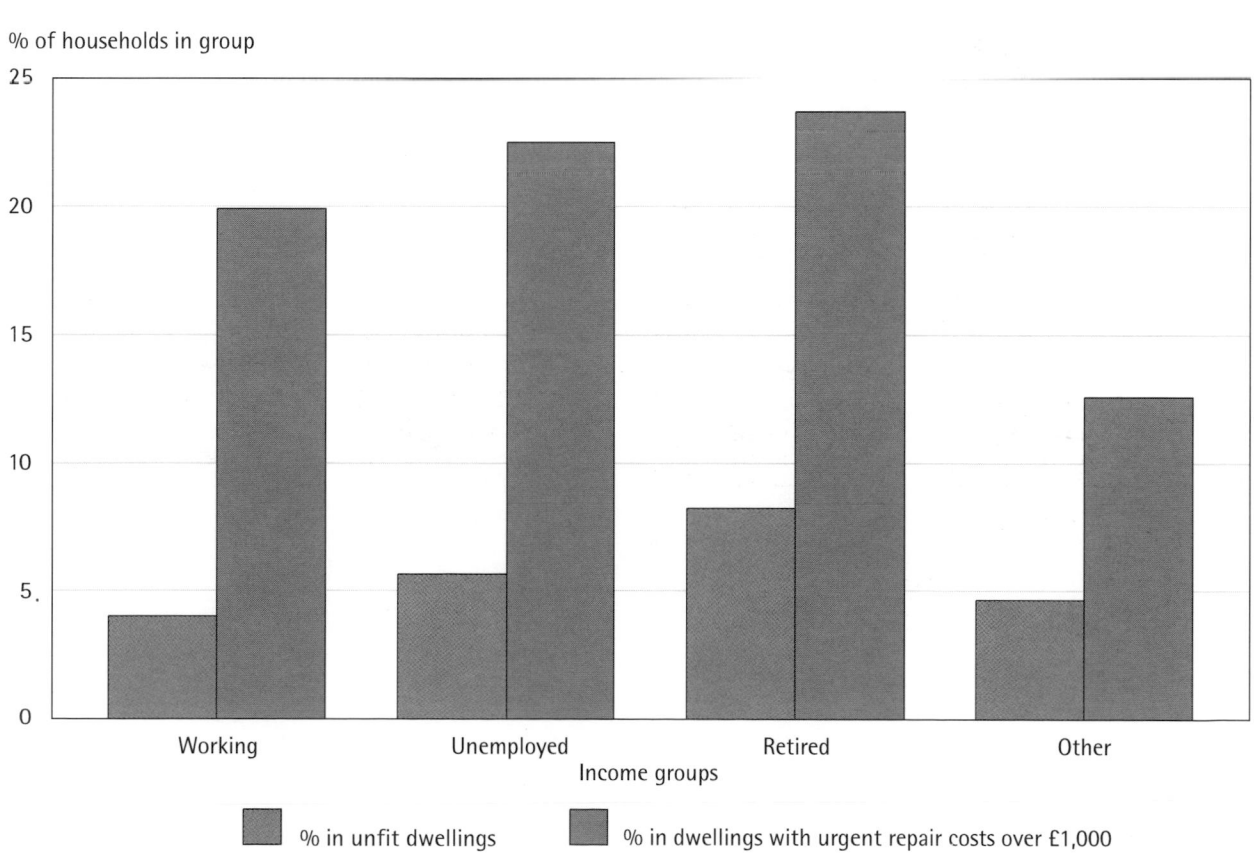

Household characteristics

The types of household which experience poor conditions are similar throughout the UK (Figures 5.8-5.11, Table A5.4). Generally both younger and older single people, and lone parent households are most likely to experience unfitness or live in BTS dwellings. The picture in Wales differs with less differentiation by household type.

The picture in relation to disrepair is less clear-cut. Lone person households are again very likely to experience problems but in England multi-adult households (41.5%), lone parent households (30%), and families with dependent children (29%) are more likely to experience poor conditions. Single pensioners are more likely to experience disrepair in their homes than pensioner couples. Two-adult households and small families are the best housed.

Figure 5.8: Households living in poor conditions by type, England (1996)

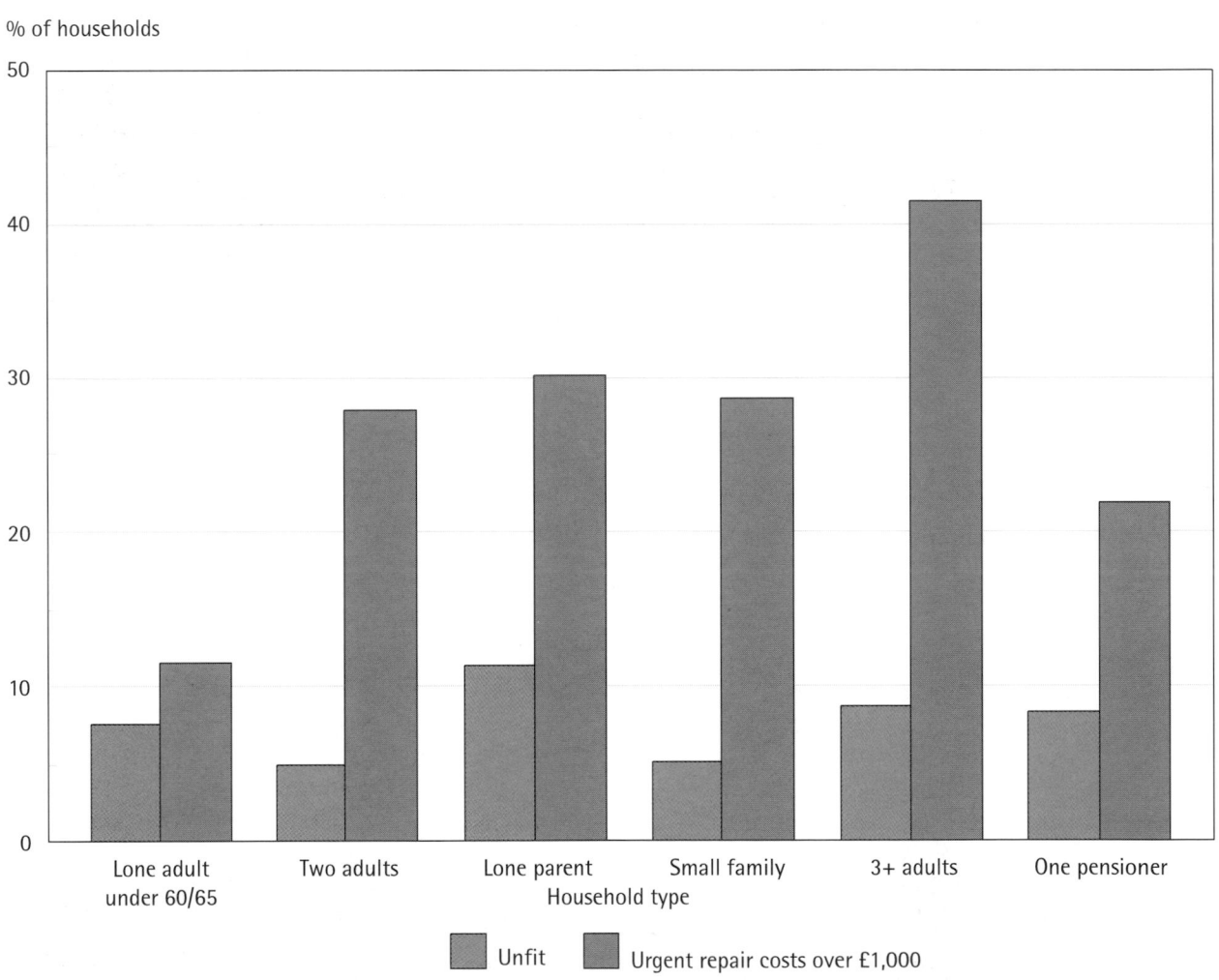

% of households

Household type

Unfit   Urgent repair costs over £1,000

Figure 5.9: Households living in poor conditions by type, Wales (1993)

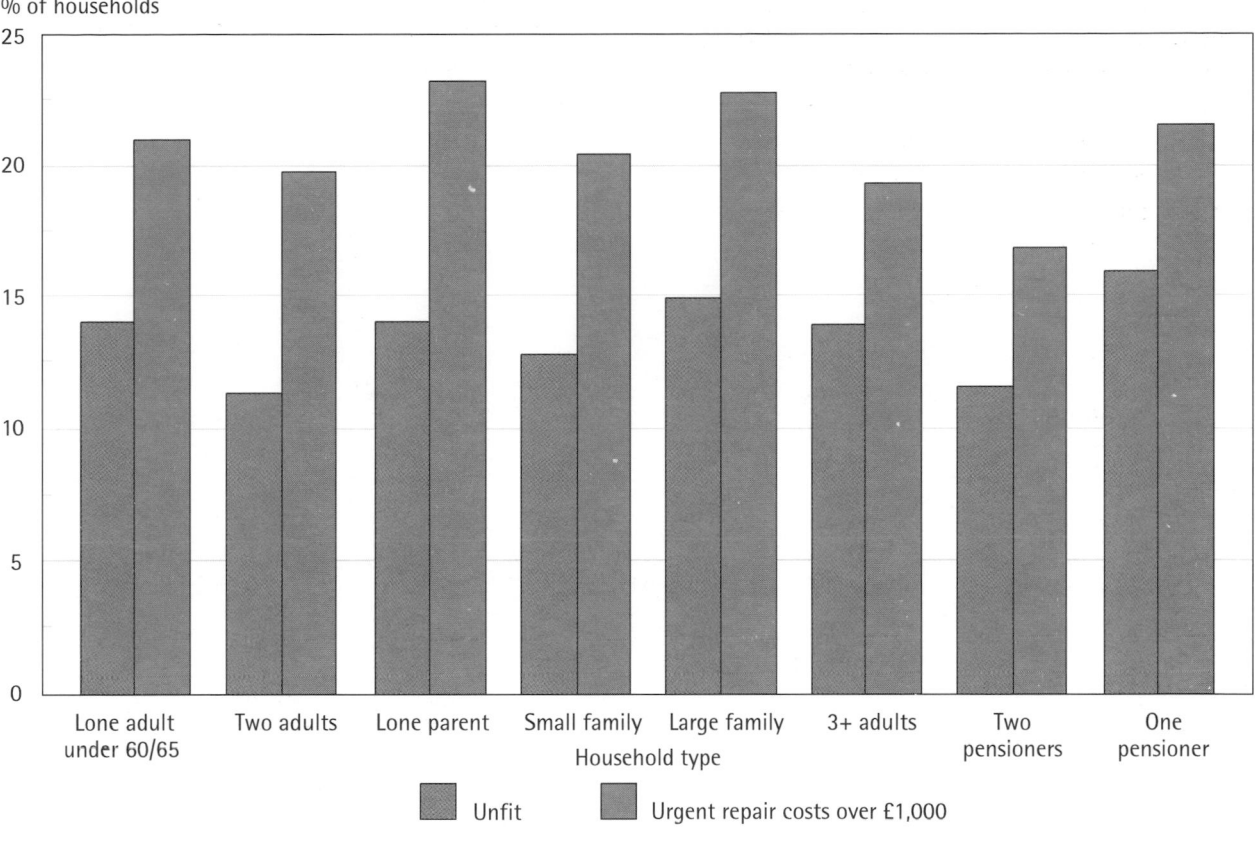

Figure 5.10: Households living in poor conditions by type, Scotland (1996)

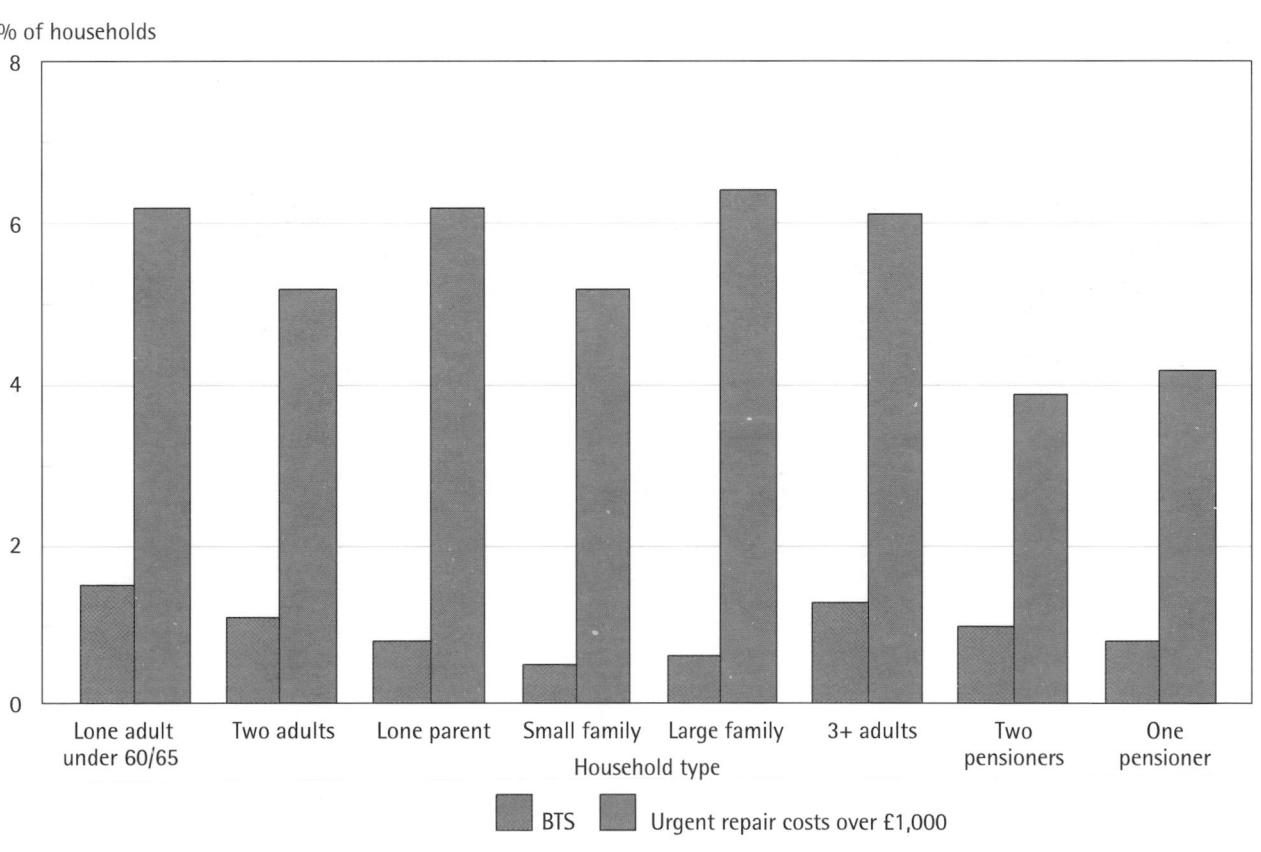

Figure 5.11: Households living in poor conditions by type, Northern Ireland (1996)

% of households

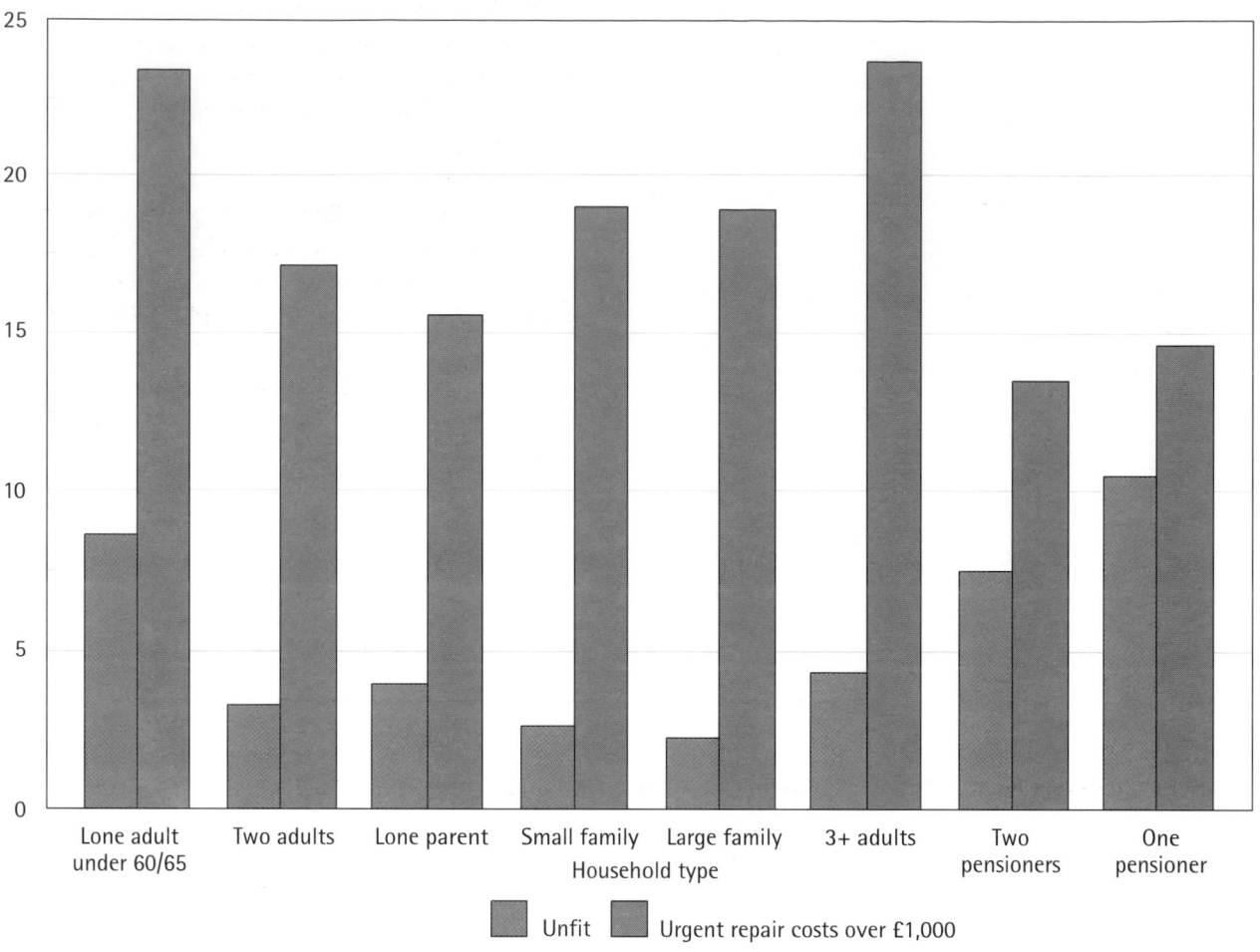

Household type

Unfit   Urgent repair costs over £1,000

Age group

Older people and younger people just starting their housing careers are the groups most likely to live in poor conditions, with middle-aged people generally better housed (Figures 5.12-5.15, Table A5.5). This same pattern exists for houses in disrepair in the four UK countries. England in particular has a severe problem in that 41% of those aged between 16-29 live in dwellings which require urgent repairs costing over £1,000. In Scotland the disparity between age and housing conditions is less striking. Northern Ireland has the highest percentage of younger people (16-29) living in unfit housing.

Within older age groups the tendency to live in poor conditions increases as the age of the head of household increases. Although a high proportion of all older households live in poorer conditions, the housing conditions of the very old (80+) are by far the worst. In England those over 85 are more than twice as likely to live in poor housing than those aged 60-64.

Detailed analysis for England (Table 5.1) shows an increase in the proportion of households living in unfit housing as the age of head of household increases from 4.3% for households headed by a person aged between 60 and 64, 66% for households headed by a person aged between 70 and 74 and up to 10.3% for households headed by someone aged 85 or more.

Table 5.1: Older households in unfit dwellings, England (1996)

Age of household head	In fit dwellings (000s)	In unfit dwellings (000s)	% in unfit dwellings
60-64	1,655	74	4.3
65-69	1,381	79	5.4
70-74	1,311	93	6.6
75-79	890	58	6.1
80-84	555	61	9.9
85 and over	270	31	10.3
All households	18,370	1,272	6.5

Source: EHCS 1996: analysis of data

Figure 5.12: Households living in poor conditions by age group, England (1996)

% of households

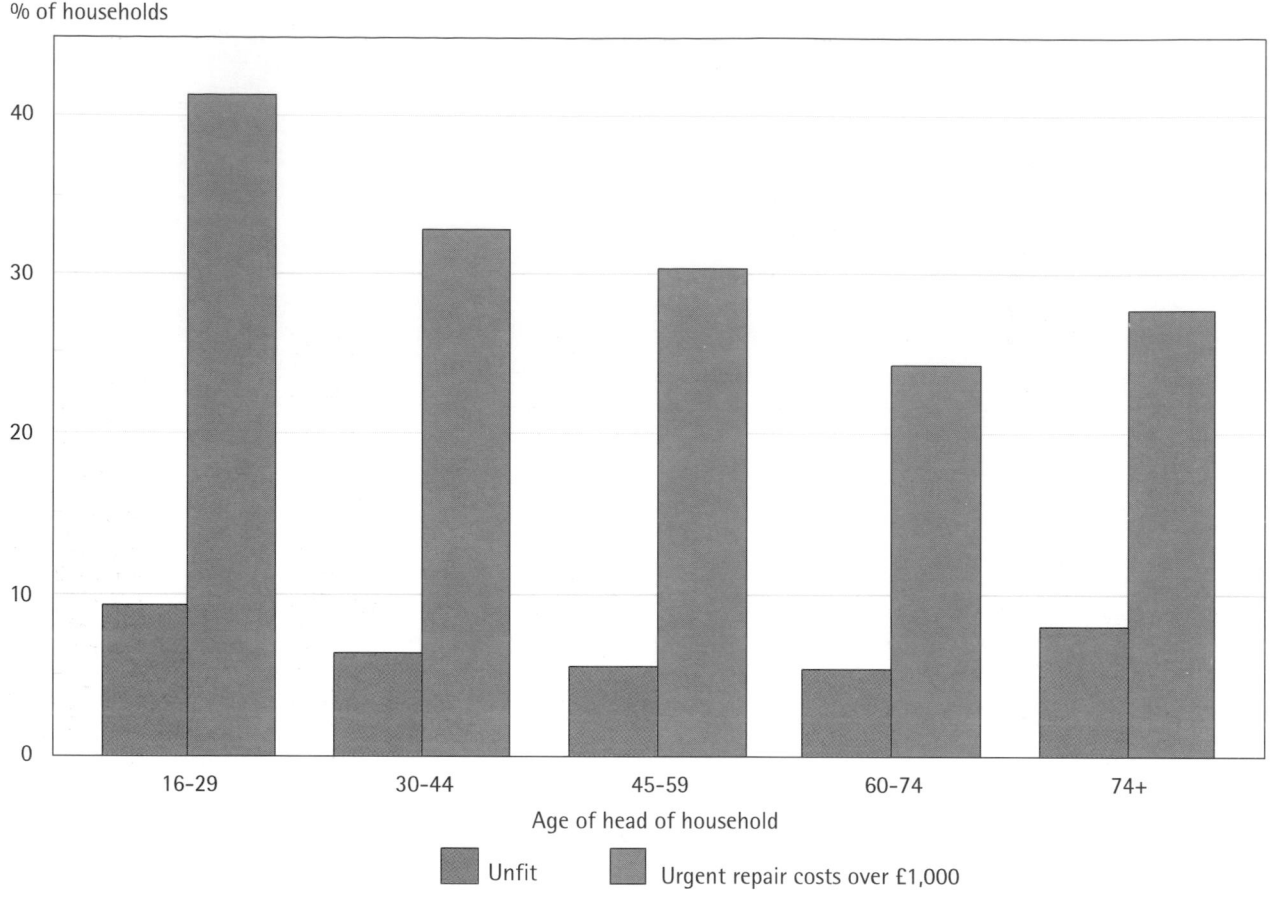

Age of head of household

Unfit   Urgent repair costs over £1,000

Figure 5.13: Households living in poor conditions by age group, Wales (1993)

% of households

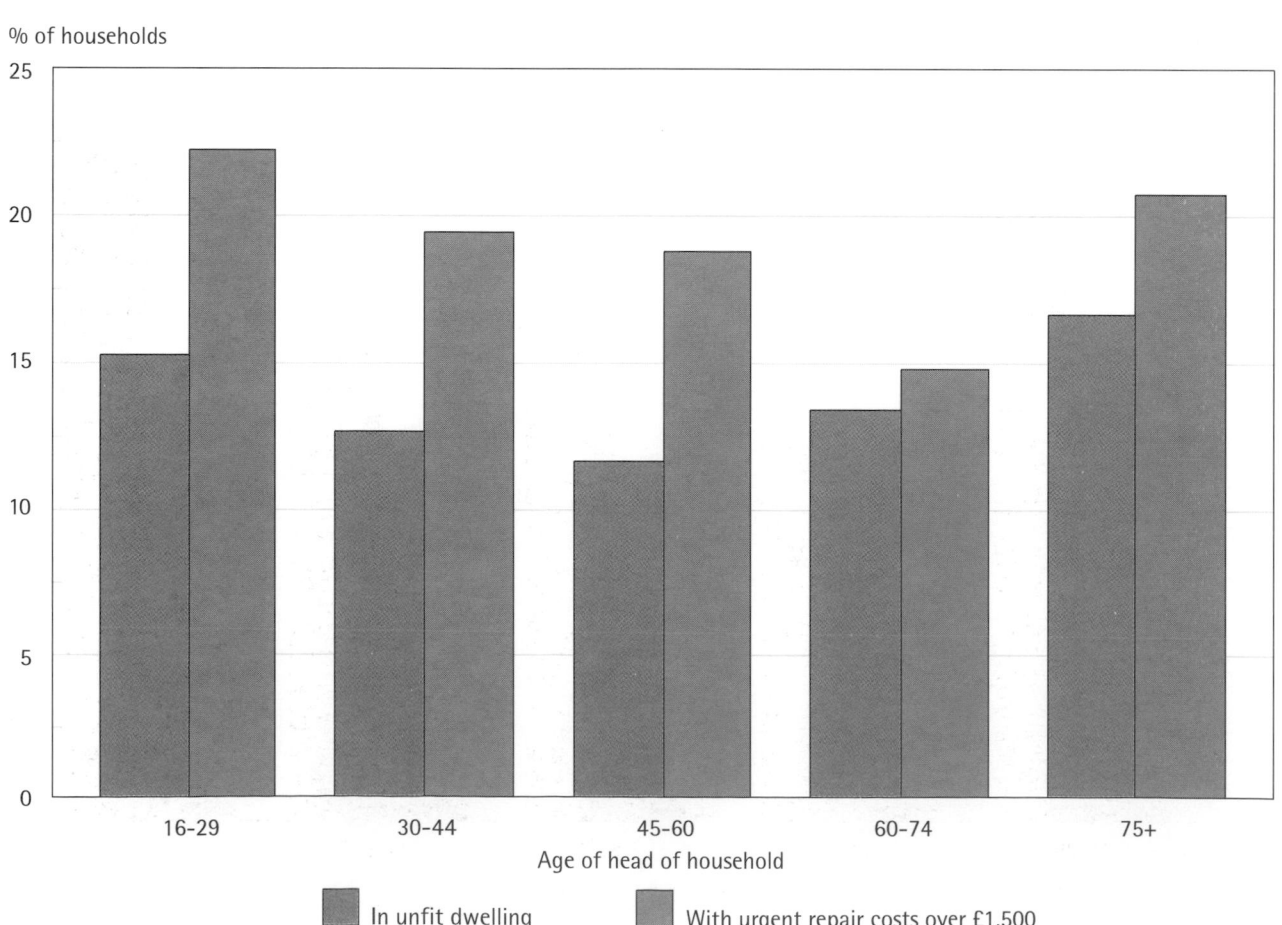

Age of head of household

In unfit dwelling   With urgent repair costs over £1,500

Figure 5.14: Households living in poor conditions by age group, Scotland (1996)

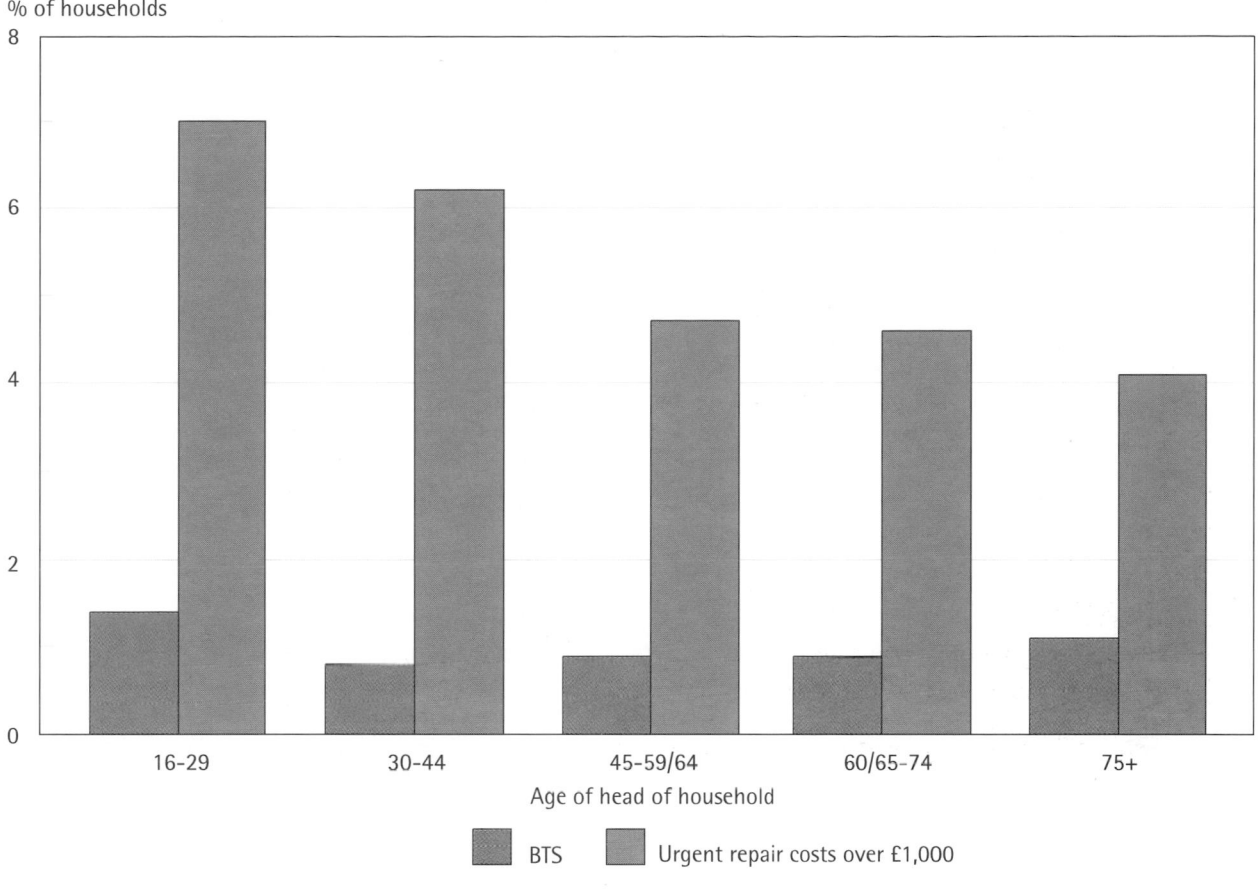

Figure 5.15: Households living in poor conditions by age group, Northern Ireland (1996)

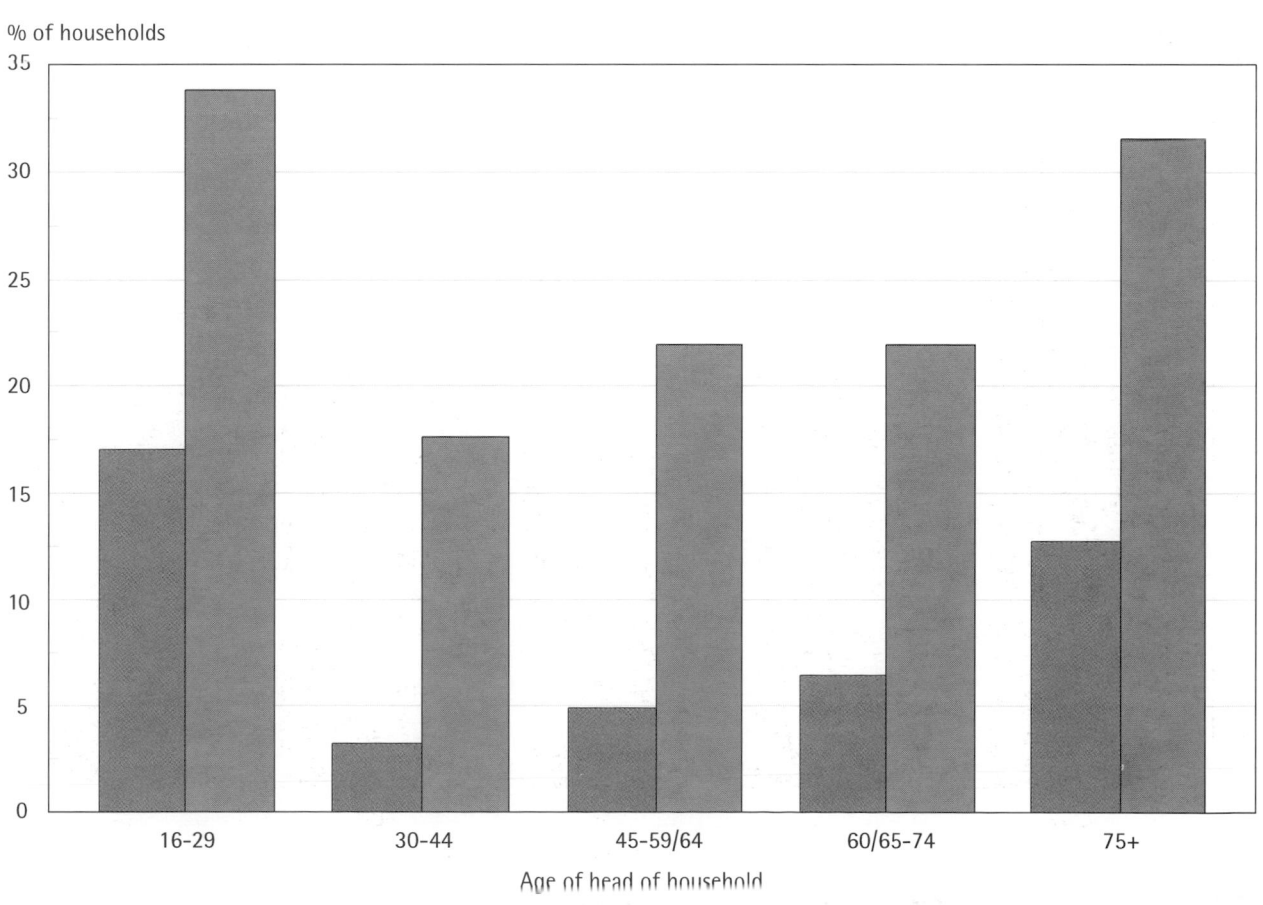

Gender of household head

Table 5.2 shows the proportion of households living in unfit dwellings by the age and gender of the household head for England in 1996. Some 8% of households headed by a woman were living in unfit housing, compared to 6% of the households headed by a male. Throughout each of the age bands households headed by females are more likely to experience unfit living conditions than a household that is headed by a male, although the differential narrows between younger and older age groups. This difference is most notable for those households headed by a female between the ages 30-44. Table A5.6 shows fuller details.

Table 5.2: Households in unfit dwellings by age and gender of household head, England (1996)

Age of house- hold head	Male headed households			Female headed households			Difference (female-male, %)
	In fit dwellings	In unfit dwellings		In fit dwellings	In unfit dwellings		
15-29	1,895	192	9.2%	723	81	10.1%	0.9
30-44	4,400	251	5.4%	962	101	9.5%	4.1
45-59	3,740	207	5.3%	825	60	6.8%	1.5
60-74	2,851	143	4.8%	1,259	87	6.5%	1.7
75+	863	73	7.8%	853	76	8.2%	0.4
All	13,748	866	5.9%	4,622	406	8.1%	2.2

Source: EHCS 1996: analysis of data

Length of residence

Figure 5.16 shows that house conditions are closely linked to length of residence with those living in the same property for up to two years, or 20 years and over, being the most likely to experience poor housing conditions (see also Table A5.7). The same picture holds for households in Northern Ireland. In Scotland differences in levels of BTS or disrepair are relatively small. More detailed analysis of data for England shows that these differences are broadly the same across all tenures (Table A5.8). The association between length of residence and poor condition in the owner-occupied sector may be explained by age factors. The majority of households resident in their homes for a long period are older people who, in general, are more likely to live in poor conditions, as shown above. It may also be the case that some homeowners buy dwellings in relatively poor condition, invest heavily during the early years of residence in a particular dwelling, and subsequently neglect repair, improvement and maintenance.

In other tenures, the cause of the link between length of residence and poor conditions is more difficult to explain, although it may simply be that older dwellings, which tend to be in poorer condition, are more likely to have long-standing residents than newer ones, and that in the social rented sector, households allocated to poor condition dwellings do not stay in them for a very long period.

Figure 5.16: Households living in poor conditions by length of residence, England (1996)

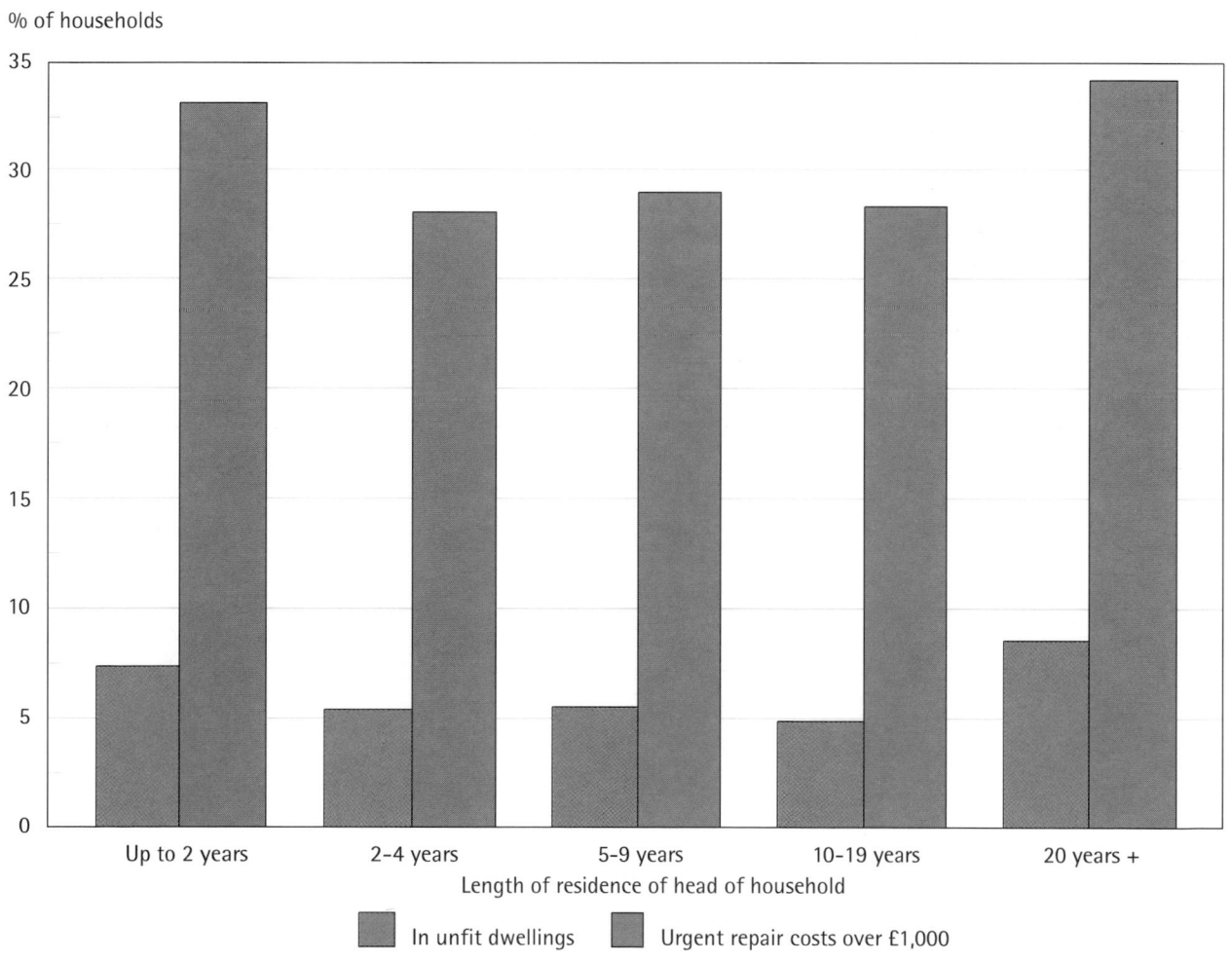

% of households

Length of residence of head of household

■ In unfit dwellings   ■ Urgent repair costs over £1,000

Ethnic origin

Data on ethnic origin and poor housing conditions is only available for England and Scotland (Figures 5.17 and 5.18, Table A5.9). In both countries households with a head from a minority ethnic community were generally more likely to live in poor conditions than those from the white community. Sample numbers are too small to permit further analysis. Asian households in particular are the most likely to be living in households that are unfit or in poor condition.

Figure 5.17: Households living in poor conditions by ethnic origin, England (1996)

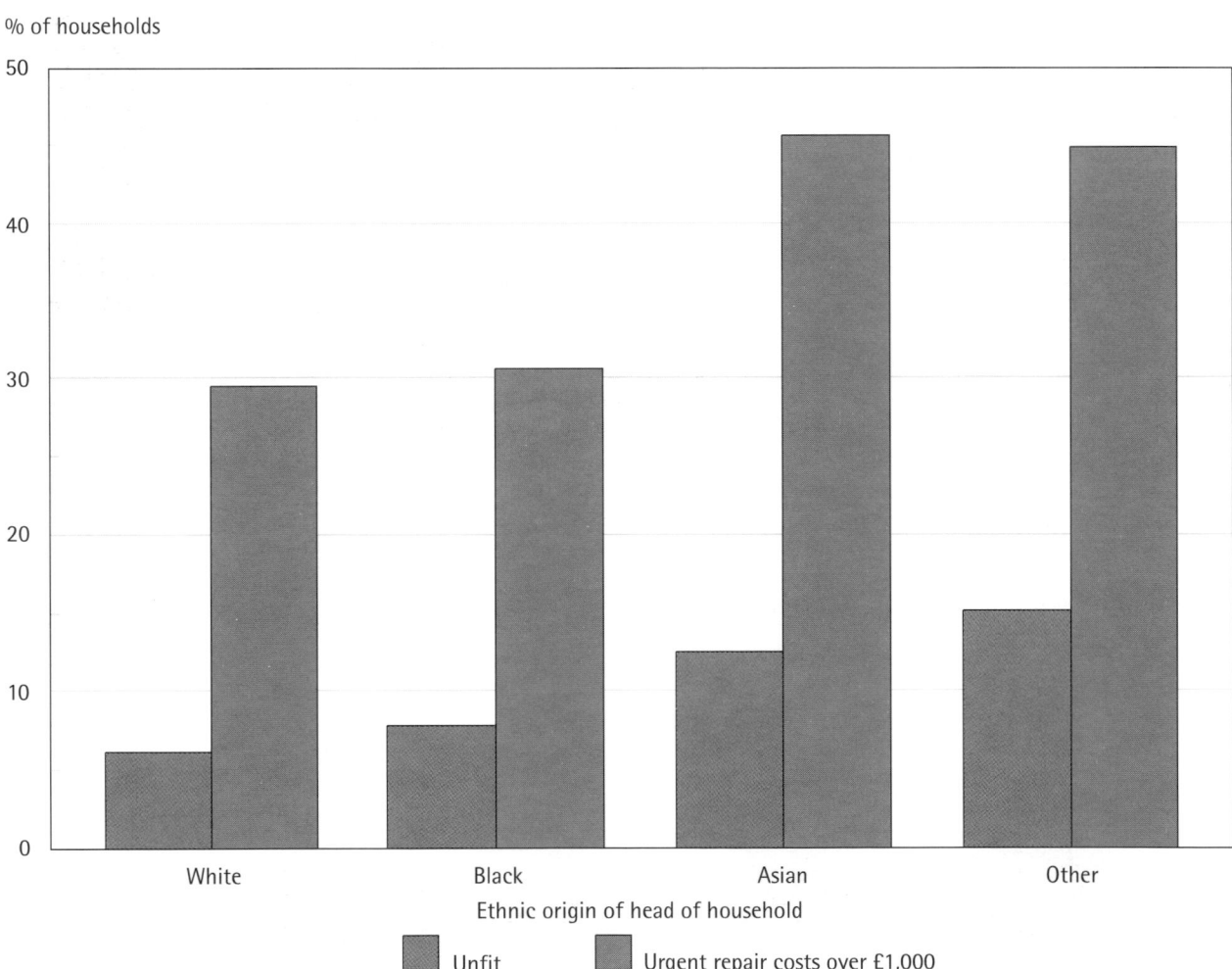

% of households

Ethnic origin of head of household

Unfit   Urgent repair costs over £1,000

Figure 5.18: Households living in poor conditions by ethnic origin, Scotland (1996)

% of households

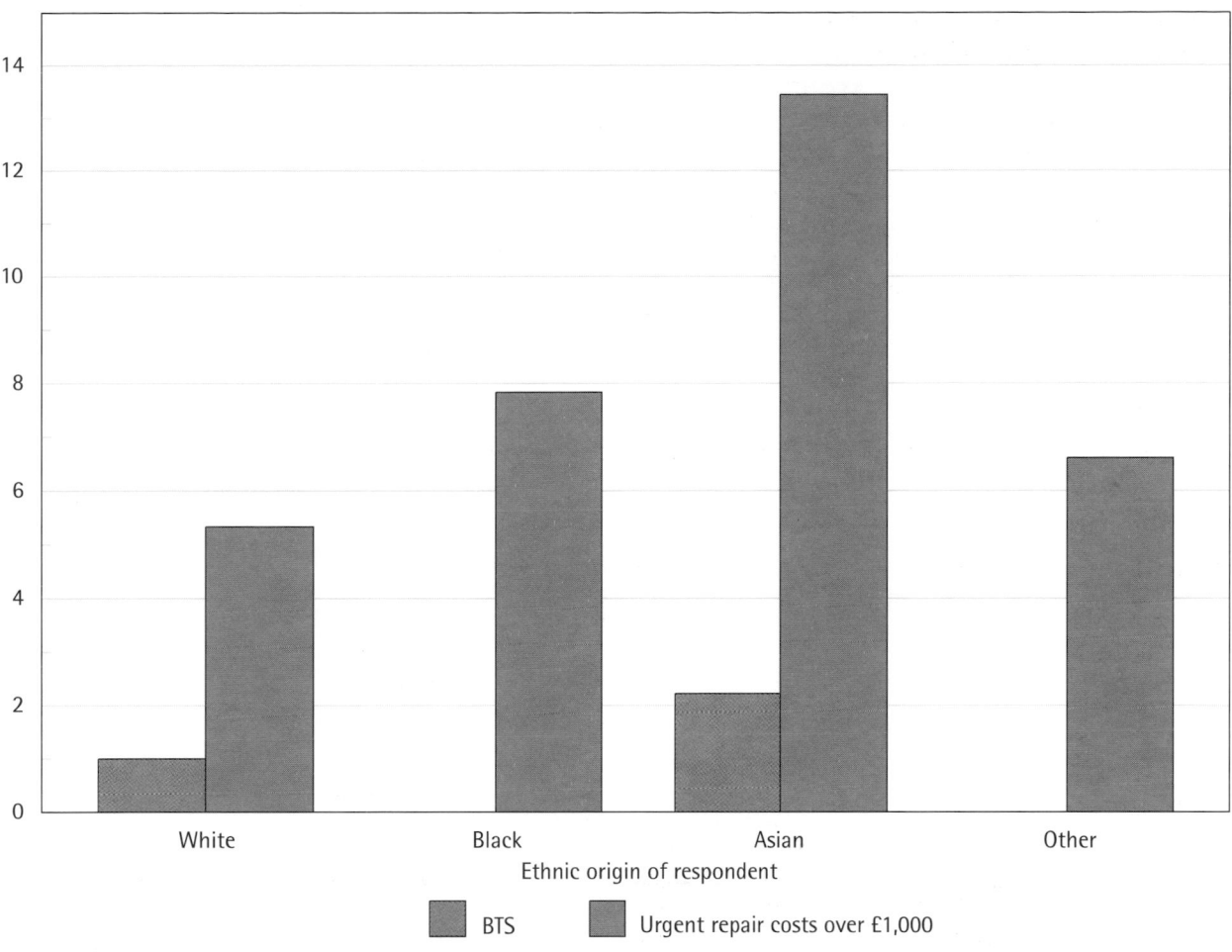

An overview of households living in poor conditions

Figures 5.19-5.22 (Table A5.10) combine information on tenure and household income in England to provide a profile of households living in unfit or BTS housing. Similar data on disrepair is included in Table A5.11.

Low-income homeowners (with incomes of under £8,000 per annum at 1991 prices) form the largest group in Wales, Scotland and Northern Ireland, accounting for roughly one third of the unfit households. In England, the links between low income homeownership and poor conditions is less pronounced. In Scotland another large group of households in BTS dwellings are those on low

incomes in the private rented sector, who account for 23% of the total. This is also a significant group occupying unfit dwellings in Northern Ireland (14%). England and Wales differ, with low-income local authority tenants forming the next largest tenure group of occupants of unfit housing. In Wales this group accounts for a quarter of those living in unfit dwellings.

However, low-income households do not account for all those in unfit or BTS housing. In all four countries there is a significant group of middle-income owners (17%-25%) in poor conditions. This percentage has increased between 1991 and 1996. There is also a smaller group of high-income owners, 15% in England (10% in 1991) and 6-7% elsewhere.

Figure 5.19: Households living in unfit dwellings by income and tenure, England (1996)

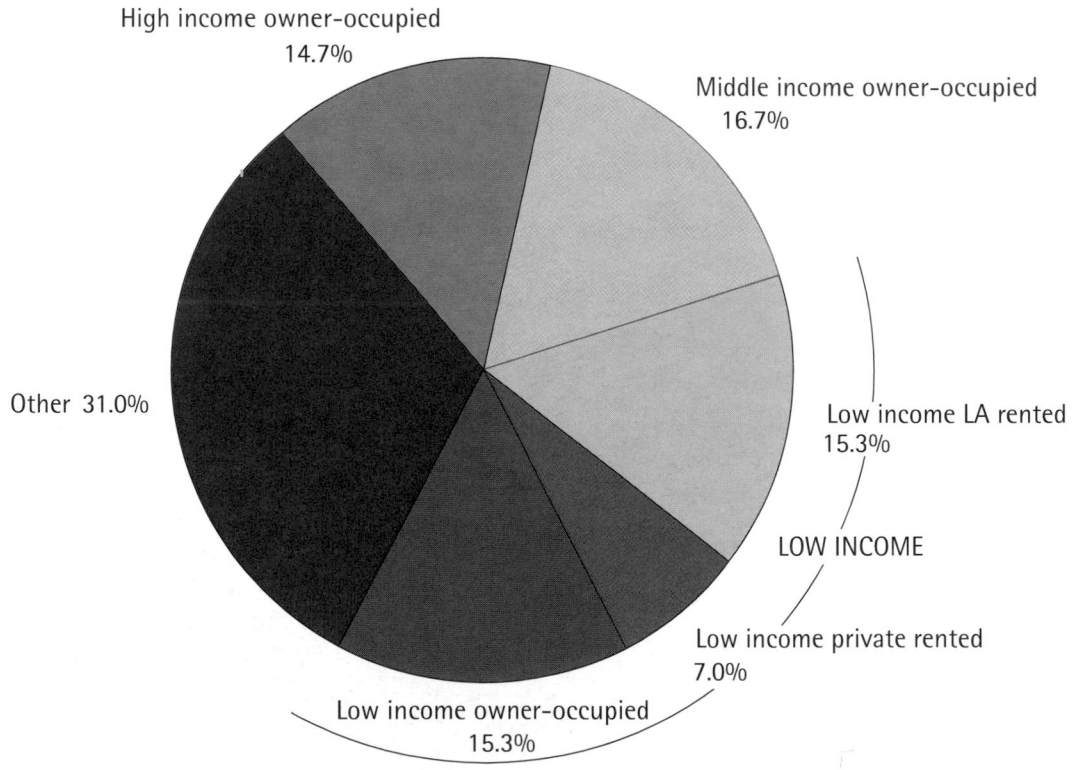

Figure 5.20: Households living in unfit dwellings by income and tenure, Wales (1993)

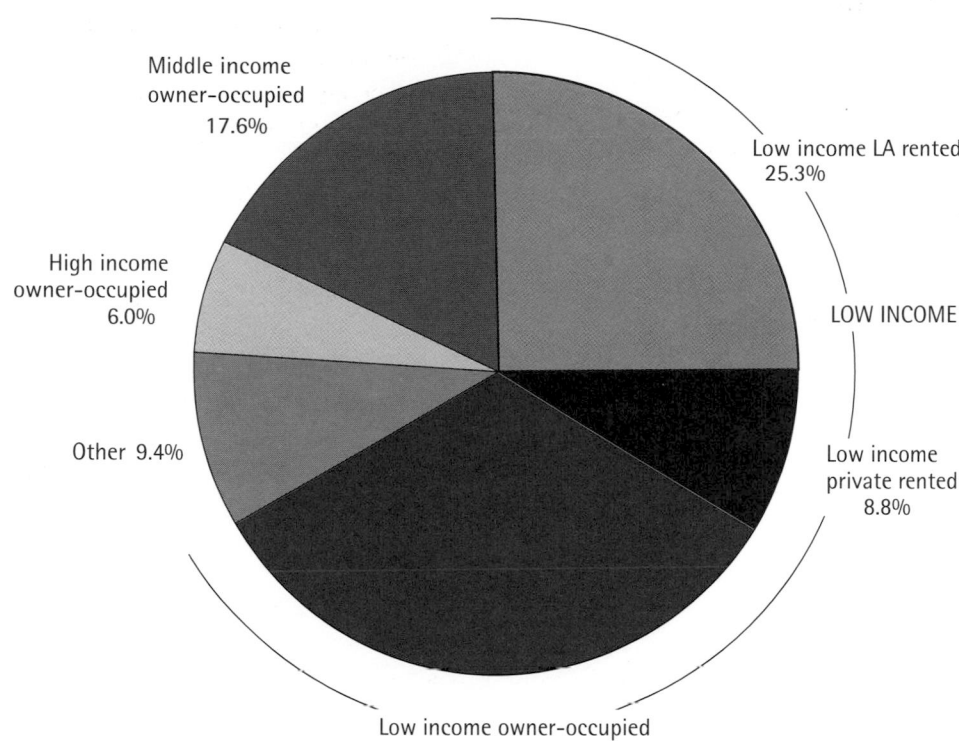

Middle income owner-occupied 17.6%

High income owner-occupied 6.0%

Other 9.4%

Low income LA rented 25.3%

LOW INCOME

Low income private rented 8.8%

Low income owner-occupied 33.0%

Figure 5.21: Households living in unfit dwellings by income and tenure, Scotland (1996)

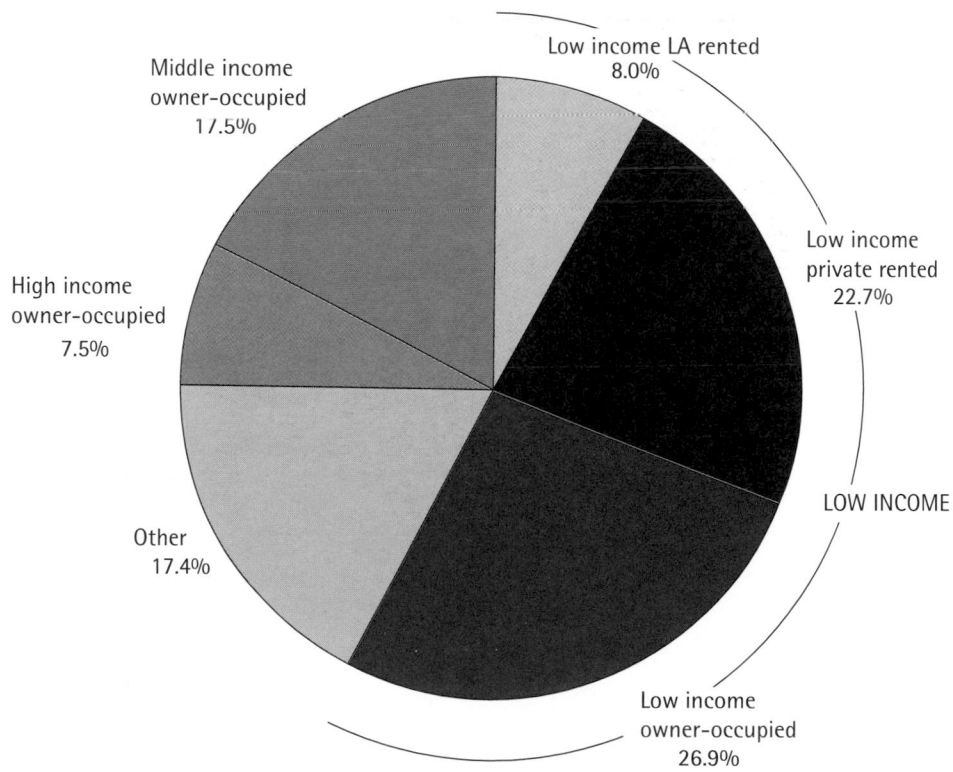

Middle income owner-occupied 17.5%

Low income LA rented 8.0%

High income owner-occupied 7.5%

Other 17.4%

Low income private rented 22.7%

LOW INCOME

Low income owner-occupied 26.9%

Figure 5.22: Households living in unfit dwellings by income and tenure, Northern Ireland (1996)

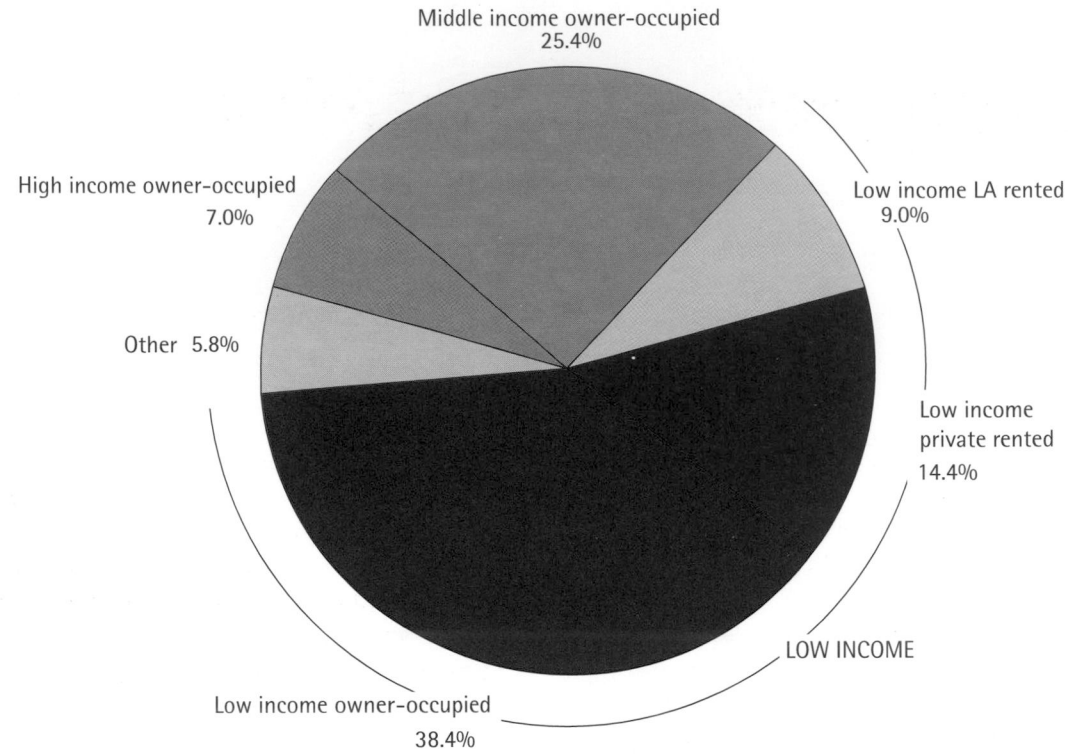

6

Housing renewal policies

It is not practical to provide a detailed historical account of the development of housing renewal policies in the UK in a report of this size. A fuller account can be found in Leather and Mackintosh (1992).

In England, demolition and rehabilitation have been the two main programmes of public sector investment in poor condition housing in the postwar period. Demolition programmes were dominant from the 1960s to the late 1970s as local authorities cleared the worst of the remaining 19th-century slum properties. Subsequently clearance has dwindled, to a mere 1,000 properties in 1997/98.

Rehabilitation policies in the private sector have been pursued through the provision of a range of grants to owners and tenants, and through area (or neighbourhood) renewal policies. From the mid-1960s onwards, there was increasing interest in renovation as a complement and eventually as an alternative to clearance. National house condition surveys revealed that there were many more sub-standard dwellings than had previously been thought and it was clear that even at the then high rates of clearance it would take many decades to deal with the backlog. Resident opposition to clearance also grew stronger as programmes moved from dwellings which were mainly privately rented into areas with higher levels of homeownership where the limited compensation provisions of the time, and the prospect of rehousing into the council sector were less attractive. The 1969 Housing Act extended the range of grants previously available to include more generous assistance with improvement as well as the installation of missing basic amenities. It also provided local authorities with powers to declare General Improvement Areas (GIAs) on which renovation efforts were focused.

The 1969 Housing Act envisaged renovation and a complement to clearance, with action taking place in areas of basically sound housing with high rates of homeownership which would not have been included in clearance programmes for many years. However, it soon became clear that opposition to clearance was forcing local authorities to use renovation powers in areas of poorer condition housing, with high levels of social deprivation, as an alternative to clearance. The 1974 Housing Act provided additional powers, including a new repair grant, higher grant rates, and an additional type of improvement area – the Housing Action Area (HAA). There was more emphasis in HAAs in the involvement of local authorities and housing associations in acquiring and renovating poor condition properties. Despite this emphasis the majority of grants were in practice provided to individual properties outside HAAs and GIAs.

During the 1980s, emphasis shifted towards the renovation of the publicly-owned housing stock, including, not only the oldest public sector houses built mainly during the 1919-45 period, but also a substantial number of flats and maisonettes built during the 1960s and 1970s in high- or medium-rise estates. The estates action programme, which provided earmarked allocations to specific local authority estates from resources top-sliced from the overall local authority capital programme, expanded rapidly during the late 1980s and early 1990s. But from 1995, estates action resources in England were subsumed into the new Single Regeneration Budget, which amalgamated resources from a large number of programmes under a new heading, with uncommitted resources allocated by competition. This emphasis on economic regeneration, and on funding partnerships between public and private sectors, has led to a decline in the level of local authority estate renovation funded from this programme.

In the housing association sector, involvement in the acquisition and rehabilitation of private sector dwellings declined in the late 1980s and 1990s. One cause for this was the introduction of a new Housing Association Grant (HAG) regime which relied on attracting an increasing element of private funding and which placed the risk element in the renovation process on housing associations. Rehabilitation projects became less attractive. Research also suggests that the supply of low-cost formerly private rented dwellings in inner-city areas also declined, and that local authorities have looked to housing associations more to provide new accommodation for rehousing needs. More recently, with growing concern about the over-supply of social rented housing in the market of the North of England and the Midlands, and evidence of market collapse being localised in areas of private housing in some inner cities, The Housing Corporation has begun to look at ways in which associations (now known as Registered Social Landlords) can make a more direct contribution to housing renovation through acquisition, clearance and involvement in group repair schemes.

In the private sector in the 1980s there was a move away from grants for improvement towards repair grants. In 1990, the whole system of renovation grants was revised. Tests of the applicant's resources were introduced for all types of grant. Improvement, repair and intermediate grants were merged into a single renovation grant (with variations for work in houses in multiple occupation and to the common parts of dwellings). For the first time a dedicated disabled facilities grant (DFG) was introduced to assist with adaptations. Finally, the minor works assistance grant was introduced to cover a variety of small jobs. Renovation grants for work to make dwellings fit for human habitation, and DFGs for most adaptation work to dwellings to assist with mobility and access to facilities, were made available as of right, subject to the test of resources.

Over the 1990-96 period, it became clear that the demand for grant aid exceeded the resources which the government was prepared to make available in England. Demand management mechanisms included the introduction of a maximum grant level and the lowering of this

level to £20,000. To resolve this crisis, the 1996 Housing Grants, Construction and Regeneration Act abolished mandatory renovation grants, and replaced minor works assistance with the home repair grant, a similar grant but with a higher cost limit, broader purposes and wider eligibility.

In Wales, the legislative framework was as for England. Renewal policies in Wales were also generally similar to those in England until the mid-1980s. However, the shift in resources in favour of public sector renovation which occurred in England did not take place in Wales, and levels of funding for private sector grants and related programmes have continued at a consistently higher level (pro rata to the size of the dwelling stock) than in England, reflecting the high priority given to private sector housing renovation by the Welsh Office. Although the 1989 Local Government and Housing Act changes to the grant system were applied in Wales, there were differences in the allocation and ear-marking of grant resources, and the maximum limit for grant in Wales is higher than in England. The changes to grant provision introduced in the 1996 Housing Grants, Construction and Regeneration Act will apply to Wales.

In Scotland, the predominance of the tenement dwelling in the poor condition privately-owned stock has shaped housing renewal policy. As in England and Wales, there was a shift of emphasis from clearance to renovation which led to new legislation in 1969. As well as extending grant provision as in England, local authorities were given powers to declare Housing Treatment Areas (HTAs) in neighbourhoods with a high proportion of unfit housing. Local authority powers to compel owners to carry out repairs, especially in HTAs, were stronger than in England and Wales. Use of HTA powers was, however, more limited than the use of GIA powers in England and Wales. Again paralleling developments in England and Wales, new legislation in 1974 introduced HAAs, although there were marked differences from the English equivalent. The main emphasis was on dwelling eligibility criteria rather than social factors, and powers of compulsion were much stronger than in England, reflecting the need for coordinated action to deal with the problems of improving and repairing tenement buildings. In some parts of Scotland, particularly Glasgow, there was also a strong emphasis on the acquisition of poor condition dwellings by community-based housing associations, on a much greater scale than occurred in England. The 1989 Act grant system changes in England and Wales were not applied in Scotland, which has continued with the earlier powers, subject only to minor amendment. However, a recent Green Paper on housing in Scotland proposed the introduction of means testing and this has received widespread support.

There is growing acceptance that the framework of housing renewal policy needs a radical overhaul to make better use of the limited public resources going into the stock renovation, to encourage more private investment, to deal more effectively with declining areas of other housing and to boost the level of replacement of obsolete housing. Stimulating debate on changes in policy is one of the aims of Joseph Rowntree Foundation programme of research which this report accompanies.

In Northern Ireland, the 1989 Act changes to the grant system were introduced in 1992, with the addition of a new replacement grant.

Table 6.1 shows some key stages in the development of housing renewal policy over the 1945-96 period.

Table 6.1: Key stages in the development of housing renewal policy, Britain (1954-96)

1954	Beginning of postwar clearance programme
1967	First national house condition surveys in England and Wales
1965-8	Re-appraisal of policy
1969	Housing Act: boost to grants as complement to clearance; area renewal via General Improvement Areas (GIAs); in Scotland parallel legislation introduced Housing Treatment Areas (HTAs)
1974	Housing Act: grants for repair introduced; Housing Action Areas (HAAs) as an alternative to clearance; capital grant (HAG) awarded to Housing Associations to finance acquisition and rehabilitation; in Scotland 1974 Housing (Scotland) Act introduced HAAs
1979	Introduction of Priority Estates Project in England to target funds on poor condition public sector estates
1980	Housing Act: extension of repair grants to all pre-1919 dwellings
1982-84	Boom in grant-take up throughout UK due to increase in grant percentages; development in England and Wales of enveloping (form of simultaneous block renovation)
1985	Review of policy in England and Wales proposes targeting of grants via a means test and the introduction of equity-sharing loans; launch of the Estate Action Programme in England to target resources on poor condition public sector estates
1987	Further consultation papers; government funding for experimental Home Improvement Agencies in England and Wales to help older owners with renovation
1989	Local Government and Housing Act in England and Wales: new renovation, disabled facilities and minor works grants; means testing of grant aid; new fitness standard; GIAs and HAAs replaced by Renewal Areas; reduction in government subsidy for grant payments
1990	1989 Act comes into operation in England and Wales
1991	Longer-term funding for 120 Home Improvement Agencies
1992	1989 Act system introduced in Northern Ireland; first review of 1989 Act system in England and Wales
1993	Second review of 1989 Act system in England and Wales and publication of consultation papers
1996	Housing Grants, Construction and Regeneration Act in England and Wales providing for abolition of mandatory renovation grants, replacement of minor works assistance with home repair grant; introduction of relocation grants

7

Tackling poor housing conditions

Clearance

Figure 7.1 shows the number of dwellings demolished under slum clearance powers in Britain for each year since 1969 (see also Table A7.1). The level of demolition has declined sharply from more than 80,000 dwellings per annum in the early 1970s to some 1,000 in 1997/98. This represents an annual replacement rate of less than one in every 23,000 dwellings.

The rate of clearance since 1978 has been heavily skewed, with 80% of authorities carrying out virtually no clearance during this period (virtually no clearance is less than 10 per 1,000 private dwellings). As Map 7.1 shows, the highest rates of clearance (and the largest absolute numbers of cleared properties) are found in cities and metropolitan districts in the North West, North East, Yorkshire and Humberside, and the Midlands. Table 7.1 shows authorities with the highest level of clearance relative to the size of the privately owned dwelling stock in their area. Only two authorities, Blackburn, Middlesbrough, have cleared more than 100 properties per 1,000 private sector dwellings. Other authorities with high levels of slum clearance include Sheffield, Kingston-upon-Hull, Salford, Bolton and Oldham.

Table 7.1: Authorities in England and Wales with the highest rate of demolitions and closures per 1,000 private sector dwellings (1978–97)

Local authority	Demolitions 1978–97	
	No	Per 1,000
Blackburn	7,170	163.77
Middlesbrough	4,793	119.47
Sheffield	13,423	91.09
Kingston-upon-Hull	6,450	90.81
Salford	5,115	81.47
Bolton	5,374	63.72
Oldham	4,085	60.37
Sandwell	4,501	59.43
St Helens	3,060	56.58
Hartlepool	1,375	50.40
South Tyneside	2,004	50.32
Derby	3,601	47.63
Burnley	1,538	46.34
Hyndburn	1,378	46.34
Southwark	2,090	44.14
Rochdale	2,718	44.08
Merthyr Tydfil	749	41.98
Stoke on Trent	3,209	41.32
Blaenau Gwent	865	40.44
Rotherham	2,777	37.83
Tameside	2,531	36.85
Nottingham	2,652	35.70
Wigan	3,376	34.74
Rossendale	773	33.99
Gateshead	1,806	32.75
Derwentside	879	32.50
Newcastle upon Tyne	2,462	32.05
Leeds	6,817	31.44
Redcar and Cleveland	1,424	31.36
Tower Hamlets	917	29.00

Source: Local housing statistics (various years)

Figure 7.1: Dwellings demolished or closed, Britain (1969-97)

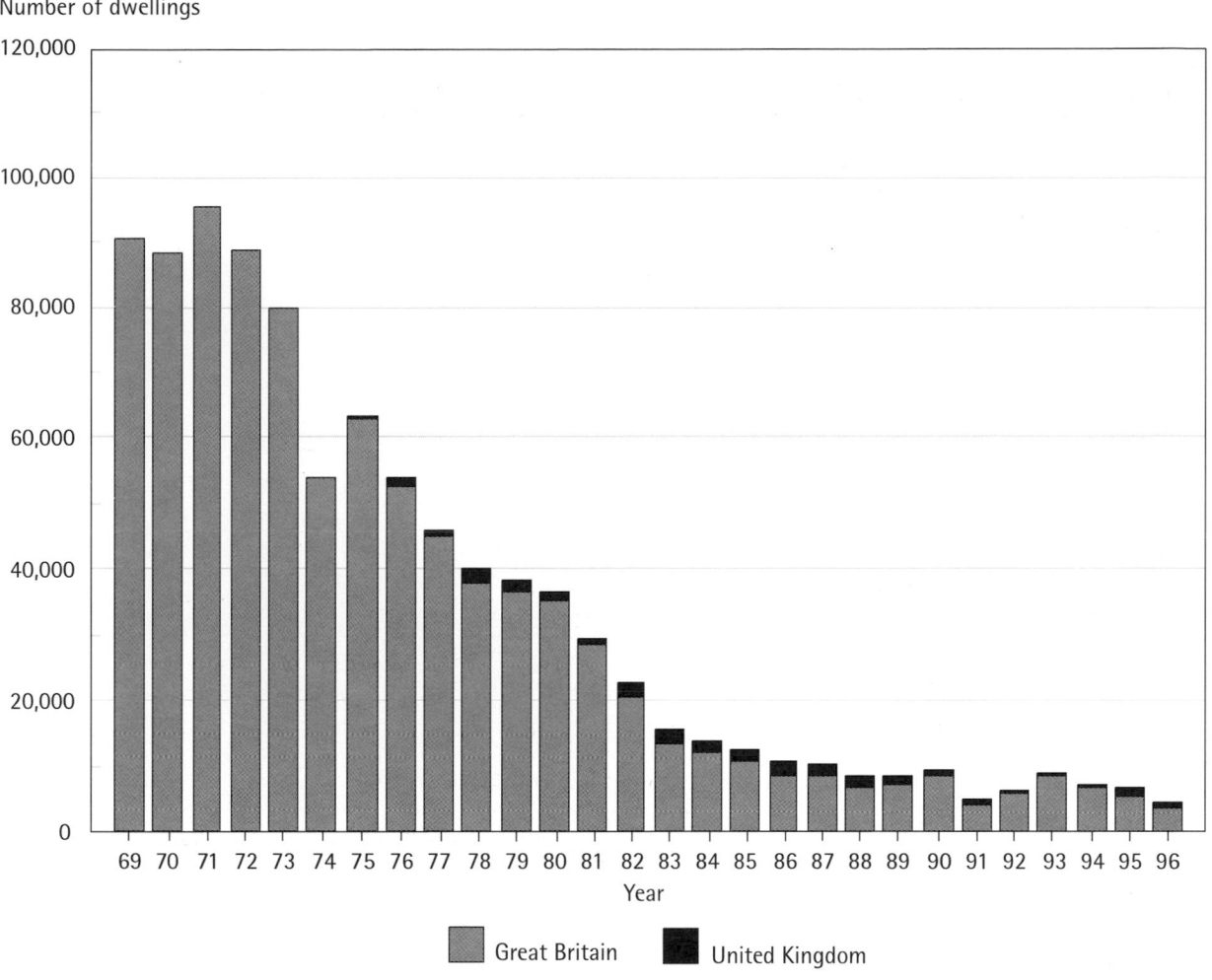

Number of dwellings

Great Britain figures for 1995 and 1996 do not include demolitions in England as these are not available

The amount of dwelling clearance fell from the higher levels attained in the 1960s and early 1970s because of a shift in emphasis towards the renovation of the older housing stock. The present level of clearance is widely regarded by professionals as too low but with a high proportion of older houses in individual ownership it is both difficult and expensive to provide appropriate rehousing. The 1996 Housing Grants, Construction and Regeneration Act introduced relocation grants which aim to assist low-income owners to purchase a better condition dwelling than the one they currently occupy, and hence make clearance a more acceptable solution. Problems of low demand in the North and the Midlands – in both social rented and private sectors – may also lead to some boost in clearance. It is doubtful, however, whether this will lead to any long-term increase in the overall level of slum clearance unless additional capital resources are made available.

Map 7.1: Dwellings demolished or closed per 1,000 privately owned dwellings, England and Wales (1978–97)

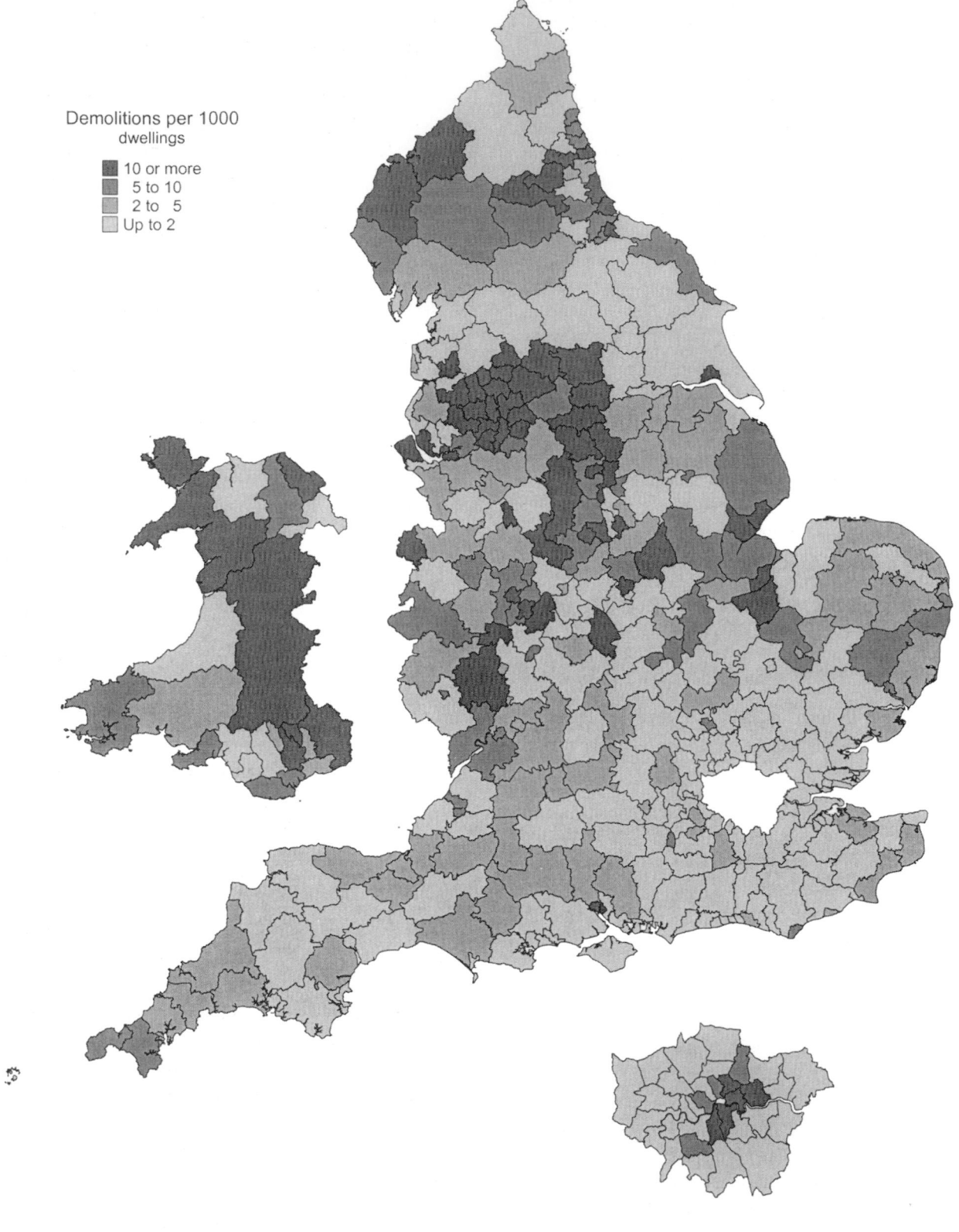

Grants to owners

Capital grants to assist homeowners (and at times tenants) to improve, repair and adapt their homes have been available for almost 50 years, but the programme of grant aid began in earnest in 1969. In 1990, the grant system was substantially revised. Prior to 1990, *intermediate* (previously standard) grants were available to provide missing amenities and associated repairs. *Improvement* grants were for more substantial works including extensions, kitchen and bathroom facilities, attic conversions, and the subdivision of dwellings. They also included provision for repairs. *Repair* grants (available on a limited basis from 1975 and more widely after 1980) were exclusively for substantial repair work. Grant aid provided in any individual case was a percentage of the cost of qualifying work up to a set maximum (the eligible cost limit). Grant percentages and eligible cost limits varied. With the exception of grants to provide amenities, or those provided to assist with work carried out as a result of a *statutory notice* served by a local council, all grants were provided at the discretion of local authorities.

The 1989 Local Government and Housing Act introduced a new system of grant aid which came into operation in England and Wales in 1990. A similar system was introduced in Northern Ireland in 1992, but in Scotland the old system remains in operation and is substantially similar to that described above.

Under the 1989 Act system, which was amended in 1996, there are three main types of grant. *Renovation* grants cover all types of improvement and repair work. They are available to owner-occupiers for all works of repair and improvement, at the discretion of the local authority. Prior to 1996 they were available as of right for works to make dwellings fit for human habitation. The amount of grant payable is assessed by a test of the applicant's financial resources and may vary from nothing to 100% of the qualifying costs of work. *Disabled facilities* grants (DFG) cover adaptations and other work to enable a disabled person to live in a dwelling. This grant is also subject to a test of resources. Grant for some types of work is mandatory. *Home repairs assistance* (usually a grant and always discretionary) is available to older people and those on certain means-tested benefits up to a maximum of £2,000 per grant.

The overall level of grant provision

Figures 7.2 to 7.5 show the changing pattern of grant provision in the UK between 1969 and 1997 and Tables A7.2-A7.5 provide detailed figures. In England, grant take-up grew slowly, but rose to a peak in 1973-74 when higher percentage grants were made available in certain economically depressed areas. After a lower level of take-up in the later 1970s there was a second boom in the 1982-84 period stimulated by another increase in grant rates. This applied particularly to repair grants for which the rate was increased to 90% of eligible costs for all owners of dwellings built before 1919. The level of take-up subsequently declined until 1990. Under the new system output initially declined further, even if the new DFGs (which do not address renovation) are included in the total. The level of provision remains well below levels achieved during the 1980s.

In Wales the pattern of take-up mirrored that in England, with a boom in improvement grants in the 1972-74 period and another in repair grants during the early 1980s. Although a decline followed in the mid-1980s this was less pronounced than in England and from the later 1980s, provision again picked up, reaching a level close to the all-time peak of 27,000 per annum in 1990. Under the 1989 grant system the overall level of output (including DFG but excluding minor works assistance; MWA) has fallen from late 1980s levels to around 11,000 grants per annum, but this represents a less severe fall than in England because private sector renovation has received higher priority.

In Scotland the level of grant provision was relatively low in the 1970s but Scotland again benefited from the repair grants boom of the 1980s. Although provision fell from the 60,000 grants provided in 1984, it remained steady at a level above 20,000 per annum until 1995, but since then has decreased steadily to under 13,000 in 1998. Some commentators have linked this decline to changes in the funding arrangements for grant aid in the mid 1990s.

In Northern Ireland the data is less complete. There were relatively few grants provided until the newly formed NIHE took over this task early in the 1970s. The level of provision then built up very rapidly with a strong emphasis on repair grants and continued throughout the mid-1980s. After 1986 there was a fall in provision. Since the introduction of the new grant system in 1992 Northern Ireland has experienced an increase in the number of grants, to around 8,000 in 1997 (excluding MWA).

Figure 7.2: Grants by type, England (1969–97)

Number of grants

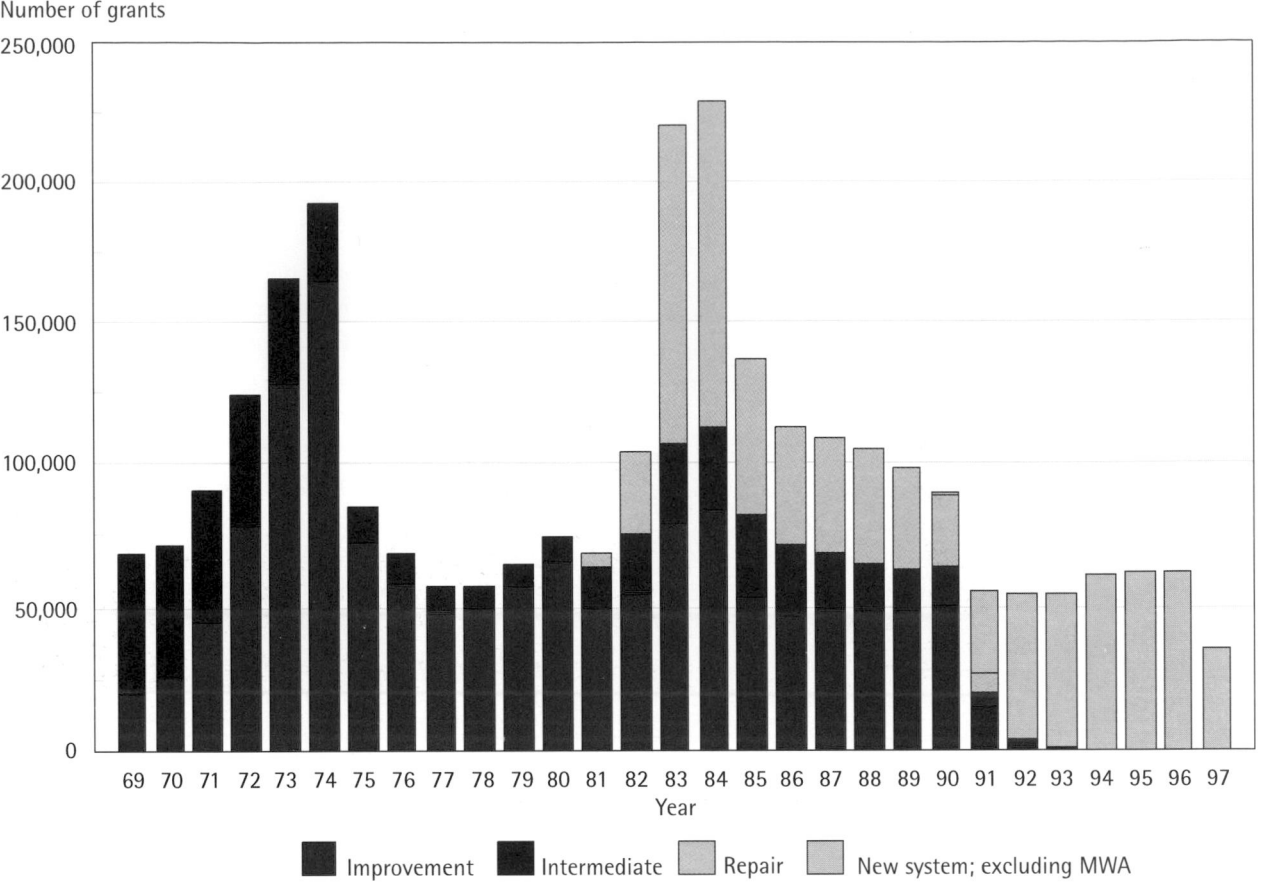

Figure 7.3: Grants by type, Wales (1969–97)

Number of grants

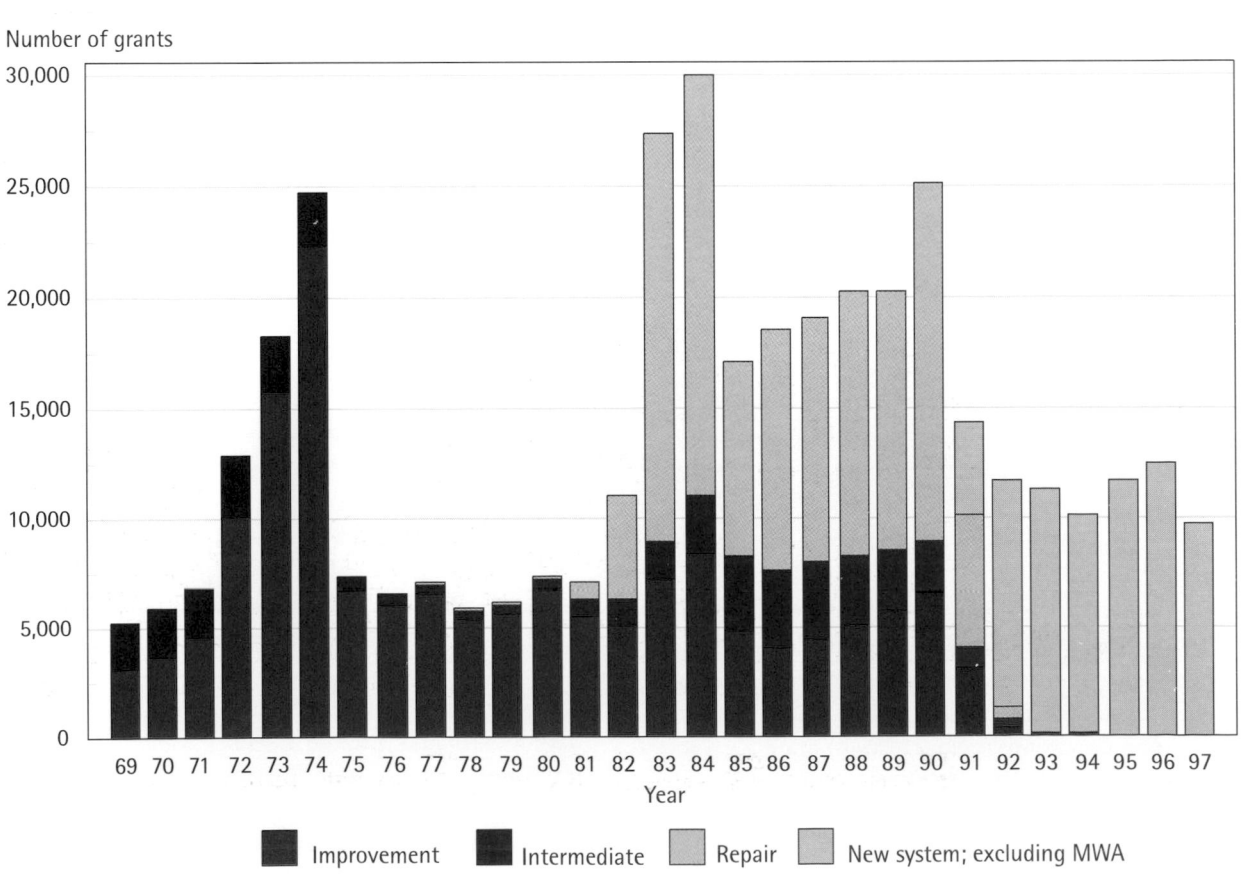

Figure 7.4: Grants by type, Scotland (1969–97)

Number of grants

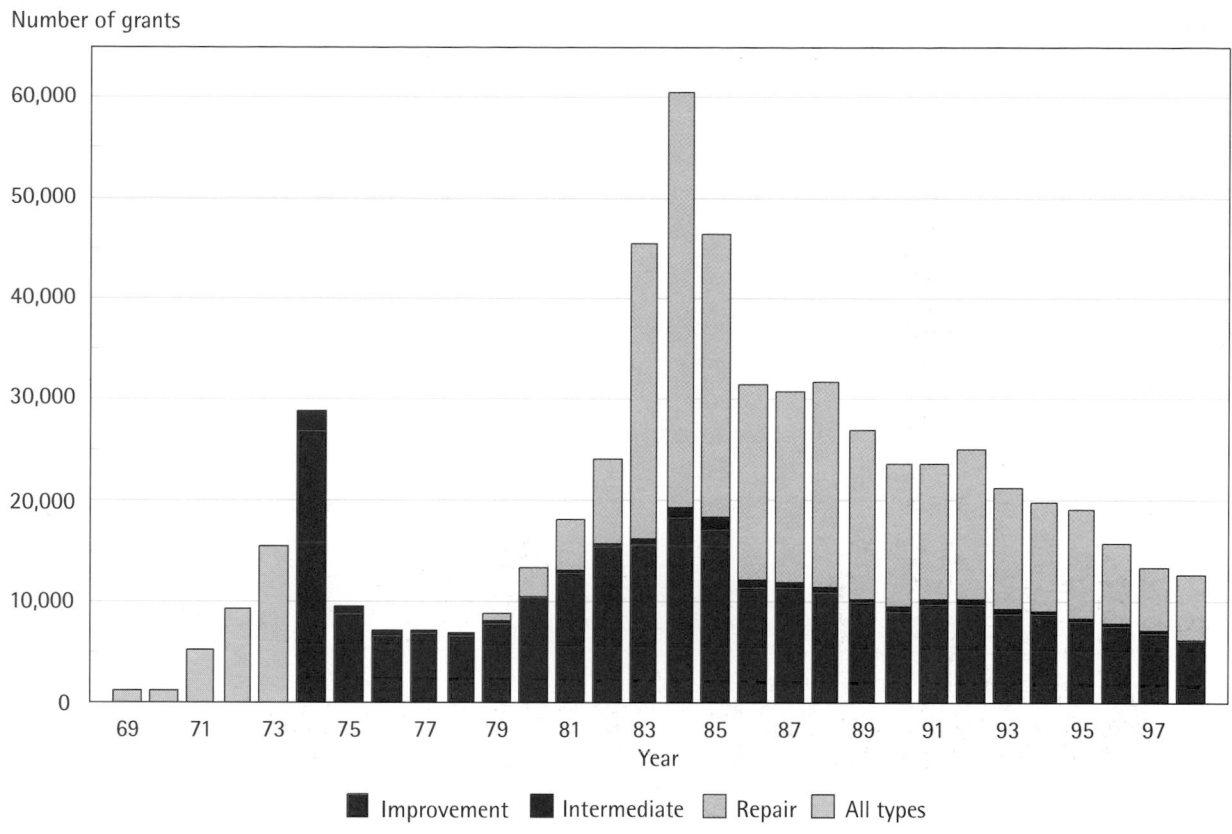

■ Improvement ■ Intermediate ▨ Repair ▢ All types

Figure 7.5: Grants by type, Northern Ireland (1977–97)

Number of grants

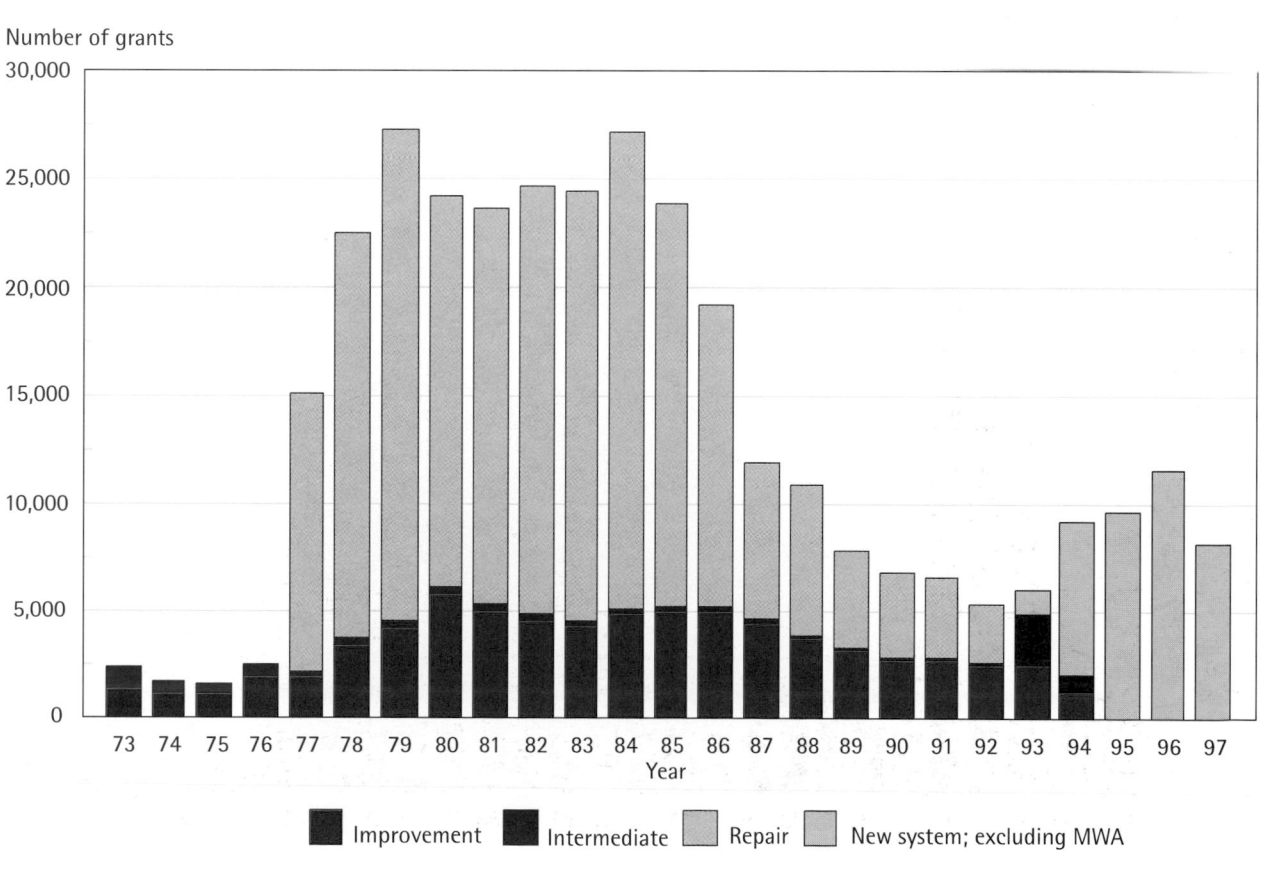

■ Improvement ■ Intermediate ▨ Repair ▢ New system; excluding MWA

Grants per 1,000 dwellings

Figure 7.6 examines the number of grants in each country in comparison to the size of the housing stock (Table A7.6). This is difficult to estimate accurately because of changes over time in the nature of the dwelling stock eligible for grant, but, accepting this limitation, it is clear that until the late 1980s investment levels in Northern Ireland generally exceeded those elsewhere in the UK. For a 10-year period between 1977 and 1985 provision exceeded 70 grants per 1,000 private sector dwellings. After a slow start the number of grants in Scotland per 1,000 privately-owned dwellings increased rapidly in the late 1970s and has generally remained above the level in England or Wales. Grant provision in Wales has exceeded that in England and in the late 1980s became comparable in terms of grants per 1,000 dwellings with Scotland and Northern Ireland. In England, provision has remained consistently the lowest, at less than five grants per 1,000 private sector dwellings since 1991, except in the two boom periods in the early 1970s and early 1980s, despite the fact that the proportions of pre-1919 and interwar dwellings exceed those in both Scotland and Northern Ireland. As a result Glasgow, Belfast and Cardiff have received far higher levels of investment in private sector renovation than most comparable cities in England.

Figure 7.6: Grants per 1,000 privately owned dwellings, UK (1969–97)

Grants per 1000 private dwellings

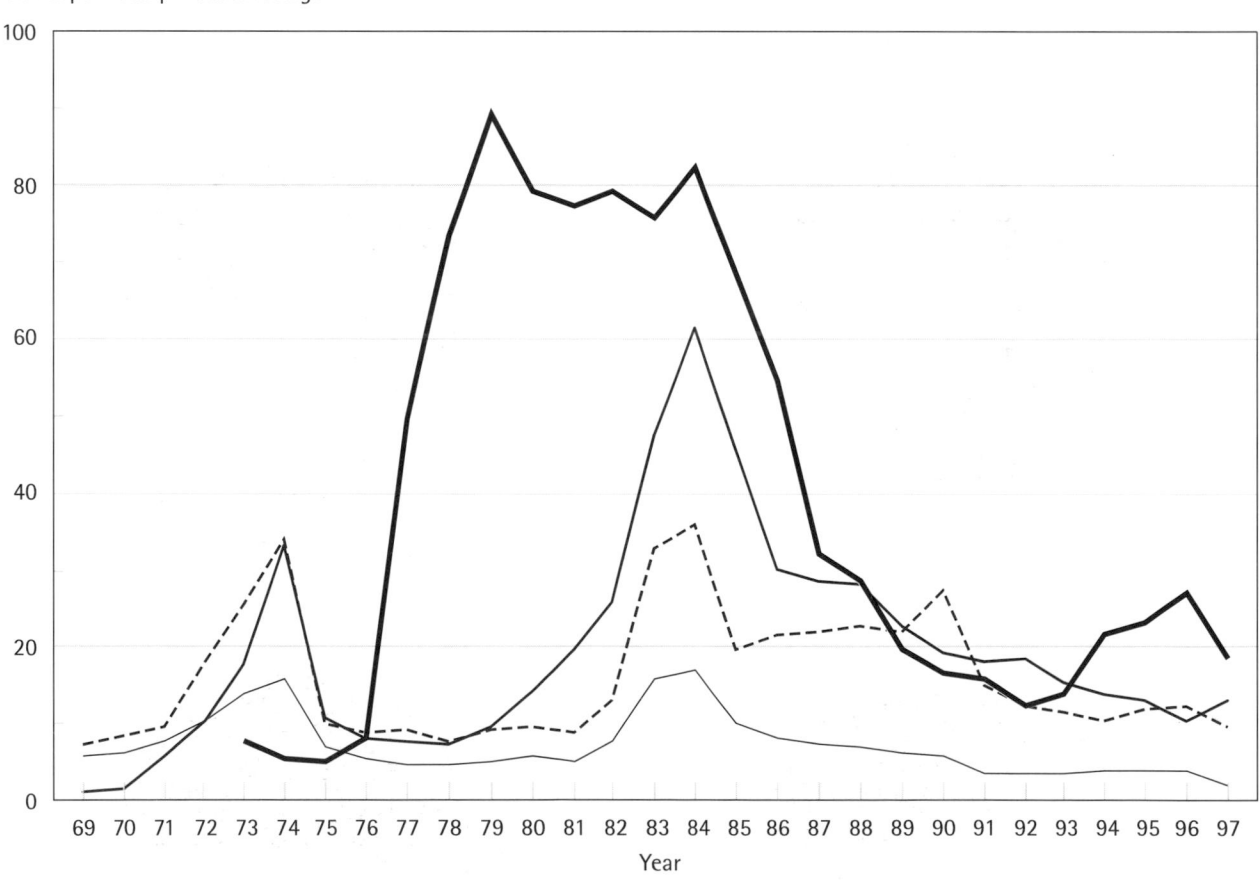

Type of grant

Figures 7.7 shows details of the types of grant provided under the old grant system (in Scotland still the current system). In England, 58% of grants provided under the old system between 1969 and 1994 were improvement grants, with the residue evenly split between repair and intermediate grants. The profile varied, with improvement grants reaching a peak of around 80% of all grants in the late 1970s, becoming displaced by repair grants in the early 1980s, and regaining some ground to account for over 50% of grants at the end of the 1980s (Table A7.7). In Wales, there were fewer improvement grants (49%) under the old system and more repair grants (38%). Improvement grants accounted for 90% of all grants in the 1970s but declined to about 25% after the extension of repair grants to all pre-1919 properties in the early 1980s. In

Scotland, information on grants by type was not available before 1974. In overall terms, 47% of grants during the 1974-94 period were improvement grants and 50% were repair grants. As in Wales, there was a strong focus on improvement grants in the 1970s, but these were subsequently displaced by repair grants to an even greater extent than in Wales. The proportion of repair grants has declined during the 1990s from a peak of over 60% but still accounts for over 50% of grants provided. In Northern Ireland, repair grants account for three quarters of all grants provided under the old system over the 1977-94 period for which information is available. Such grants were available at an earlier stage than in the rest of the UK, accounting for 85% of grants in 1977. There was a steady decline in the proportion of repair grants to about 50% in 1992, the last year of the old system in Northern Ireland.

Figure 7.7: Grants by type under the old system (1969-94)

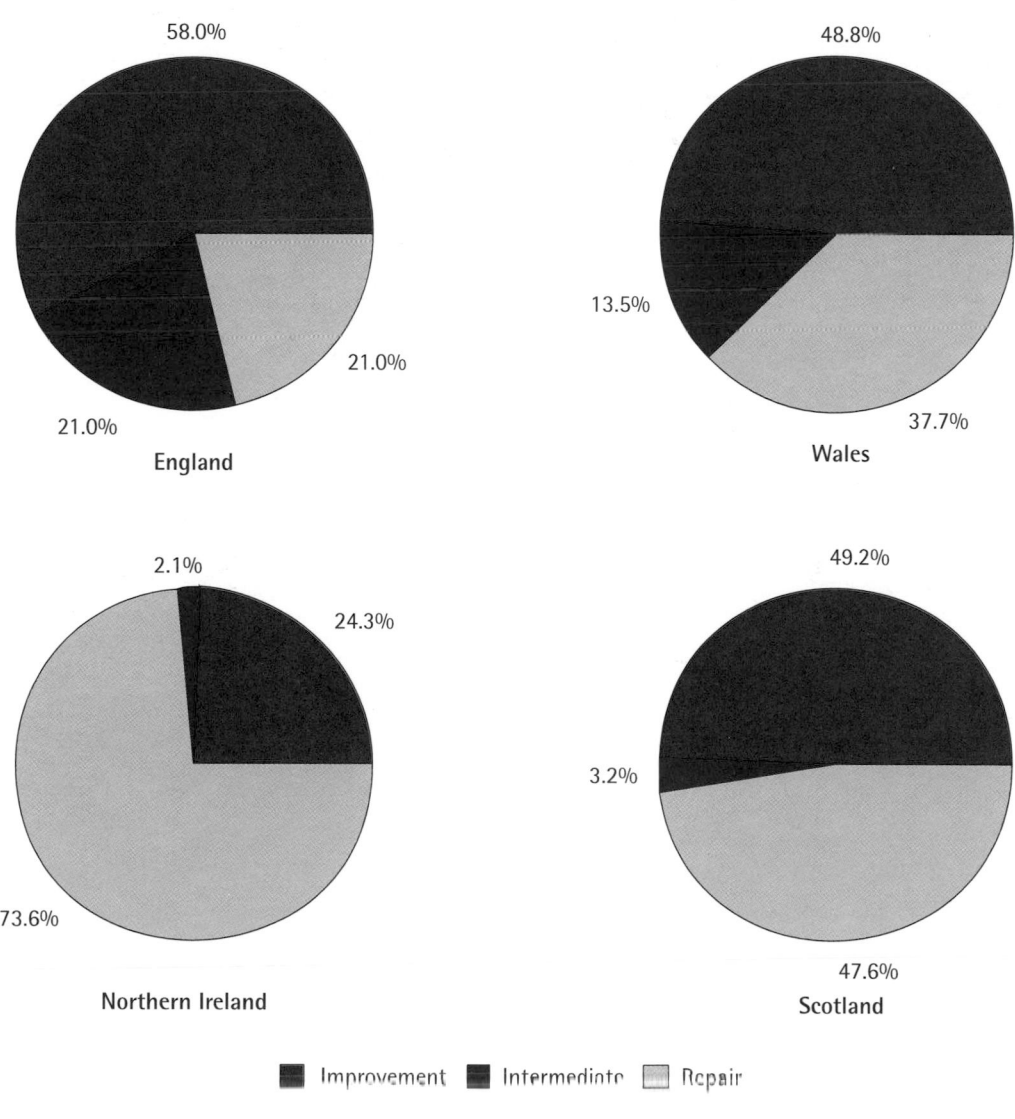

These findings reveal a different focus in renovation policy between England and the remainder of the UK under the old renovation grant system. In England there was emphasis on the more comprehensive improvement grants, while in Scotland, Wales and Northern Ireland grant aid focused more on repair work. This may, in part, explain the higher per dwelling provision of grants outside England, as repair grants were typically worth far less than improvement grants. Average grant levels are examined further below.

Mandatory renovation grants were the main type of grant provided under the 1989 system in both England and Wales between 1990 and 1996 (Figure 7.8; Table A7.8; Table A7.9). Since 1997

all renovation grants have been discretionary (see above); in 1997, in England, 59% of grants were of this type. In Wales the equivalent figure was 71% (Table A7.8; Table A 7.10). DFGs were the other main type of grant provided, accounting for 34% of grants in England and 26% in Wales. Almost all DFGs are mandatory. HMO (houses in multiple occupation) grants formed only 3% of all grants provided and there were very few common parts grants. If home repairs assistance (formerly MWA) were to be added into the total, these grants would form 23% of all grants provided in England and 20% in Wales. Table A7.11 shows the breakdown of grant provision in Northern Ireland for 1993 – the first year that the new system operated – to 1997.

Figure 7.8: Grants by type under the new system, England and Wales (1997)

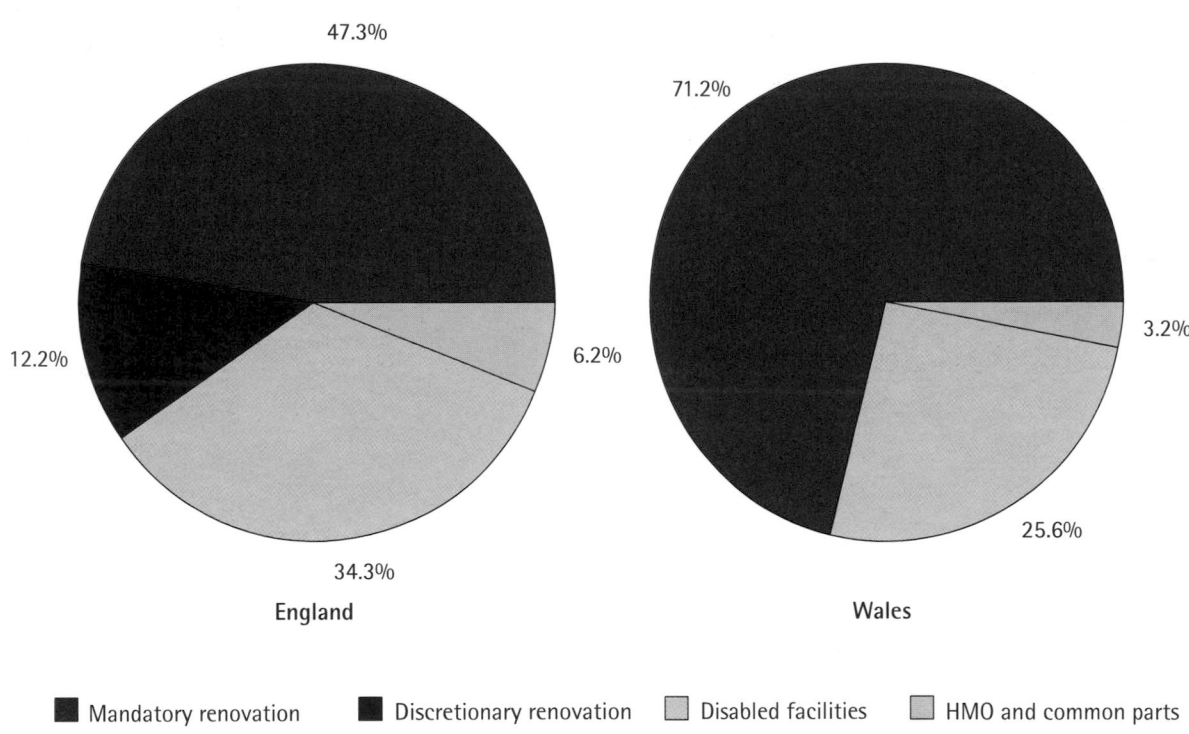

England

Wales

■ Mandatory renovation   ■ Discretionary renovation   ▢ Disabled facilities   ▢ HMO and common parts

Looking specifically at home repair assistance (formerly MWA), Table 7.2 shows the split in provision between the types of grant available (see also Table A7.12). Staying put grants to assist older people to continue living independently at home have been consistently the most significant type of assistance, accounting for 89% of all MWA provided in 1996/97 in England.

Thermal insulation has been the other main purpose (36% of MWA in 1990/91, declining to 8% in 1996/97. The other three types of MWA have only rarely been provided, although in 1995/96 elderly adaptation grant made up 4.3% of MWA. This increase was at the expense of thermal insulation grants.

Table 7.2: Minor works assistance by type, England (1990–97)*

Year	Thermal insulation Number	%	Patch and mend† Number	%	Staying put‡ Number	%	Elderly adaptation§ Number	%	Lead pipes¶ Number	%
1990/91	5,512	35.9	1	0.0	9,454	61.5	407	2.6		
1991/92	5,823	20.7	118	0.4	21,934	78.1	208	0.7		
1992/93	5,309	19.3	21	0.1	21,749	79.2	384	1.4		
1993/94	4,080	14.2	125	0.4	24,121	83.7	210	0.7	284	1.0
1994/95	3,364	11.2	37	0.1	25,899	86.4	406	1.4	273	1.0
1995/96	1,684	5.3	33	0.1	28,137	89.1	1,358	4.3	335	1.1
1996/97	2,632	8.3	6	0.01	28,479	89.3	574	1.8	196	0.6

Source: Housing and Construction Statistics (various years)

* MWA has been replaced by Home Repairs Assistance;
† Grant for a temporary improvement to a property which is in a clearance area or will be within 12 months;
‡ Repairs, improvements or adaptations to properties owned or tenanted by a person aged 60 or more;
§ Adaptations to property to enable an older person, not the owner or tenant, who is or who proposes to be resident in the property to be cared for by a friend or relative;
¶ Replacement of lead water service pipes (introduced from September 1992).

The local pattern of grant provision

There have been substantial variations in the numbers of grants paid by individual local authorities, as a result of differences in size, variations in housing conditions, and differences in the enthusiasm with which renewal policies were pursued. Map 7.2 shows the number of grants of all types provided under the old grant system per 1,000 private sector dwellings in the period 1978-91 in England and Wales. There are no clear patterns in the distribution but there are concentrations of authorities with high levels of grant activity – especially in Wales, but also in the South West, East Anglia, the Midlands, North East Lancashire and the North East. The authorities with the highest rates of grant provision overall are predominantly Welsh including both urban and rural districts (Table 7.3). In England the majority of authorities with high levels of provision are rural and few large urban authorities have given a large number of grants relative to the size of their stock.

Table 7.3: Authorities in England and Wales with the highest rate of 1985 Act grant payments per 1,000 private sector dwellings (1978–94)

| Local authority | 1985 Act grants | |
	Number	Per 1,000
Rhondda	19,599	772.80
Islwyn	10,831	571.00
Cynon Valley	8,547	436.16
Merthyr Tydfil	6,589	422.59
Blaenau Gwent	7,497	385.80
Carmarthen	6,667	384.51
Neath	7,292	369.16
Llanelli	7,943	349.66
South Pembrokeshire	4,532	345.22
Arfon	5,315	340.74
Lliw Valley	6,416	330.50
Taff-Ely	9,454	327.71
Meirionnydd	3,397	307.39
Dwyfor	2,704	303.62
Rhymney Valley	8,400	297.03
Cardiff	25,676	293.06
Swansea	15,157	279.95
Port Talbot	4,005	279.32
Blackburn	10,146	269.85
Bolsover	5,518	268.09
Leicester	18,091	263.40
Brecknock	3,305	261.32
Hastings	6,848	256.31
Waveney	9,091	254.66
Ogwr	10,152	248.84
Burnley	7,128	247.01
Allerdale	6,726	245.98
Preseli	5,085	244.22
Wear Valley	3,940	230.26
Wandsworth	17,861	228.37

Source: Local housing statistics (various years)

Map 7.2: Grants under the old system per 1,000 privately owned dwellings, England and Wales (1978–94)

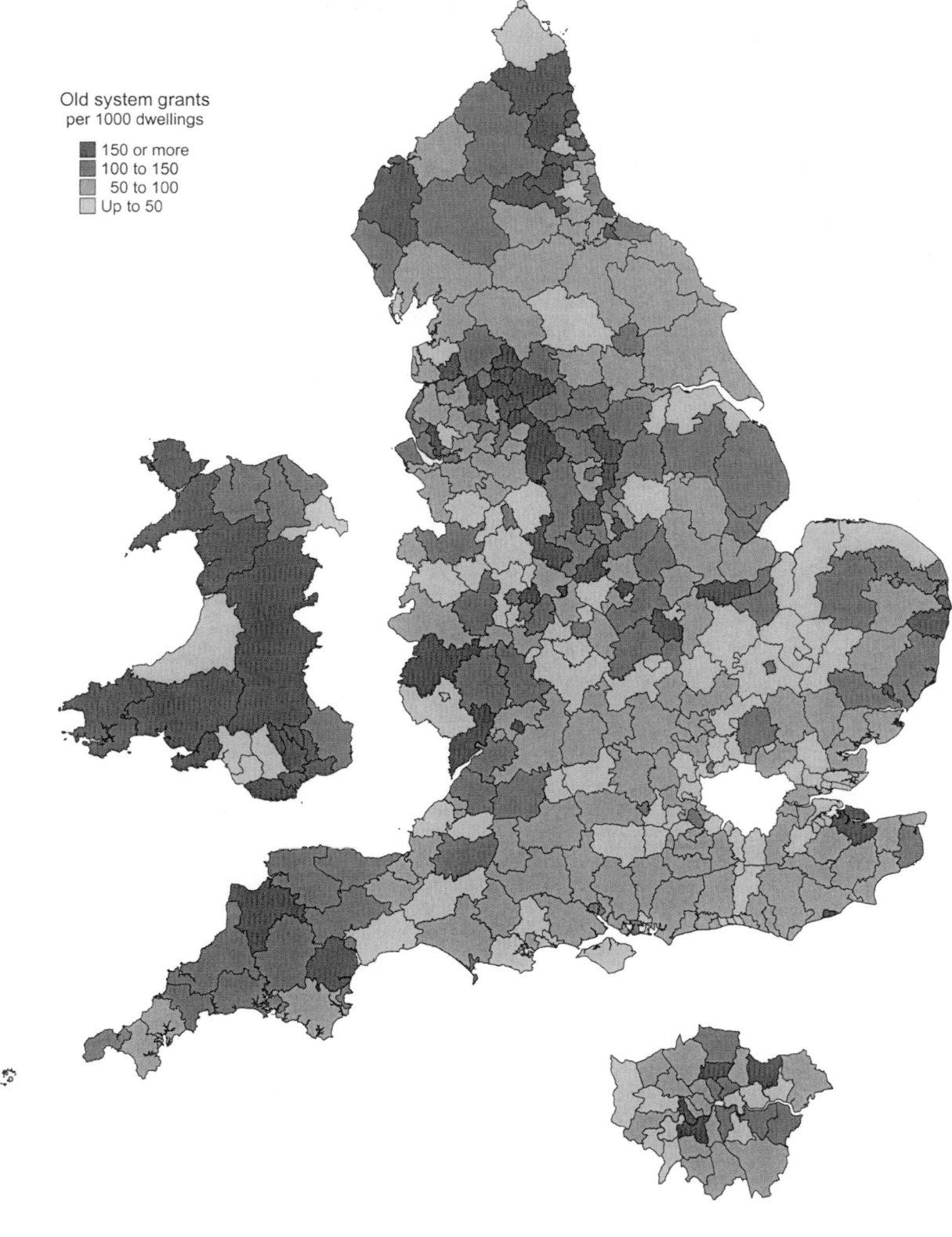

Old system grants
per 1000 dwellings

- ■ 150 or more
- ■ 100 to 150
- ▨ 50 to 100
- ▢ Up to 50

Data for Scotland at local authority level is not available for an extended period, but Map 7.3 shows overall levels of grant activity per 1,000 households by area in Scotland over the 1990-97 period. Rural areas in north Scotland such as Eilean Siar (previously the Western Isles), and Orkney and Shetland provided the highest number of grants per household, followed by some of the larger cities (Aberdeen, Glasgow, Dundee).

Map 7.3: Grants per 1,000 households by area, Scotland (1990–97)

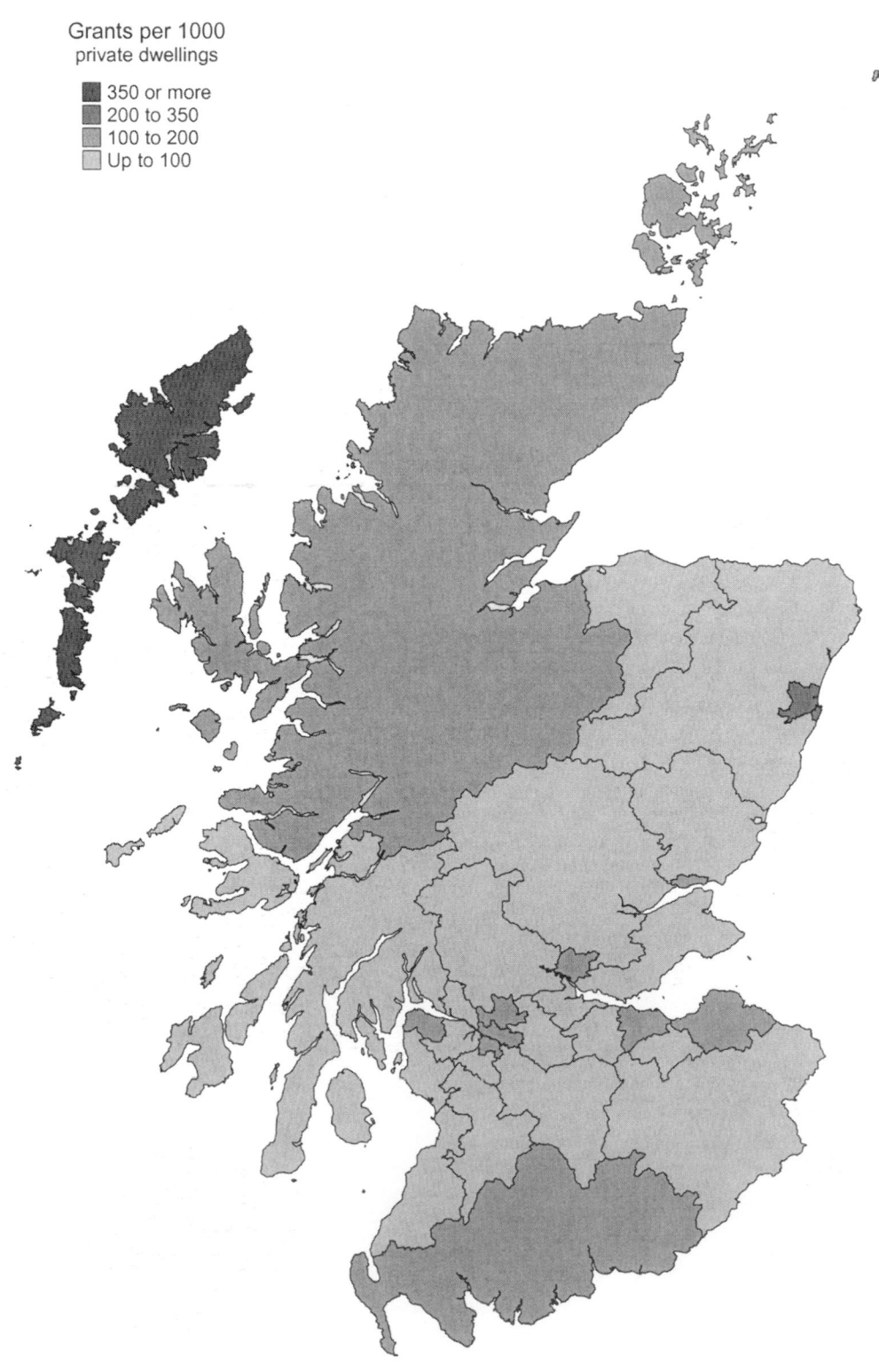

Grants per 1000
private dwellings

- 350 or more
- 200 to 350
- 100 to 200
- Up to 100

The pattern of grant provision under the new system

Map 7.4 shows the number of renovation grants provided per 1,000 private dwellings in England and Wales during the period 1990-97. As with grants under the old system the picture is dominated by Welsh authorities (Table 7.4), predominantly from South Wales but not exclusively so. In England authorities providing high numbers of grants relative to their stock include Wansbeck, Leicester, Kingston upon Hull, Rugby, Barrow-in-Furness, Swale, Norwich, Charnwood, Derwentside and Hastings. Relatively few grants have been given in London and the South East.

Map 7.4: Renovation grants per 1,000 privately owned dwellings, England and Wales (1990–97)

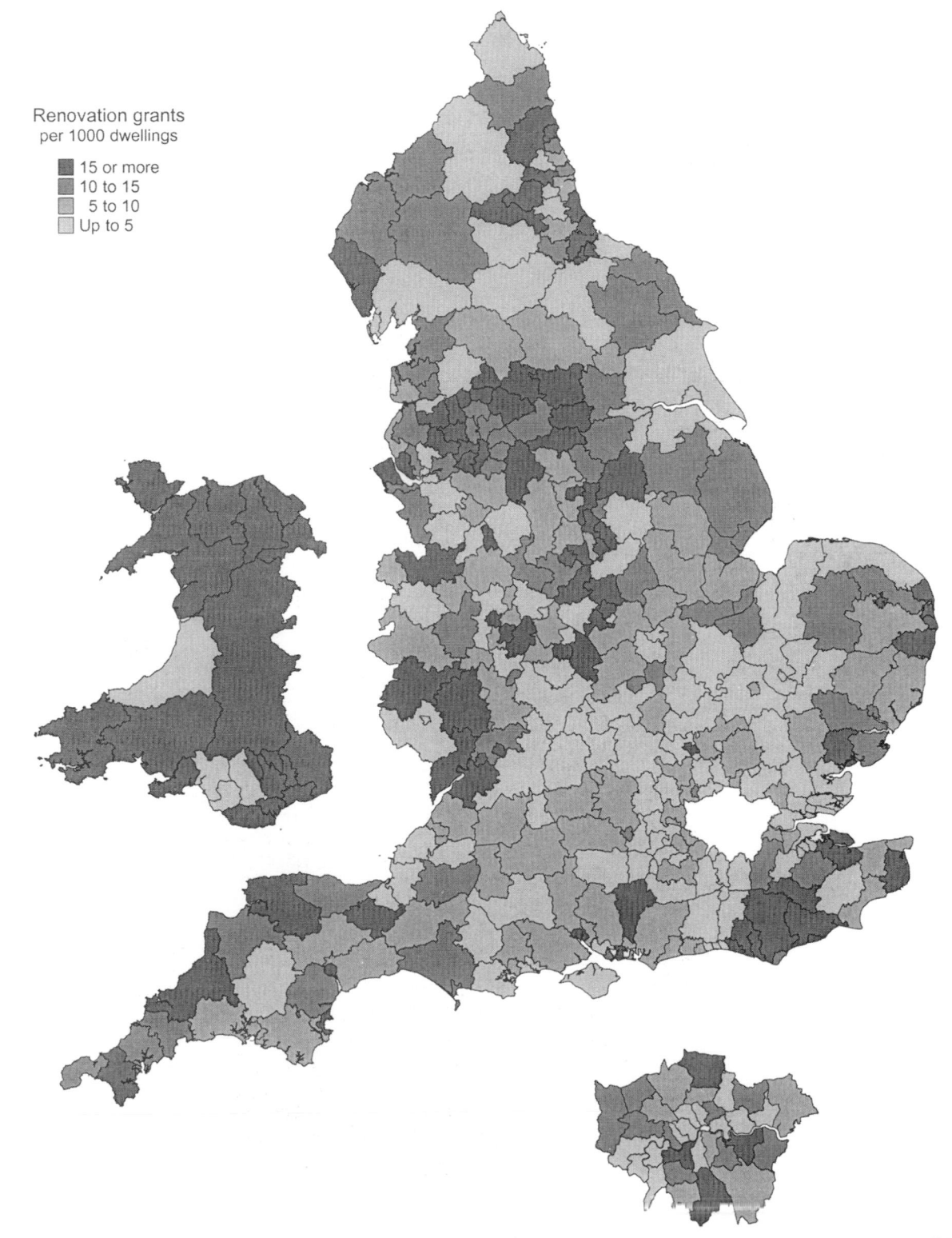

Table 7.4: Authorities in England and Wales with the highest rate of renovation grant payments per 1,000 private sector dwellings (1990–96)

Local authority	Renovation grants	
	No	Per 1,000
Neath and Port Talbot	3,711	87.75
Caerphilly	3,881	82.14
Rhondda Cynon Taff	5,836	79.94
Blaenau Gwent	1,519	79.93
Wansbeck	959	59.08
Ceredigion	1,113	51.28
Gwynedd	1,799	50.60
Carmarthenshire	2,563	48.86
Pembrokeshire	1,622	47.78
Cardiff	3,994	45.17
Isle of Anglesey	930	44.53
Bridgend	1,756	43.22
Merthyr Tydfil	655	42.01
Swansea	2,661	40.72
Leicester	2,970	38.8
Vale of Glamorgan	1,383	38.61
Kingston upon Hull	2,584	38.1
Rugby	1,105	37.6
Powys	1,363	37.33
Barrow-in-Furness	1,007	36.6
Swale	1,440	33.2
Norwich	1,009	32.1
Charnwood	1,560	30.2
Derwentside	785	29.6
Conwy	1,094	29.02
Hastings	892	28.3
Denbighshire	837	28.2
Newport	1,066	27.8
Torfaen	624	27.5
Pendle	859	26.2

Source: Local housing statistics (various years); Welsh Housing Series (various years)

Table 7.5: Authorities in England and Wales with the highest rate of disabled facilities grant payments per 1,000 private sector dwellings (1990–96)

Local authority	DFGs	
	No	Per 1,000
Rotherham	3,259	45.0
Caerphilly	2,009	42.5
Ellesmere Port	1,047	41.4
Swansea	2,295	35.1
Neath and Port Talbot	1,345	31.8
Caradon	900	28.6
Waveney	1,136	27.4
Vale of Glamorgan	979	27.3
Cardiff	2,414	27.3
West Oxfordshire	830	25.7
Knowsley	919	25.4
Stockton-on-Tees	1,301	23.4
Torfaen	532	23.4
Pembrokeshire	714	21.0
Burnley	681	20.6
Calderdale	1,369	20.4
Newark	671	18.7
Norwich	586	18.6
Exeter	554	16.5
Leeds	3,531	16.5
Manchester	1,681	16.0
Wychavon	586	15.9
Barnsley	1,021	15.3
Swale	657	15.1
Flintshire	648	15.1
South Somerset	773	14.7
Bromsgrove	448	14.5
West Somerset	201	18.9
Havant	567	14.5
Northampton	886	14.3

Source: Local housing statistics (various years); Welsh Housing Series (various years)

Map 7.5 shows the number of DFGs given per 1,000 private dwellings over the same period. The level of provision is lower than for renovation grants. Table 7.5 shows the authorities providing the most grants of this type relative to their dwelling stock. Welsh authorities are again prominent, many being the same authorities as in Table 7.4. The English authorities differ from those in Table 7.4 and include both metropolitan districts (such as Rotherham, Barnsley, Leeds, Manchester, Calderdale and Knowsley), towns (such as Burnley, Norwich, Northampton and Exeter) and more rural districts (such as Caradon, West Somerset and South Somerset). There is no spatial pattern to the distribution of authorities active in the provision of DFG.

Map 7.5: Disabled facilities grants per 1,000 privately owned dwellings, England and Wales (1990–96)

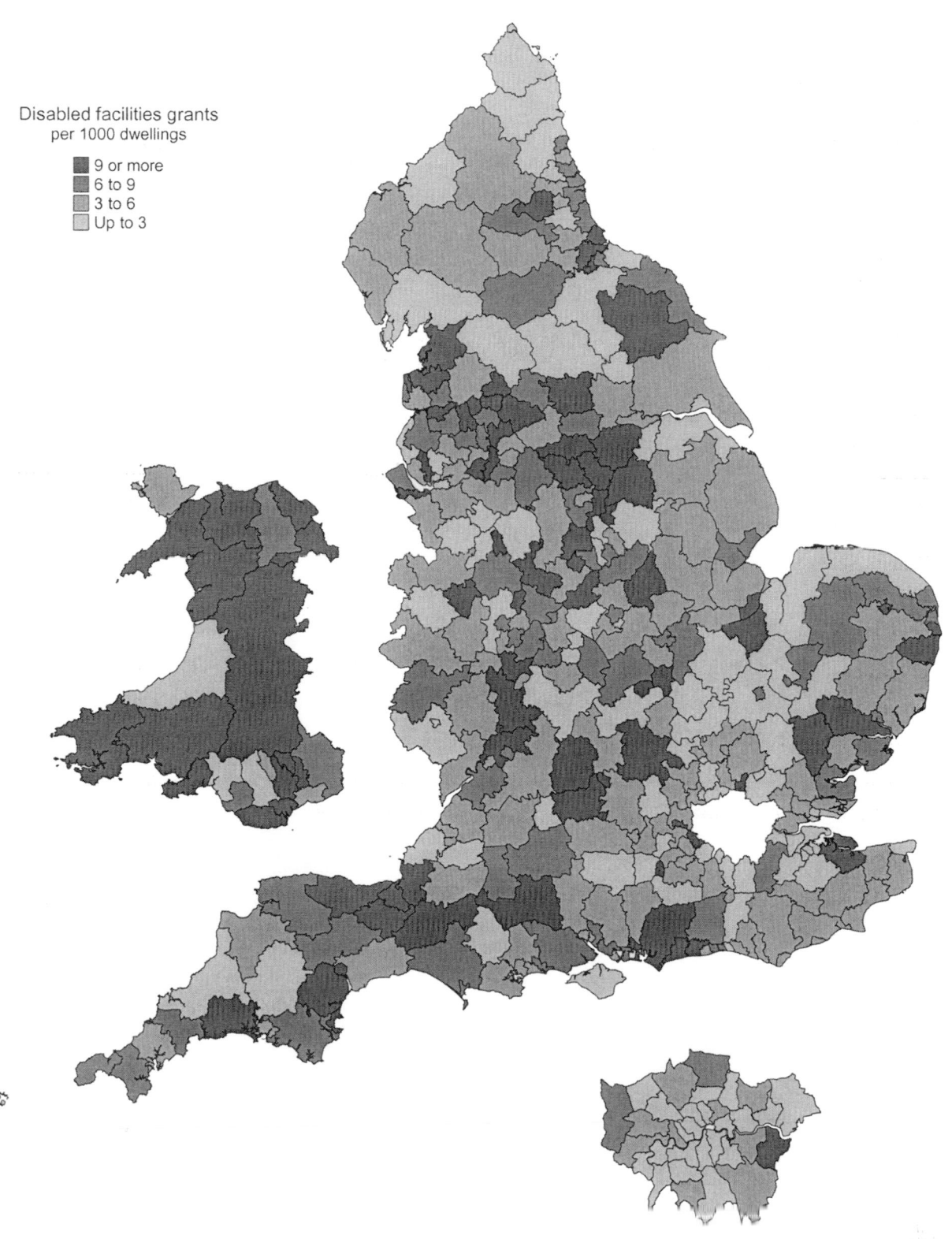

Disabled facilities grants
per 1000 dwellings

- 9 or more
- 6 to 9
- 3 to 6
- Up to 3

Map 7.6 shows the distribution of MWA. The level of provision is much higher. Again there are high levels of provision in South Wales but otherwise the pattern is scattered with more rural areas active in providing MWA than for renovation grants or DFGs (Table 7.6). There is some limited evidence that areas with well-established HIAs provide higher levels of MWA (see below for further discussion of the role of HIAs in relation to MWA). Some local authorities appear never to have provided MWA since its inception.

Table 7.6: Authorities in England and Wales with the highest rate of minor works assistance payments per 1,000 private sector dwellings (1990–96)

Local authority	MWA grants	
	No	Per 1,000
Blaenau Gwent	1,285	67.6
Merthyr Tydfil	927	59.5
Blackburn	2,544	58.6
Caerphilly	2,651	56.1
Oxford	1,991	55.1
Rhondda Cynon Taff	3823	52.4
Swale	2,213	50.9
Pembrokeshire	1,669	49.2
Cardiff	4,335	49.0
Torfaen	1,023	45.0
Newport	1,701	44.4
Derwentside	1,081	40.7
Conwy	1,504	39.9
North East Lincolnshire	2,006	39.0
Wychavon	1,346	43.2
Exeter	1,255	37.4
St Helens	1,985	36.9
Wychavon	1,346	36.5
Carmarthenshire	1,904	36.3
Bridgend	1,458	35.9
Middlesbrough	1,409	35.4
Bournemouth	2,336	35.4
Mid Devon	851	35.3
West Lindsey	1,007	35.1
South Shropshire	543	34.7
Wealden	1,880	34.7
Burnley	1,112	33.7
Manchester	3,419	32.5
Stroud	1,216	32.0
Powys	1,145	31.3

Source: Local housing statistics (various years); Welsh Housing Series (various years)

Map 7.6: Minor works assistance per 1,000 privately owned dwellings, England and Wales (1990–96)

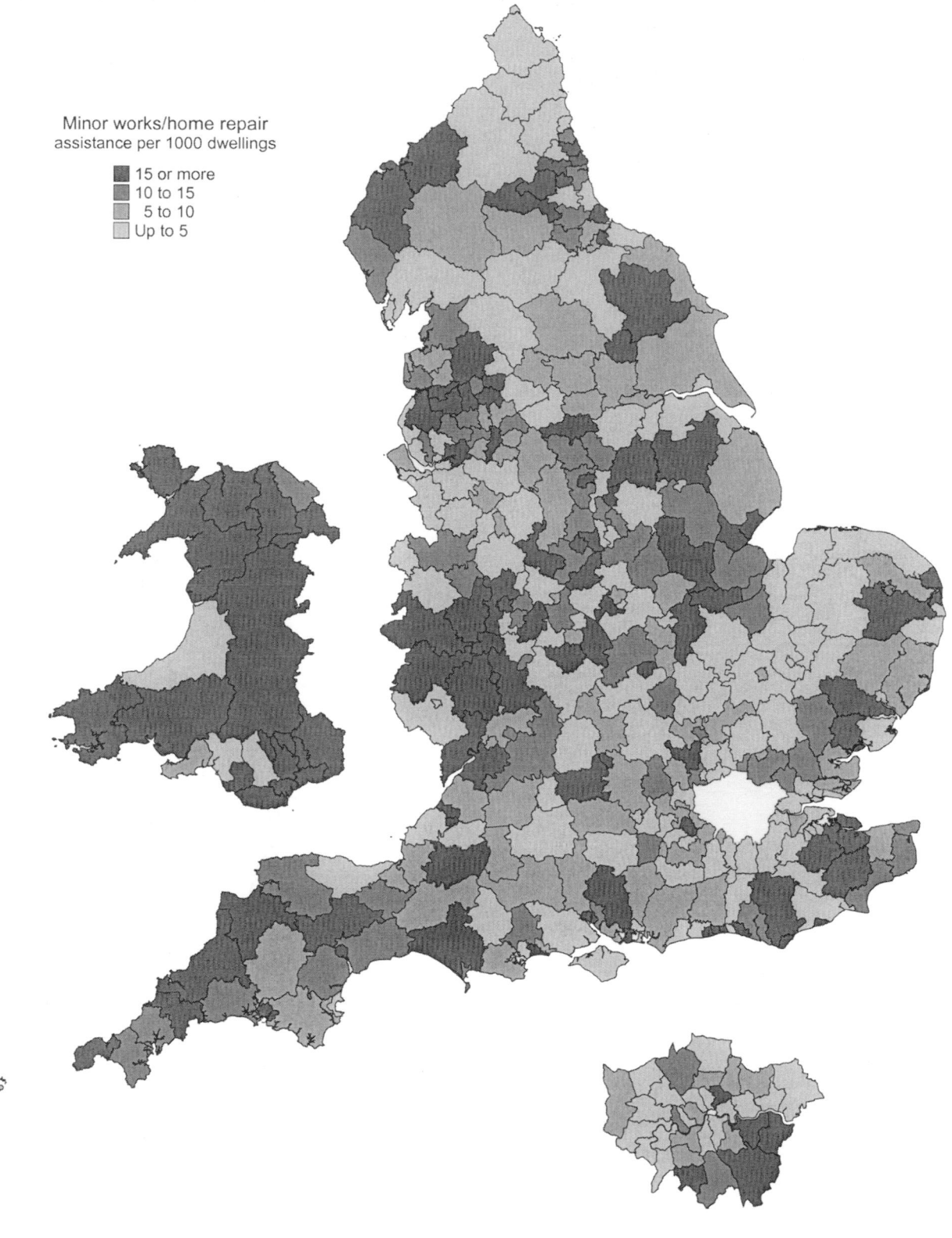

Minor works/home repair
assistance per 1000 dwellings

- 15 or more
- 10 to 15
- 5 to 10
- Up to 5

Average value of grant

Figure 7.9 shows the average value of grants of various types between 1979 and 1997 under both the old and new grant systems (see also Table A7.13). Average values have been updated to 1993/94 price levels. Average grant levels under the old system (an amalgamation of repair and improvement grants) were generally similar for England and Wales. Average values rose from about £4,000 in 1979 to almost £8,000 in the mid-1980s before falling again in the late 1980s. After the start of the new grant system in 1990, the average values of the residual completions under the old system rose as if in sympathy with the higher grants provided at the same time under the new system. Average renovation grant levels under the new system then increased sharply, from £5,000 in 1990 to about £10,000 in 1994 in England, and from £10,000 in 1990 to £18,000 in 1994 in Wales. All these values are expressed in constant price terms. In Scotland, grants also increased, but more steadily, rising from about £3,500 in 1979 to £7,500 in 1990. Since then there has been a slight fall in real terms in England, Scotland and Wales. The average value of grants in Northern Ireland was higher than in the rest of the UK throughout the period, reaching almost £11,000 in the mid-1980s, subsequently falling back to £10,000. Since the introduction of the new grant system in 1992 there has been an increase in the average grant value in Northern Ireland. This peaked in 1995 at over £18,000, but has since levelled off to a value similar to Wales. Northern Ireland and Wales have much higher average grant values than England and Scotland.

In part, the large increases in average grant levels under the new system are due to the higher grant percentages paid under the new system in England, Wales and Northern Ireland. Under the new renovation grant system, grant is not assessed as a fixed percentage, but covers the residual cost of work after the owner's contribution has been assessed. Table 7.7 shows that on average, renovation grants covered 88% of the total costs of grant-aided work in 1996/97, with DFGs covering an average of 93%. Some 60% of renovation grants and 80% of DFGs covered 100% of the cost of works in 1996/97. For both types of grant the proportion which covered all the costs of work has remained fairly constant since the introduction of the new system. The absence of an upper limit on grant payments between 1990 and March 1993 also contributed to the increase in the average grant. A limit of £50,000 per grant was imposed from April 1993, and this was subsequently reduced to £20,000 (£24,000 in Wales) in January 1994. But it is also likely that the extent of work carried out with grant aid has increased because grant aid is being targeted on the properties in poorest condition.

Table 7.7: 100% grants and average grant as % of costs of work, renovation grants and disabled facilities grants, England (1990-97)

	100% grants as % of all grants		Aggregate grant as % of aggregate cost of works	
	Renovation	DFG	Renovation	DFG
1990/91	56	79	89	93
1991/92	59	77	87	90
1992/93	57	77	90	85
1993/94	61	81	85	91
1994/95	59	78	88	92
1995/96	58	81	89	92
1996/97	60	80	88	93

Source: Housing and Construction Statistics (various years)

Figure 7.9: Average value of grants, UK (1979–96)

Average value £

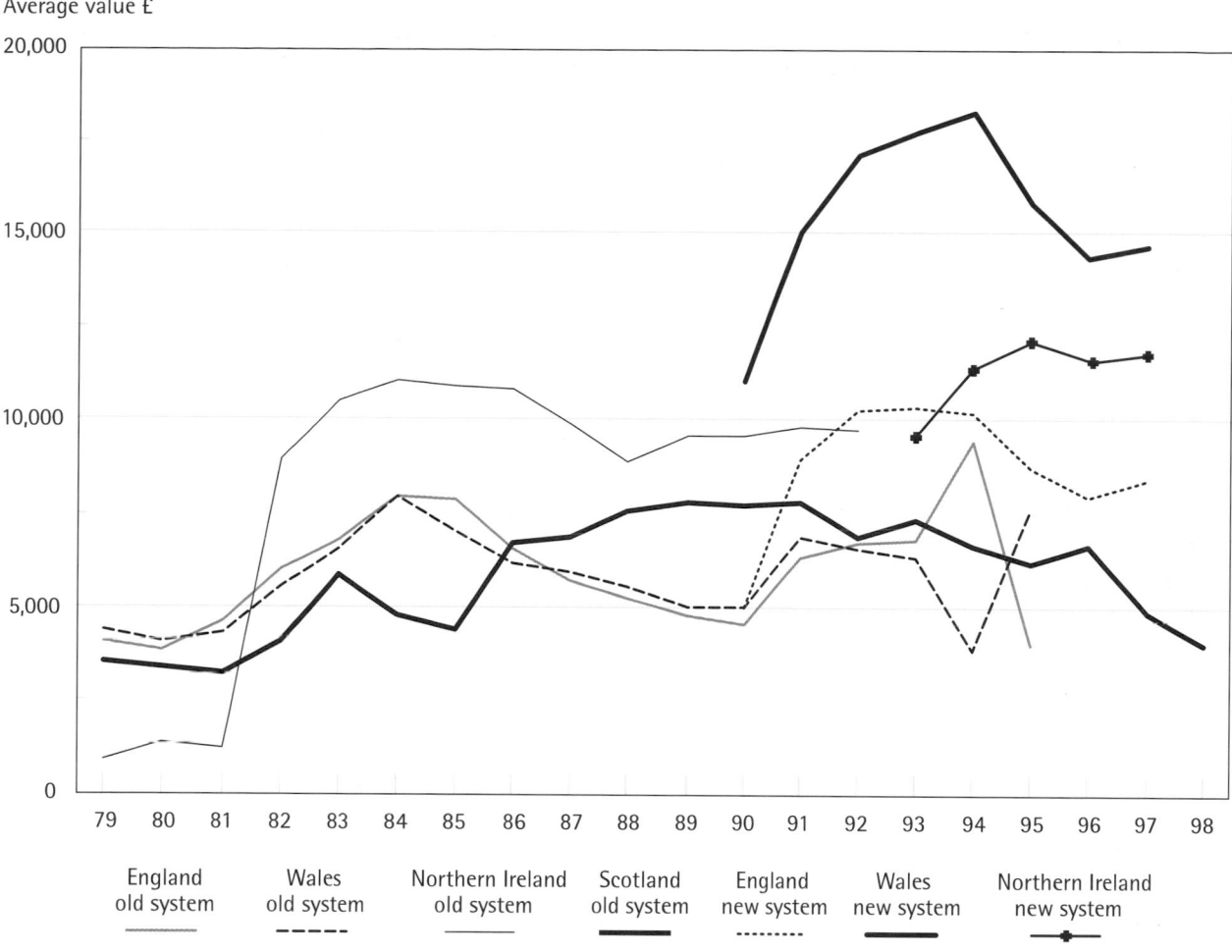

England old system	Wales old system	Northern Ireland old system	Scotland old system	England new system	Wales new system	Northern Ireland new system

However, average grant values conceal substantial local variations. Map 7.7 shows the average value of mandatory renovation grants by local authority district in England and Wales in 1996/97 and Table 7.8 lists authorities with the highest average grant levels. Almost half the authorities are Welsh, demonstrating the impact of higher levels of resources in Wales. Some 10% of authorities gave mandatory renovation grants with an average value of under £5,000 in 1996/97, 52% gave grants averaging £5,000-£9,999, 25% averaged between £10,000-£14,999, and a further 8% averaged between £15,000-£19,999. Only 5% (32) of authorities gave grants with an average exceeding £20,000 (Table 7.8). Variations of this magnitude suggest that there is considerable scope for the application of local discretion in identifying unfitness and determining appropriate solutions. In England the highest average grants occurred mainly in rural areas, where the number of grants was small, but several London boroughs such as Tower Hamlets rate high.

Table 7.8: Authorities in England and Wales with the highest rate average payments for mandatory renovation grants (1996/97)

Local authority	Average grant	Number
Flintshire	64,465	43
South Lakeland	58,663	9
Hackney	55,456	116
Tower Hamlets	38,772	50
Barking and Dagenham	35,756	60
Kensington and Chelsea	28,562	56
South Oxfordshire	26,434	26
Wrexham	25,552	145
Newport	24,675	120
Waltham Forest	24,531	24
Isle of Anglesey	22,122	98
Pembrokeshire	21,335	161
Allerdale	21,213	16
Denbighshire	21,169	166
Sandwell	20,407	275
Torfaen	20,098	102
The Wrekin Telford	19,632	39
Blaenau Gwent	19,559	188
Tameside	19,383	52
Merthyr Tydfil	18,459	133
Ceredigion	18,371	175
Eden	18,063	33
South Ribble	17,480	24
Southwark	17,447	156
Oldham	17,403	93
Maldon	17,387	22
Gwynedd	16,935	293
Winchester	16,889	28
Lambeth	16,873	59
South Shropshire	16,764	30

Note: Data for Wales are for the calendar year after 1994.

Sources: Unpublished data supplied by the DoE; Welsh Housing Statistics 1997 (Welsh Office, 1997)

Map 7.7: Average value of mandatory renovation grants, England and Wales (1996/97)

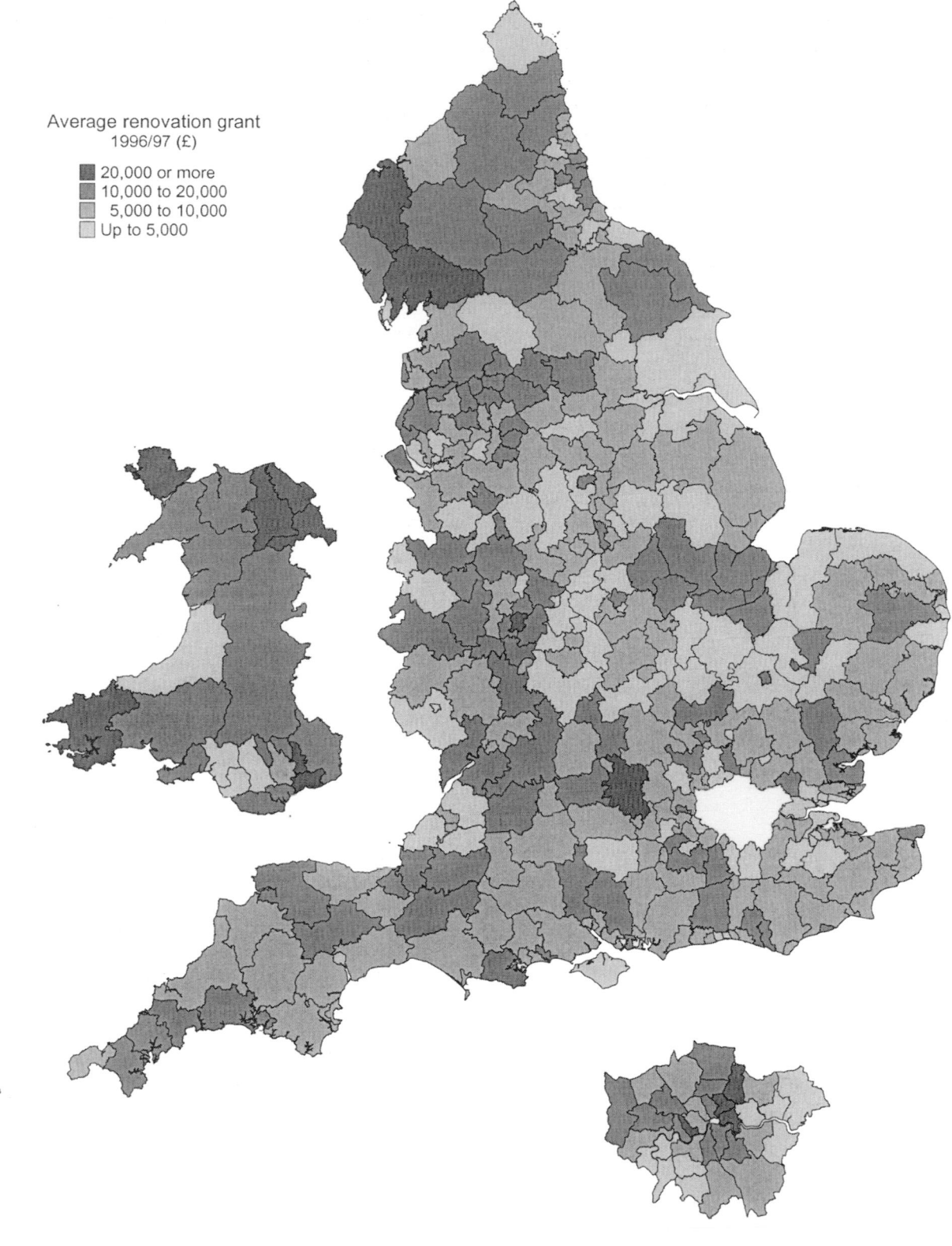

Average renovation grant
1996/97 (£)

- 20,000 or more
- 10,000 to 20,000
- 5,000 to 10,000
- Up to 5,000

Map 7.8 shows average values of disabled facilities grants in 1996/97 and Table 7.9 shows authorities providing the highest average value DFGs. Some 8% of authorities provided DFGs averaging under £2,500 in 1996/97. The largest group (55%) provided grants averaging between £2,500-£4,999. A further 24% averaged between £5,000-£7,499 and 8% averaged between £7,500-£9,999. Only 5% averaged £10,000 or more.

Map 7.9 shows average improvement grant levels by area in Scotland for 1997. There is substantial variation, with average grants exceeding £10,000 in three areas, but under £3,000 in six areas. The substantial variation between the larger urban areas that existed in previous years has diminished, as Dundee, Glasgow and Edinburgh average £7,000-£9,000, although Aberdeen is still very low in comparison averaging only £2,500.

Table 7.9: Authorities in England and Wales with the highest rate average payments for mandatory disabled facilities grants (1996/97)

Local authority	Average mandatory DFG	Number of grants
Hackney	30,236	44
Barking and Dagenham	27,272	120
Flintshire	24,645	31
Ealing	17,456	131
Brent	15,228	17
Isle of Anglesey	15,143	7
Cambridge	13,634	44
South Oxfordshire	13,620	20
Harrow	15,588	21
Mole Valley	12,241	21
Ceredigion	11,625	32
Tower Hamlets	11,170	54
Rother	11,102	17
Peterborough	11,096	24
Haringey	10,946	46
Congleton	10,851	6
Merthyr Tydfil	10,591	22
Lambeth	10,015	83
Alnwick	9,905	8
Castle Point	9,864	12
Hastings	9,831	13
Redbridge	9,624	69
Coventry	9,525	66
Hart	9,477	5
Hillingdon	9,412	119
Cardiff	9,380	242
Camden	9,372	17
Dacorum	9,274	22
Enfield	9,035	133
Sandwell	8,959	83

Note: Data for Wales are for the calendar year after 1994.

Sources: Unpublished data supplied by the DoE; Welsh Housing Statistics 1997 (Welsh Office, 1997)

Map 7.8: Average value of mandatory disabled facilities grants, England and Wales (1996/97)

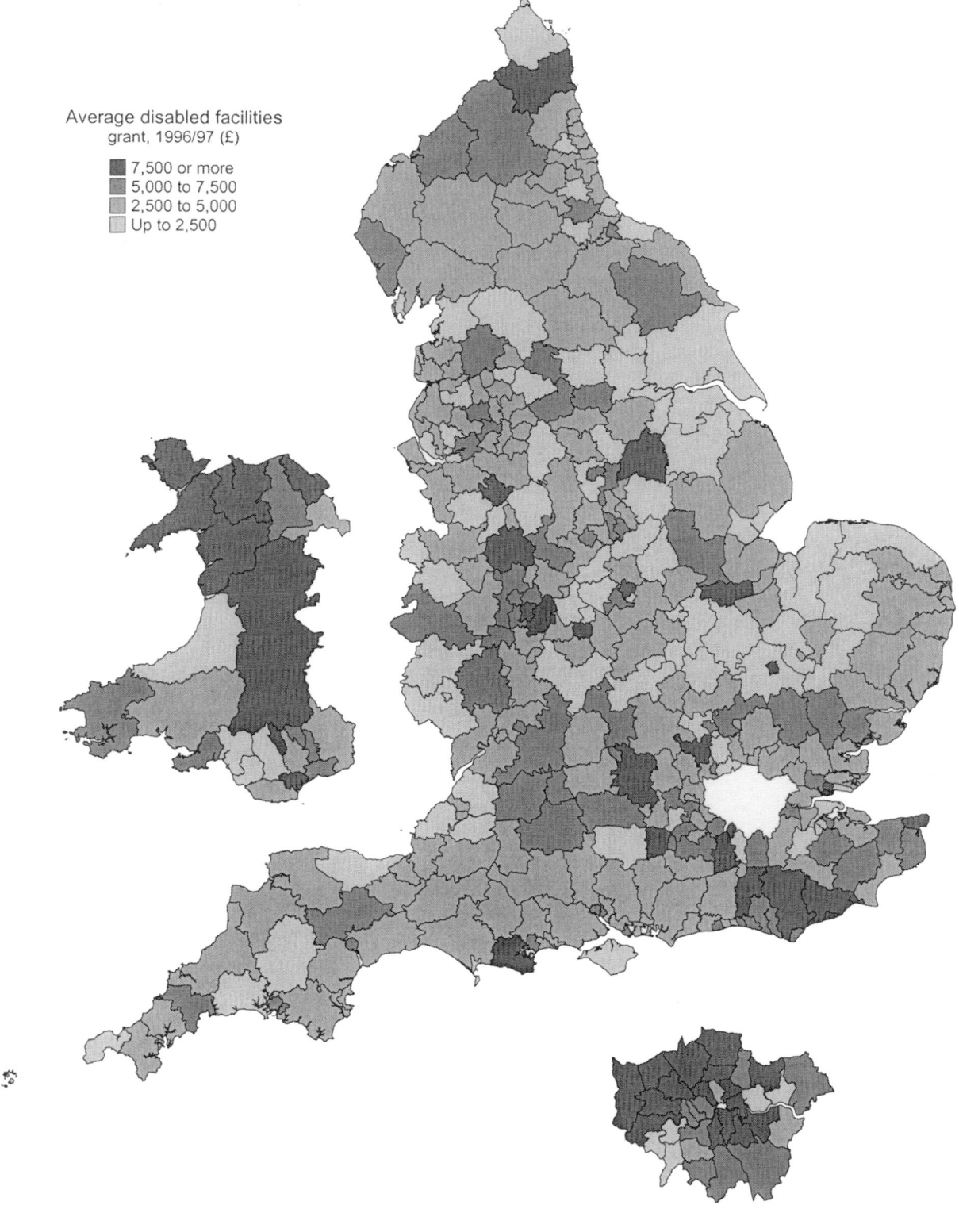

Average disabled facilities
grant, 1996/97 (£)

- 7,500 or more
- 5,000 to 7,500
- 2,500 to 5,000
- Up to 2,500

Map 7.9: Average value of improvement grants by area, Scotland (1997)

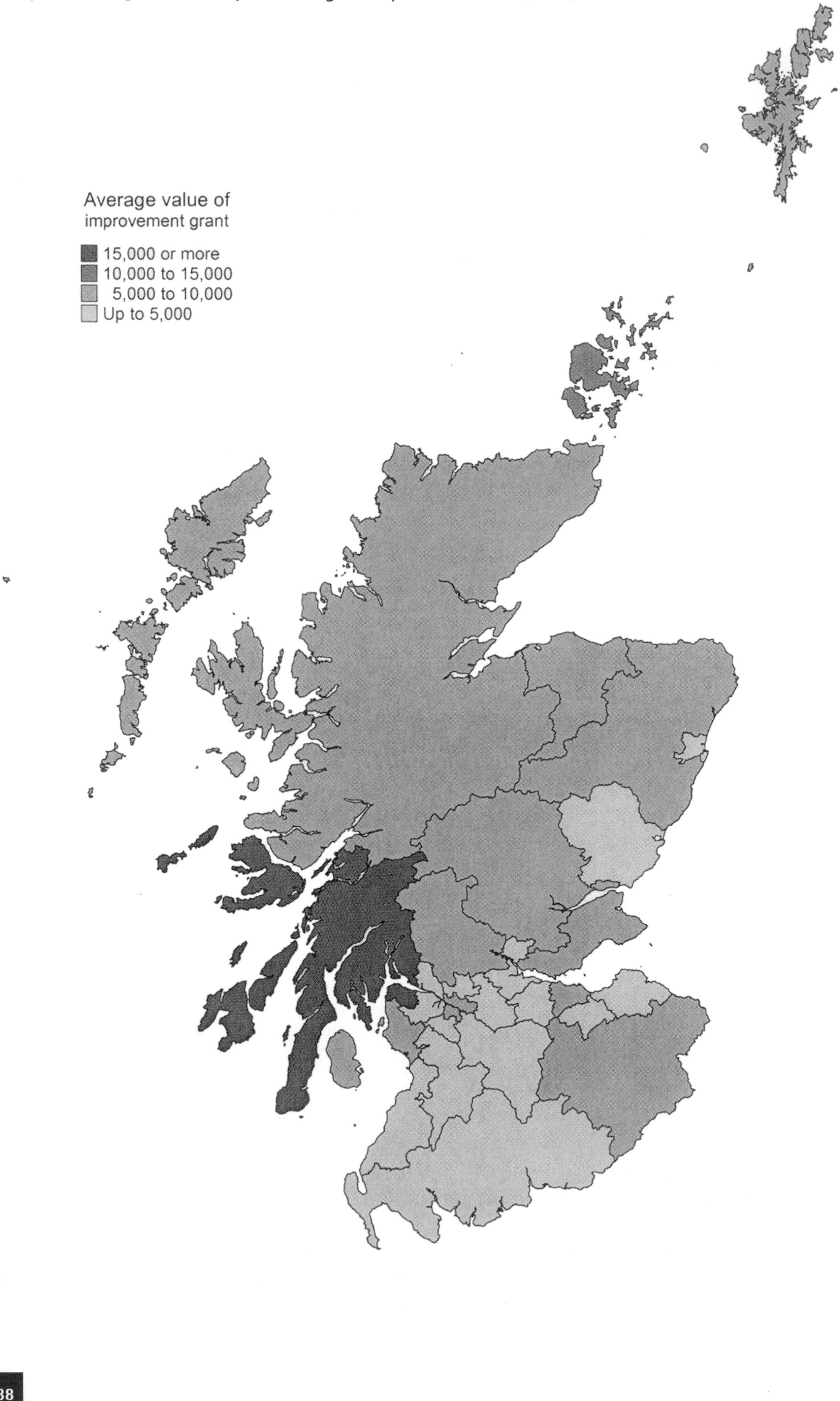

Average value of
improvement grant

- 15,000 or more
- 10,000 to 15,000
- 5,000 to 10,000
- Up to 5,000

Grants and poor conditions

It is difficult to measure the impact of grant investment on poor housing conditions. At the national level there has been some improvement in the proportion of dwellings lacking amenities, but unfitness and disrepair remain serious problems with relatively little change between the last two national house condition surveys. Local level data on changes in house condition is rarely available so it is impossible to demonstrate the impact of grant investment over a period of time.

It is to be expected that those authorities with large numbers of pre-1919 dwellings would have given more grants. Figure 7.10 indicates that this is generally the case, but there is a substantial amount of variation, with some authorities which have high levels of pre-1919 dwellings giving very low numbers of grants – particularly inner London boroughs – while at the other extreme some authorities have provided a much larger number of grants than might be expected, for example, Rhondda, Leicester and Wandsworth.

Figure 7.10: Grant payments by number of pre–1919 dwellings, England and Wales (1978–94)

Grants 1978-94

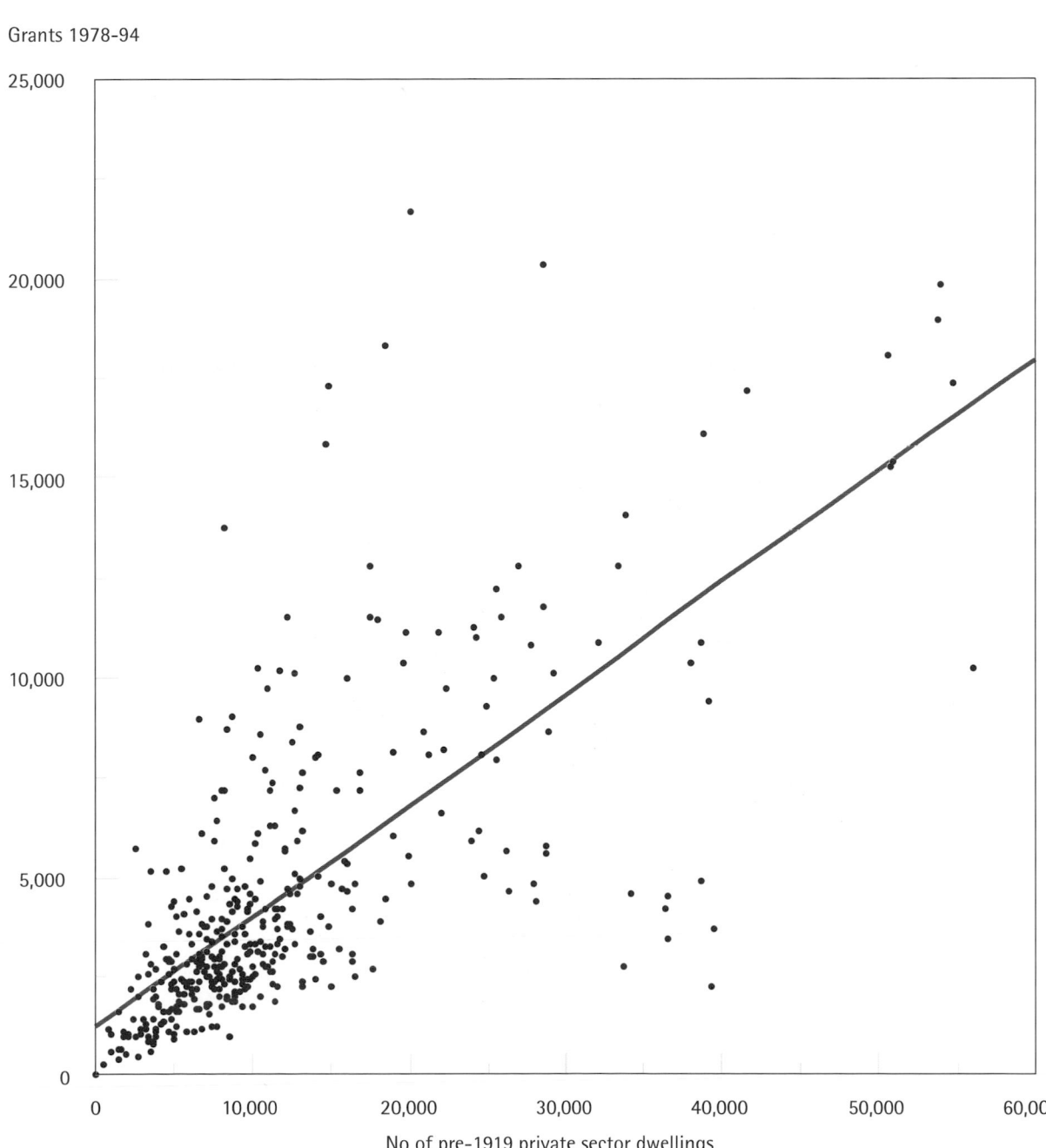

No of pre-1919 private sector dwellings

Grant recipients

The 1986 EHCS provides information on grant recipients during the period 1981-86 when the old grant system was in operation. Some 82% were owner-occupiers and 15% were landlords. Households with incomes of under £3,000 per annum were under-represented, taking up 13% of all grants, while those with an income of between £3,000-£9,000 were over-represented receiving 55% of all grants. Those with incomes of more than £12,000 received 33% of all grants. In terms of age, younger households aged between 17-39 received a disproportionate share of grants (46%). At the other extreme those aged 75 and over were under-represented (3% of grants).

Specific surveys into the distribution of grants undertaken over the same period also showed that households headed by older people were under-represented among those taking up grants. The socioeconomic characteristics of grant recipients were similar to the population as a whole with the majority of grants (59% in England and 57% in Wales) going to people in skilled manual or non-manual occupations. The average income of grant recipients (£7,000 in England and £5,200 in Wales) was similar to the national average in 1982 but those receiving improvement grants were better off than those receiving repair or intermediate grants. After 1982 the shift to higher percentage repair grants led to an increase in the number of recipients who were older or who had been resident for 10 years or more.

There has been no published monitoring of the characteristics of grant recipients under the new grant system apart from a study carried out for the DoE in the system's early period of operation. This showed that older people received a higher proportion of grants under the new system than under the old one. During the first two years of operation, 48% of renovation grant approvals were awarded to people over 60, a much higher proportion than under the old system. In addition, 75% of DFG approvals were awarded to those aged 60 or more. As a result of the test of resources, grants were closely targeted on those with low incomes. In total, 60% of those who had grants approved were in receipt of some form of state benefit.

In terms of tenure, private landlords have fared badly under the new system compared with the old system (Table 7.10). In 1990/91, 93% of renovation grants went to owner-occupiers and only 7% to landlords. Subsequent years have seen the proportion of renovation grants to landlords increase only slowly to reach 14% in England in 1996/97 and 8% in Wales. DFGs are less focused on owner-occupiers but this group nevertheless have continued to receive about two thirds of these grants since 1990/91 in England (about three quarters in Wales). Local authority tenants have been the next largest group of recipients, although the proportion of grant that they are receiving has declined over recent years (from 27% in England for 1990/91 to 18% in 1996/97). Tenants of private landlords in England have accounted for about 10% of DFGs. Private landlords and housing associations as landlords have received insignificant numbers of DFGs, both in England and in Wales.

Properties receiving grants

Monitoring by the DoE has shown that in the first 18 months of the new grant system, three quarters of renovation grant approvals related to dwellings built before 1919. One fifth of approvals were for dwellings built after 1945. However more than 80% of approvals related to properties which were unfit for human habitation. Grants under the new system are thus more closely targeted on the poorest condition properties than those under the old system, which placed more importance on dwelling age. As might be expected, DFG approvals were fairly evenly spread across the dwelling stock and only a quarter were unfit. For MWA, 39% of dwellings where a grant was approved were built before 1919, with 21% dating from the interwar period and 39% from the postwar period. Almost 90% of MWA approvals were for dwellings which were fit.

Table 7.10: Grants by tenure of recipient, England and Wales (1990–96) (% of grants)

England		Owner-occupier	Private landlord	Housing associations	Private tenant	LA tenant	All recipients
Renovation	1990/91	92.6	6.4	1.0	0.0	0.0	100.0
	1991/92	92.0	7.2	0.2	0.6	0.0	100.0
	1992/93	88.8	10.1	0.8	0.3	0.0	100.0
	1993/94	87.4	11.7	0.7	0.2	0.0	100.0
	1994/95	87.0	12.2	0.6	0.2	0.0	100.0
	1995/96	84.0	14.6	1.2	0.2	0.0	100.0
	1996/97	84.0	14.1	1.7	0.2	0.0	100.0
DFG	1990/91	67.5	0.2	0.2	5.1	27.0	100.0
	1991/92	63.2	0.4	0.9	5.1	30.4	100.0
	1992/93	66.2	0.5	0.3	6.5	26.5	100.0
	1993/94	65.4	0.5	0.9	7.4	25.8	100.0
	1994/95	68.5	0.7	0.7	8.0	2.1	100.0
	1995/96	66.9	0.3	1.5	8.8	22.5	100.0
	1996/97	68.8	0.5	2.0	10.3	18.4	100.0

Wales		Owner-occupier	Landlord including housing association		Private tenant	LA tenant	All recipients
Renovation	1990	100.0	0.0		0.0	0.0	100.0
	1991	97.9	2.0		0.1	0.0	100.0
	1992	95.7	4.1		0.2	0.0	100.0
	1993	93.6	6.0		0.3	0.0	100.0
	1994	92.9	6.8		0.3	0.0	100.0
	1995	93.2	6.4		0.3	0.0	100.0
	1996	92.2	6.8		1.0	0.0	100.0
	1997	91.1	8.4		0.5	0.0	100.0
DFG	1990	81.5	0.0		3.7	14.8	100.0
	1991	74.7	2.0		2.4	21.0	100.0
	1992	76.7	2.2		3.2	17.8	100.0
	1993	74.0	1.7		4.7	19.6	100.0
	1994	72.8	2.4		4.0	20.7	100.0
	1995	76.4	0.9		4.1	18.5	100.0
	1996	78.9	2.1		2.6	16.4	100.0
	1997	79.1	2.0		3.7	15.2	100.0

Notes: Renovation grants not available to local authority tenants. Grants to private tenants include grants to housing association tenants. Separate information on grants to private landlords and to housing associations as landlords is not available for Wales.

Sources: Housing and Construction Statistics (various years); Welsh Housing Statistics (various years)

Area renewal

General Improvement Areas and Housing Action Areas

Since the 1960s, local authorities have had powers to declare special areas on which they will focus their housing renewal activities. In some circumstances, households in these areas have been eligible for additional types of grant or grants at higher rates. From 1969, local authorities could declare GIAs and, from 1975, HAAs. There are no comprehensive official statistics on the number of areas declared or the number of dwellings included within these areas in England and Wales, but Thomas (1985) estimated that by 1982 just over 500 HAAs had been declared in England, containing around 173,000 dwellings – less than 10% of the potential level estimated from 1971 Census data. The 1981

EHCS estimated that only 408,000 dwellings fell within potential HAAs but, even on this lower estimate, less than a quarter of dwellings with potential for area action were included in current declared areas.

Figure 7.11 shows the number of grants provided to private owners in GIAs or HAAs during the period 1975-89 and the proportion of all grants which this represents. The number of grants in declared areas rose slowly from the mid-1970s to a peak of 35,000 in 1983 and declined thereafter to about 12,000 in 1989. As a proportion of all grants provided, grants in GIAs and HAAs were never very significant, reaching a peak of 22% in 1982, but rarely exceeding 15%. Area improvement has never been a dominant element of renewal programmes in England except in a small number of local areas where these policies have been pursued more intensively.

Figure 7.11: Grants in HAAs and GIAs, England (1975-89)

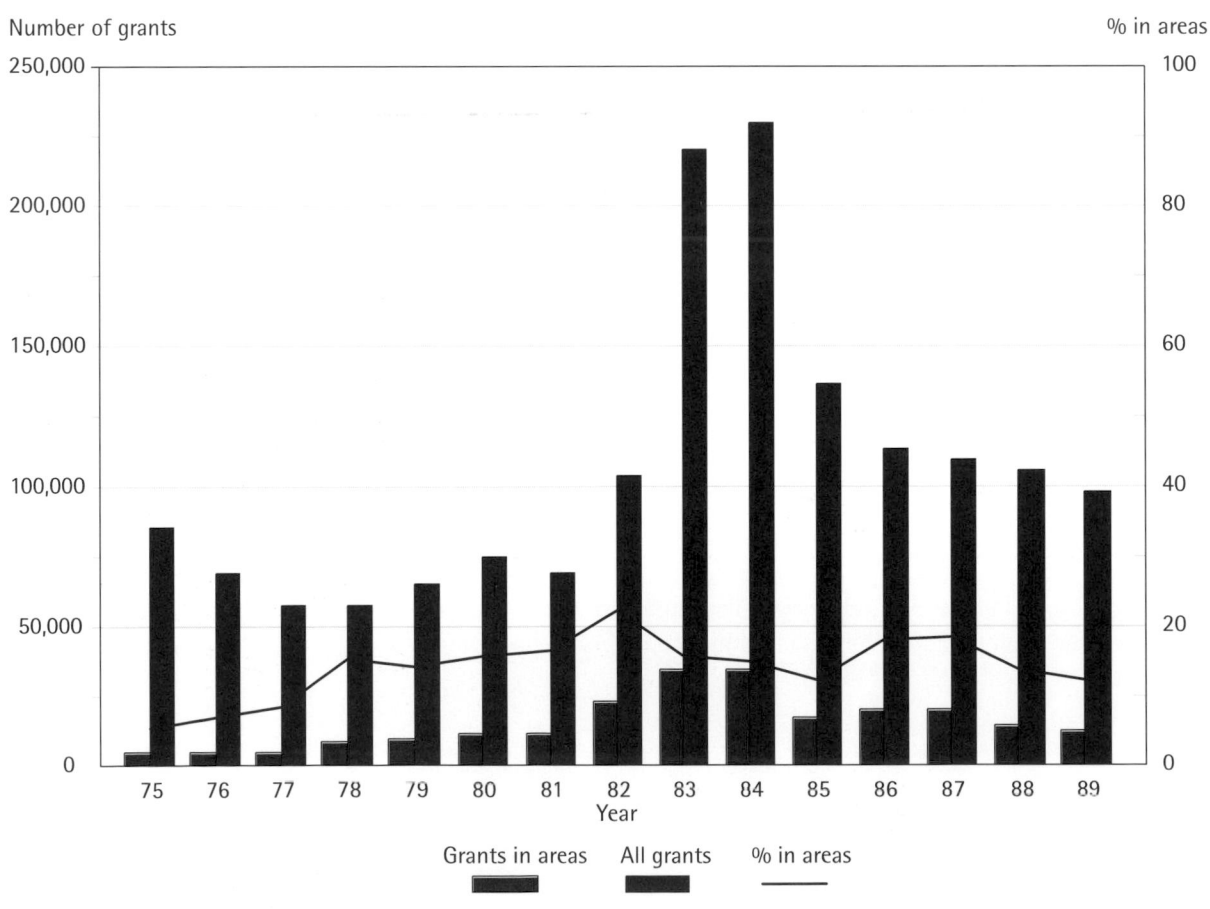

Renewal areas

Renewal Areas replaced HAAs and GIAs as the statutory mechanism for area-based private sector housing renewal in July 1990. By March 1995, some 84 renewal areas had been declared in England, together with a further 20 in Wales. In the last three years 30 new renewal areas have been declared in England, but in Wales the number of renewal areas increased only slightly. Table A7.14 lists renewal areas in England declared by June 1998, in order of declaration, together with the number of dwellings in each area. Table A7.15 shows equivalent information for Welsh renewal areas. Map 7.10 shows the location of these areas.

Map 7.10: Location of renewal areas, England and Wales (1998)

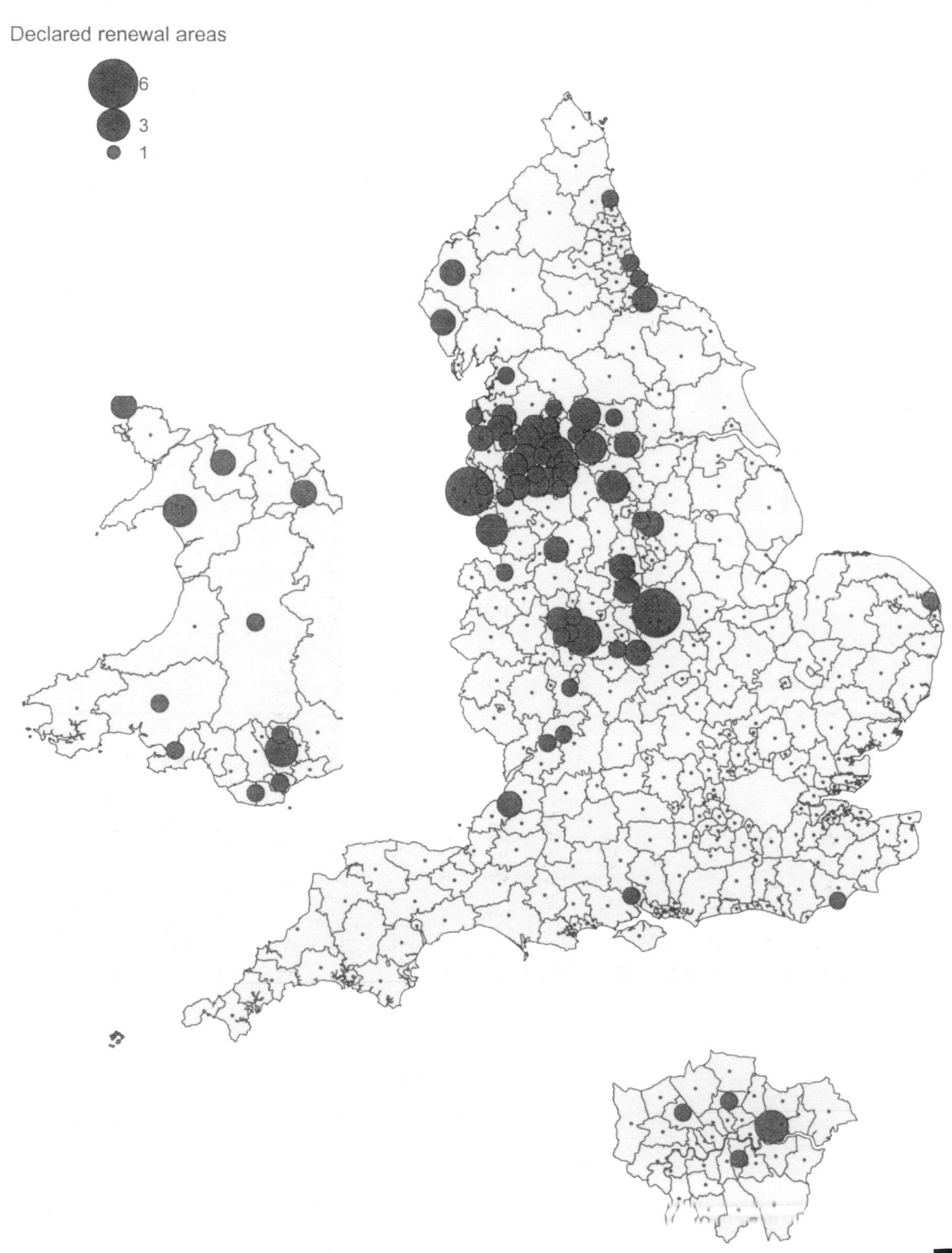

In total, some 160,000 dwellings were included in renewal areas in England (an extra 34,000 dwellings since 1995), an average of just under 1,400 per area. In Wales, the total number of dwellings was 19,600 (19,272 in 1995) or 933 dwellings per area on average. It is difficult to form a judgement on whether this is a satisfactory level of renewal area activity, particularly because no explicit target for renewal area declarations has been set out, as this is a matter for individual local authorities. The number of dwellings in declared areas in England is equivalent to 10% of unfit private sector dwellings in 1996, but, of course, not all unfit dwellings are in areas which would be eligible for renewal area status and not all dwellings in renewal areas are unfit or privately owned.

Table 7.11 shows the distribution of renewal areas in England by standard region. So far, renewal areas are predominantly located in the North of England (64%) and the Midlands (25%). One region, the North West had 37% of the declared renewal areas, with the West Midlands having the next largest proportion (14%). There were only seven renewal areas (8%) in the South of England and East Anglia had one declared area.

The average number of dwellings in renewal areas was 1,500, but the range was very wide,

with the largest area having 4,535 dwellings and the smallest only 335. Figure 7.12 shows that in England the size distribution is skewed towards smaller areas, with the median (1,193 dwellings) well below the mean (Table A7.16). Over 42% of declared areas had less than 1,000 dwellings, and 65% had less than 1,500 dwellings. However, there was a significant group of larger areas (15%) with more than 2,500 dwellings. In Wales renewal areas are significantly smaller, with no areas having more than 2,500 dwellings, and 50% of areas having less than 1,000.

Overall levels of activity in declared renewal areas for which data is available for the years 1990/91 to 1993/94 are shown in Figure 7.13. Total expenditure increased from £8.1 million in 1990/91, to £47.7 million in 1991/92, £86.0 million in 1992/93, and £110.8 million in 1993/94. Increasing the latter figure pro rata for missing data would boost total spend in 1993/94 to £123.4 million. In terms of the source of investment, in 1993/94, 59% of investment in renewal areas came from local authority sources (including government subsidy where appropriate), 34% from housing associations (including HAG and LAHAG), and 7% from private sources. Private spending has declined since 1991/92, while housing association investment peaked in 1992/93.

Table 7.11: Renewal areas by standard region, England

Region	Renewal areas		Local authorities declaring renewal areas	
	Number	%	Number	%
North East	6	5	5	8
Yorkshire and Humberside	15	12	7	11
East Midlands	13	11	5	8
Eastern	1	1	1	1
London	6	5	4	6
South East	2	2	2	3
South West	4	3	3	5
West Midlands	16	14	10	15
North West	42	38	24	37
Merseyside	10	9	4	6
Total	114	100	65	100

Figure 7.12: Size distribution of declared renewal areas, England and Wales

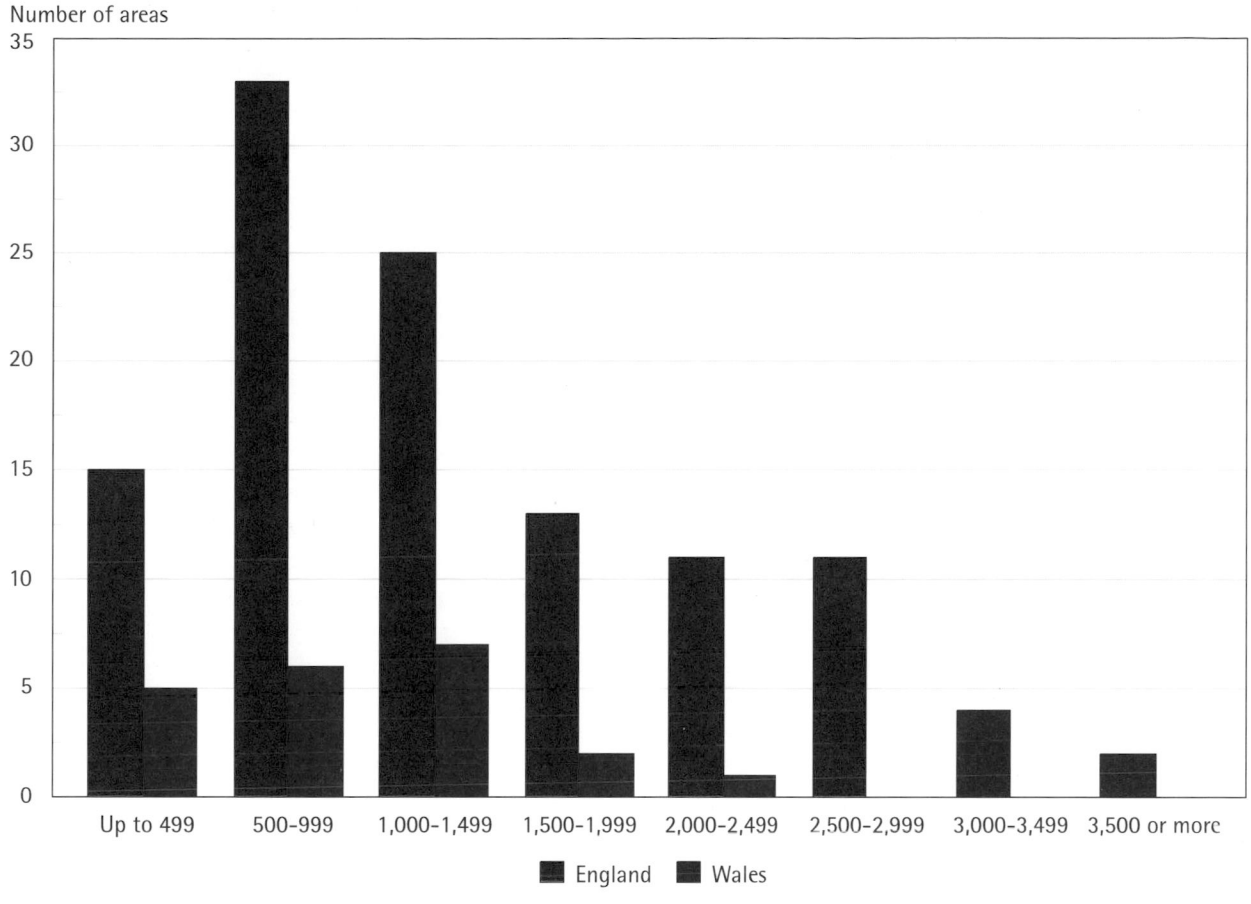

Number of areas

England ■ Wales

Figure 7.13: Changing proportion of spending in renewal areas by source, England

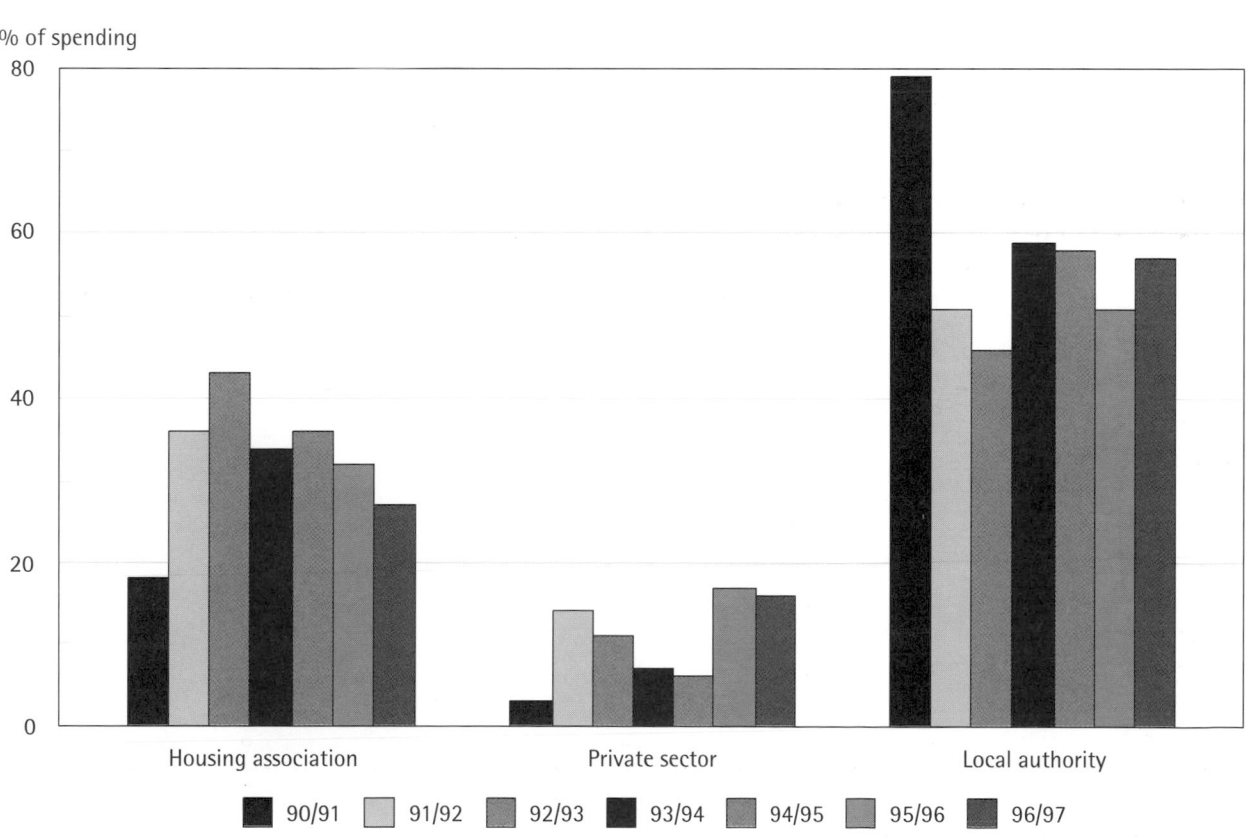

% of spending

90/91 ■ 91/92 ■ 92/93 ■ 93/94 ■ 94/95 ■ 95/96 ■ 96/97

The breakdown of expenditure between programmes also changed over this period, with the proportion accounted for by grants steadily increasing over the period to reach 29% of the total by 1993/94 (Table A7.17). Since 1991, new build by housing associations and the private sector has remained the largest component of renewal area investment, accounting for 38% of the total in 1993/94. In the same year, demolitions accounted for 13% of spending, followed by group repair (10%) If demolition costs are added to new build, over 50% of renewal area expenditure was on new development, indicating the extent to which activities in these areas go beyond housing renovation.

The proportion of renovation, HMO and common parts grants provided in renewal areas was, as might be expected, small, increasing from 1% in 1990/91 but reaching only 6% in 1993/94. Just over 2,000 dwellings were included in completed group repair schemes in 21 authorities. About 1,400 minor works grants and 400 DFG have been provided in renewal areas.

Group repair

Table 7.12 shows progress with group repair schemes in England since 1990. Group repair schemes are now under the 1996 Housing Grants, Construction and Regeneration Act. After a slow start, the number of dwellings in schemes started increased to over 2,700 in 1998. Completions have followed this trend, reaching over 2,400 in 1998. In recent years the level of overall progress with group repair has improved with almost 11,500 dwelling completions under group repair since 1991. The number of started schemes in 1998, and the number of dwellings involved is a good positive indication for group repair schemes.

Most group repair takes place in declared renewal areas. Some 50% of completions up to March 1999 were in the North West region, followed by Yorkshire and Humberside (21%). There has been almost no completed group repair work in the North East region, and none in London or the South East.

Table 7.12: Group repair schemes and dwellings in schemes, England (1991–98)

| Period | Starts | | Completions | |
	Schemes	Dwellings	Schemes	Dwellings
1991	47	721	11	170
1992	42	735	51	798
1993	127	1,526	57	706
1994	113	1,572	132	1,667
1995	141	2,091	132	1,904
1996	168	2,275	136	1,779
1997	114	1,583	125	1,913
1998	184	2,783	154	2,406
Total		13,286		11,343

Note: Group repair schemes after 1997 under the 1996 Housing Construction, Grants and Regeneration Act.

Source: DoE Building Stock Research Division, unpublished paper

Area renewal in Scotland

The mechanism for area-based renewal in Scotland has remained the Housing Action Area (HAA) since 1974. A recent study by Robertson and Bailey (1996) provides some details of activity over the 1978-92 period. Unlike the position in England and Wales before 1990, there were three basic types of HAA: HAA for demolition, HAA for improvement, and areas with a combination of the two. By the end of 1996, approximately 1,700 HAAs had been declared, of which 257 were HAAs for demolition, with the majority of the remainder being HAAs for improvement (Table 7.13).

Declarations rose steadily from about 50 in 1981 to a peak of around 125 in 1987. New declarations remained at close to 100 per annum until 1991 after which there was a steep decline in activity. HAAs in Scotland typically contain far fewer dwellings than those in England and Wales. The average HAA over the 1978-92 period contained just 41 dwellings, and only 22% of HAAs for improvement contained over 200 dwellings. The size of HAA being declared has also grown smaller over time.

Table 7.13: Housing Action Area declarations and completions, Scotland (1978–97)

	Completed		Outstanding		All		
At cnd 1991/92	No	Dwellings	No	Dwellings	No	Dwellings	Average no dwellings
HAA for demolition	238	7,887	19	558	257	8,445	33
HAA for improvement	923	37,850	419	16,353	1,342	54,203	40
HAA for both	46	4,667	9	699	55	5,366	98
Total at end 1991/92	1,207	50,404	447	17,610	1,654	68,014	41
At end 1996/97	1,357	na	336	na	1,693	na	na

Sources: Robertson and Bailey (1996); Scottish Housing Bulletin (various)

Figure 7.14 shows the contribution to improvement made by various sources in completed Scottish HAAs for improvement. Housing associations have been the dominant force for improvement, but their contribution was at its greatest in the early 1980s (Table A7.18). Since 1992-97, grant take-up by individual owner-occupiers dominated the profile of activity, as in England and Wales, but in recent years this ratio has balanced out between housing associations and owner-occupiers both accounting for about one third of the grant up take in HAA s. In general, area-based housing renewal in Scotland has been more significant as a proportion of all grant activity than area-based renewal in England and Wales, but has still accounted for a relatively small proportion of all renovation activity.

Figure 7.14: Improvements in Scottish HAAs by source (1979–97)

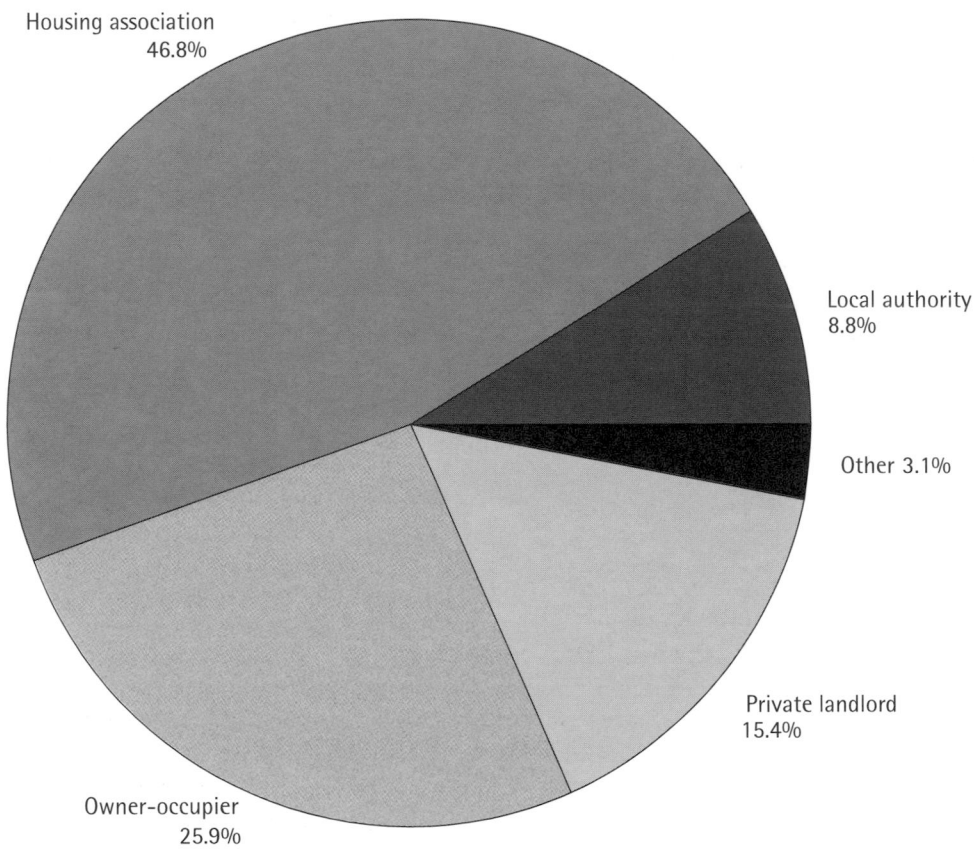

Improving the local authority stock

Chapter 4 showed that the overall condition of the housing stock owned by local authorities in England, Wales and Northern Ireland was proportionately better than the privately-owned stock. Nevertheless, substantial house condition problems were found to be present in the public sector. The 1996 EHCS showed that 227,000 local authority dwellings (6.8% of the total) were unfit for human habitation – a figure only marginally below that for the dwelling stock as a whole. Similarly, in Wales 8.2% of the local authority stock (20,000 dwellings) was unfit in 1998, although this figure is for social housing rather than just local authority housing. In Scotland, the proportion of this sector dwellings falling BTS was 0.5%, with only housing association properties performing better. However, the private rented sector was much higher at 4.1%.

The majority of poor condition local authority dwellings were constructed after 1945. In addition to the need for improvements to amenities and repairs in the traditionally-built housing stock, there are substantial problems of repair in the non-traditional stock. An estimated 500,000 low rise dwellings of non-traditional construction using prefabricated reinforced concrete (PRCs) were built in Britain between 1945 and 1965, together with approximately 1 million dwellings built using industrialised or system building methods (Diacon, 1991). Many of the latter took the form of medium- or high-rise blocks of flats. Problems with non-traditional construction are particularly severe in Scotland.

Renovations to local authority stock

Figures 7.15-7.16 show the level of renovations to local authority stock during the period 1969-96 (see also Table A7.19). England shows a minor peak in the 1972-74 period (when much investment was financed through the improvement grant system), and a substantial build-up of expenditure during the 1980s. This reached a maximum in the late 1980s when many local authorities made use of accumulated capital receipts to improve the condition of their stock. The number of local authority dwellings renovated overtook the number of private sector dwellings renovated in 1978, and although the position was reversed for a short period during the grant boom of 1982-84, by 1990 local authority

renovation was running at almost three times the level of private sector renovation. After falling back from the 1990 peak of 230,000 renovations to about 175,000 in 1992, activity has continued to increase to an all-time high of almost 330,000 dwellings in 1996. The growth in local authority stock renovation has not, however, been at the expense of private sector renovation, but as a result of a shift in resources from new construction by local authorities.

In Scotland, there were similar peaks in the early 1970s and late 1980s. Except during the 1982-84 period, the level of local authority renovation has consistently exceeded the number of private sector grants, with about 78,000 dwellings renovated in 1990 compared with 23,000 private sector grants. As in England, the level of activity has risen in the 1990s to a new all-time peak of almost 100,000 dwellings.

In Northern Ireland, the level of public sector renovation also generally exceeded the provision of grants in the limited period for which comparative data is available, but in contrast to England and Scotland, figures declined from over 50,000 dwellings in 1984 to less than 10,000 dwellings in 1990. The level then fell further to under 7,000, before rising to around 9,500 in 1994, but this reduced by 50% in the following year and then to 4,000 in 1996. This is a historically low figure for Northern Ireland.

In contrast to the remainder of the UK, the level of local authority renovation in Wales has generally been much lower than the level of grant provision to the private sector. In 1984 only 2,300 public sector dwellings were renovated while some 30,000 grants were provided to private owners. However, since 1988, the level of public sector renovation has increased sharply, rising from around 10,000 dwellings per annum to over 20,000 in 1993 and 1994, while the number of private dwellings improved with a grant under the new system has fallen in comparison with activity under the old system. 1996 saw a dramatic decrease in the number of renovations to local authority stock to under 5,000.

Figure 7.15: Renovations to local authority stock, England (1969–96)

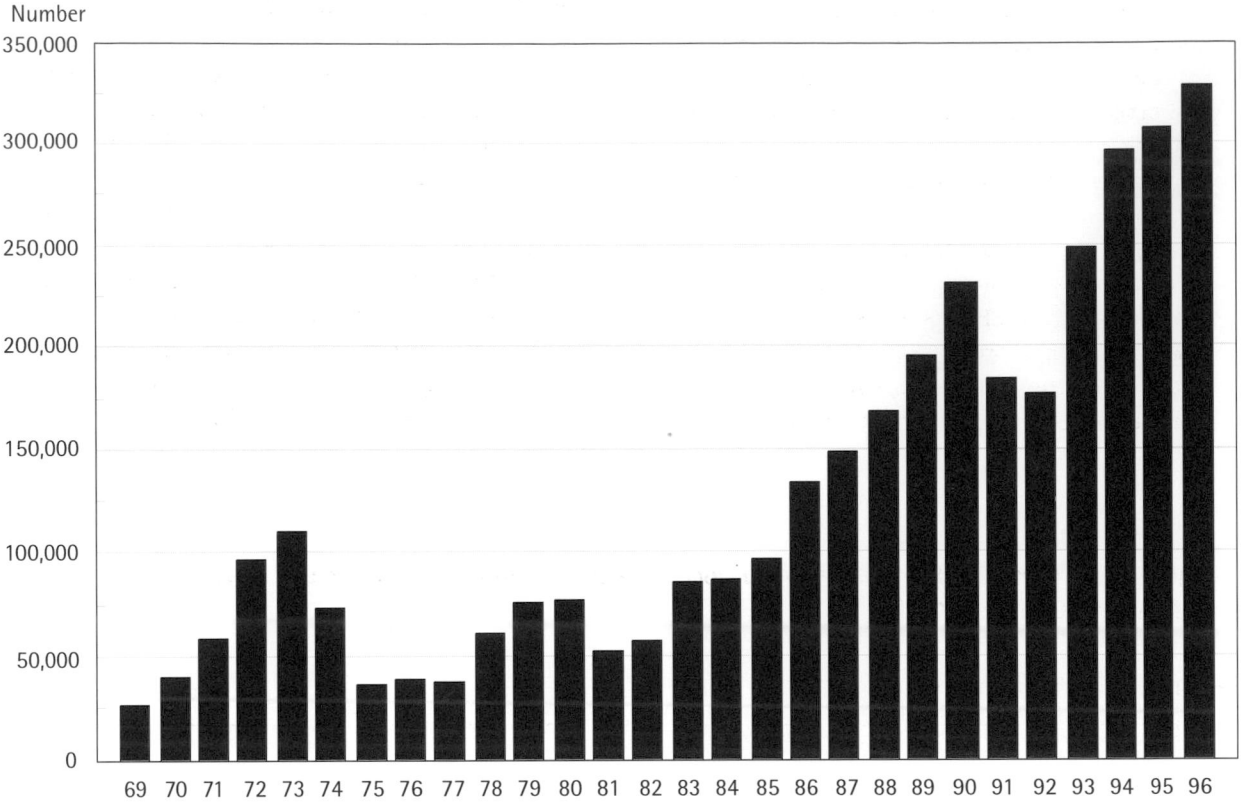

Figure 7.16: Renovations to local authority stock, Wales, Scotland and Northern Ireland (1969–96)

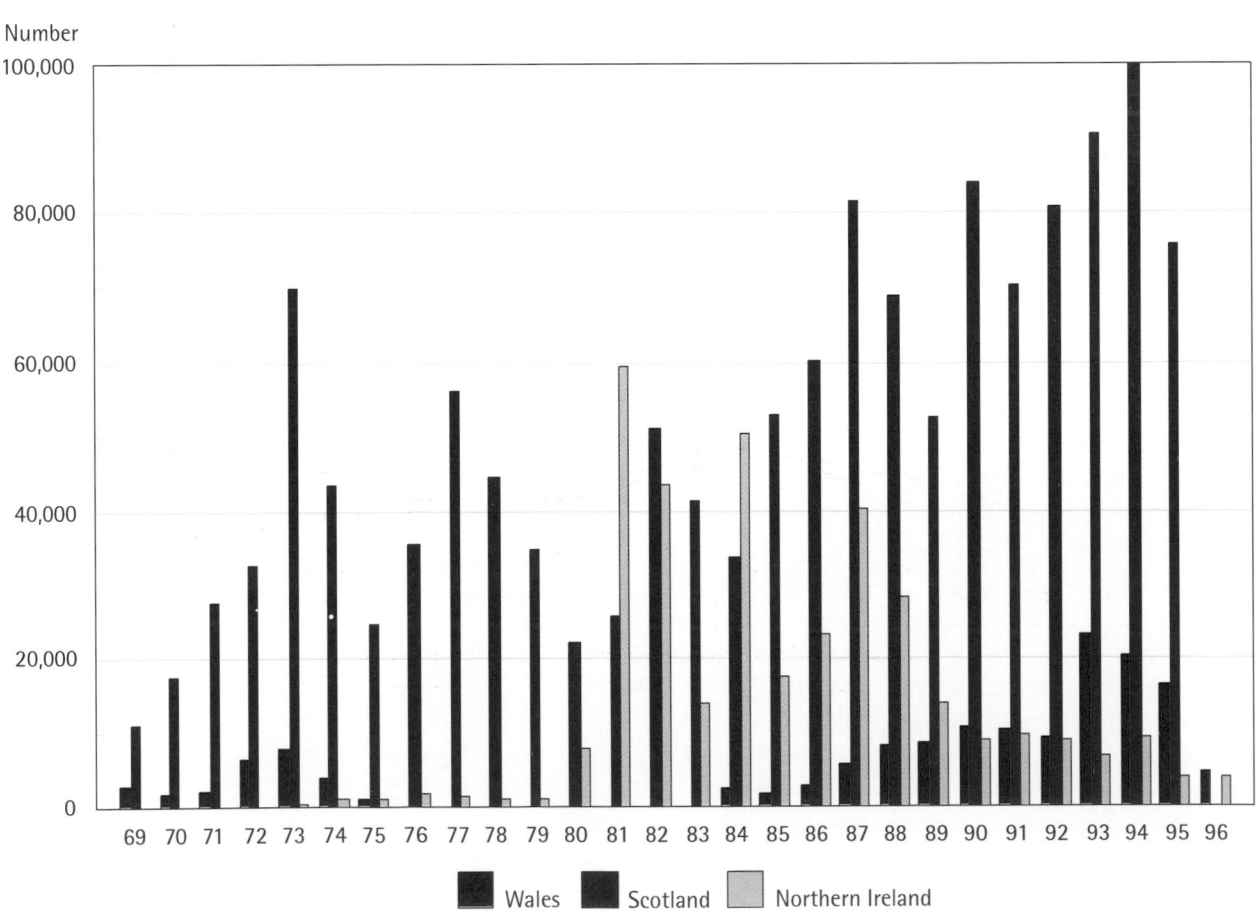

■ Wales   ■ Scotland   □ Northern Ireland

Average value of local authority renovation work

Figure 7.17 shows the average value of local authority renovations in comparison with those carried out in the private sector with the assistance of a grant and those undertaken by housing associations, all at constant 1993/94 prices (see also Table A7.20). Data limitations make it possible to only produce this information for England. In addition, experience with the collection of data on local authority stock renovation in the EHCS suggests that local authority records on dwelling stock renovation often record the number of dwellings in a renovation scheme and the total cost rather than the number of dwellings where work was carried out. This would lead the true average cost of work to be understated. During the 1970s the average value of local authority renovations substantially exceeded grants to the private sector, although this difference was reduced when owners' contributions were also taken into account. During the 1980s average private grant levels overtook local authority renovation costs, although both declined steadily in real value at much the same rate. In the 1990s, however, the gap has widened rapidly as private sector grant values increased in real terms under the new renovation grant system. Housing association renovations are discussed below.

Figure 7.17: Average value per dwelling of local authority, housing association and private sector renovations, England (1979–96)

Average value in 1993/94 prices (£)

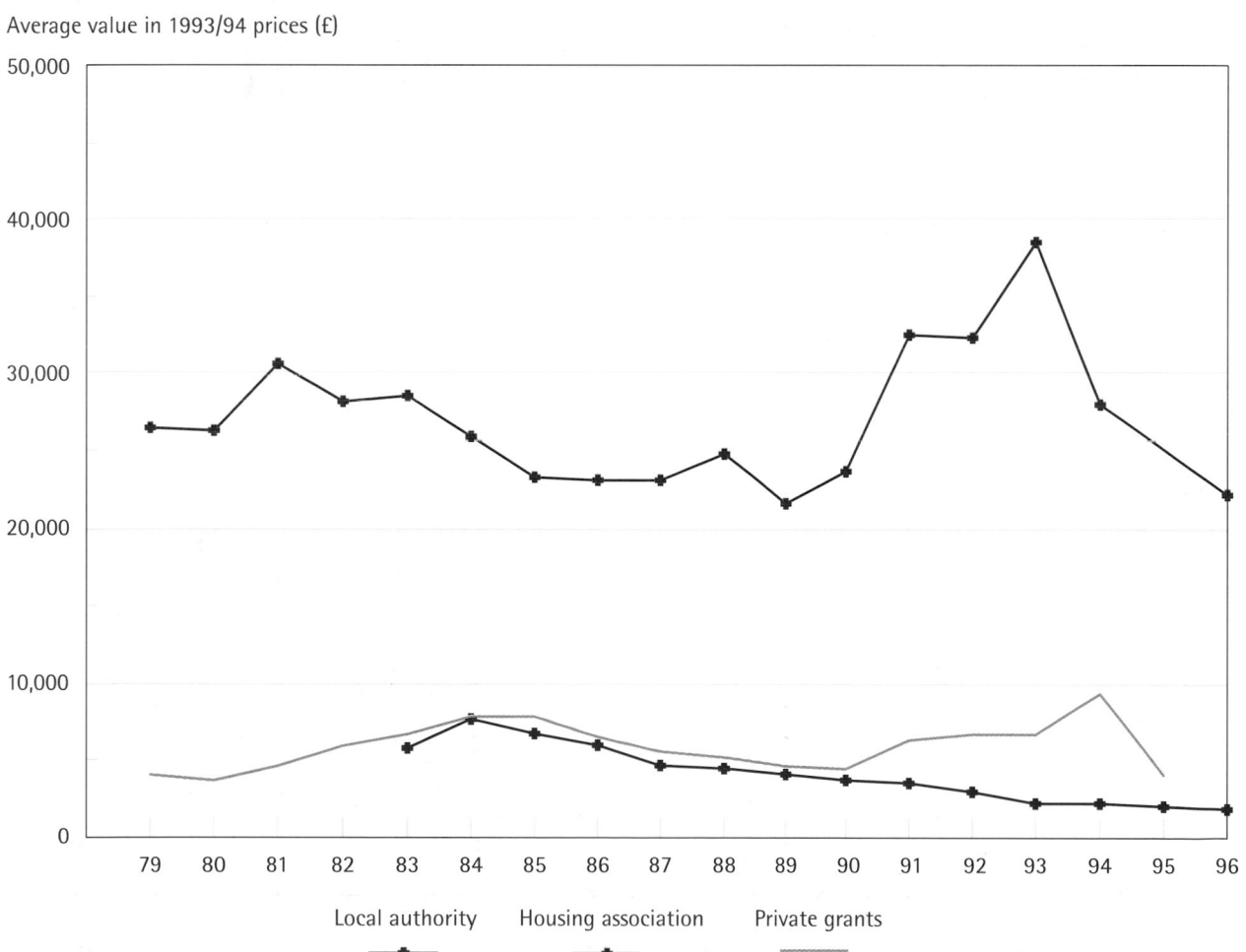

Local authority   Housing association   Private grants

The pattern of local authority renovation

Map 7.11 shows the number of renovations carried out by local authorities to their own stock between 1978-94 per 1,000 public sector dwellings, and Table 7.14 shows the authorities with the highest rate of renovation per 1,000 dwellings. Although the data should be treated with caution because of the variations in what constitutes a 'renovation', the map suggests that activity levels have generally been highest in the South East and South West of England and in parts of the Midlands. It is notable that the majority of metropolitan districts with large public sector stocks have not been able to achieve as much renovation relative to the size of their stock as smaller districts, probably because subsidy systems have not compensated them fully for higher new building costs.

Estates Action

The Estates Action initiative was developed in 1985 as a way of renovating run down estates. Local authorities were able to bid for centrally allocated resources to improve estates which had higher than average levels of vacancies, arrears, tenant turnover, vandalism or other indicators of social and economic problems. The initiative aimed to improve the condition of the housing stock, to set up estate-based management in which tenants have greater input, and to develop new forms of management such as tenants' cooperatives and trusts. It also aimed to increase levels of private sector investment and to encourage diversification of tenure. Resources for this initiative increased steadily from the launch of the scheme to reach over £373 million in 1994/95, or about 12% of total local authority gross capital expenditure in England. Nearly 500,000 dwellings were improved under the Estates Action Programme between 1987 and 1995. From April 1994 the Estates Action Programme was incorporated into the Single Regeneration Budget.

Table 7.14: Authorities in England and Wales with the highest rate of renovation to their own stock per 1,000 council dwellings (1978-96)

Local authority	LA renovations 1978-96	
	No	Per 1,000
Solihull	59,734	4,586
Elmbridge	18,612	3,937
Wolverhampton	20,411	3,782
Woking	12,792	3,166
Stafford	9,205	2,715
Kingston upon Thames	13,545	2,492
Enfield	36,558	2,491
Bristol	8,4991	2,479
North East Lincolnshire	29,149	2,461
Rother	7,313	2,330
South Kesteven	7,896	2,282
North Kesteven	9,847	2,223
Shepway	8,455	2,100
Cherwell	10,043	2,084
Mid Bedfordshire	7,198	2,068
North Somerset	14,881	2,061
Oadby and Wigston	3,029	2,023
Bournemouth	11,324	1,990
St Albans	12,323	1,980
Ribble Valley	2,855	1,980
Walsall	13,177	1,963
Charnwood	13,443	1,934
Welwyn Hatfield	21,128	1,917
Sunderland	76,788	1,892
Portsmouth	21,223	1,808
Thanet	6,693	1,786
Stratford on Avon	10,623	1,761
Wandsworth	35,698	1,745
Merton	15,044	1,708
Bolsover	11,207	1,707

Source: Local housing statistics (various years)

Map 7.11: Renovations to local authority stock per 1,000 publicly owned dwellings, England and Wales (1978–96)

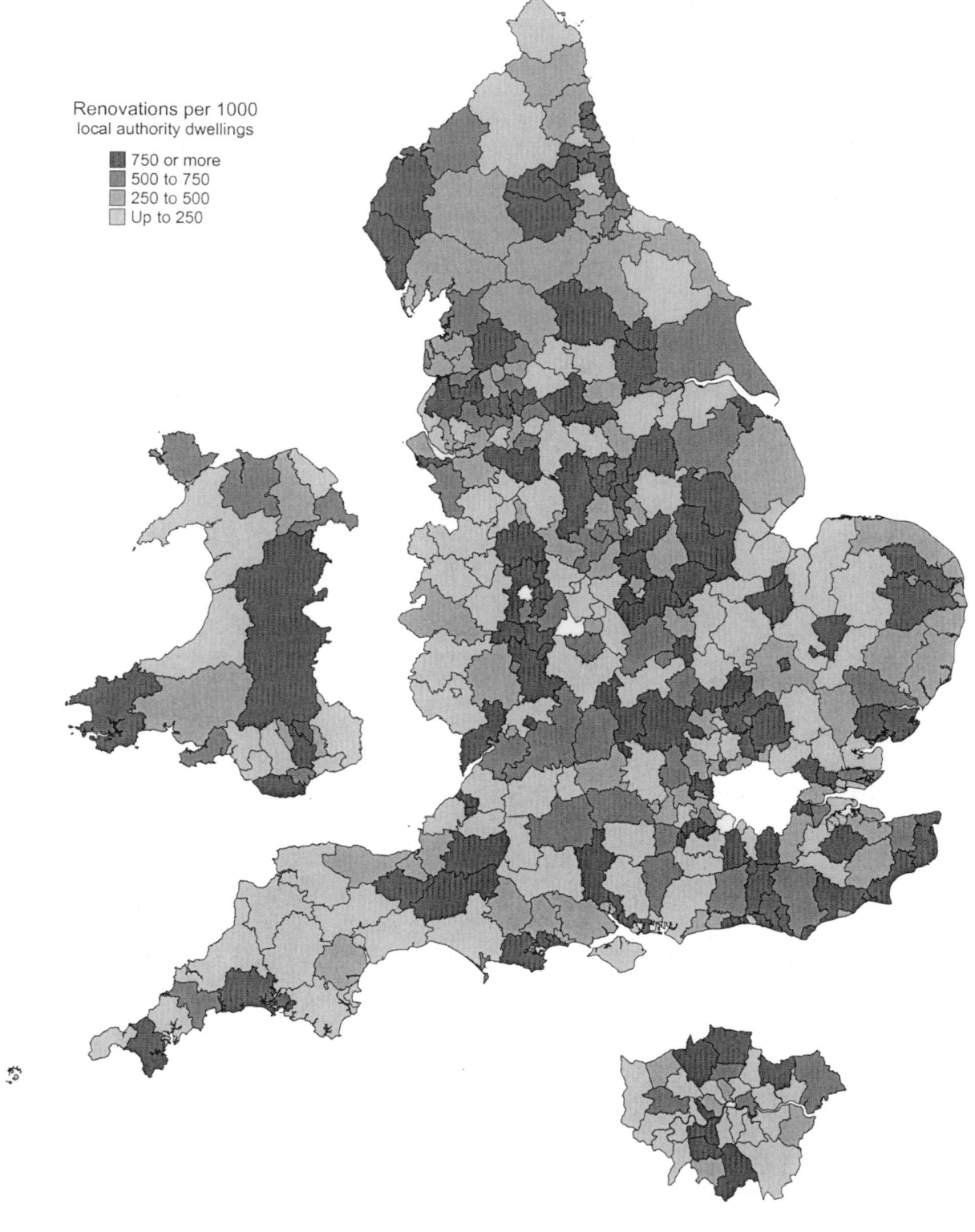

Renovations per 1000
local authority dwellings

- 750 or more
- 500 to 750
- 250 to 500
- Up to 250

The role of housing associations

Figures 7.18 and 7.19 show renovations by housing associations in England, and in Wales, Scotland and Northern Ireland, over the period 1969-97 (see also Table A7.21). In England, there was a rapid increase in the level of renovations as a result of the introduction of Housing Association Grant (HAG) in 1975. The level of renovation activity fluctuated between 10,000 and 20,000 throughout the 1980s before falling to below 6,000 per annum for most of the 1990s, although in recent years a slight increase has been witnessed. This decline has been partly attributed to the new arrangements for funding housing associations introduced by the 1988 Housing Act. Lower levels of HAG and the requirement that associations should bear any cost over-runs in full have made rehabilitation much less attractive than new-build schemes. A similar decline has occurred in the remainder of the UK.

In the past, the majority of housing association renovation work has been undertaken on dwellings purchased from private sector owners, so this activity has made an important contribution to the alleviation of poor housing conditions in the private sector. In England, the level of housing association renovation varied between 2% and 5% of the level of private sector renovation until 1975, after which it rose rapidly to a peak of 33% in 1977. It remained over 20% until 1982, but declined to between 7% and 12% towards the end of the 1980s. However, as Table 7.15 shows, housing association renovations have been heavily concentrated in areas with a high proportion of private sector housing in poor condition. The impact of this investment was therefore much greater than this proportion would suggest. In Scotland, the level of housing association involvement in rehabilitation was similar, reaching a peak equivalent to 31% of the private sector grant renovation programme in 1979, but subsequently declining to only 2-4% in the 1980s. In Northern Ireland and Wales housing association investment has been relatively insignificant in comparison to the programme of private grants.

Table 7.15: Authorities in England and Wales with the highest rate of housing association renovation per 1,000 private sector dwellings (1978-96)

Local authority	HA renovations 1978-96	
	No	Per 1,000
Liverpool	12,994	101.34
Islington	3,042	94.73
Hackney	2,986	92.98
Kensington and Chelsea	5,069	85.59
Hammersmith and Fulham	3,701	77.01
Manchester	8,076	76.66
Westminster	5,415	65.98
Tower Hamlets	1,909	65.26
Brent	4,466	59.22
Camden	3,111	58.44
Winchester	1,668	52.48
Lambeth	3,081	51.34
Haringey	3,202	48.96
Wandsworth	4,164	46.71
Nottingham	3,187	43.19
Leicester	3,253	42.52
Birmingham	10,069	37.85
St Helens	1,930	35.92
Salford	2,101	35.44
Newcastle upon Tyne	2,567	33.82
Copeland	764	33.27
Allerdale	1,066	32.57
South Tyneside	1,239	31.43
Sefton	2,995	30.66
Woking	885	28.41
City of London	78	26.03
Wirral	2,880	25.17
Southwark	1,129	24.60
Newham	1,359	24.37
Greenwich	1,244	23.91

Source: Local housing statistics (various years)

Figure 7.18: Renovations to housing association stock, England (1969-96)

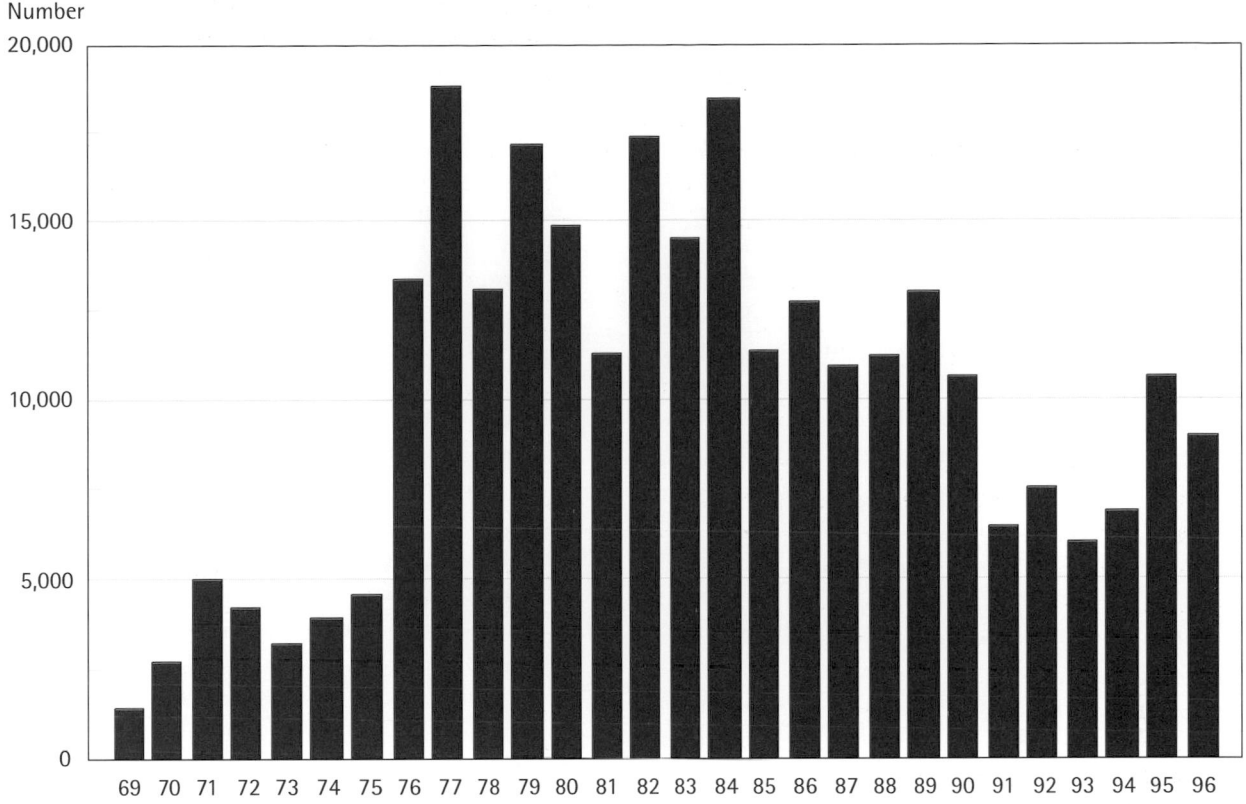

Figure 7.19: Renovations to housing association stock, Wales, Scotland and Northern Ireland (1969-97)

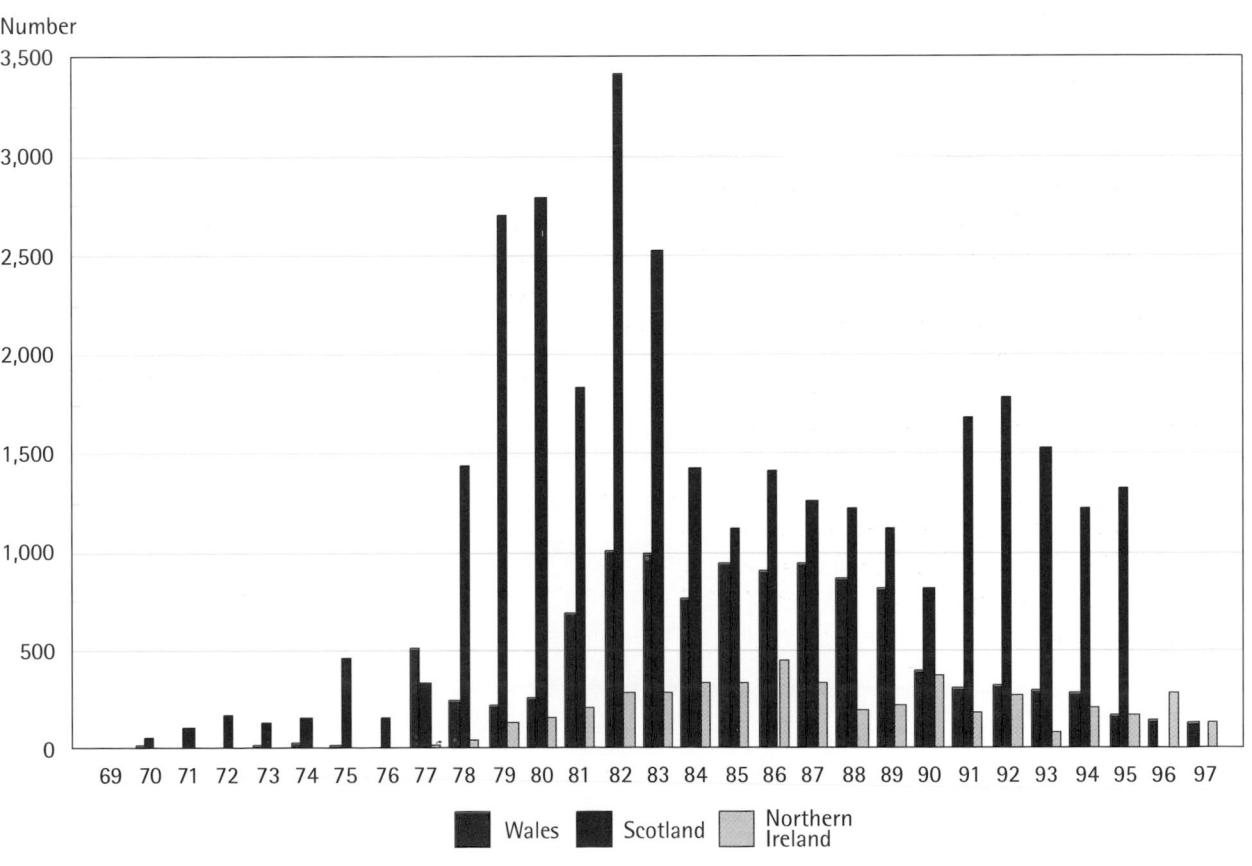

Average value of housing association renovation work

Figure 7.17 shows that the average value of housing association rehabilitation jobs in England has been much greater than the equivalent figures for local authority or private sector renovation work, although since it reached its peak in 1993 of 38,597 it has since decreased to £22,148 in 1996. This partly reflects the fact that housing associations have often purchased and improved dwellings which were in much poorer condition than those in the private sector, but, in addition, housing association work has generally achieved much higher standards than the private improvement grant programme. It should also be noted that a small proportion of grants appearing in the figures for private sector renovation were awarded to housing associations.

The pattern of housing association renovation

Map 7.12 shows the number of housing association renovation jobs per 1,000 private sector dwellings for the period 1978-96 for districts in England and Wales. Housing association investment is heavily concentrated in urban areas, even taking account of the relative size of the private sector stock. Comparing the map with the distribution of improvement grants to private owners, it is clear that housing association activity has been much more important in London than renovation by private owners, reflecting the high proportion of privately-rented older housing in the capital which housing associations have been able to acquire over the period covered by the data. Table 7.15 shows authorities where housing association renovation has been proportionately greatest. The table is heavily dominated by the London boroughs and the larger metropolitan areas or cities, indicating that the housing association renovation programme was targeted on these areas to a much greater degree than the programme of grants to private owners.

Map 7.12: Renovations to housing association stock per 1,000 privately owned dwellings, England (1978–96)

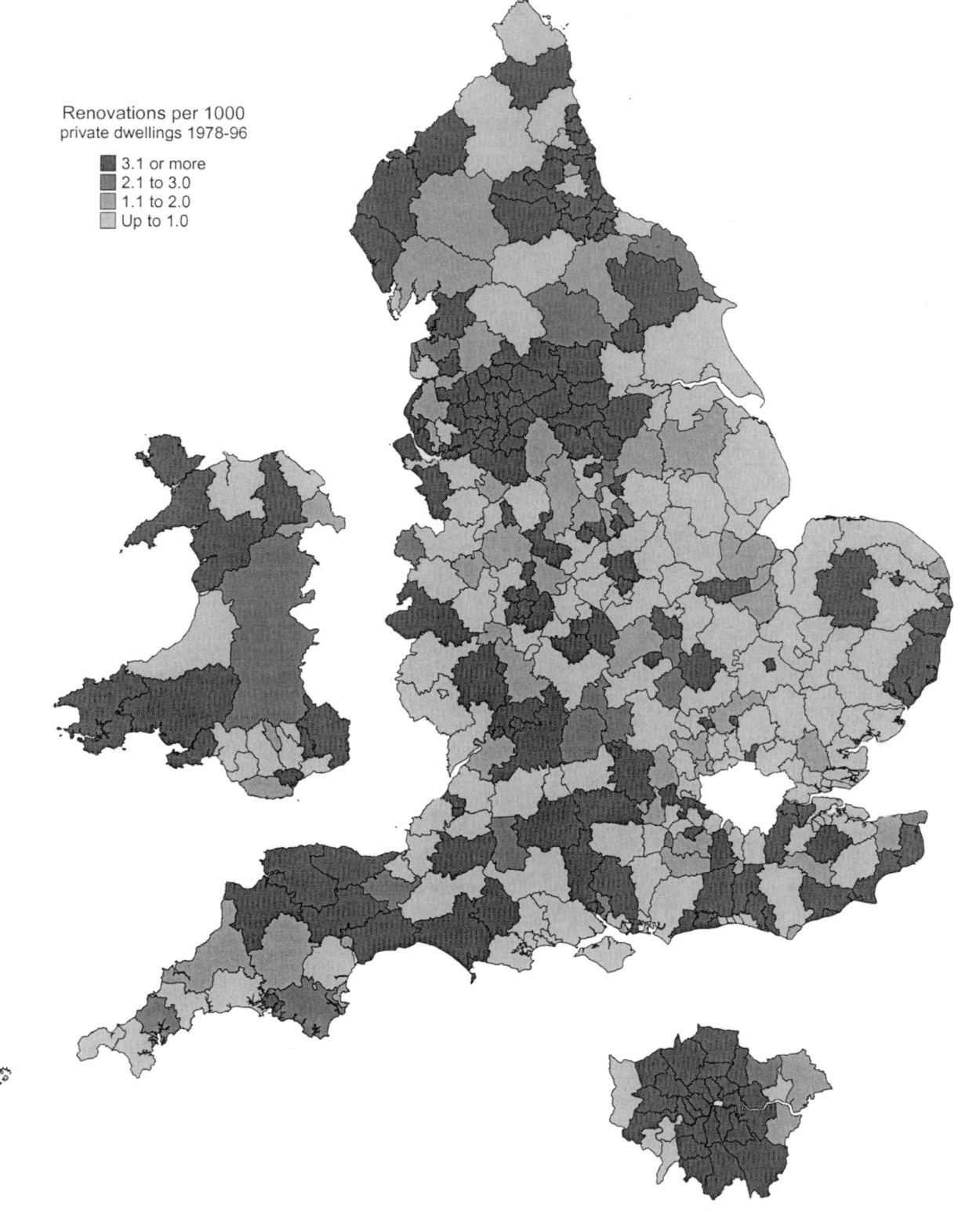

Renovations per 1000
private dwellings 1978-96

- 3.1 or more
- 2.1 to 3.0
- 1.1 to 2.0
- Up to 1.0

Dealing with adaptations

Since the mid-1970s, grants have also been available to assist private owners with the costs of adapting dwellings to meet the needs of disabled people. Until 1990, this assistance was provided through the mechanisms of improvement and intermediate grants, but a separate grant – the DFG – now provides this form of help. Figures 7.20 and 7.21 show the number of grants provided for people with disabilities in England and Wales since 1975 and the proportion of all grants which this represents (see also Tables A7.22 and A7.23). In both England and Wales, the number of grants awarded has followed a similar pattern to the level of grant provision as a whole, with a peak in the 1982-84 period in both countries, paralleling the peak in other types of grant. There was a further boost in Wales in the late 1980s. In England, total spending in grants for people with disabilities rose to around £60 million per annum at 1993/94 prices in the mid-1980s, and remained at that level before reaching a peak of almost £80 million in 1990. It then fell under the new system of DFGs to about £56 million in 1991, but subsequently continued to rise steeply in real terms to reach an all-time high of about £90 million for 1995 and 1996. However, 1997 saw another drop back to the 1991 figure. In comparison to total grant provision, the proportion of spending on grants for people with disabilities also rose, slowly in the 1970s and then more sharply in the 1980s, to reach a peak of 22% of all spending on private sector grants in 1990. The proportion fell again in the early 1990s under the new grant system, but rose again to reach 22% in 1997. Although actual spending has declined

in recent years, DFGs represent an increasing proportion of all grant aid. In Wales, spending at 1993/94 prices rose from £6 million in the early 1980s to around £9 million in 1990. The increase resumed quickly after a slight drop under the new grant system in 1991, and reached £12 million in 1993, falling slightly in 1994, followed by another increase to £14 million in 1996. Spending on grants for disabled people as a percentage of all grant spending has been consistently lower in Wales than in England, peaking at around 10% in 1989, before falling to 6% in 1992 and rising again to 11% in 1997, which is still half the proportion that is allocated to DFGs in England.

MWA grants can be used to meet the costs of adaptations and this is often thought to be a significant source of additional funding for minor adaptations. However, a special analysis of HIA records revealed that only 10% of the MWA grants dealt with by agencies in 1994/95 were for adaptation work. If this proportion were applied across all MWA grants in England and Wales, this would add a further £2.5 million to total spending on adaptations for people with disabilities.

Total expenditure on adaptations for people with disabilities is not centrally recorded. In 1994, local authorities in England and Wales provided grants to the value of £96 million at cash prices, including MWA. Data for Scotland is not available but assuming expenditure amounted to 8% of all grant provision, this would add a further £7 million, bringing the total to £103 million. Assuming an average grant rate of 90% would bring an additional £9 million through contributions from private owners.

Figure 7.20: Grants for people with disabilities, England (1979–97)

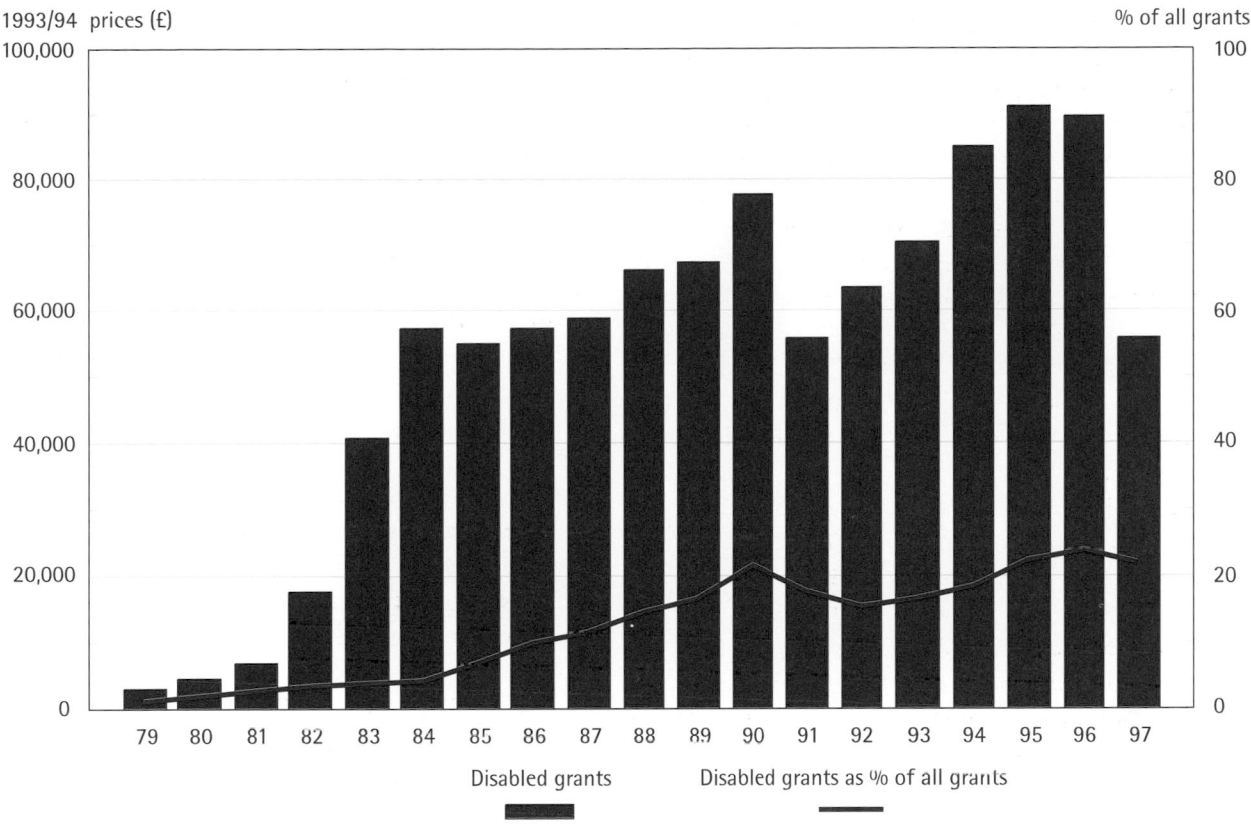

Figure 7.21: Grants for people with disabilities, Wales (1979–97)

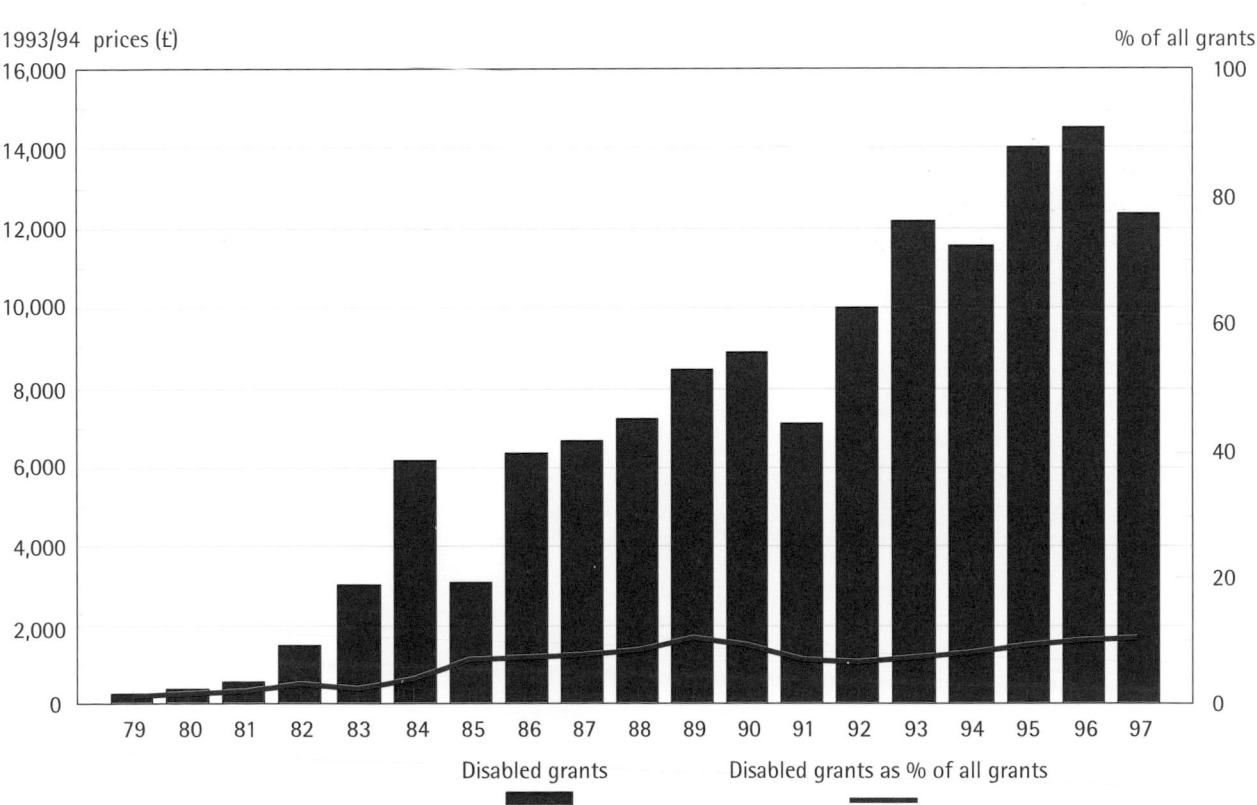

Expenditure on equipment and adaptations by social services departments in Britain is estimated at £75 million (Laing and Buisson Ltd, 1993). Spending on adaptations undertaken by local authorities from their housing revenue accounts (HRA) is not separately recorded, and the production of a reliable estimate is highly problematic. Most previous work has been based on small samples. The sums involved are potentially much greater than those spent through social services sources or through the renovation grant system. In most authorities, minor adaptations for council tenants are funded from HRA, and in perhaps two thirds of authorities major adaptations are also funded from this source or from capital. In total, local authorities in Britain spent around £2.75 billion on the repair and maintenance of council dwellings in 1994/95, together with £2.4 billion in capital expenditure. Assuming that only 2% of the total from each source is spent on adaptations would produce expenditure of around £100 million. Housing associations also spend revenue resources on adaptations and The Housing Corporation provides an annual capital sum from its ADP budget. No estimate is available of the former but the latter provided about £11 million in 1994/95, or about £12 million if additional sums are assumed for housing associations in Scotland (Tai

Cymru in Wales does not provide capital funds for housing association adaptations). Adding in revenue spending at about the same level as that assumed for local authorities (2%) would produce a further £11 million in housing association spending, bringing the total to £23 million. Finally, individuals also invest their own resources in equipment and adaptations. Published data from the annual Family Expenditure Survey does not permit the identification of spending on adaptations and equipment so no reliable estimate of this spending is possible.

Therefore, a total of more than £300 million in public resources was spent on equipment and adaptations in 1994/95. Adding an estimated £100 million in local authority spending on council dwellings produces a total of just of £300 million. Known private spending of £9 million linked to grant aid, and additional private spending, must also be added to this sum. Table 7.16 summarises these estimates.

The pattern of grant provision for disabled people

Map 7.5 shows the local pattern of provision of DFGs in England and Wales, Table 7.9 shows the most active authorities, and Table 7.10 shows the distribution of DFGs by tenure.

Table 7.16: An estimate of spending on equipment and adaptations, Britain (1994/95)

Source	Estimated spending (£m)
DFG, MWA and other local authority grants to private owners and tenants	97
Spending by social services authorities on equipment and adaptations	75
Spending by health authorities on equipment and adaptations	5
Capital and revenue spending by local authorities on adaptations to their own stock	104
Capital and revenue spending by housing associations on adaptations to their own stock	23
Total public/social rented sector spending	304
Private contributions to local authority grants	9
Other private spending	not known

Sources: Authors' estimates, based on data from Housing and Construction Statistics (various years); Wilcox (1995); Laing and Buisson Ltd (1993)

Home improvement agencies

HIAs provide practical help to older, disabled and low-income households with repair, improvement and adaptation work to their homes. They help clients to diagnose house condition problems, obtain estimates from competent builders, raise finance to meet the costs of work, and ensure that work is carried out properly. The government, local authorities, housing associations and a number of charities provide funding to meet the running costs of these organisations. Anchor Housing Trust, with 56 agencies, is the largest provider. In 1999, 210 HIAs were in operation in England, together with 21 in Wales, and 33 in Scotland. In Northern Ireland, the Housing Executive takes a leading role in funding three projects. Overall less than two thirds of local authority districts have such projects. There are concentrations in urban areas of the North East, North West, Midlands, South Wales, and in south coast resorts in Kent, Sussex and Hampshire. The South West, East Anglia, Lincolnshire, Yorkshire and rural areas of northern England have relatively few projects.

Table 7.17 provides a profile of the clients helped by government-funded HIAs in England and Wales (1996/97) and Scotland (1997/98) and the work which these clients carried out. A high proportion of the clients helped are vulnerable because of age, illness, disability or low income. The majority of jobs carried out involve repairs to the structure or external envelope of the dwelling or the provision or renewal of basic amenities and services such as wiring or heating. An increasing proportion of jobs include adaptations for disabled people.

HIAs have played an important role in assisting local authorities to target grants under the new renovation grant system, and a high proportion of their clients use funding from this source, particularly MWA for older people. In 1996/97, HIAs in England dealt with about 7% of all renovation grants, 11% of DFGs and 44% of home repair (minor works) assistance.

Table 7.17: Output of government-funded home improvement agencies in England, Wales and Scotland (1996/97)

	England	Wales	Scotland
Clients aged 75 or over (%)	45	48	39
Clients ill or disabled (%)	67	91	77
Clients on low income (%)	75	69	78
Clients helped with advice (number of enquiries)	26,192	8,091 (4,356)	5,789
Clients helped with building work (number of jobs completed)	25,945	2,002 (3,719)	2,069
Total cost of work completed (£ million)	42.92	10.5	8.2
Jobs involving adaptations (%)	23	60	15
Jobs involving essential work (%)	86	93	100
Jobs funded by renovation grant* (%)	7	7	64
Jobs funded by DFG (%)	11	27	na
Jobs funded by HRA (%)	44	26	na

* In Scotland, improvement and repair grants. The percentage in Scotland refers to the proportion of total works costs funded by grant, not the proportion of jobs.
Note: England's figure for total cost of work completed excludes VAT.

Sources: Care and Repair England (1997); Care and Repair Wales (1997); Care and Repair Scotland (1998)

Energy efficiency

The 1995 Home Energy Conservation Act places a duty on housing authorities to publish measures likely to significantly improve energy efficiency in their area. Programmes already underway include the Home Energy Efficiency Scheme (HEES) which provides grants to those receiving benefit for energy saving measures, and a network of Energy Advice Centres supported by the Energy Saving Trust.

Figure 7.22 shows the uptake of HEES by tenure at December 1998. It shows that nearly 60% of recipients were in local authority accommodation, owner-occupiers received 21% of grants, and just 4% went to private rented dwellings, although this tenure is the least energy efficient. Figure 7.23 shows take-up of grants by dwelling type with

most grants going to terraced or semi-detached dwellings. There has been very little change in the proportion of dwelling types receiving grants since 1993. Figure 7.24 shows the take up of HEES by dwelling age (June 1997). This shows that the majority of grants were allocated to post-1965 housing (67%), whereas in 1993 they were more evenly allocated. Unfortunately HEES data does not utilise the commonly accepted dwelling age bands.

To encourage householders to undertake energy conservation measures, a three-year pilot scheme of local energy advice centres was set up by the Energy Saving Trust. These have now been reorganised and renamed Energy Efficiency Advice Centres. There are now fewer centres, each covering a wider area.

Figure 7.22: Take-up of HEES by tenure, England (1990–97)

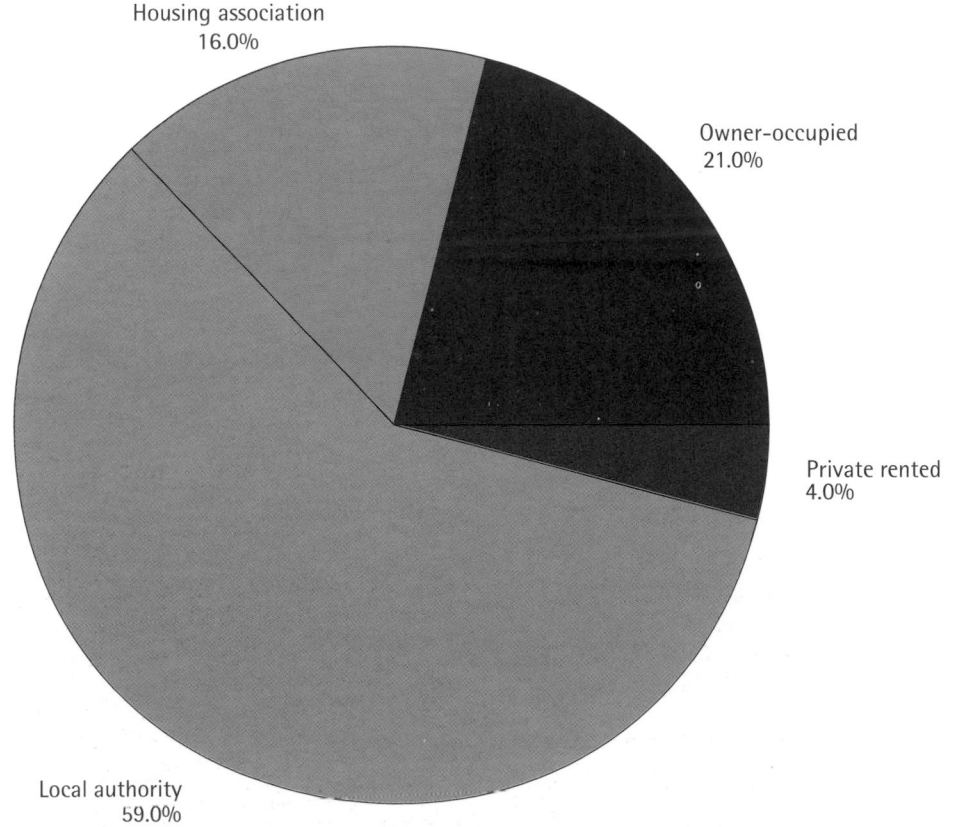

Housing association
16.0%

Owner-occupied
21.0%

Private rented
4.0%

Local authority
59.0%

Figure 7.23: Take-up of HEES by dwelling type, England (1990–97)

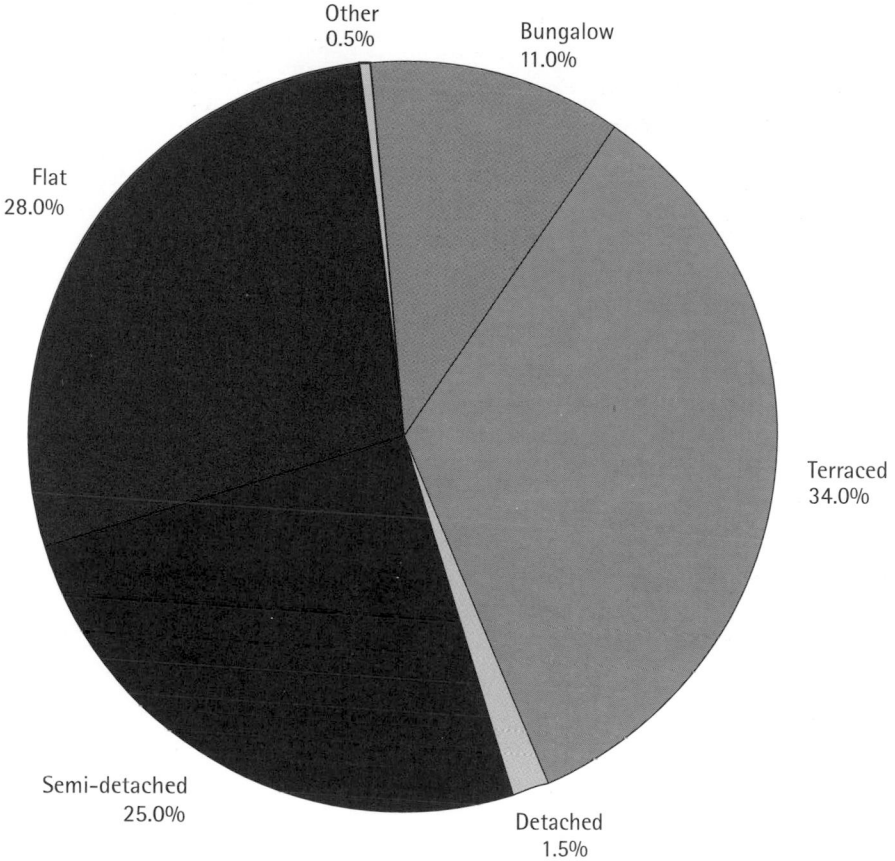

Figure 7.24: Take-up of HEES by dwelling age, England (1990–97)

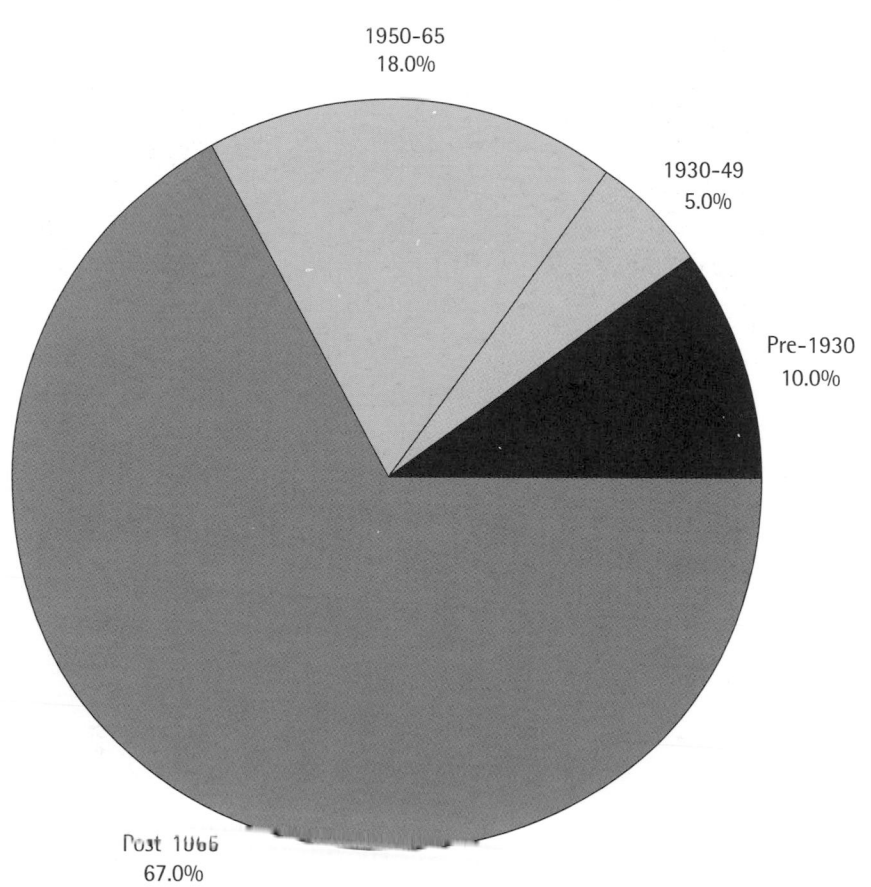

8

Public investment in housing renovation

Renovation's share of public expenditure

Renovation took an increasing share of public expenditure during the 1980s while new building declined. In England, local authority renovation increased from 20% in 1979/80 to almost 50% in 1989/90. After falling back slightly in subsequent years the programme increased again to account for 47% of capital spending in 1997/98. Expenditure on grants to private owners reached a peak of 24% in 1983/84, and remained at around 15% before falling to 8% in 1989/90. However, this has been subject to a gradual increase since then and has remained at around 15% in the last three years. (Figure 8.1; Table A8.1). During the 1990s the programme's share of spending has risen as a result of the need to meet mandatory demand for renovation grants and

through earmarking of resources through specified capital grant. The Housing Corporation programme, although in decline since 1993, still accounts for a fifth of total capital spending on housing. An increasing proportion of this is for new-build rather than renovation activity, but despite this, renovation is likely to continue to dominate local authority investment programmes.

In Wales (Figure 8.2; Table A8.2) new building fell even more dramatically than in England. Local authority renovation also increased its share of total expenditure from 20% to 40% during the 1980s, but was overtaken in importance by grants to private owners which reached over 40% of total investment in the early 1990s. Similar to the situation in England, the Tai Cymru programme has recently increased in significance.

Figure 8.1: Percentage shares of public expenditure on housing by programme, England (1979-97)

% total public capital expenditure
50
40
30
20
10
0
79/80 80/81 81/82 82/83 83/84 84/85 85/86 86/87 87/88 88/89 89/90 90/91 91/92 92/93 93/94 94/95 95/96 96/97 97/98
Year
LA new build
LA renovation
LA lending to HAs
Private sector renovation
LA mortgages
Housing Corporation

Figure 8.2: Percentage shares of public expenditure on housing by programme, Wales (1981-97)

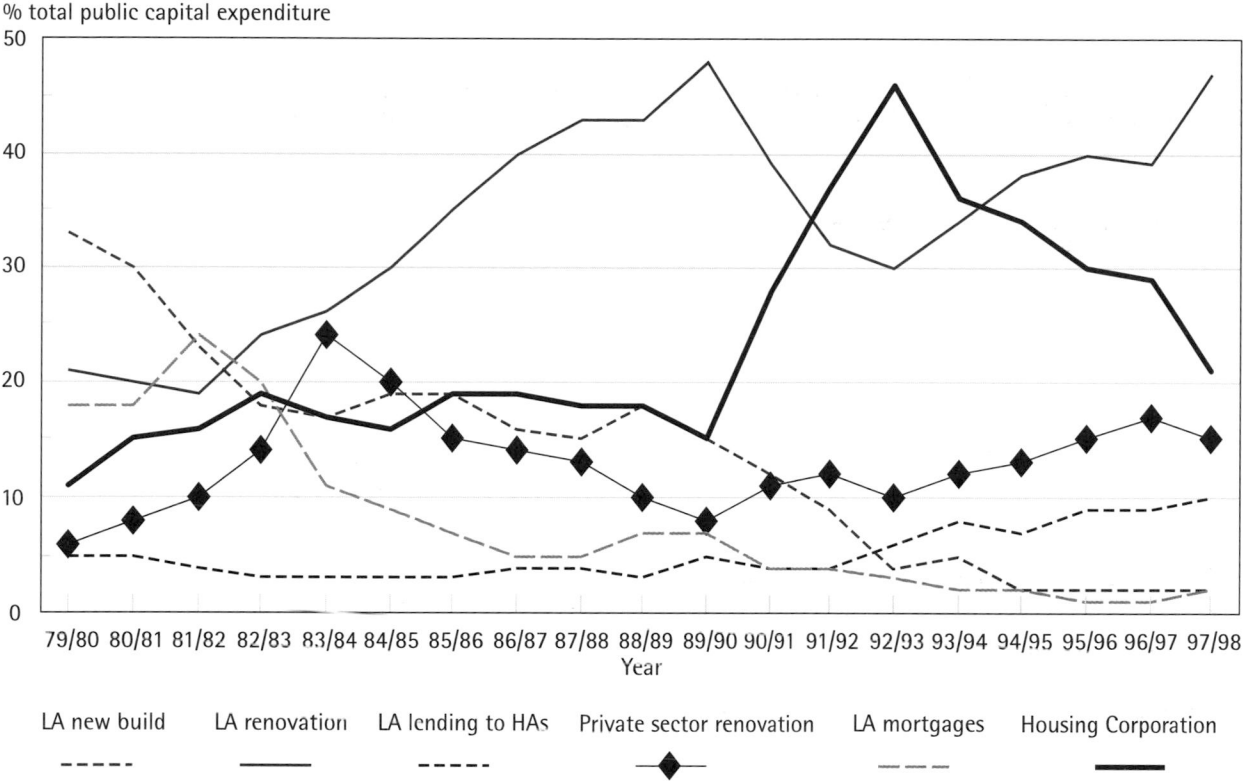

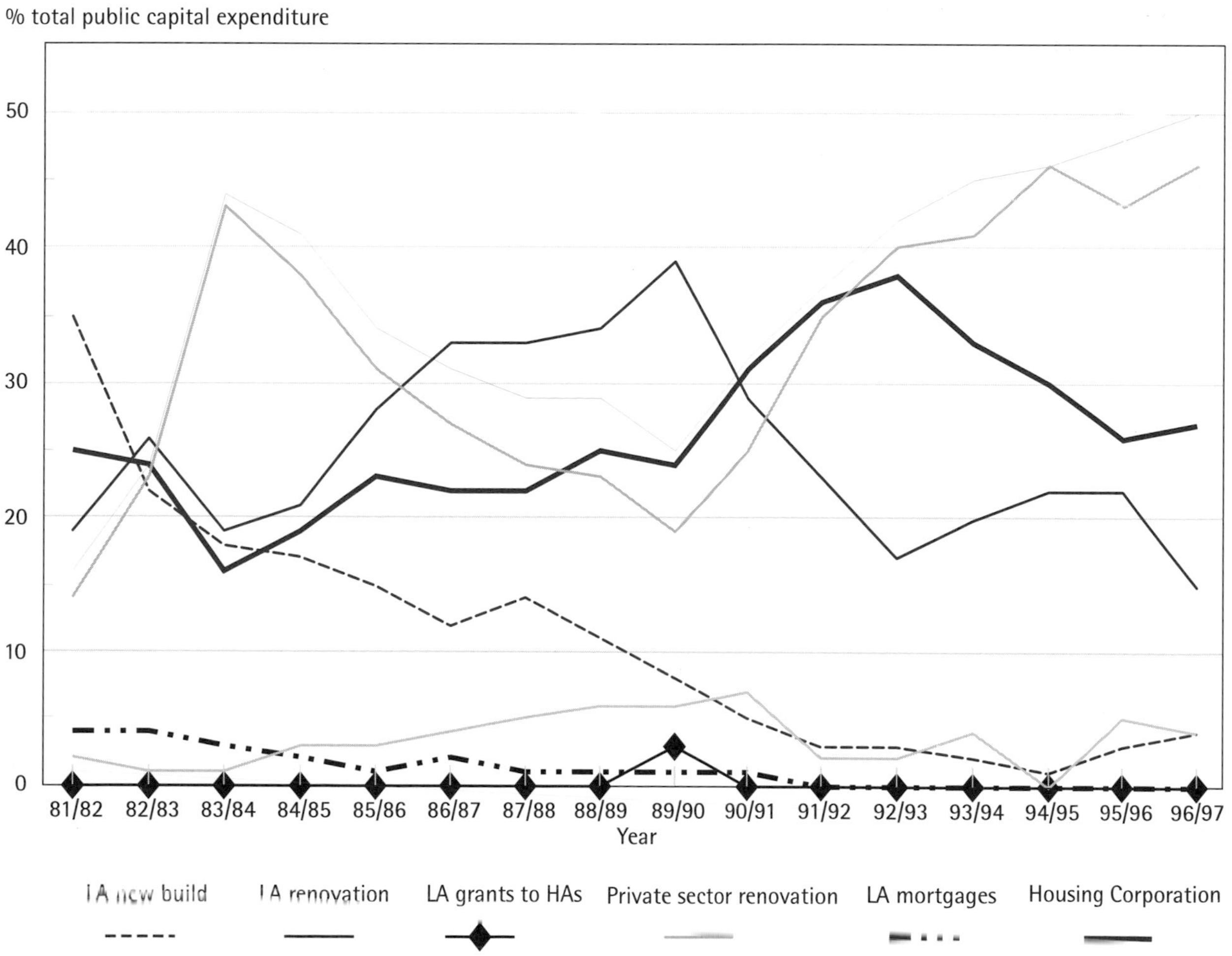

% total public capital expenditure
50
40
30
20
10
0
81/82 82/83 83/84 84/85 85/86 86/87 87/88 88/89 89/90 90/91 91/92 92/93 93/94 94/95 95/96 96/97
Year
LA new build
LA renovation
LA grants to HAs
Private sector renovation
LA mortgages
Housing Corporation

Detailed data on expenditure within the housing programme is not available for Scotland. In Northern Ireland, data is only available for the latter part of the 1980s. As in England and Wales, public sector renovation (of NIHE stock) has increased to about 40% of the programme, but expenditure on grants to private owners declined to less than 20% of the total (Figure 8.3; Table A8.3). New building by the Housing Executive has also declined to about 25% of the total programme, but this level of expenditure remains substantially higher than in England or Wales. Support for the voluntary sector has historically been low in Northern Ireland at around 20% of total expenditure.

Figure 8.3: Percentage shares of public expenditure on housing by programme, Northern Ireland (1985–97)

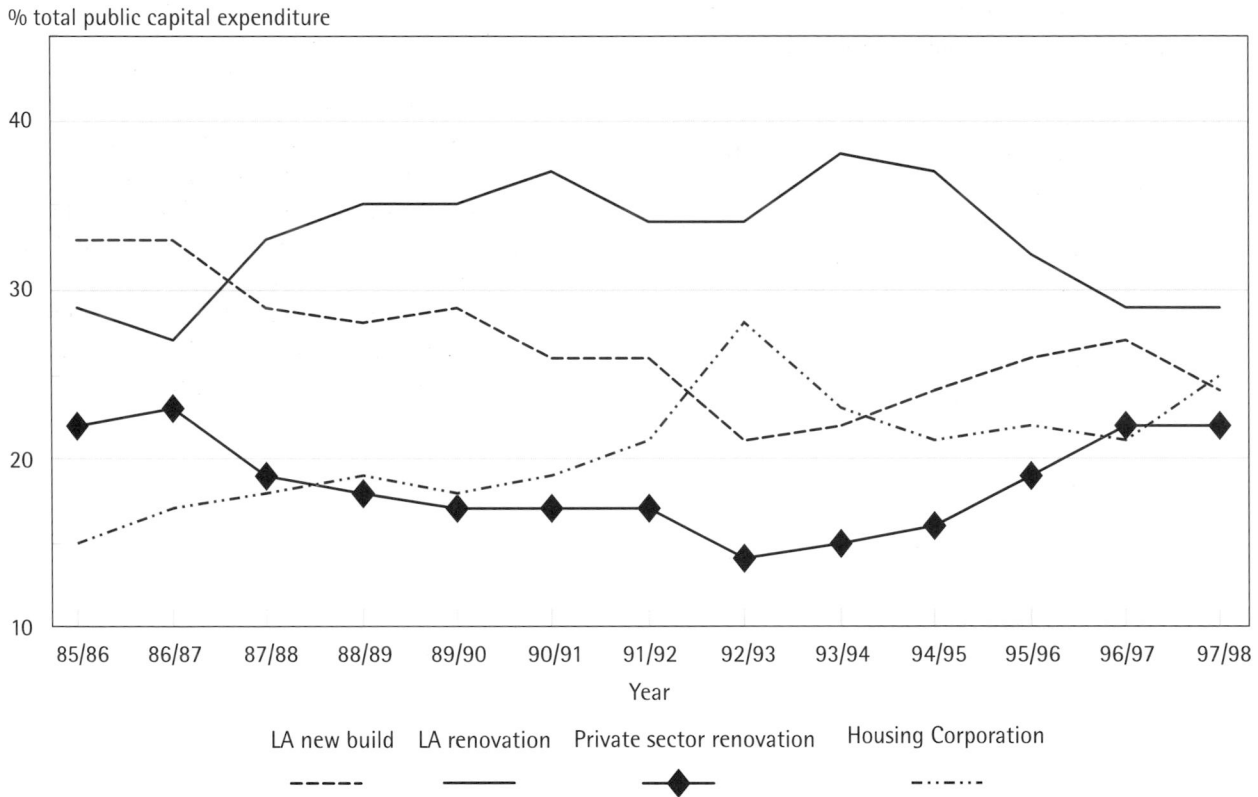

Renovation expenditure

Figures 8.4 to 8.6 show expenditure on the renovation of local authority, housing association, and private stock in England, Wales and Northern Ireland since 1979. In England, expenditure increased from £1.1 billion in 1981/82 to a peak of £3.6 billion in 1989/90, before falling back sharply to under £2 billion in the later 1990s. Expenditure on local authority renovation has taken the main share of spending throughout the 1979-98 period, accounting for over half of all renovation expenditure in most years (Figure 8.4; Table A8.4). Private sector renovation spending only approached spending on the local authority stock in the early 1980s during the repair grants boom. Investment in renovation by housing associations remained consistently below both other programmes. When expressed in constant prices it is striking how consistent total spending by housing associations and the aggregate value of grants to private owners have been over a long period. However, as Chapter 7 showed, increases in housing association unit costs and private grant levels have reduced the volume of output over

the period by a substantial amount, while reductions in unit costs since 1990 have sustained the volume of local authority renovation output (see Figures 7.9 and 7.17).

In Wales, expenditure increased from only £106 million in 1981/82 at 1993/94 prices to £291 million in 1993/94 (Figure 8.5; Table A8.5). As in England, renovation of the local authority stock increased up to 1989 and has subsequently reduced, although it remains higher than in the early 1980s. Spending on grants to private owners has increased and, in real terms, in the 1990s has exceeded levels achieved during the early 1980s boom. In contrast to England, spending on private grants is around twice that on renovation of the local authority stock. Housing association renovation investment has been relatively insignificant. In Northern Ireland, expenditure on renovation has fallen since the mid-1980s from £142 million to only £114 million in 1994/95 (Figure 8.6; Table A8.6). Within this overall decline, renovation of Housing Executive stock has increased while expenditure on grants to private owners has fallen sharply.

Figure 8.4: Public expenditure on housing renovation, England (1979-97)

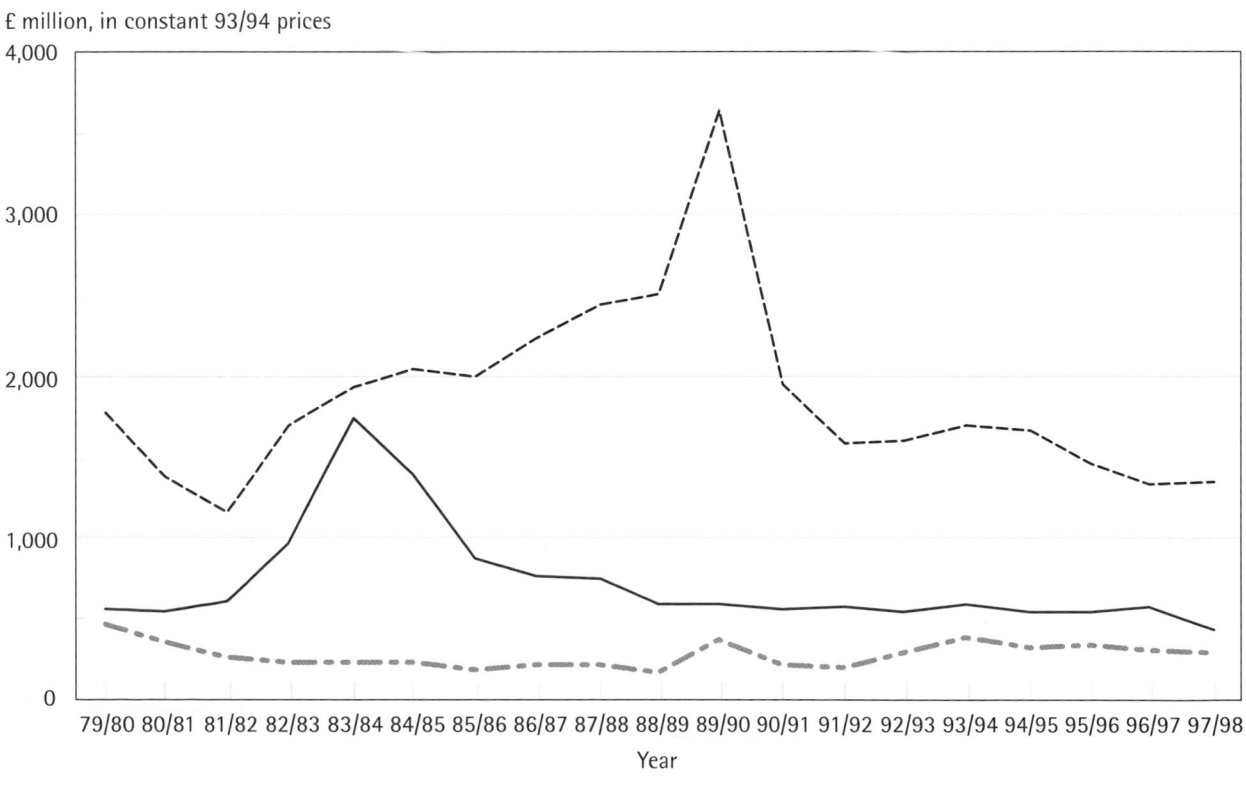

£ million, in constant 93/94 prices

LA renovation   Private sector renovation   HA renovation

Figure 8.5: Public expenditure on housing renovation, Wales (1981–97)

£ million, in constant 93/94 prices

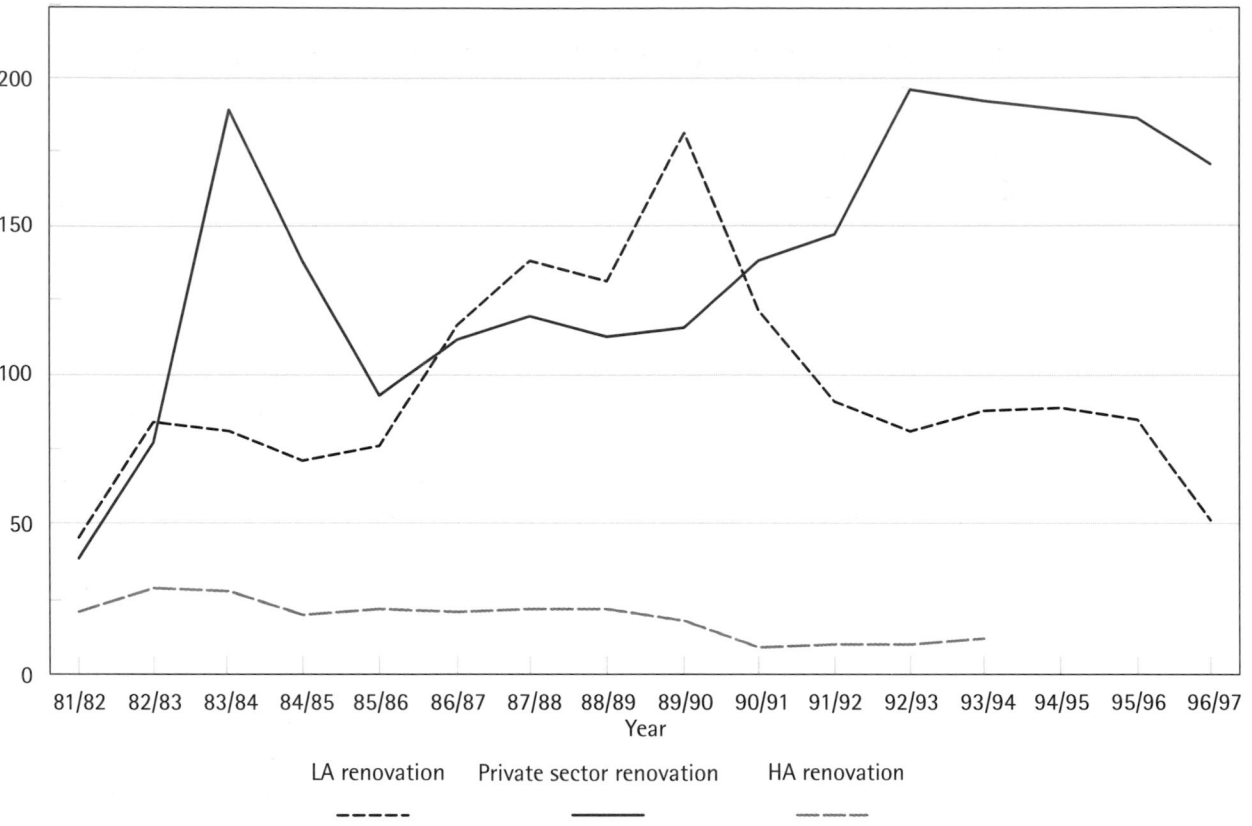

Figure 8.6: Public expenditure on housing renovation, Northern Ireland (1985–97)

£ million, in constant 93/94 prices

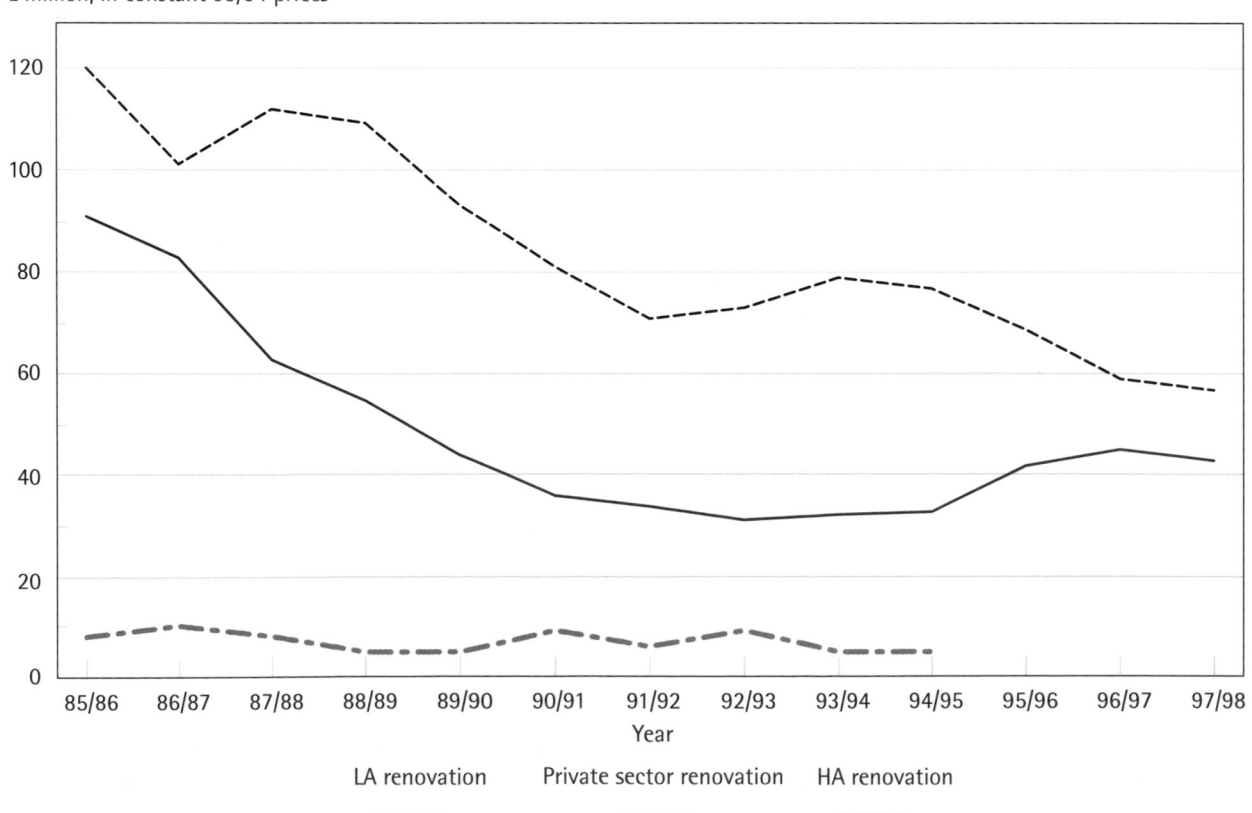

9

Private investment in housing renovation

Private expenditure

In addition to public expenditure on renovation, there is a large volume of expenditure undertaken by individual households or owners using their own resources. Relatively little is known about this investment. The annual Family Expenditure Survey (FES) (see for example CSO, 1998) records some details of expenditure on repair, maintenance and decoration but this information is incomplete as it excludes expenditure financed by borrowing. Accepting this limitation, Figure 9.1 (see also Table A9.1) shows variations in household expenditure over the period 1986-97. In cash terms this shows a steady increase over the period, from £253 per annum in 1986 to £386 in 1993. This fell in the next two years, but rose again to £391 in 1996/97. Adjusting this spending to constant 1993/94 prices reveals a fall between 1986 and 1988. This was followed by an increase in spending between 1989 and 1991 when the average across all households exceeded £400. In subsequent years the total fell back to only £336 in 1994, increasing since to £354 (1996/97). These figures represent aggregate expenditure of about £8.1 billion in 1994.

Figure 9.1: Household expenditure on repair, maintenance and decoration, UK (1986–97)

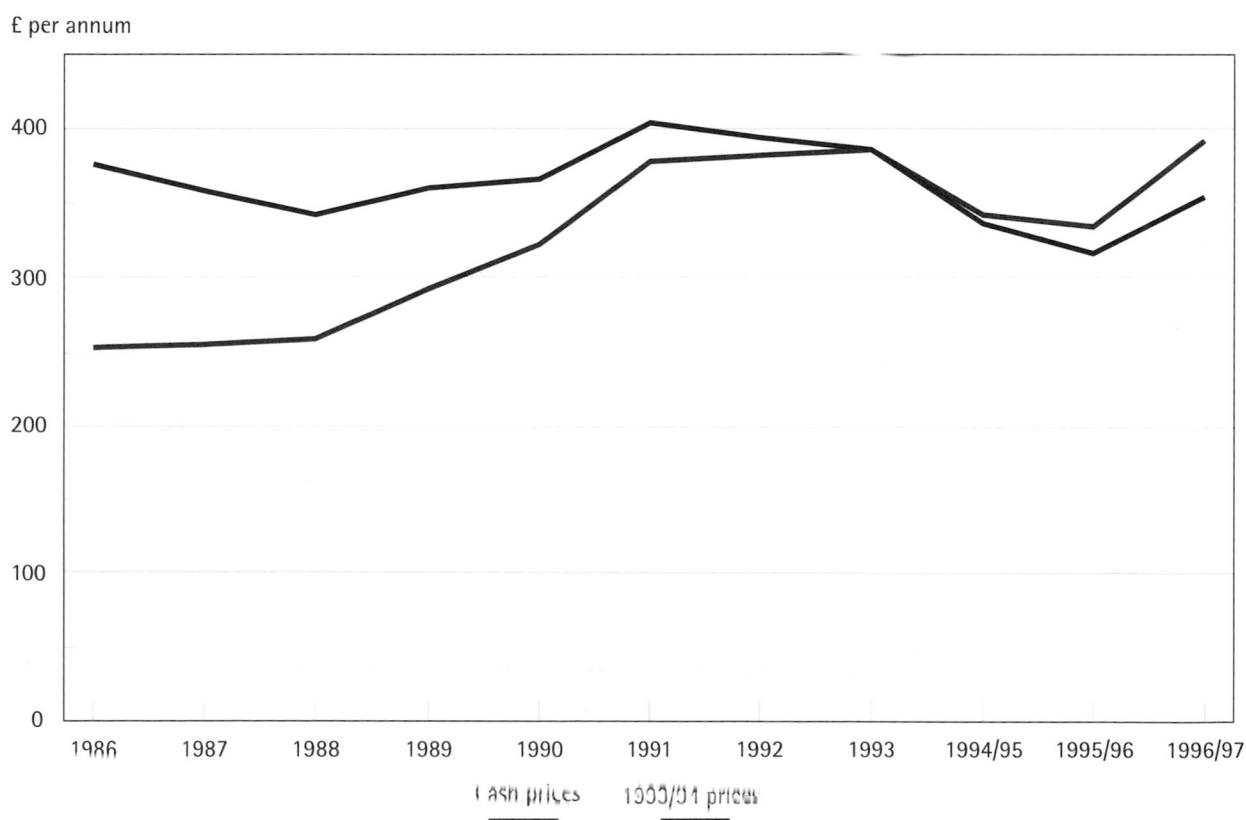

£ per annum

As might be expected, homeowners spend more than those in other tenures on repair, maintenance and decoration (Figure 9.2; Table A9.1). On average, homeowners spent about £480 per year in 1996, but those with a mortgage spent about £550 while outright owners spent £500. Private tenants in unfurnished accommodation spent about £80, local authority tenants £75, housing association tenants £70. Spending by those renting furnished accommodation has more than doubled since 1994 from £31 to £72.

Expenditure in 1997 was greatest among the 50-64 age group at about £550 per annum, followed by 30-49 at £450 per annum, and least among those under 30 and over 75 (Table A9.2). Among homeowners, spending was highest in Wales, the North East, London and Eastern, and lowest in the South West, Yorkshire and Humberside, the East Midlands, North West and the West Midlands (Table 9.1). This may be related to the age profile of the dwelling stock, with expenditure lowest in the regions with the highest proportion of postwar stock.

Table 9.1: Expenditure on repairs, maintenance and decoration by region, UK (1996-97) (£ per annum)

Region	Owned outright	Buying with mortgage	All owner-occupiers
North East	–	705	794
Yorkshire/Humberside	418	434	428
East Midlands	268	589	465
Eastern	406	714	613
London	502	715	657
South East	677	604	630
South West	406	375	387
West Midlands	543	456	491
North West	449	492	471
England	501	557	537
Wales	462	–	829
Scotland	722	400	496
Northern Ireland	207	703	527
United Kingdom	506	575	551

Source: CSO (1997)

Figure 9.2: Household expenditure on repair, maintenance and decoration, by tenure, UK (1986-97) (1993/94 prices)

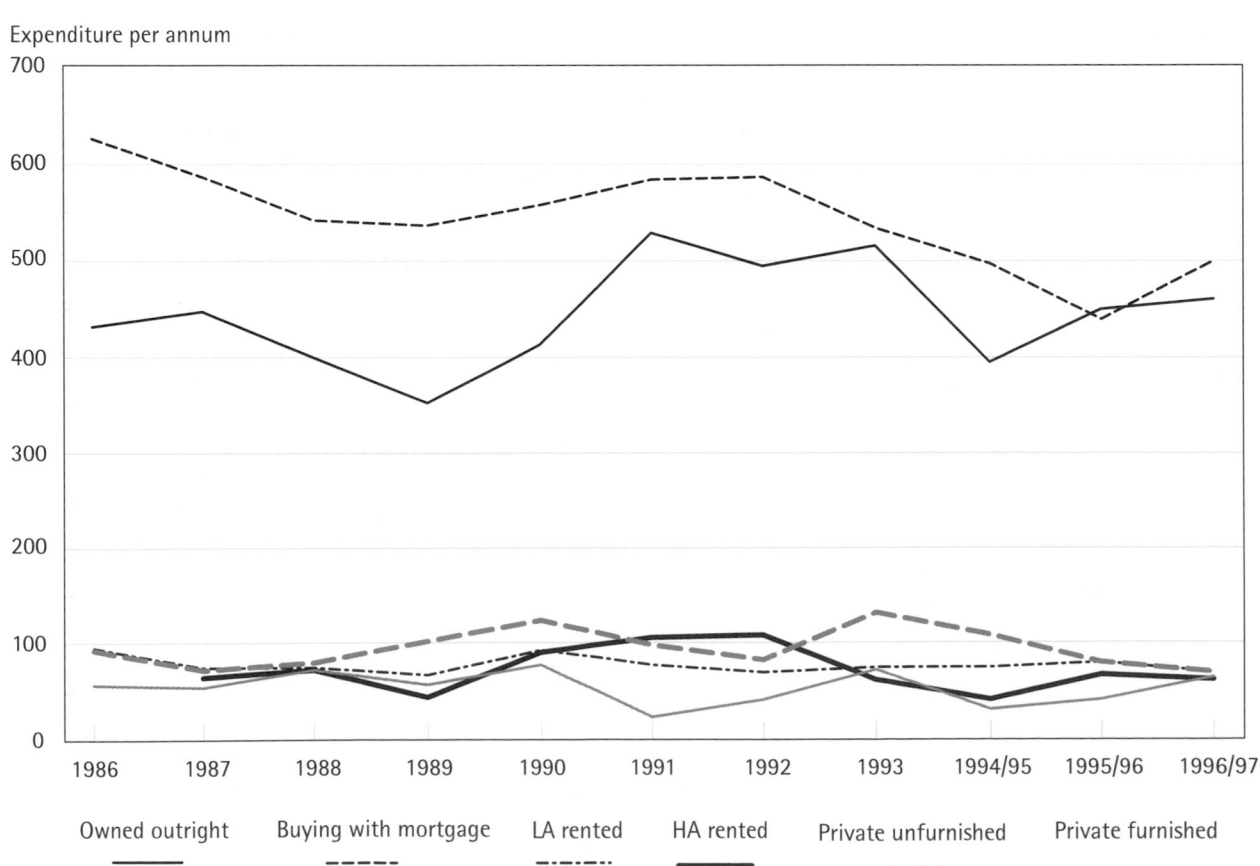

Expenditure per annum

Owned outright   Buying with mortgage   LA rented   HA rented   Private unfurnished   Private furnished

Expenditure on repairs, maintenance and decoration generally increases with income (Table 9.2), both for households as a whole and for homeowners, but the proportion of total income devoted to these items decreases as income rises (Table 9.3), with the exception of those in the highest income decile, where there is a sharp increase in spending which is reflected in an increase in the proportion of income devoted to repair work.

Table 9.2: Average weekly spending on repairs, maintenance and decoration by income, owner-occupiers, UK (1996-97)

Income decile	Lower boundary of decile	All tenures	Outright owners	Buying on mortgage	All owner-occupiers
1 (Lowest)	0	1.66	5.48	2.66	4.68
2	85	1.96	4.42	2.7	3.96
3	127	3.40	6.41	4.47	5.79
4	175	5.85	10.56	6.25	8.76
5	239	6.23	9.77	7.10	8.32
6	313	6.12	9.48	6.72	7.57
7	394	7.18	8.90	7.75	8.02
8	485	8.12	10.85	8.30	8.80
9	602	12.7	14.59	13.63	13.78
2 (Highest)	793	21.88	23.76	23.11	23.22

Source: CSO (1997)

Table 9.3: Average weekly spending on repairs, maintenance and decoration by income as a percentage of income, owner-occupiers, UK (1996-97)

Income decile	All tenures	Outright owners	Buying on mortgage	All owner-occupiers
1 (Lowest)	2.8	9.1	4.4	7.8
2	1.7	3.8	2.3	3.4
3	2.1	4.0	2.8	3.6
4	2.6	4.7	2.8	3.9
5	2.1	3.4	2.4	2.9
6	1.7	2.6	1.8	2.1
7	1.6	2.0	1.7	1.8
8	1.5	2.0	1.5	1.6
9	1.7	2.0	1.9	1.9
10 (Highest)	2.6	2.8	2.7	2.7

Source: CSO (1997)

Table 9.4 shows more detail from the Family Expenditure Survey on the nature of spending on repairs, maintenance, decoration and related matters in Britain in 1994-97. Some of the groupings seem rather idiosyncratic but this is the form in which the survey results are presented. The items are ranked in ascending order of expenditure, averaged not across all households but across those who incurred expenditure under each heading. Some 46% of all households did not undertake any spending at all on repairs, maintenance, decoration and related matters. Those who did, spent on average £14 per week or £730 per annum. Some three quarters of households purchased house contents insurance, at an average cost of £124. Roughly half of those spending on repairs, or a quarter of all households, invested in central heating repairs, investing £149 per annum on average. Only 7% of households invested in tools, costing £284 where they did so. A total of 15% spent an average of £418 per annum on materials other than paint, wallpaper, plaster and wood, or in the hire of equipment. About 24% spent an average of £588 on home maintenance falling outside any of the other categories in the table. Only 10% of households invested resources on doors, or

electrical and other fitting but those who did so invested over £700 on average. Only 2% of households admitted to work on the somewhat heterogeneous grouping of DIY improvements to double glazing, kitchen units or sheds, but those who did so invested £2,160. The largest average spent was incurred by those who carried out work on house extensions (7%) whose average spend was £2,653.

The 1991 English and 1996 Scottish House Condition Surveys also obtained details of work undertaken by private owners. The 1991 EHCS recorded details of all building work carried out in 1991 and of major work carried out over the 1987-91 period. In 1991, three quarters of households in England carried out work to their dwellings. Owner-occupiers (84%) were the most likely group to do work (Table 9.5). The average value of work carried out during the year (allowing for the notional costs of DIY inputs) was £1,648. Work by owner-occupiers (including those who carried out no work) averaged about £2,200, while tenants carried out work averaging around £500. Figure 9.3 (Table A9.3) shows the distribution of households by the value of work carried out for each tenure.

Table 9.4: Spending on repairs, maintenance and decoration and related matters, UK (1997/98)

Spending category	% of all households with any spend	Average spend across all households	Average spend if spent at all	
			Per week	Per annum
House contents insurance	75.1	1.80	2.40	124.61
Central heating repairs	24.5	0.70	2.86	148.51
Tools	7.3	0.40	5.46	283.92
Other materials, hire of equipment	14.9	1.20	8.03	417.76
House maintenance	23.8	2.70	11.31	588.02
Paint, wallpaper, plaster, and wood	11.4	1.40	12.29	639.02
Doors, electrical and other fittings	9.6	1.30	13.58	706.17
Central heating installation	1.7	0.60	36.28	1,886.42
DIY improvements: double glazing, kitchen units, sheds	1.7	0.70	41.54	2,160.07
House extensions	7.3	7.96	51.02	2,652.81
Total spend on repairs, maintenance and decoration	54.2	7.60	14.01	728.61

Source: CSO (1998)

Figure 9.3: Value of expenditure on building work by tenure, England (1991)

% of households by tenure

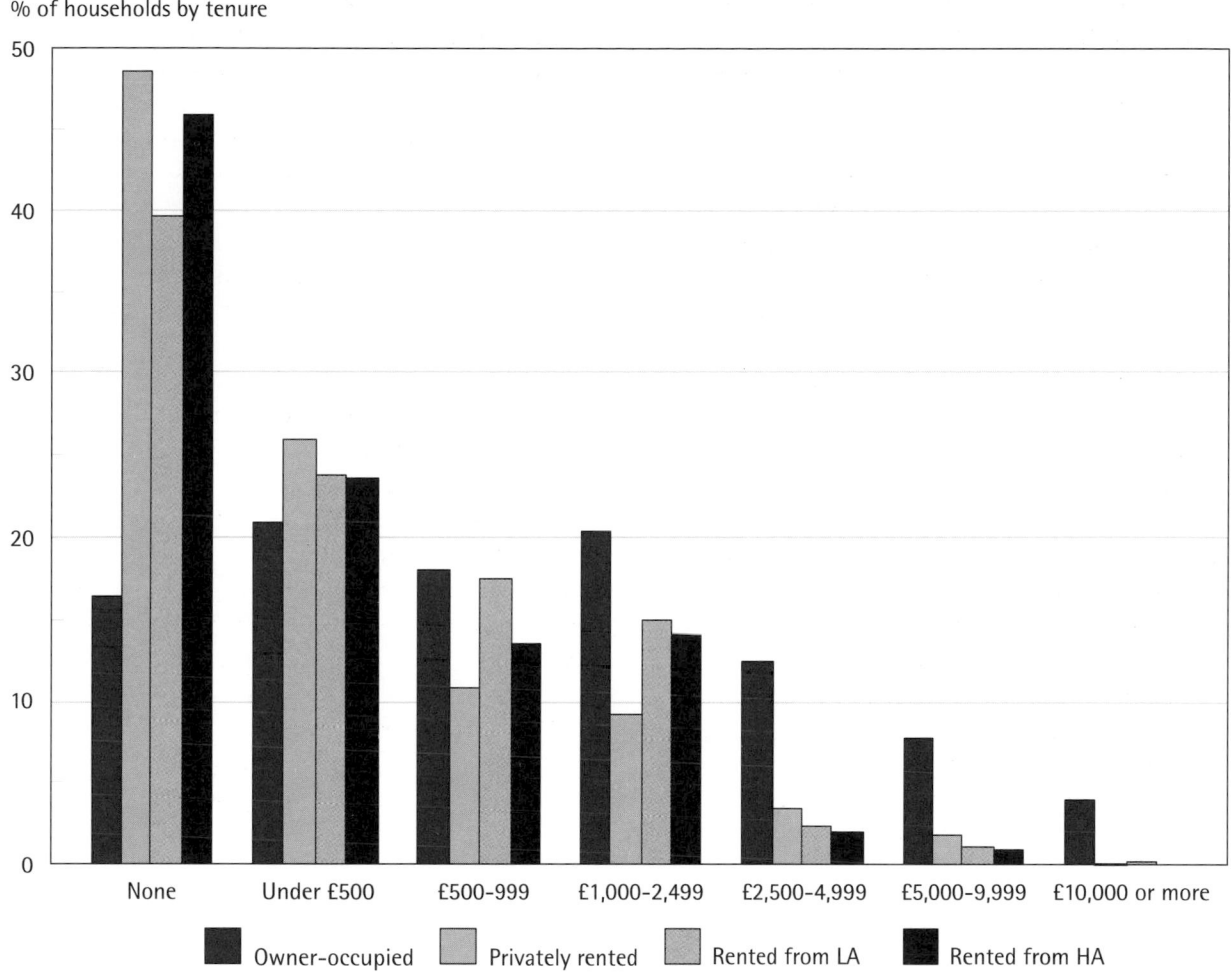

Owner-occupied　Privately rented　Rented from LA　Rented from HA

Table 9.5: Value of work carried out by households by tenure, England (1991)

Tenure	% doing any work	Total value (£m)	% of total wk done	Average (£)	No of cases (000s)
All work 1991					
Owner-occupied	83.5	27,930	88.7	2,170	12,872
Privately rented	51.4	918	2.9	540	1,700
Rented from LA	60.4	2,330	7.4	601	3,877
Rented from HA	54.4	315	1.0	477	662
All households	74.9	31,493	100.0	1648	19,111
Major work 1987–91					
Owner-occupied	86.0	73,360	96.3	5,699	12,872
Privately rented	63.1	1,077	1.4	634	1,700
Rented from LA	39.8	1,579	2.1	407	3,877
Rented from HA	51.0	202	0.3	305	662
All households	73.4	76,218	100.0	3,988	19,111

Source: 1991 EHCS: analysis of data

In aggregate, work to the value of some £31.5 billion was identified as being completed by residents in 1991, of which the majority (£28 billion, or 89%) was carried out by owner-occupiers. This compares with about £7.2 billion of expenditure which can be inferred from the Family Expenditure Survey for 1991. The latter figure excludes DIY work and some work funded by loans, but the difference is nevertheless very difficult to reconcile. The EHCS, as a specialist survey, is likely to provide the most accurate indication of total spending, while the FES may provide an indication of trends over time.

The survey also looked at major work over the 1987-91 period. Some 86% of owners completed major work in this period (Table A9.3). In the rented sector about two thirds of private tenants carried out major works, but the proportions of housing association and local authority tenants were smaller (51% and 40% respectively). The average value of major work completed by homeowners over the period (£5,700) was significantly greater than for tenants. The aggregate value of work over the period was £73.2 billion, of which 96% was carried out by homeowners. Estimates of work by landlords for the 1987-91 period are not available.

In addition to work by those resident in dwellings, the 1991 EHCS made estimates of work by landlords and other owners (Table 9.6). Freeholders carried out work to the value of £0.2 billion, private developers £0.8 billion, private landlords £2.0 billion, local authorities as landlords £3.9 billion, and housing associations as landlords £0.4 billion. The total value of work by owners and residents was £38.9 billion.

Table 9.6: Value of work carried out by landlords and others, England (1991)

All work 1991	Total value (£bn)	Average value (£)
Freeholders	0.2	na
Private developers	0.8	na
Private landlords	2.0	1,240
Local authorities	3.9	986
Housing associations	0.4	723

Source: DoE Building Stock Research Division, unpublished tables based on 1991 EHCS

Table 9.7 shows the type of work carried out within the overall totals. In 1991, only about a quarter of work by value was related to dwelling repair. A further quarter of work involved internal decoration, and the remaining 50% related to improvements. Not surprisingly, there were substantial variations in this pattern by tenure, with tenants more likely to invest in internal decorations (around two thirds of the value of work by local authority or housing association tenants and 50% of work by private tenants). Homeowners devoted only 17% of investment to internal decorations, but improvements (53%) still predominate over repairs (30%).

Table 9.7: Type of work by tenure, England (1991)

		Owner-occupied	Private rented	LA rented	HA rented	All households
All work 1991						
Improvements	Total value of work (£m)	14,666	293	577	73	15,609
	Mean value (£)	1,139	172	149	110	817
	% of all work	53	32	25	23	50
Repairs	Total value of work (£m)	8,463	169	252	36	8,920
	Mean value (£)	657	100	65	54	467
	% of all work	30	19	11	11	28
Internal decor	Total value of work (£m)	4,751	451	1,501	206	6,910
	Mean value (£)	369	266	387	312	362
	% of all work	17	49	64	65	22
Total	Total value of work (£m)	27,881	914	2,330	315	31,439
Major work 1987–91						
Improvements	Total value of work (£m)	46,329	630	1,045	113	48,118
	Mean value (£)	3,599	371	270	171	2,518
	% of all work	68	70	75	72	68
Repairs	Total value of work (£m)	21,801	271	353	45	22,469
	Mean value (£)	1,694	159	91	68	1,176
	% of all work	32	30	25	28	32
Total	Total value of work (£m)	68,130	901	1,399	158	70,587

Source: EHCS 1991: analysis of data

Figures 9.4-9.10 provide a profile of the average value of work by selected household and dwelling type characteristics. Tables A9.4 and A9.5 provides details of these and additional characteristics. There are clear links between household characteristics and the average value of work carried out. The average value of work rises from £800 for those with an income of under £4,000 per annum to £3,000 for those with an income of over £24,000 per annum (Figure 9.4). In terms of the age of household head the value of work remains fairly level from the ages of 25-54, but falls off for older age groups to less than £350 for those over 85 (Figure 9.5). In terms of household type, families with children carry out the most work (averaging about £2,500). Couples under retirement age and multi-adult households average around £2,000, pensioner couples and lone-parent households carry out work averaging around £1,000, and lone-adult households (£850) and lone pensioners (£550) carry out least work (Figure 9.6). There is also a relationship between length of residence and the value of work carried out (Figure 9.7), with the amount of work at a peak of around £2,000 for those resident for 1-2 years (the pro rata annual rate for those resident under a year would probably be similar) and declining steadily thereafter.

Figures 9.8-9.10 show variations in the value of work carried out by occupants in relation to selected dwelling characteristics. Here the links are less easy to demonstrate. Although occupant characteristics such as incomes would be expected to have a significant impact on investment, the need to spend would also be expected to be important. In terms of dwelling age, which earlier chapters have shown to be an important influence on dwelling condition, the oldest dwellings (pre-1850) generated the highest average value of work (£2,700) (Figure 9.8). A second peak occurs for dwellings in the 1919-44 age group (£1,950). Otherwise, the value of work is somewhat, but not substantially, higher for dwellings built in the 1850-1918 period (£1,600) than for postwar dwellings (£1,500). In general, therefore, the extent of variation in expenditure by age is not substantial.

Figure 9.9 shows variations in the value of work in 1991, and for the period 1987-91 for major work, in terms of general repair cost in 1991. The pattern is complex, but spending is highest on dwellings considered to have no general repair costs in 1991 and lowest on those with the highest costs. In between these extremes there is a peak in spending for dwellings with costs in the £5,000-£9,999 band, but otherwise little variation. The pattern is the same for work carried out in 1991 and for work carried out over the 1987-91 period. Finally Figure 9.10 shows the relationship between the value of work carried out and dwelling value. There is a clear increase in the value of work carried out as dwelling value increases, from less than £1,000 for dwellings valued at under £40,000 to over £4,000 for dwellings worth more than £160,000. Higher levels of investment in higher value dwellings arise because high value dwellings are generally bigger and, other things being equal, require more to be spent on them, because those living in these dwellings have higher incomes, and perhaps because higher dwelling values make it more likely that an investment will be recovered.

Figure 9.4: Average value of work carried out by household income, England (1991)

Average value (£)

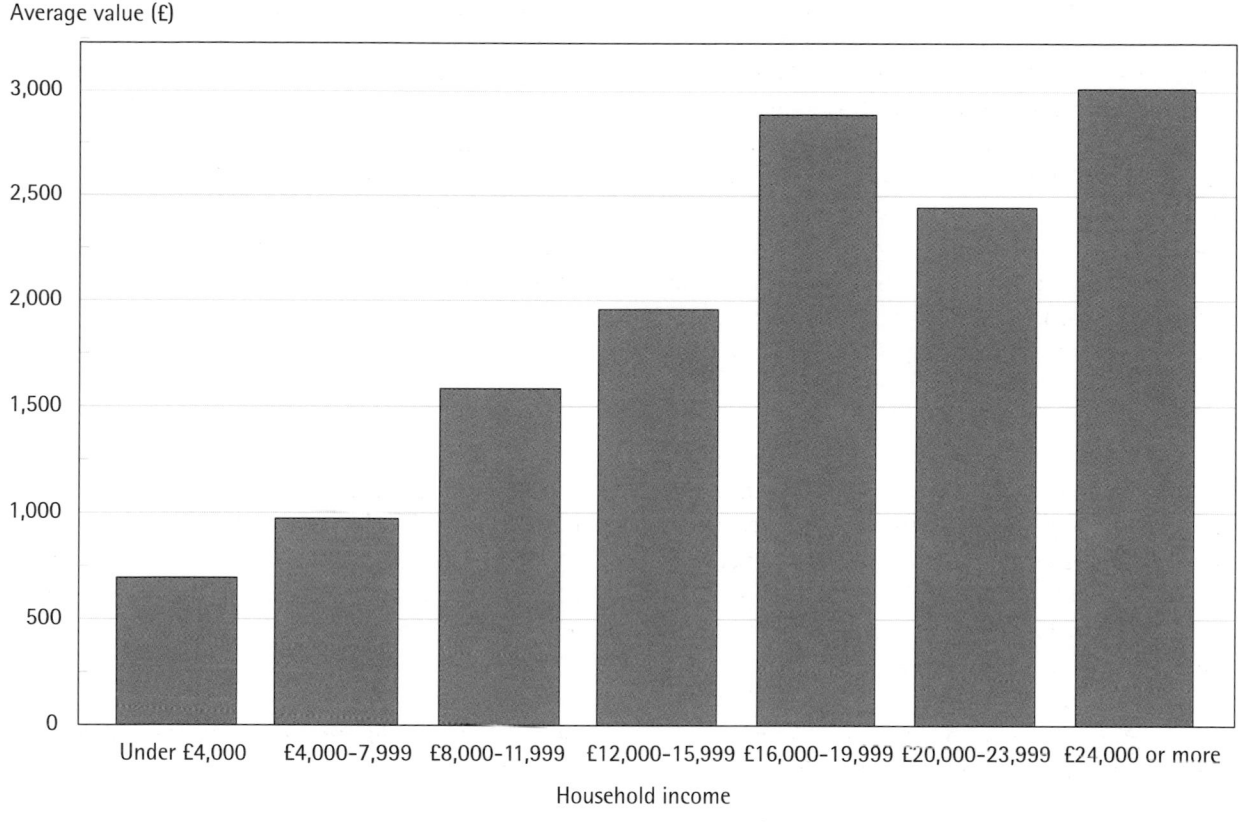

Household income

Figure 9.5: Average value of work carried out by age of household head, England (1991)

Average value (£)

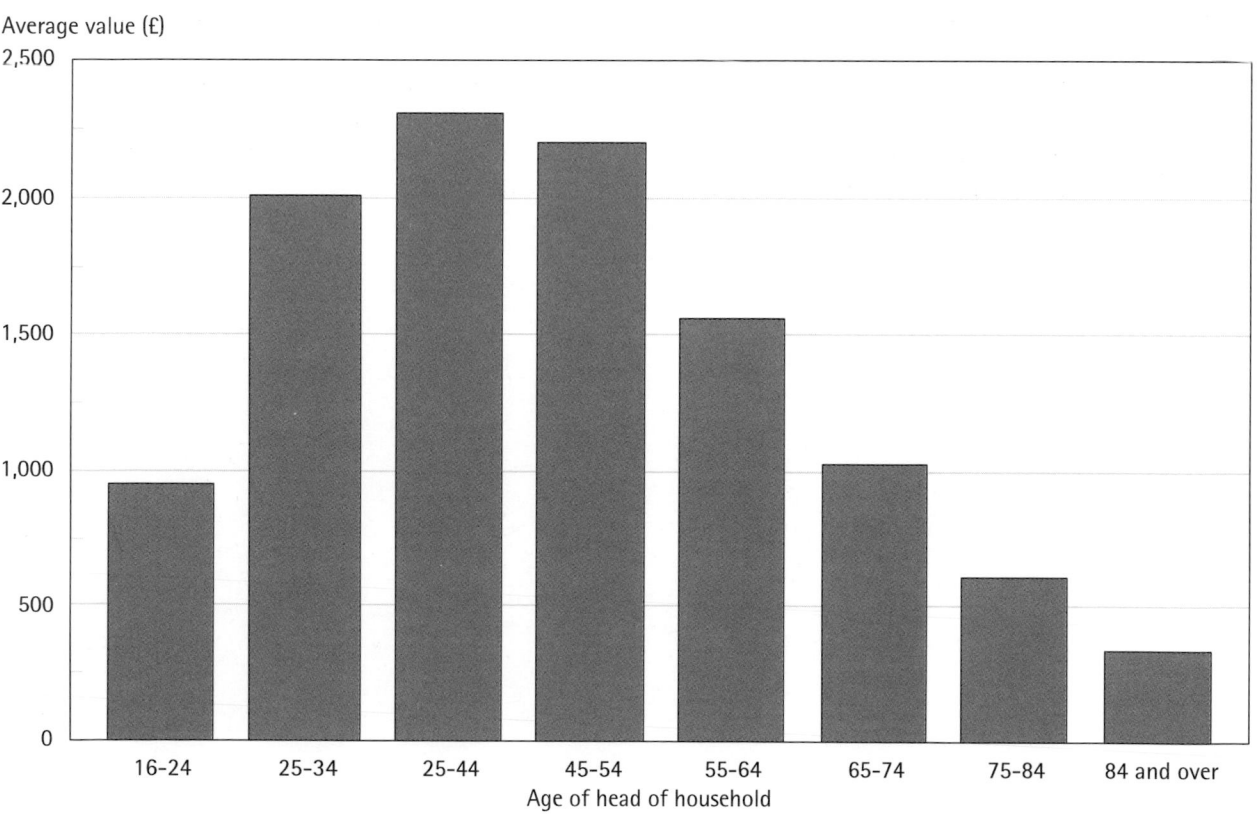

Age of head of household

Figure 9.6: Average value of work carried out by household type, England (1991)

Average value (£)

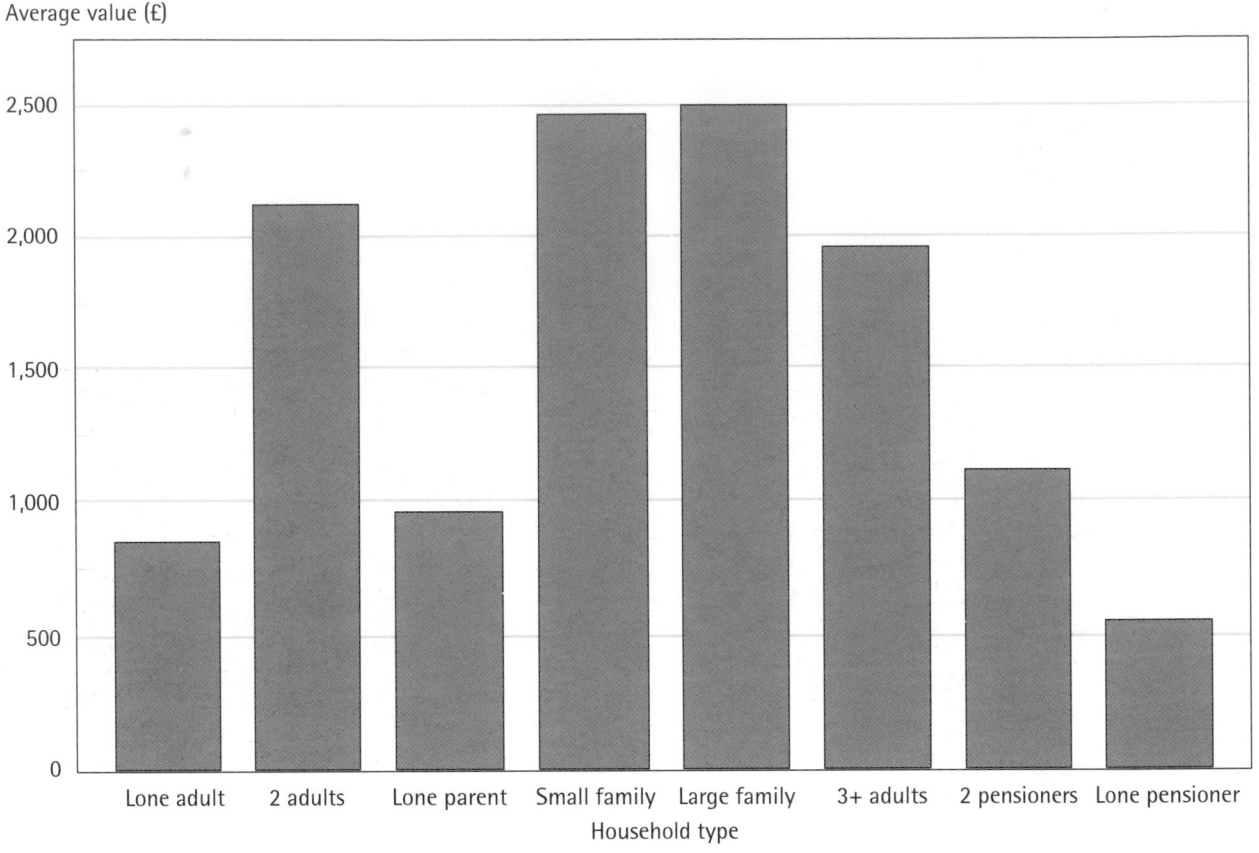

Figure 9.7: Average value of work carried out by length of residence, England (1991)

Average value (£)

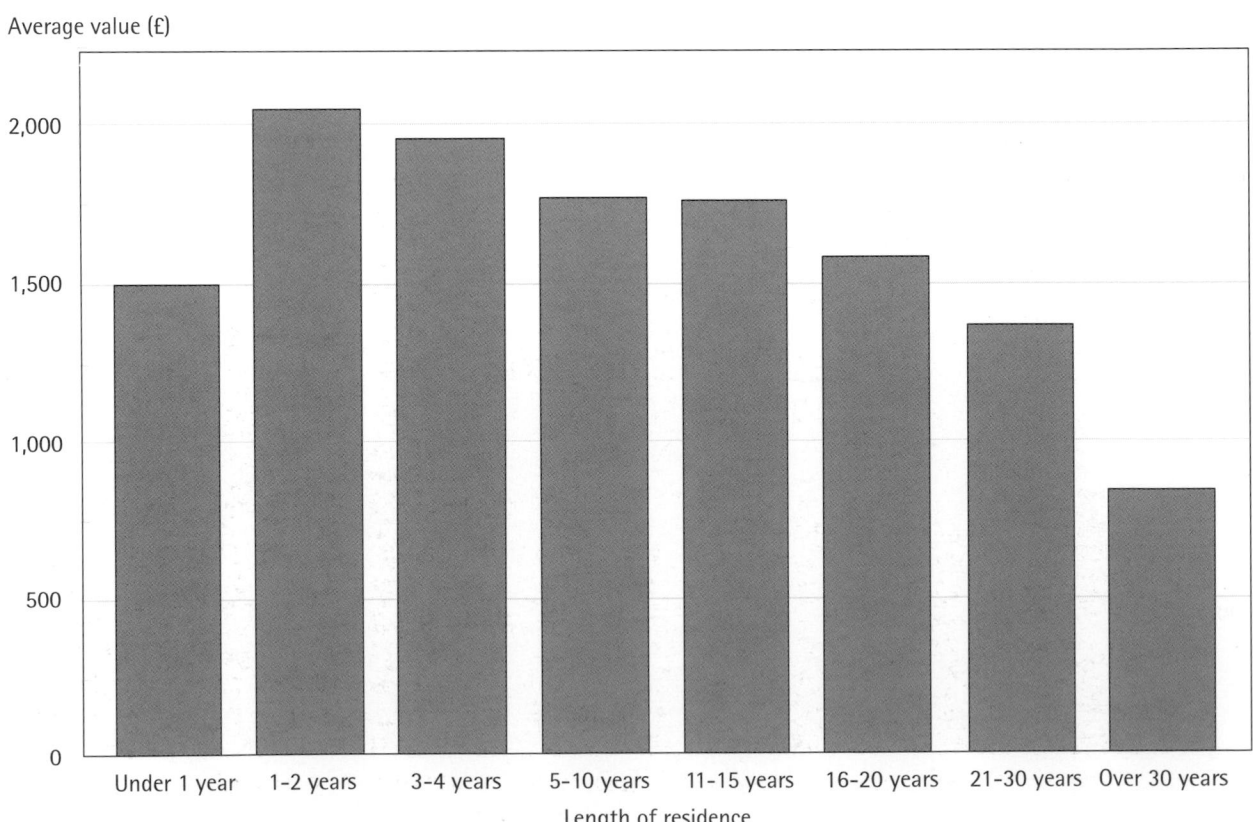

Figure 9.8: Average value of work carried out by age of dwelling, England (1991)

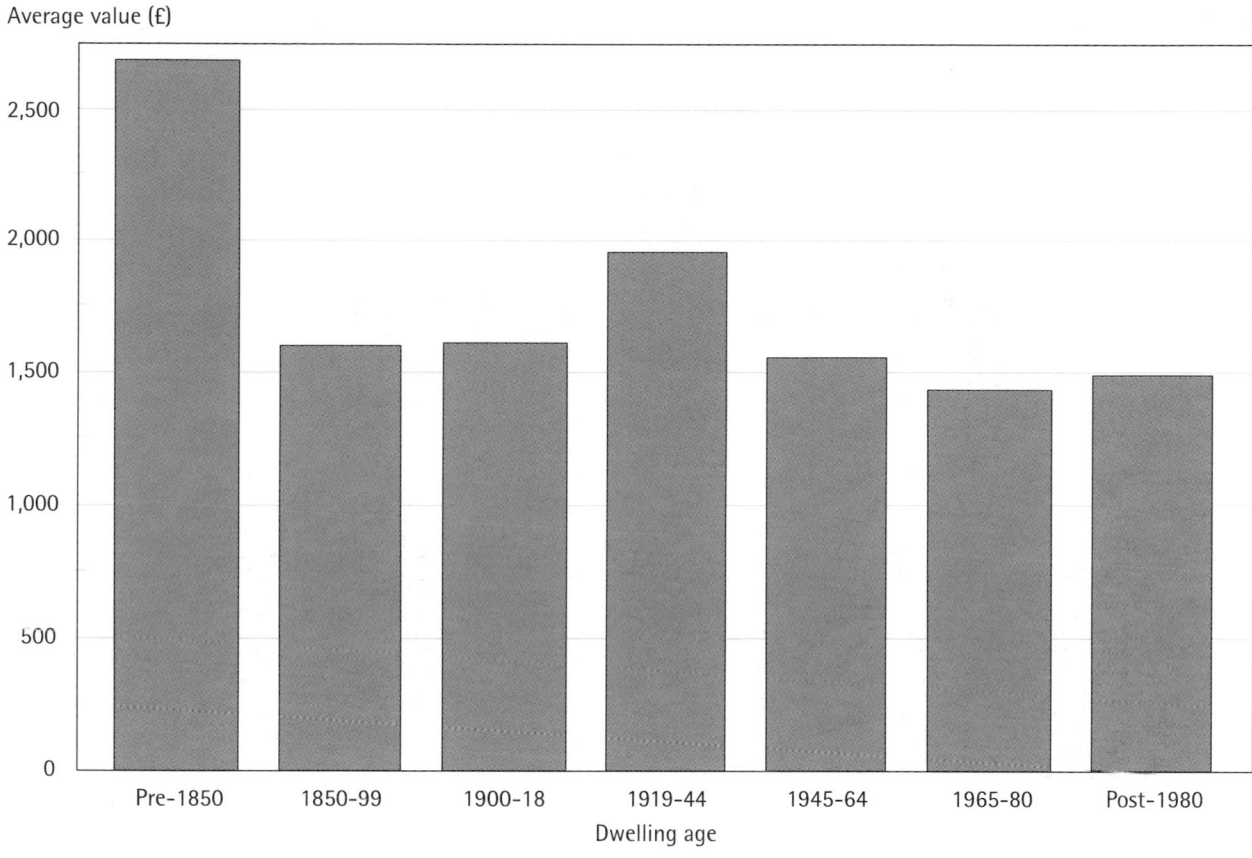

Figure 9.9: Average value of work carried out by general repair cost, England (1991)

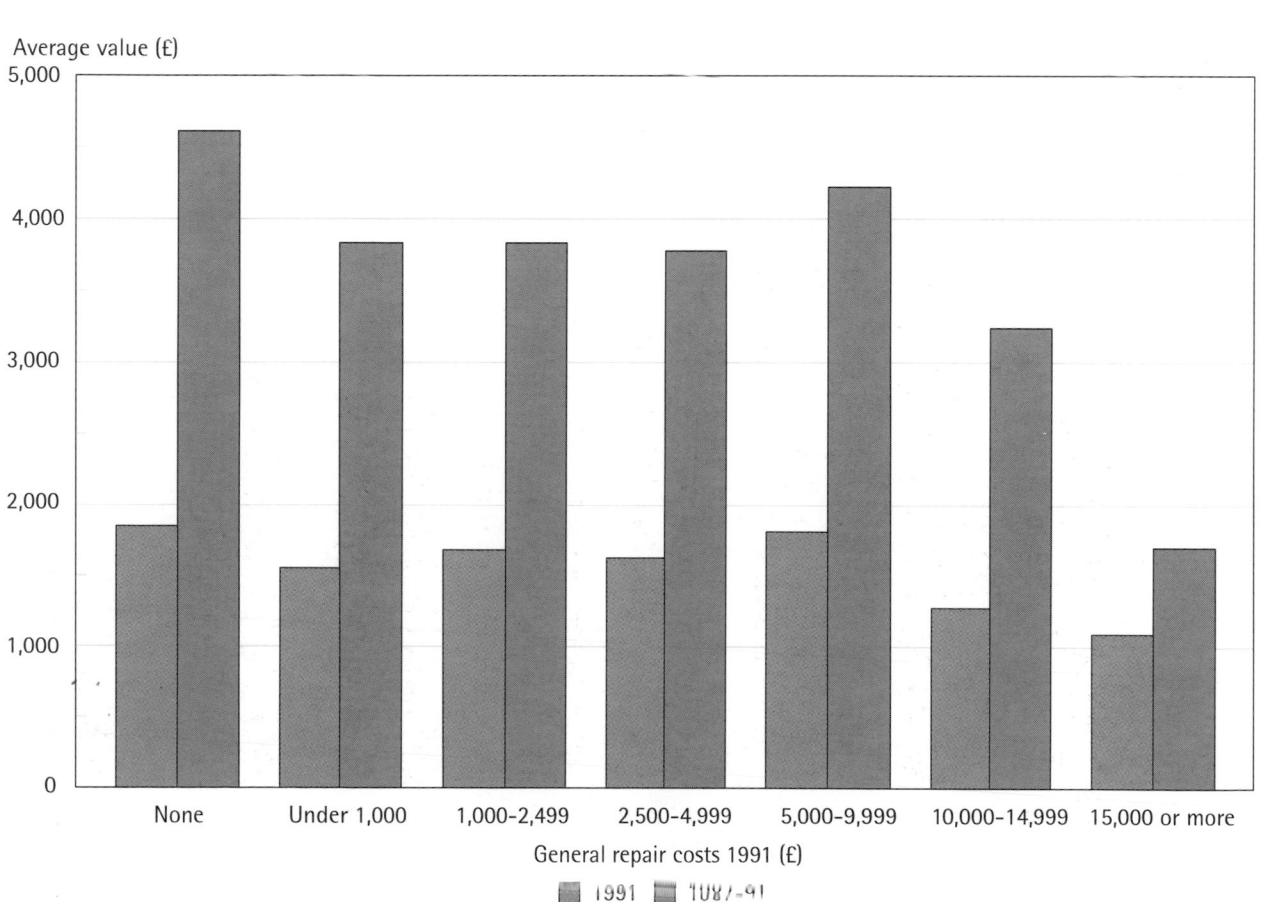

Figure 9.10: Average value of work carried out by value of dwelling, England (1991)

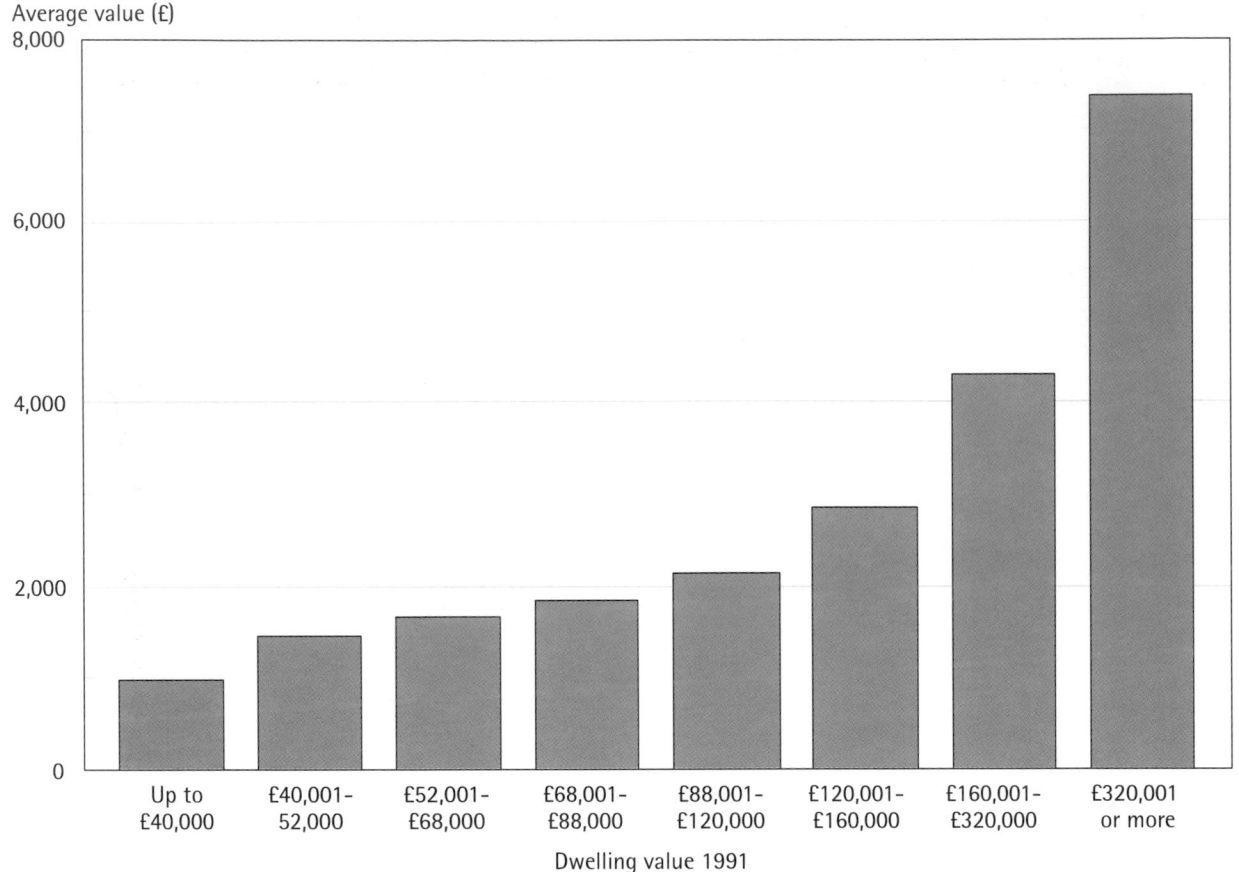

Average value (£)

Dwelling value 1991

Table 9.8 shows work done in 1996 by households in Scotland. The proportion of households carrying out any work was apparently much lower in Scotland (59%) than in England (75%). Owner-occupiers reported average expenditure of about half the amount undertaken in England and tenants reported very small levels of spending.

Table 9.8: Value of work carried out by households by tenure, Scotland (1996)

Tenure	Major work			Minor work		
	% doing any work	Total value (£m)	Average (£)	Total value (£m)	Average (£)	No of cases (000s)
Owner-occupied	58.1	1,561	1,301	217.5	189	706
Privately rented	47.7	38	234	9	58	77
Rented from LA	59.3	74	110	63	97	400
Rented from HA	50.0	5.5	64	6	75	43
All households	57.8	1,679	791	295	145	1,215

Source: SCHS 1996: analysis of data

Building society lending

Information on the amount of lending by building societies for renovation work (rather than house purchase) is not available. Figure 9.11 shows the extent of lending on pre-1919 dwellings and more specifically on pre-1919 terraced houses and converted flats (see also Table A9.6). This showed a significant increase on the late 1970s, levelled off during the 1980s, fell slightly in the early 1990s, and has remained at this level to the present date.

Figure 9.11: Building society lending by type of property, Britain (1973-98)

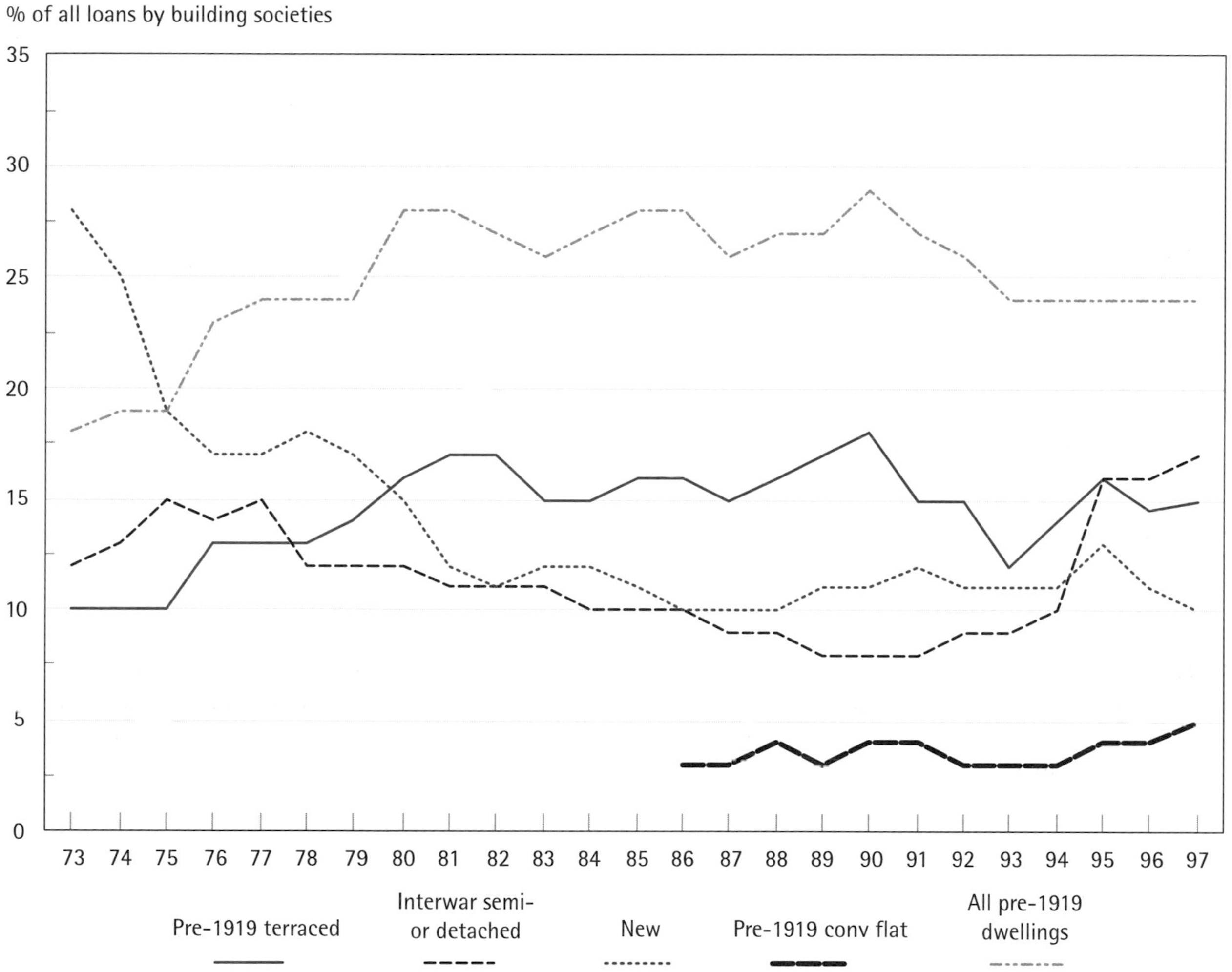

% of all loans by building societies

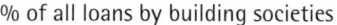

Figure 9.12 shows variations in the propensity of first-time buyers to purchase dwellings of a particular age over time (see also Tables A9.7 and A9.8). First time buyers remain more likely to buy pre-1919 dwellings than existing owners, and less likely to buy newer dwellings, but in recent years the difference between the age profiles of dwellings bought by first time buyers and existing owners have become significantly less.

Figure 9.12: Ratio of first time buyers to existing owners by age of dwelling, Britain (1998)

Ratio of first-time buyers to previous owners

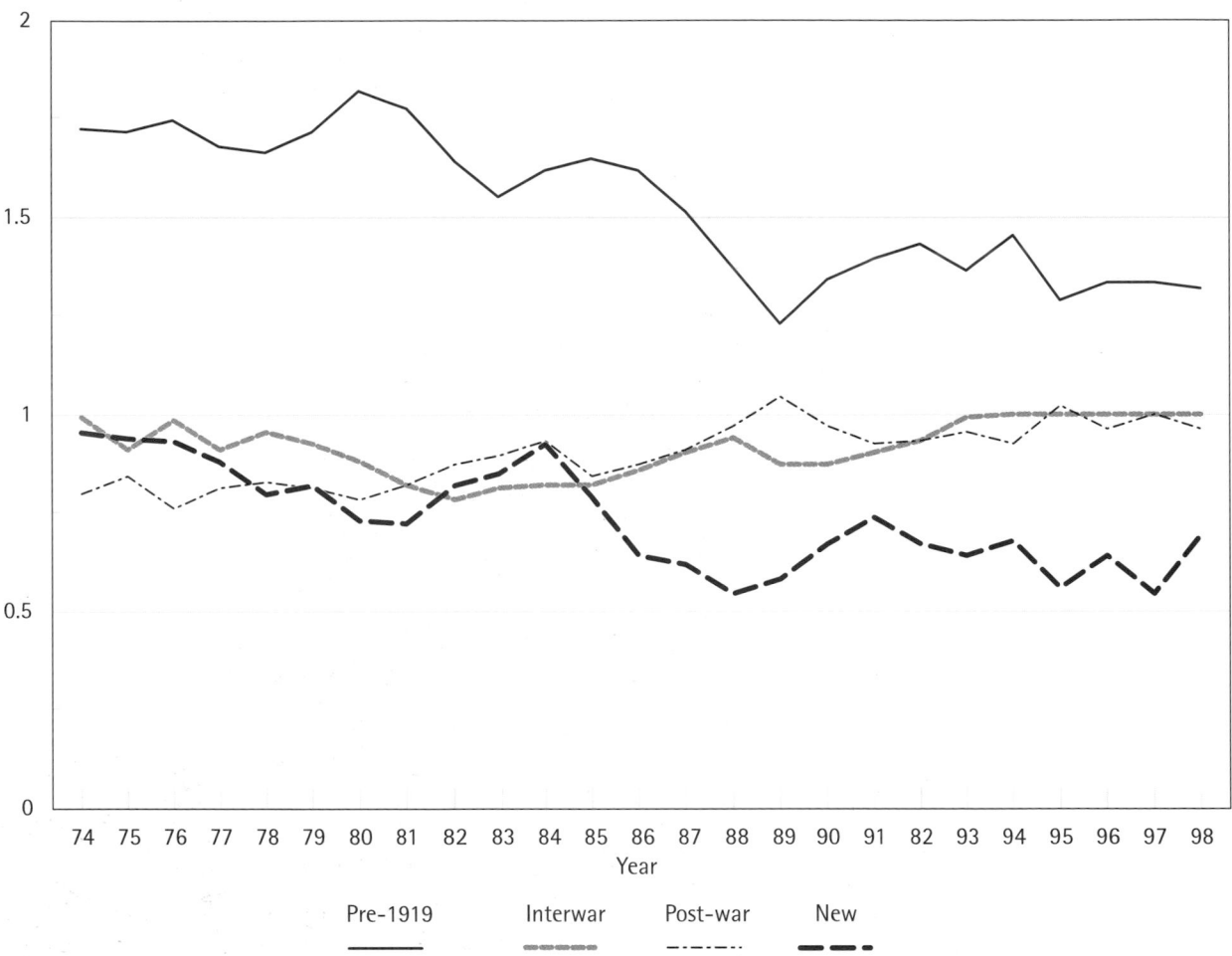

Map 9.1 shows variations in the average price of a terraced house by postcode district in 1998. Although the North–South split dominates the picture, the map also shows high price concentrations in rural area in the north. Values in Wales (especially the South Wales valley), the North East, Humberside and South Yorkshire, and parts of the North West are often extremely low, averaging under £30,000.

Map 9.1: Average price of a terraced dwelling by postcode district, England and Wales (1998)

Average price terraced house 1998

- £75,000 or more (545)
- £50,000 to £75,000 (614)
- £30,000 to £50,000 (783)
- Up to £30,000 (272)

Building industry output

Evidence on the volume of renovation activity is also provided by official statistics on building industry output. Figure 9.13 shows output on housing repair and maintenance work by sector over the period 1985-97 at cash prices (see also Table A9.9). For the private sector the total output is broadly consistent with the Family Expenditure Survey but investment as a whole is less than the EHCS recorded for 1991, even allowing for DIY work. Figure 9.13 clearly shows the importance of private investment which significantly exceeded public investment throughout the 1985-91 period. The impact of the period of boom in the economy (1987-90) followed by the subsequent recession in 1991 and later years is also apparent, although private investment has begun to steadily increase over the last three years.

Figure 9.14 shows output by size of firm (see also Table A9.10). It can be seen that the repair and maintenance sector is heavily dominated by small firms with seven or less employees, which in 1994 accounted for two thirds of the aggregate value of repair and maintenance work done, including jobs in the public sector. For private sector jobs alone the proportion would be higher.

Figure 9.13: Output on housing repair and maintenance, Britain (1985-97)

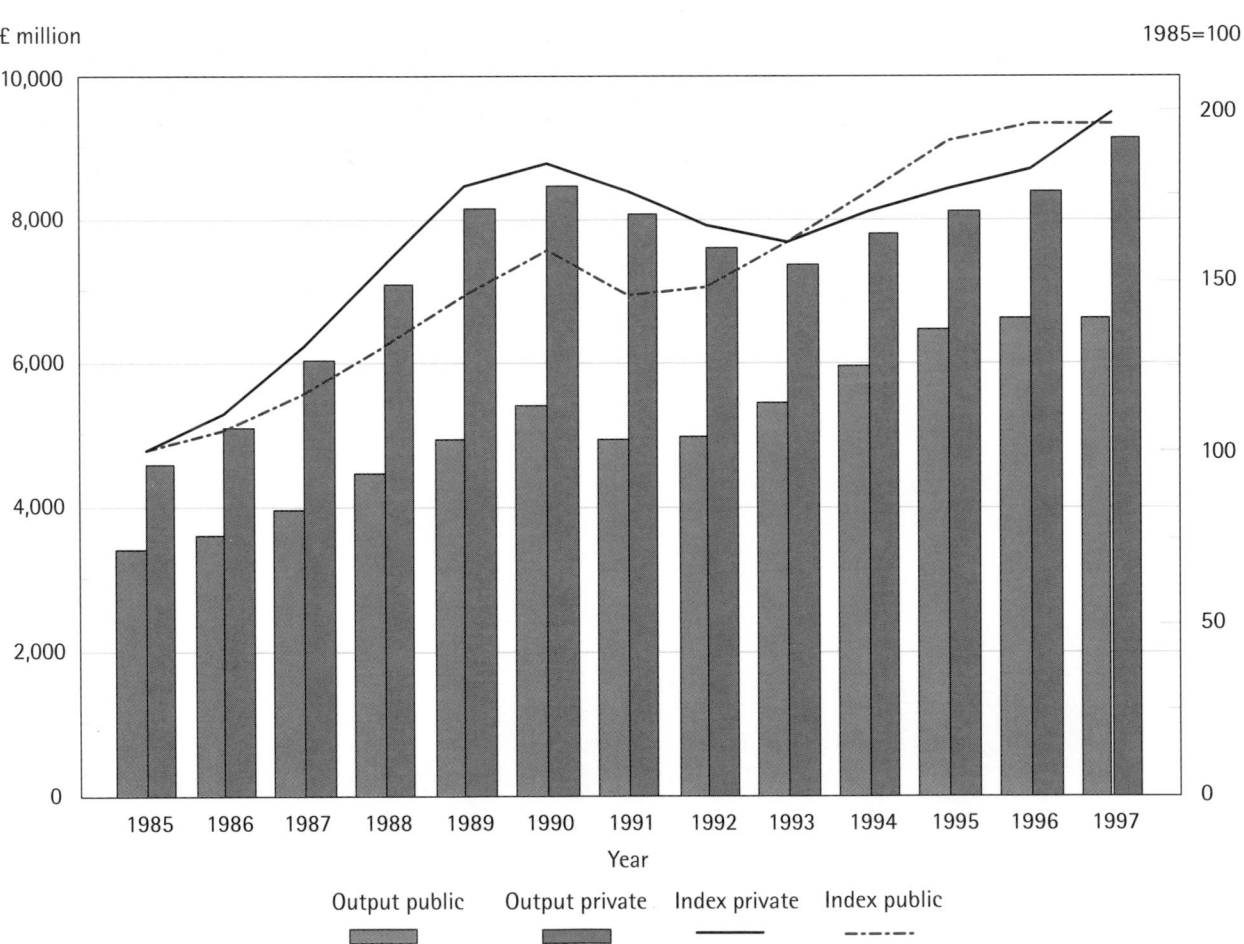

£ million   1985=100

Output public   Output private   Index private   Index public

Figure 9.14: Output on housing repair and maintenance by size of firm, Britain (1990, 1992, 1994, 1996)

Value of work done (£ million)

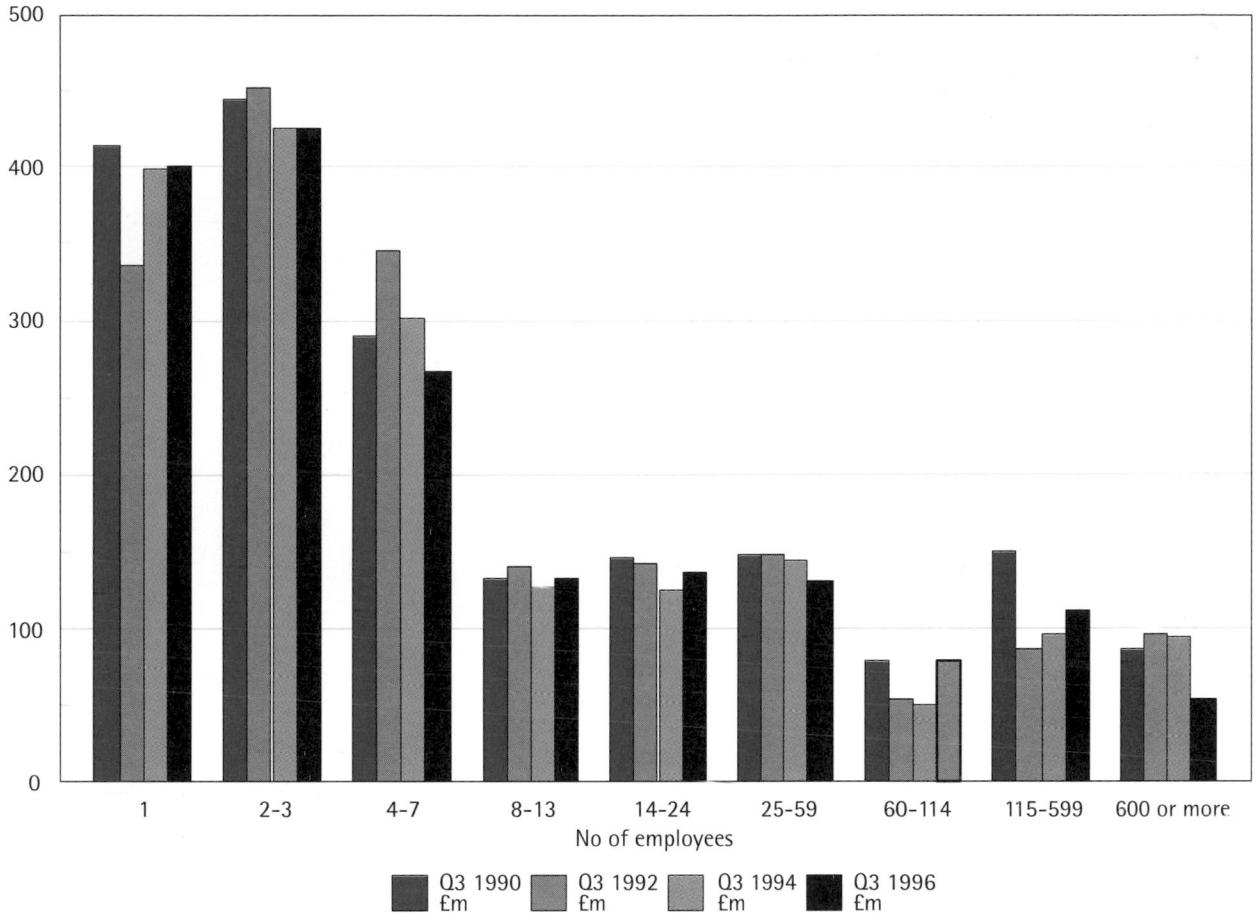

No of employees

Q3 1990 £m   Q3 1992 £m   Q3 1994 £m   Q3 1996 £m

10

European comparisons

Comparison of housing conditions within the UK is difficult because of differences in the indicators used in national surveys and differences in definitions. These problems also make it difficult to produce comparisons of housing conditions between the UK and Europe. Figures 10.1 to 10.5, drawing on data assembled by the EU (1996), provide some limited information.

Figure 10.1 shows that the proportion of dwellings which are in owner-occupation is lower in the UK than in Eire, Greece and Spain but higher than in countries of northern Europe such as France, Denmark, the Netherlands and Germany. In terms of the age of the stock, the UK has the second highest proportion of pre-1919 housing, with France having just 1% more, followed by Belgium, Austria and Luxembourg (Figure 10.2). Combining evidence on homeownership and age of the stock suggests that the UK has a more substantial proportion of privately-owned older houses than other European countries except Eire and Belgium.

Figure 10.3 shows that the UK has the lowest rate of demolition in the EU. Other countries with an ageing housing stock (Austria, France and Belgium) have higher levels of clearance.

Figure 10.4 shows the proportion of dwellings with a bath/shower in each EC country. The UK ranks highly on this indicator, with 99% of dwellings, in comparison with countries such as Belgium, Portugal, Greece and Italy where the proportion is less than 90%.

Finally, Figure 10.5 shows the proportion of dwellings with central heating in each EU country. The UK performs less well on this indicator (86%) in comparison with other countries with a similar climate. Of the northern European countries, only Belgium and Eire have fewer dwellings with central heating.

Figure 10.1: Proportion of owner-occupied dwellings in the European Community

% owner-occupied dwellings

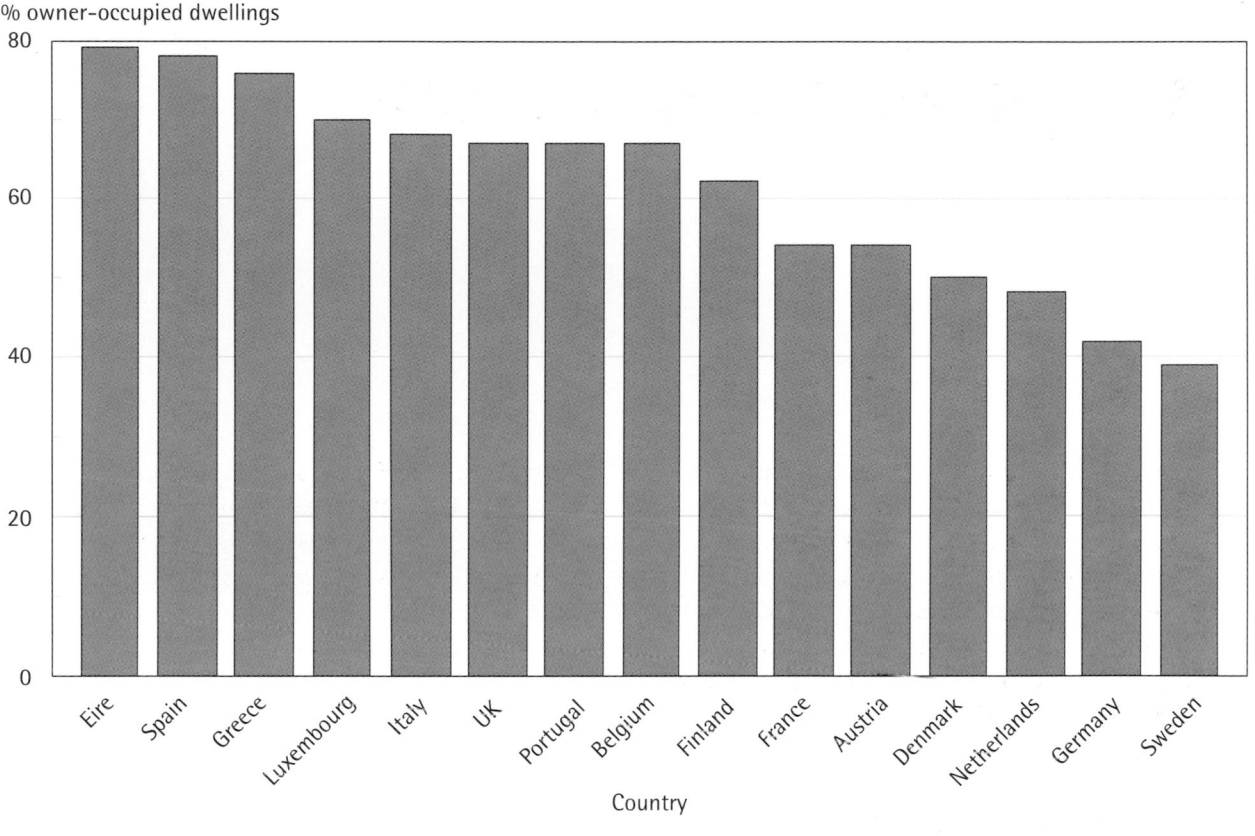

Country

Figure 10.2: Proportion of pre-1919 dwellings in the European Community

% pre-1919 dwellings

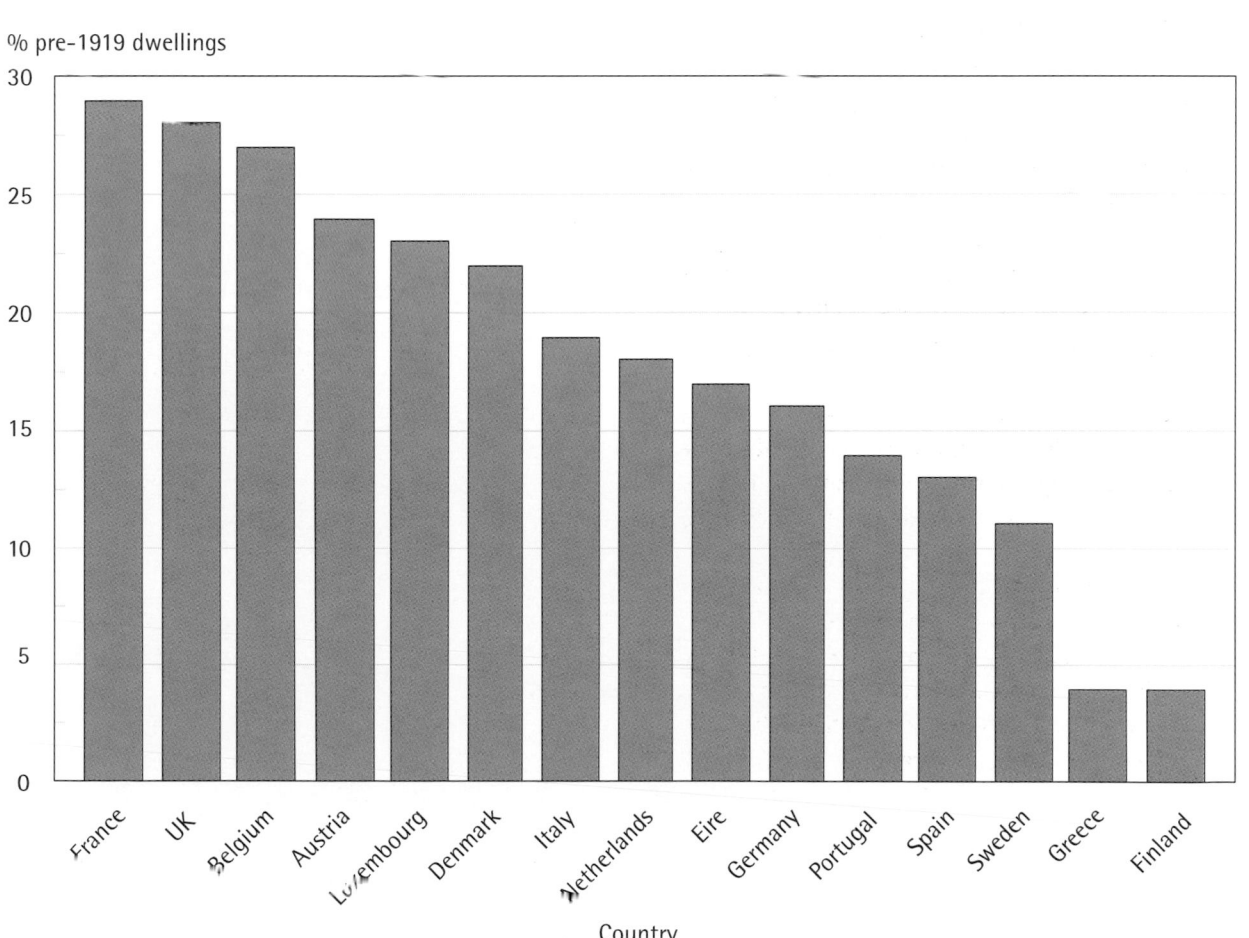

Country

Figure 10.3: Decreases in dwelling stock per 1,000 dwellings in the European Community

Decrease per 1,000 dwellings

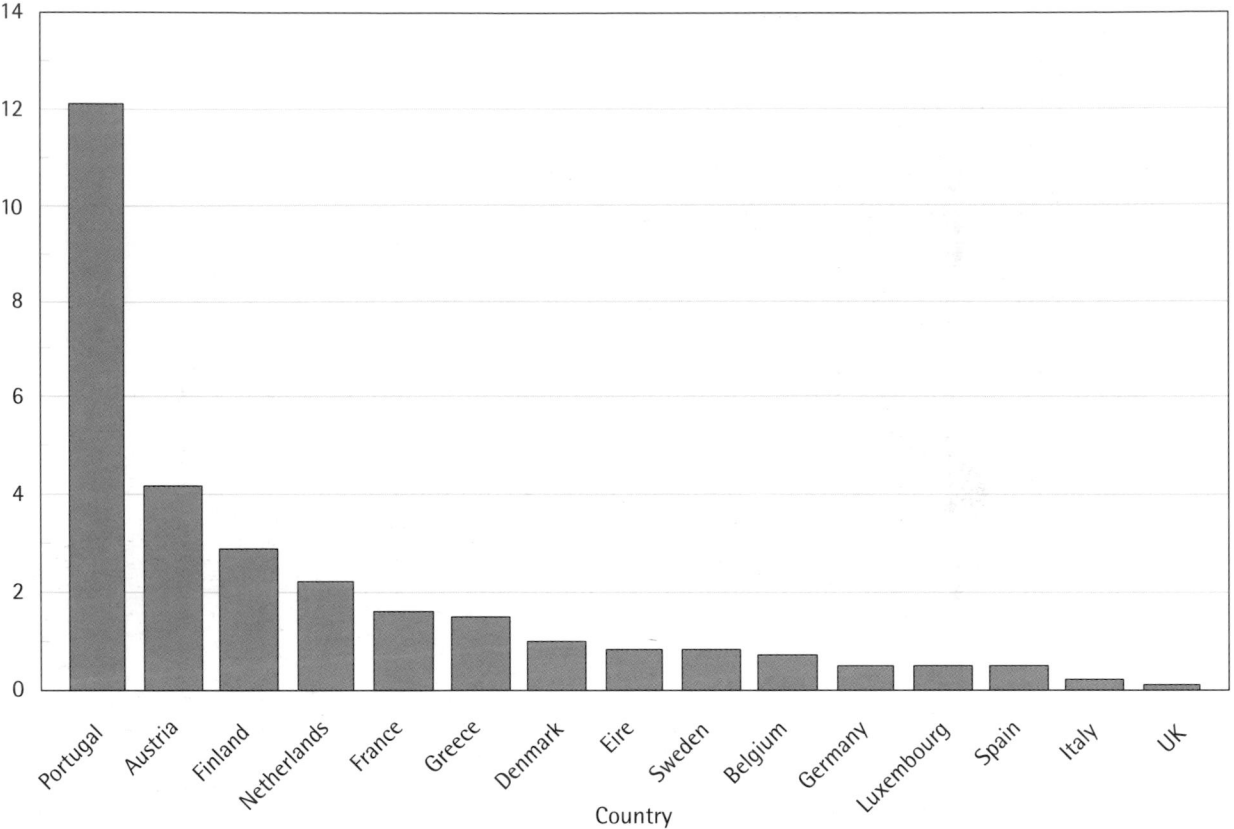

Country

Figure 10.4: Proportion of dwellings with a bath/shower in the European Community

% dwellings with bath/shower

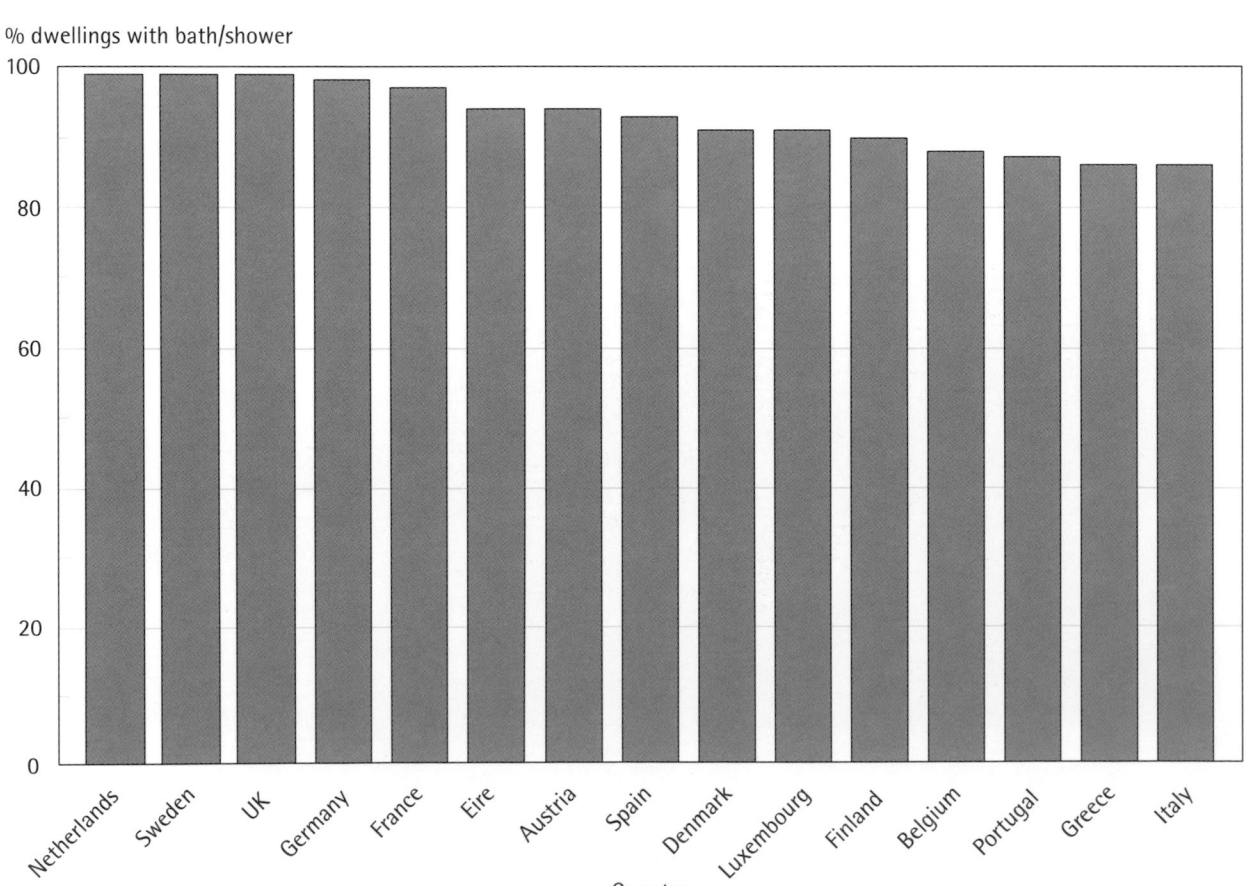

Country

Figure 10.5: Proportion of dwellings with central heating in the European Community

% dwellings with central heating

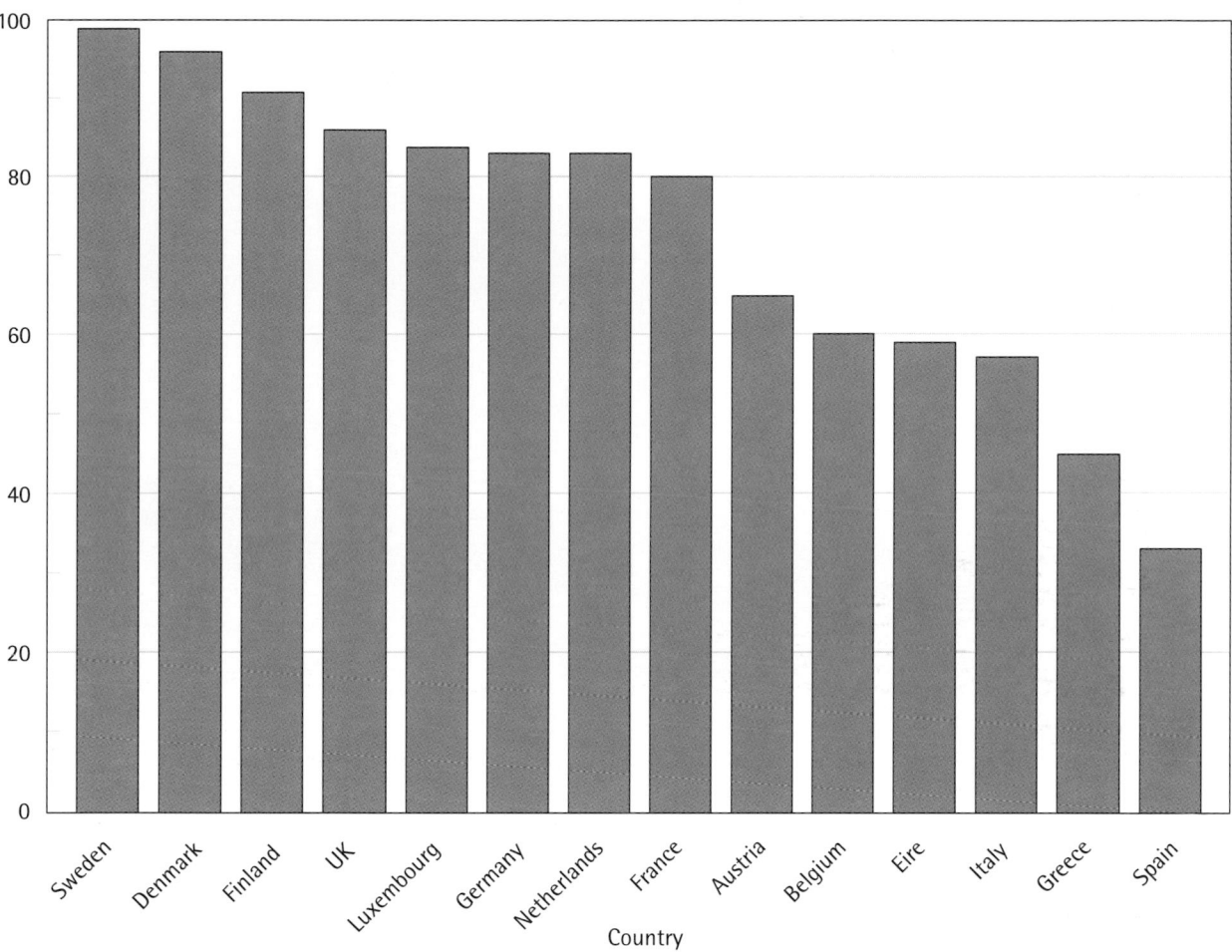

Country

References and sources

Care and Repair (1998) *Report on agency performance 1997/98*, Nottingham: Care and Repair

Council of Mortgage Lenders (various years) *Housing Finance*, London: CML.

CSO (Central Statistical Office) (various years) Reports of the annual Family Expenditure Survey (under various titles, such as *Family spending: A report on the 1996-97 FES*), London: HMSO.

Department of Finance and Personnel Northern Ireland (various years) *Northern Ireland Annual Abstract of Statistics*, Belfast: Department of Finance and Personnel.

Department of Health and Social Services Northern Ireland and Registrar General Northern Ireland (1997) *The Northern Ireland Census 1996: Summary Report*, Belfast: HMSO.

Department of the Environment for Northern Ireland (1992) *Housing Statistics 1991*, Belfast: HMSO.

Diacon, D. (1991) *Deterioration of the public sector housing stock*, Aldershot: Avebury.

DoE (Department of the Environment) (1988) *English House Condition Survey 1986*, London: HMSO.

DoE (1993) *English House Condition Survey 1991*, London: HMSO.

DoE (1995) *Energy efficiency in council housing: Strategic guide: Condition of the stock*, London: DoE.

DoE (1996) *English House Condition Survey 1991, Energy Report*, London: HMSO.

DoE (1998) *English House Condition Survey 1996*, London: HMSO.

DoE (unpublished) 'Data on age of stock and poor housing conditions by local authority district', Mimeo.

DoE and Welsh Office (various years) *Local Housing Statistics England and Wales*, London: HMSO.

DoE, Scottish Development Department and Welsh Office (various years) *Housing and Construction Statistics Great Britain*, (see especially the annual publication covering the previous decade), London: HMSO.

Dunster J. et al (1994) *Domestic energy fact file: Owner occupied homes, local authority homes, private rented homes*, Watford: Building Research Institute.

European Commission (1996) *Statistics on Housing in the European Community*, Brussels: European Commission.

Laing and Buisson Ltd (1993) *Care of elderly people: Market survey 1992/93*, London: Laing and Buisson Publications Ltd.

Leather, P. (1995) 'Performance of Welsh Care and Repair projects, 1994/95', Mimeo.

Leather, P. (2000) *Crumbling castles? Helping owners to repair and maintain their homes*, York: Joseph Rowntree Foundation.

Leather, P. and Morrison, T. (1997) *The state of UK housing: A factfile on dwelling conditions*, Bristol/York: The Policy Press/Joseph Rowntree Foundation.

Leather, P. and Mackintosh, S. (1992) *Maintaining home ownership: The agency approach*, London: Longman/Institute of Housing.

Murtagh, B. and McPeake, J. (1990) *Dwelling conditions and household characteristics: A follow up to the 1987 House Condition Survey*, Occasional Papers in Housing Research, Belfast: NIHE.

NIHE (Northern Ireland Housing Executive) (1998) *1996 Northern Ireland House Condition Survey*, Belfast: NIHE.

OPCS (Office of Population Censuses and Surveys) (1992) *1991 Census County Monitors*, London: OPCS.

OPCS (1994) *1993 General Household Survey*, London: HMSO.

OPCS (1996) *1995 General Household Survey*, London: HMSO.

Robertson, D. and Bailey, N. (1996) *Review of the impact of housing action areas*, Edinburgh: Scottish Homes.

Scottish Homes (1996) *Scottish House Condition Survey 1996*, Edinburgh: Scottish Homes.

Scottish Office (various years) *Scottish Abstract of Statistics*, Edinburgh: Scottish Office.

Scottish Office (various years) Statistical Bulletin, Housing Series, Edinburgh: HMSO.

Thomas, A. (1985) *Housing and urban renewal*, London: Allen and Unwin.

Welsh Office (1994) *1993 Welsh House Condition Survey*, Cardiff: Welsh Office.

Welsh Office (various years) *Welsh Housing Statistics*, Cardiff: Welsh Office.

Welsh Office (1999) *1998 Welsh House Condition Survey, Preliminary Tables*, Cardiff: Welsh Office.

Wilcox, S. (1995) *Housing finance review 1994/95*, York: Joseph Rowntree Foundation.

Wilcox, S. (1999) *Housing finance review 1999/2000*, York: Joseph Rowntree Foundation.

Appendix A: Detailed tables

Table A3.1: Average repair costs, UK (England, Northern Ireland and Scotland 1996, Wales 1993)

	Urgent repairs (£)		General repairs (£)		Comprehensive repairs (£)		Repair costs for unfit/ BTS dwellings (£)	
	Occupied	Vacant	Occupied	Vacant	Occupied	Vacant	Occupied	Vacant
England	1,280	3,841	1,830	4,854	3,420	6,762	5,233*	10,777
N Ireland	1,006	6,996	1,599	8,522	na	na	na	na
Wales	na	na	na	na	953	na	4,470§	na
Scotland	220	na	782	na	2,597	na	1,350†	na

* Mean general repair cost for unfit dwellings; † Mean cost of repairs to BTS dwellings; ‡ Mean total cost to make fit; § Mean repair cost for unfit dwellings; ¶ Total repair costs.
Note: Definitional and other problems preclude most comparisons between countries – see notes to Table 3.1.

Table A3.2: Unfitness by urban–rural location, UK

			Urban	Rural	Total	% urban
England (1996)*	Occupied	% unfit	6.7	3.7		
		Unfit 000s	1,103	148	1,251	88
	All dwellings	% unfit	7.8	4.9		
		Unfit 000s	1,277	195	1,472	
Northern Ireland (1996)†	Occupied	% unfit	4	7.9		
		Unfit 000s	15.989	15.786	31.775	50
	All dwellings	% unfit	5.2	11.6	7.3	
		Unfit 000s	20.951	23.200	44.151	
Wales (1993)*		% Unfit	13.3	13.1		
		Unfit 000s	124	27	151	82
Scotland (1996)*		% BTS	0.8	1.8		
		BTS 000s	14	7	21	66

* Occupied dwellings only; † Rural includes isolated rural dwellings and dwellings in small settlements.
Sources: 1991 EHCS, 1996 SHCS, 1996 NIHCS: analysis of data; 1993 WHCS: special tabulations

Table A4.1: Age of dwelling stock

	Pre-1919	1919-44	1945-64	1965+	Total stock
	Number of dwellings (000s)				
England	4,752	3,900	4,244	7,439	20,335
Northern Ireland	121	70	129	284	602
Wales	368	157	244	361	1,132
Scotland	456	318	590	759	2,123
Great Britain	5,576	4,375	5,078	8,559	23,590
United Kingdom	5,697	4,445	5,207	8,843	24,192
	% of dwellings				
England	23.4	19.2	20.9	36.6	100
Northern Ireland	20.0	11.5	21.4	47.2	100
Wales	32.5	13.9	21.6	31.9	100
Scotland	21.5	15.0	27.8	35.8	100
Great Britain	23.6	18.5	21.5	36.3	100
United Kingdom	23.5	18.4	21.5	36.6	100

Notes: Figures for England, Scotland and Northern Ireland are for 1996, figures for Wales are for 1993; Table includes vacant dwellings, except in Wales.
Sources: DoE (1996); Scottish Homes (1996); NIHE (1996); Welsh Office (1994)

Table A4.2: Type of dwelling stock

	Detached house	Semi-detached house	Terraced house	Purpose built flat	Converted flat	All dwellings
	Number of dwellings (000s)					
England	4,165	6,053	6,204	3,025	880	20,327
Northern Ireland	189	141	222	41	9	602
Wales	267	367	385	83	29	1,131
Scotland	367	450	500	767	39	2,123
Great Britain	4,799	6,870	7,089	3,875	948	23,581
United Kingdom	4,988	7,011	7,311	3,916	957	24,183
	% of dwellings					
England	20.5	29.8	30.5	14.9	4.3	100
Northern Ireland	31.4	23.4	36.9	6.8	1.5	100
Wales	23.6	32.4	34.1	7.3	2.5	100
Scotland	17.3	21.2	23.6	36.1	1.8	100
Great Britain	20.4	29.1	30.1	16.4	4.0	100
United Kingdom	20.6	29.0	30.2	16.2	4.0	100

Notes: Figures for England, Scotland and Northern Ireland are for 1991, figures for Wales are for 1993; Table includes vacant dwellings, except in Wales.
Sources: DoE (1996); Scottish Homes (1996); NIHE (1996); Welsh Office (1994)

Table A4.3: Age and type of dwelling stock (% of whole stock)

	Pre-1919	1919–44	1945–64	Post-1964	All ages
England					
Terraced house	12.5	5.3	4.2	8.5	30.5
Semi-detched house	3.5	9.4	9.1	7.8	29.8
Detached house	2.9	2.9	3.5	11.2	20.5
Converted flat	3.8	0.3	0.0	0.2	4.3
Purpose-built flat	0.7	1.3	4.1	8.8	14.9
All types	23.4	19.2	20.9	36.5	100.0
Northern Ireland					
Terraced house	6.8	4.6	8.3	17.3	37.0
Semi-detached house	1.9	3.2	7.0	11.2	23.3
Detached house	10.3	3.5	4.3	13.3	31.4
Converted flat	1.0	0.2	0.2	0.1	1.5
Purpose-built flat	0.0	0.0	1.6	5.2	6.8
All types	20.0	11.5	21.4	47.1	100.0
Wales					
Terraced house	18.6	2.4	4.5	6.4	31.9
Semi-detached house	4.1	7.6	11.6	9.2	32.5
Detached house	6.5	2.4	3.2	11.5	23.6
Converted flat	1.8	0.4	0.2	0.2	2.6
Purpose-built flat	0.2	0.4	2.1	4.8	7.5
All types	31.2	13.2	21.6	32.1	100.0
Scotland					
Terraced house	2.7	1.6	8.9	10.3	23.6
Semi-detached house	2.6	3.6	7.2	7.7	21.2
Detached house	4.7	1.9	1.8	8.8	17.3
Converted flat	1.6	0.1	0.1	0.0	1.8
Purpose-built flat					
Tenement	8.6	2.3	6.0	6.1	22.9
Four in block	1.2	5.4	2.7	1.2	10.5
Tower/deck	0.0	0.0	1.1	1.5	2.7
All types	21.5	15.0	27.8	35.7	100.0
Great Britain					
Terraced house	11.9	4.8	4.6	8.6	29.9
Semi-detached house	3.4	9.5	9.3	6.5	29.1
Detached house	3.2	2.8	3.3	9.6	20.3
Converted flat	3.5	0.3	0.2	0.5	4.0
Purpose-built flat	1.5	2.1	4.4	7.9	16.5
All types	23.6	18.5	21.6	36.2	100.0
United Kingdom					
Terraced house	11.8	4.8	4.7	8.8	30.0
Semi-detached house	3.4	8.7	9.0	7.9	29.0
Detached house	3.4	2.8	3.4	11.1	20.6
Converted flat	3.4	0.3	0.0	0.2	3.9
Purpose-built flat	1.5	1.8	4.4	8.5	16.2
All types	23.5	18.4	21.6	36.5	100.0

Notes: Figures for England, Scotland and Northern Ireland are for 1991, figures for Wales are for 1993. Table includes vacant dwellings, except in Wales.

Sources: DoE (1996); Scottish Homes (1996); NIHE (1996); Welsh Office (1994)

Table A4.4: Dwellings in poor condition by age

			Pre-1919	1919–44	1945–64	Post-1964	All ages
England 1996							
Unfit	All	Number (000)	715	377	216	163	1,471
		%	15.1	9.7	5.1	2.2	
	Occupied	Number (000)	595	329	176	151	1,251
		%	12.5	8.4	4.2	2.0	
Urgent repairs over £1,000	All	Number (000)	2,606	1,575	1,222	993	6,396
		%	54.8	40.4	28.8	13.3	
	Occupied	Number (000)	2,397	1,465	1,153	957	5,972
		%	54.4	37.6	27.2	12.9	
Northern Ireland 1996							
Unfit	All	Number (000)	25	8	7	4	44
		%	20.6	12.1	5.4	1.4	
	Occupied	Number (000)	17	6.2	6	3	32
		%	14	9	4.4	1	
Urgent repairs over £1,000	All	Number (000)	56	24	29	31	140
		%	46.9	35.1	22.2	10.9	
	Occupied	Number (000)	47	21	25	29	122
		%	39	31	19	10	
Wales 1993 (occupied dwellings only)							
Unfit	Occupied	Number (000)	75	27	28	22	152
		%	20.3	16.9	11.6	6.0	
Repairs over £1,500	Occupied	Number (000)	125	37	45	24	231
		%	33.8	23.4	18.2	6.8	
Scotland 1996							
Below tolerable standard	Occupied	Number (000)	15	2.6	2	0.9	21
		%	3.3	0.8	0.3	0.1	
Urgent repairs over £1,000	Occupied	Number (000)	66	20	17	10	113
		%	14.4	6.4	2.8	1.3	

Sources: DoE (1996); Scottish Homes (1996); NIHE (1996); Welsh Office (1994)

Table A4.5: Poor condition dwellings by age (%)

	Pre-1919	1919-44	1945-64	Post-1964
Unfit/BTS				
England	48.6	25.6	14.7	11.1
Northern Ireland	56.4	19.0	15.7	8.9
Wales	54.4	15.9	19.0	10.7
Scotland	73.2	12.8	9.7	4.3
Disrepair				
England	40.8	24.6	19.1	15.5
Northern Ireland	40.3	17.3	20.4	21.9
Wales	54.2	16.1	19.8	9.9
Scotland	55.2	22.3	13.6	8.9

Notes: Figures for England, Scotland and Northern Ireland are for 1996, figures for Welsh disrepair are for 1993, Welsh unfitness are for 1998. Data available for occupied stock only in Wales and Scotland.
Sources: DoE (1996); Scottish Homes (1996); NIHE (1996); Welsh Office (1994)

Table A4.6: Dwellings in poor condition by type

		Terraced house	Semi-detached house	Detached house	Converted flat	Purpose-built flat	All types
England 1996							
Unfit	Number (000)	668	327	127	142	209	1,473
	%	10.8	5.4	3.0	16.1	6.9	7.2
Urgent repairs	Number (000)	2,422	1,788	1,055	447	679	6,391
over £1,000	%	39.0	29.5	25.3	50.8	22.4	31.4
Northern Ireland 1996							
Unfit	Number (000)	15	6	21	1	1	44
	%	6.2	4.6	11.0	17.0	2.3	7.3
Urgent repairs	Number (000)	46	24	63	3	4	140
over £1,000	%	20.1	17.2	33.7	31.1	10.2	23.3
Wales 1993 (occupied dwellings only)							
Unfit	Number (000)	46	45	23	14		98
	%	11.4	6.8	6.1	16.9	7.3	8.5
Repairs over	Number (000)	100	69	50	11		230
£1,500	%	37.4	18.8	13.0	9.8		20.3
Scotland 1996 (occupied dwellings only)							
Below tolerable	Number (000)	2	3	5	2	9	21
standard	%	0.4	0.7	1.2	5.0	1.2	0.1
Urgent repairs	Number (000)	15	19	30	6	43	113
over £1,000	%	3.1	4.1	8.3	14.9	5.6	5.3

Notes: Figures for England, Scotland and Northern Ireland are for 1996, unfit figures for Wales use 1999 preliminary data, urgent repairs are for 1993. Data available for occupied stock only in Wales and Scotland.
Sources: DoE (1996); Scottish Homes (1996); NIHE (1996); Welsh Office (1994)

Table A4.7: Poor condition dwellings by type (%)

	Terraced house	Semi-detached house	Detached house	Converted flat	Purpose-built flat
Unfit/BTS					
England	45.4	22.2	8.6	9.6	14.2
Northern Ireland	32.1	17.3	45.7	2.0	3.0
Wales	47.5	27.3	16.5	2.6	6.1
Scotland	8.8	14.4	21.5	9.5	45.8
Disrepair					
England	37.9	28.0	16.5	7.0	10.6
Northern Ireland	31.8	14.8	47.8	3.4	2.2
Wales	43.5	30.0	21.7	4.8	
Scotland	13.7	16.4	26.9	5.1	37.9

Notes: Figures for England, Scotland and Northern Ireland are for 1996, unfit figures for Wales uses 1999 preliminary data, repairs use 1993. Data available for occupied stock only in Wales and Scotland.
Sources: DoE (1996); Scottish Homes (1996); NIHE (1996); Welsh Office (1994)

Table A4.8: Unfitness/BTS by age and type of dwelling stock in combination (% of whole stock)

	Pre-1919	1919–44	1945–64	Post-1964	All ages
England					
Terraced house	29.5	10.6	2.4	2.9	45.4
Semi-detached house	4.5	9.6	6.5	1.6	22.2
Detached house	3.3	2.8	0.9	1.6	8.6
Converted flat	9.2	0.4	0.0	0.0	9.6
Purpose-built flat	2.1	2.1	5.0	5.0	14.2
All types	48.6	25.5	14.8	11.1	100.0
Northern Ireland					
Terraced house	17.3	7.4	3.8	3.3	31.8
Semi-detached house	4.1	3.4	6.0	1.3	14.8
Detached house	32.3	8.1	4.8	2.6	47.8
Converted flat	2.6	0.4	0.5	0.0	3.5
Purpose-built flat	0.0	0.0	0.9	1.3	2.2
All types	56.3	19.2	16.0	8.5	100.0
Wales					
Terraced house	32.9	5.5	3.5	3.4	45.3
Semi-detached house	4.9	8.0	11.4	5.6	29.8
Detached house	8.0	1.9	1.9	3.6	15.3
Flat	3.7	2.2	2.0	1.6	9.5
All types	49.5	17.6	18.7	14.2	100.0
Scotland					
Terraced house	0.6	0.1	0.1	0.1	12.7
Semi-detached house	0.4	0.2	0.1	0.0	12.2
Detached house	0.6	0.3	0.1	0.0	22.1
Converted flat	0.4	4.3	0.0	3.1	7.5
Purpose-built flat					
Tenement	1.5	0.2	0.1	0.0	39.9
Four in block	0.1	0.1	0.0	0.0	5.5
Tower/deck	0.0	0.4	0.0	0.0	0.1
All types	73.2	12.8	9.7	4.3	100.0
Great Britain					
Terraced house	29.0	10.2	2.4	2.9	44.4
Semi-detached house	4.4	9.3	6.5	1.7	22.0
Detached house	3.4	2.7	0.9	1.6	8.7
Flat	10.8	2.5	4.8	4.8	23.0
All types	47.6	24.8	14.6	11.0	98.0
UK					
Terraced house	28.8	10.1	2.4	2.9	44.2
Semi-detached house	4.4	9.3	6.5	1.7	21.9
Detached house	3.8	2.8	1.0	1.7	9.2
Flat	10.7	2.5	4.7	4.8	22.7
All types	47.7	24.7	14.6	11.0	98.0

Notes: Figures for England, Scotland and Northern Ireland are for 1996, figures for Wales are for 1993. Table includes vacant dwellings in England and Northern Ireland. Converted flats includes dwellings with mixed residential/non-residential uses. Data on converted and purpose-built flats not available separately for Wales.
Sources: DoE (1996); Scottish Homes (1996); NIHE (1996); Welsh Office (1994)

Table A4.9: Tenure by country, UK (1998)

	Owner-occupied	Privately rented	Rented from LA	Rented from HA	All dwellings
	No of dwellings (000s)				
England	14,033	2,304	3,353	1,008	20,698
Northern Ireland	412	25	135	15	587
Wales	828	81	248		1,157
Scotland	1,365	155	632	116	2,268
Great Britain	16,290	2,565	4,188	1,173	24,216
UK	16,702	2,590	4,323	1,188	24,803
	% of dwellings				
England	67.8	11.1	16.2	4.9	
Northern Ireland	70.2	4.3	23.0	2.6	
Wales	71.6	7.0	21.4		
Scotland	60.2	6.8	27.9	5.1	
Great Britain	67.3	10.6	17.3	4.8	
UK	67.3	10.4	17.4	4.8	

Note: Increase in private owned stock in Northern Ireland from 1993-94 of 13,000 apportioned pro rata between owner-occupation and private renting.
Sources: DoE (1998); Scottish Homes (1998); NIHE (1998); Welsh Office (1999)

Table A4.10: Age of dwellings by tenure, Great Britain (1996)

	Pre-1919	1919-44	1945-64	1965 or later	All ages
	% in each age group by tenure				
Owned outright	21	23	25	31	
With mortgage	20	21	18	41	
Local authority rented	3	18	41	38	
Housing association rented	17	11	9	63	
Privately rented	42	21	13	24	
All dwellings	20	20	23	37	
	% in each tenure by age group				
Owned outright	28	29	28	21	26
With mortgage	44	44	33	47	42
Local authority rented	3	16	32	19	19
Housing association rented	4	2	2	8	5
Privately rented	21	9	5	6	9

Source: OPCS (1996)

Table A4.11: Tenure by dwelling type, Great Britain (1996)

	Detached house	Semi-detached house	Terraced house	Purpose-built flat	Converted flat*	All types
	% in each type category by tenure					
Owned outright	33	37	22	6	2	
With mortgage	26	36	29	6	3	
Local authority rented	1	28	31	38	2	
Housing association rented	1	18	31	40	10	
Privately rented	13	19	28	16	24	
All tenures	21	32	27	15	5	
	% in each tenure by type					
Owned outright	41	29	20	11	11	25
With mortgage	52	47	44	17	26	42
Local authority rented	1	17	22	49	8	19
Housing association rented	0	2	5	13	10	5
Privately rented	6	5	9	10	45	9

* Including with business premises.
Source: OPCS (1996)

Table A4.12: Dwellings in poor condition by tenure

		Owner-occupied	Privately rented	LA rented	HA rented
England 1996		14,033	2,304	3,353	1,008
Unfit	Number (000s)	726	263	227	35
	%	5.4	15.1	6.8	3.9
Urgent repairs over £1,000	Number (000s)	3,978	940	931	124
	%	29.3	53.9	28	13.8
Northern Ireland 1996					
Unfit	Number (000s)	22	5	3	3
	%	5.9	16.3	2.4	2
Urgent repairs over £1,000	Number (000s)	91	14	16	0.5
	%	23.7	42.2	11.1	3.4
Wales 1999/93					
Unfit	Number (000s)	63	15	20	
	%	7.6	18.4	8.2	
Repairs over £1,500	Number (000s)	156	29	42	2
	%	19.9	34.3	18.7	8.4
Scotland 1996					
Below tolerable standard	Number (000s)	11	7	3	0.2
	%	0.9	4.1	0.5	0.2
Urgent repairs over £1,000	Number (000s)	62	27	22	1
	%	5.2	16.7	3.3	1.2

Notes: Figures for England, Scotland and Northern Ireland are for 1996, unfit figures for Wales are for 1999, repair figures are for 1993. Excludes vacant dwellings.
Sources: DoE (1996); Scottish Homes (1996); NIHE (1996); Welsh Office (1994)

Table A4.13: Poor condition dwellings by tenure (% dwellings in each country)

	Owner-occupied	Privately rented	LA rented	HA rented
Unfit/BTS				
England	58.0	21.0	18.2	2.8
Northern Ireland	70.7	17.8	10.7	0.8
Wales	64.2	15.1	20.7	
Scotland	51.9	32.3	14.8	1.0
Disrepair				
England	66.6	15.7	15.6	2.1
Northern Ireland	74.0	12.6	13.0	0.4
Wales	67.9	12.8	18.3	1.0
Scotland	56.5	6.7	32.5	4.3

Notes: Figures for England, Scotland and Northern Ireland are for 1996, unfit figures for Wales are for 1999, repair figures are for 1993. Excludes vacant dwellings.
Sources: DoE (1996); Scottish Homes (1996); NIHE (1996); Welsh Office (1994)

Table A4.14: Unfitness/BTS by age and tenure of dwelling (% of total dwelling stock)

	Owner–occupied	Privately rented	LA rented	HA rented	All tenures
England					
Pre-1919	29.5	14.3	1.2	1.5	46.5
1919-44	16.1	2.5	7.1	0.6	26.3
1945 -64	5.4	1.1	7.3	0.3	14.1
Post-1964	5.9	3.1	2.6	0.4	12.0
All vacant	0.5	0.4	0.1	0.1	1.1
All	57.4	21.4	18.3	2.9	100.0
Northern Ireland					
Pre-1919	29.5	7.3	1.2	0.3	38.3
1919-44	9.3	3.4	1.3	0.1	14.1
1945-64	9.5	0.9	2.5	0.0	12.9
Post-1964	2.7	1.1	2.7	0.1	6.6
All vacant	19.7	5.1	3.0	0.3	28.1
All	70.7	17.8	10.7	0.8	100.0
Wales					
Pre-1919	37.6	9.7	1.6	0.6	49.5
1919-44	9.1	1.3	6.7	0.6	17.7
Post-1945	15.0	0.9	16.8	0.2	32.9
All	61.7	11.9	25.1	1.4	100.1
Scotland					
Pre-1919	40.9	28.9	3.4	0.1	73.2
1919-44	7.2	2.0	3.6	0.0	12.8
1945-64	1.6	1.4	0.5	0.5	9.7
Post-1964	2.3	0.0	1.6	0.4	4.3
All	51.9	32.3	14.8	1.0	100.0

Notes: Figures for England, Scotland and Northern Ireland are for 1996, figures for Wales are for 1993. Excludes vacant dwellings.

Sources: DoE (1996); Scottish Homes (1996); NIHE (1996); Welsh Office (1994)

Table A4.15: Disrepair by age and tenure of dwelling (% of total dwelling stock)

	Owner-occupied	Privately rented	LA rented	HA rented	All tenures
England					
Pre-1919	26.7	10.6	0.8	0.8	38.9
1919–44	17.4	2.6	4.3	0.3	24.6
1945–64	10.5	1.1	7.3	0.4	19.3
Post-1964	10.8	1.5	3.1	0.6	16.0
All vacant	0.1	0.7	0.3	0.1	1.2
All	65.5	16.5	15.8	2.2	100.0
Northern Ireland					
Pre-1919	26.7	5.8	0.7	0.2	33.4
1919–44	11.8	2.7	0.6	0.1	15.2
1945–64	12.3	1.5	4.1	0.0	17.9
Post-1964	13.6	1.2	5.9	0.1	20.8
All vacant	9.6	1.4	1.7		12.7
All	74.0	12.6	13.0	0.4	100.0
Wales					
Pre-1919	42.1	10.4	1.0	0.5	54.0
1919–44	10.5	1.5	3.5	0.5	16.0
Post-1945	15.2	0.9	13.8	0.0	29.9
All	67.8	12.8	18.3	1.0	99.9
Scotland					
Pre-1919	13.7	3.6	1.0	1.0	19.3
1919–44	7.6	0.7	6.4	0.2	14.9
1945–64	11.6	0.9	15.4	0.6	28.5
Post-1964	23.6	1.5	9.7	2.5	37.3
All	56.5	6.7	32.5	4.3	100.0

Notes: Figures for England, Scotland and Northern Ireland are for 1996, figures for Wales are for 1993. Excludes vacant dwellings.

Sources: DoE (1996); Scottish Homes (1996); NIHE (1996); Welsh Office (1994)

Table A5.1: Poor conditions by income

Income band	In unfit/BTS dwellings		With urgent repair costs over £1,000*		All households
	(000s)	(%)	(000s)	(%)	(000s)
England					
Under £4,000	80	11.5	317	24.3	854
£4,000-7,999	420	9.4	1,591	20.6	4,886
£8,000-11,999	283	7.5	1,232	20.9	3,678
£12,000-15,999	193	5.0	947	16.3	3,109
£16,000-19,999	86	4.5	617	16.7	2,196
£20,000-23,999	80	4.3	519	11.8	1,785
£24,000 or more	131	2.8	853	16.8	3,136
Northern Ireland					
Under £4,000	11	10.5	28	26.9	104
£4,000-6,999	9	6.3	31	22.0	140
£7,000-9,999	4	5.3	13	17.7	76
£10,000-14,999	4	4.8	19	21.4	87
£15,000-19,999	2	2.3	14	21.0	65
£20,000-29,999	1	2.5	10	17.8	55
£30,000 or more	1	1.9	8	17.1	45
Scotland					
Under £4,000	10	1.0	51	4.9	1,057
£4,000-7,999	2	0.8	15	7.3	198
£8,000-11,999	4	1.1	19	5.3	361
£12,000-15,999	2	0.8	11	4.8	225
£16,000-19,999	1	0.9	6	5.0	112
£20,000-23,999	1	0.3	4	5.5	67
£24,000 or more	1	1.3	7	7.4	101
Wales*					
Under £4,000	30	19.4	42	27.3	153
£4,000-7,999	33	15.0	43	19.5	219
£8,000-11,999	11	11.2	19	20.9	94
£12,000-19,999	12	10.1	21	18.4	115
£20,000-29,999	4	7.7	11	20.6	54
£30,000 or more	3	6.6	6	13.9	41

* Repair costs over £1,500 for Wales.

Notes: Figures for England, Scotland and Northern Ireland are for 1996, figures for Wales are for 1993.

Sources: DoE (1993); Scottish Homes (1996); NIHE (1993); Welsh Office (1994)

Table A5.2: Incomes of households living in poor conditions (% of households by income)

	Under £4,000	£4,000– 7,999	£8,000– 11,999	£12,000 –15,999	£16,000– 19,999	£20,000– 23,999	£24,000 or more
Unfit/BTS							
England	6.3	33.0	22.2	15.2	6.7	6.3	10.3
Northern Ireland*	34.5	27.9	12.7	13.0	4.8	4.4	2.7
Wales†	32.3	35.5	11.8	12.9	4.3	3.2	0.0
Scotland	50.6	8.0	20.2	8.7	5.2	1.0	6.4
In disrepair‡							
England	5.2	26.2	20.3	15.6	10.1	8.5	14.0
Northern Ireland*	22.9	25.2	11.0	15.2	11.2	8.1	6.3
Wales†	29.6	30.3	13.4	14.8	7.7	4.2	0.0
Scotland	45.6	12.9	16.9	9.6	5.0	3.3	6.6

* Income bands for Northern Ireland differ slightly from those for the remainder of the UK – see Table A5.1;
† Income bands for Wales differ – see Table A5.1; ‡ For definition of disrepair see Table A5.1.
Notes: Figures for England, Scotland and Northern Ireland are for 1996, figures for Wales are for 1993.
Sources: DoE (1996); Scottish Homes (1996); NIHE (1996); Welsh Office (1994)

Table A5.3: Poor conditions by employment status

Employment status	% in unfit/BTS dwellings	% in dwellings with urgent repair costs over £1,000*
England		
Working	5.5	31.8
Unemployed	11.6	40.0
Retired	6.4	24.4
Other	8.9	38.1
Northern Ireland		
Working	4.0	19.9
Unemployed	5.7	22.5
Retired	8.3	23.7
Other	4.7	12.6
Wales		
Working	10.4	19.2
Unemployed	Unavailable	17.7
Retired		21.7
Other	na	
Scotland		
Working	0.9	5.9
Unemployed	1.1	7.2
Retired	0.8	3.8
Other	1.4	5.3

* Repair costs over £1,500 for Wales.
Notes: Figures for England, Scotland and Northern Ireland are for 1996, figures for Wales are for 1986.
Sources: DoE (1996); Scottish Homes (1996); NIHE (1996); Welsh Office (1994)

Table A5.4: Households living in poor conditions by type

Household type	% in unfit dwellings	% in dwellings with urgent repair costs over £1,000*
England		
Lone adult under 65/60	7.6	36.2
Two adults	5.8	29.1
Lone parent	11.4	40.7
Family (small and large)	5.1	31.3
3+ adults	8.7	42.6
Two pensioners	3.8	23.6
One pensioner	8.3	26.6
Northern Ireland		
Lone adult under 65/60	8.6	23.4
Two adults	3.3	17.1
Lone parent	3.9	15.6
Small family	2.6	19.0
Large family	2.3	18.9
3+ adults	4.3	23.7
Two pensioners	7.5	13.5
One pensioner	10.5	14.6
Wales		
Lone adult under 65/60	14.0	21.0
Two adults	11.3	19.7
Lone parent	14.0	23.2
Small family	12.8	20.4
Large family	14.9	22.8
3+ adults	13.9	19.3
Two pensioners	11.5	16.8
One pensioner	15.9	21.5
Scotland		
Lone adult under 65/60	1.5	6.2
Two adults	1.1	5.2
Lone parent	0.8	6.2
Small family	0.5	5.2
Large family	0.6	6.4
3+ adults	1.3	6.1
Two pensioners	1.0	3.9
One pensioner	0.8	4.2

* Repair costs over £1,500 for Wales.

Notes: Figures for England, Scotland and Northern Ireland are for 1996, figures for Wales are for 1993.

Sources: DoE (1996); Scottish Homes (1996); NIHE (1996); Welsh Office (1994)

Table A5.5: Households living in poor conditions by age of household head

Age of household head	% in unfit dwellings	% in dwellings with urgent repair costs over £1,000*
England		
16–29	9.3	41.3
30–44	6.4	32.8
45–59	5.5	30.4
60–74	5.3	24.3
75+	8.0	27.7
Northern Ireland		
16–29	17.1	33.8
30–44	3.2	17.1
45–59/64	4.9	21.9
60/65–74	6.4	22.0
75+	12.8	31.5
Wales		
16–29	15.3	22.3
30–44	12.7	19.5
45–59/64	11.7	18.8
60/65–74	13.4	14.8
75+	16.7	20.8
Scotland		
16–29	1.4	7.0
30–44	0.8	6.2
45–59/64	0.9	4.7
60/65–74	0.9	4.6
75+	1.1	4.1

Notes: Figures for England, Scotland and Northern Ireland are for 1996, figures for Wales are for 1993.
Sources: DoE (1996); Scottish Homes (1996); NIHE (1996); Welsh Office (1994)

Table A5.6: Households in unfit housing by age and gender, England (1996)

Age of household head	Male-headed households			Female-headed households			Balance (F–M)
	In fit dwellings	In unfit dwellings	% in unfit dwellings	In fit dwellings	In unfit dwellings	% in unfit dwellings	
15–19	73	6	8.2	62	6	9.0	0.8
20–24	488	63	11.4	329	37	10.0	-1.4
25–29	1,334	122	8.4	332	38	10.4	2.0
30–34	1,625	69	4.1	380	42	10.0	5.9
35–39	1,425	97	6.4	323	38	10.5	4.1
40–44	1,351	85	5.9	259	21	7.6	1.7
45–49	1,577	82	4.9	274	21	7.2	2.3
50–54	1,111	72	6.1	239	22	8.4	2.3
55–59	1,052	54	4.9	312	17	5.2	0.3
60–64	1,071	36	3.2	347	21	5.8	2.6
65–69	969	58	5.7	411	21	4.9	-0.8
70–74	810	49	5.7	501	44	8.2	2.5
75–79	511	37	6.7	379	21	5.3	-1.4
80–84	256	26	9.3	299	35	10.4	1.1
85 and over	96	10	9.9	174	20	10.5	0.6
All	13,749	866	5.9	4,621	404	8.1	2.2
15–29	1,895	191	9.2	723	81	10.1	0.9
30–44	4,401	251	5.4	962	101	9.5	4.1
45–59	3,740	208	5.3	825	60	6.8	1.5
60–74	2,850	143	4.8	1,259	86	6.4	1.6
75+	863	73	7.8	852	76	8.2	0.4
All	13,749	866	5.9	4,621	404	8.1	2.2

Source: EHCS (1996)

Table A5.7: Households living in poor conditions by length of residence (1996)

Length of residence of household	% in unfit dwellings	% in dwellings with urgent repair costs over £1,000
England		
Up to 2 years	7.4	33.1
2–4 years	5.4	28.1
5–9 years	5.5	29.0
10–19 years	4.8	28.3
20 years +	8.5	34.2 ·
Northern Ireland		
Up to 2 years	4.5	16.8
2–4 years	3.0	15.4
5–9 years	2.6	15.9
10–19 years	3.0	17.3
20 years +	10.3	31.5
Scotland		
Up to 2 years	1.3	6.0
2–4 years	0.8	5.2
5–9 years	0.7	5.0
10–19 years	0.8	5.2
20 years +	1.2	5.2

Notes: Figures for England, Scotland and Northern Ireland are for 1996.
Sources: DoE (1996); Scottish Homes (1996); NIHE (1996); Welsh Office (1994)

Table A5.8: Households in unfit housing by length of residence by tenure, England (1996) (% households living in unfit dwellings)

Length of residence	Owner-occupied	Privately rented	Local authority rented	Housing association rented
Under 1 year	4.7	13.8	7.6	2.9
1–2 years	4.7	20.8	4.8	0.5
3–4 years	4.7	10.9	6.6	2.6
5–10 years	5.3	10.8	5.1	5.5
11–15 years	4.1	15.8	5.4	6.8
16–20 years	3.5	1.8	8.1	5.7
21–30 years	4.7	26.9	7.9	2.2
Over 30 years	11.9	32.6	9.6	5.9
All	5.4	15.1	6.8	3.8
In unfit dwelling (000s)	736	274	227	35
All owners (000s)	13,581	1,817	3,340	905

Source: EHCS (1996)

Table A5.9: Households living in poor conditions by ethnic origin of household head (1991)

Ethnic origin of household head	% in unfit dwellings	% in dwellings with urgent repair costs over £1,000
England		
White	6.1	29.5
Black	7.8	30.6
Asian	12.5	45.6
Other	15.2	44.8
Scotland		
White	1.0	5.3
Black	–	7.8
Asian	2.2	13.4
Other	–	6.6

Note: data on ethnic origin not available for Wales and Northern Ireland.
Sources: DoE (1996); Scottish Homes (1996)

Table A5.10: Households living in unfit/BTS housing by income and tenure (% of all households in unfit/BTS dwellings)

Income	Owner-occupied	Privately rented	LA rented	HA rented	All tenures
England					
Under £8,000	15.3	7.0	15.3	5.4	43.0
£8,000-£15,999	16.7	6.6	10.4	3.3	37.0
£16,000 or more	14.7	2.6	1.8	1.1	20.2
All households	46.7	16.2	27.5	9.8	100.2
Northern Ireland					
Under £7,000	38.4	14.4	9.0	0.6	62.4
£7,000-£19,999	25.4	3.3	1.6	0.2	30.5
£20,000 or more	7.0	0.1	0.0	0.0	7.1
All households	70.8	17.8	10.6	0.8	100.0
Wales					
Under £8,000	33.0	8.8	25.3	1.3	68.4
£8,000-£19,999	17.6	2.8	3.3	0.4	24.1
£20,000 or more	6.0	0.2	1.4	0.0	7.6
All households	56.6	11.8	30.0	1.7	100.1
Scotland					
Under £8,000	26.9	22.7	8.0	1.0	58.6
£8,000-£15,999	17.5	5.3	6.0	0.0	28.8
£16,000 or more	7.5	4.3	0.8	0.0	12.6
All households	51.9	32.3	14.8	1.0	100.0

Notes: Figures for England, Scotland and Northern Ireland are for 1996, figures for Wales are for 1993. Income bands differ slightly for Wales and Northern Ireland reflecting availability of data. Percentage totals may not add due to rounding.

Sources: DoE (1996); Scottish Homes (1996); NIHE (1996); Welsh Office (1994)

Table A5.11: Households living in housing in disrepair by income and tenure (% of all households in dwellings in disrepair)

Income	Owner-occupied	Privately rented	LA rented	HA rented	All tenures
England					
Under £8,000	11.9	5.5	13.3	4.3	35.0
£8,000-£15,999	19.4	4.5	9.4	3.8	37.1
£16,000 or more	23.3	2.4	1.5	0.7	27.9
All households	54.6	12.4	24.2	8.8	100.0
Northern Ireland					
Under £7,000	29.5	8.8	9.7	0.3	48.3
£7,000-£19,999	30.7	3.5	3.1	0.0	37.3
£20,000 or more	13.9	0.5	0.1	0.0	14.5
All households	74.1	12.8	12.9	0.3	100.1
Wales					
Under £8,000	30.7	8.3	19.3	1.2	59.5
£8,000-£19,999	21.6	3.7	3.0	0.3	28.6
£20,000 or more	10.2	0.8	0.8	0.0	11.8
All households	62.5	12.8	23.1	1.5	99.9
Scotland					
Under £8,000	25.9	16.0	15.9	0.8	58.6
£8,000-£15,999	18.5	4.9	3.0	0.1	26.5
£16,000 or more	11.0	3.1	0.8	0.0	14.9
All households	55.4	24.0	19.7	0.9	100.0

Notes: Figures for England, Scotland and Northern Ireland are for 1996, figures for Wales are for 1993. Income bands differ slightly for Wales and for Northern Ireland.

Sources: DoE (1996); Scottish Homes (1996); NIHE (1996); Welsh Office (1994)

Table A7.1: Slum clearance, Great Britain and UK (1969-96) (number of dwellings demolished)

Year	England	Wales	Scotland	Great Britain	Northern Ireland	UK
1969	70,296	2,404	17,847	90,547	na	na
1970	68,691	2,427	17,345	88,463	na	na
1971	72,050	2,671	20,554	95,275	na	na
1972	68,205	2,029	18,518	88,752	na	na
1973	62,478	2,442	14,745	79,665	na	na
1974	40,860	1,166	12,024	54,050	na	na
1975	51,162	1,878	10,021	63,061	428	63,489
1976	44,956	1,281	6,370	52,607	1,573	54,180
1977	38,899	1,379	4,977	45,255	715	45,970
1978	32,384	1,581	3,814	37,779	2,363	40,142
1979	28,674	1,345	6,653	36,672	1,776	38,448
1980	28,315	1,232	5,815	35,362	1,403	36,765
1981	22,585	900	4,975	28,460	906	29,366
1982	16,019	1,089	3,703	20,811	2,130	22,941
1983	11,100	522	1,987	13,609	2,276	15,885
1984	9,751	568	1,736	12,055	2,071	14,126
1985	8,604	516	1,615	10,735	2,044	12,779
1986	6,744	282	1,735	8,761	2,016	10,777
1987	6,402	281	1,801	8,484	1,805	10,289
1988	5,237	272	1,175	6,684	1,873	8,557
1989	5,936	221	1,007	7,164	1,540	8,704
1990	5,934	276	2,224	8,434	1,122	9,556
1991	2,222	161	1,816	4,199	1,012	5,211
1992	1,988	84	3,685	5,757	607	6,364
1993	3,856	206	4,311	8,373	877	9,250
1994	1,990	433	4,371	6,794	617	7,411
1995	1,564	111	5,541	7,216	1,128	8,344
1996	1,124	233	3,426	4,783	1,045	5,828
Total 1969-96	718,026	27,990	183,791	929,807	31,327	464,382

Note: Data up to 1972 is for calendar years; after 1972 for financial years.

Source: Housing and Construction Statistics (various years), 1995/96 and 1996/97 data for England from DETR unpublished figures

Table A7.2: Grants by type, England (1969–97)

	Number of grants				
	Improvement	Intermediate	Repair	New system*	Total
1969	20,125	48,274	0		68,399
1970	26,097	45,196	0		71,293
1971	44,428	46,439	0		90,867
1972	78,542	45,634	0		124,176
1973	128,381	37,577	0		165,958
1974	164,525	27,823	0		192,348
1975	72,966	12,368	59		85,393
1976	57,784	10,849	85		68,718
1977	47,788	9,037	130		56,955
1978	49,496	7,940	218		57,654
1979	57,222	7,792	345		65,359
1980	65,809	8,143	513		74,465
1981	49,145	14,743	5,053		68,941
1982	54,732	20,600	28,696		104,028
1983	79,531	27,236	113,065		219,832
1984	83,958	29,003	116,146		229,107
1985	52,989	29,012	54,411		136,412
1986	46,994	24,629	41,705		113,328
1987	49,383	19,661	39,864		108,908
1988	48,213	17,107	39,983		105,303
1989	48,711	14,027	35,479		98,217
1990	51,028	12,688	25,361	896	89,973
1991	15,475	4,230	6,509	29,625	55,839
1992	2,464	671	744	51,028	54,907
1993	400	129	131	54,251	54,911
1994	135	40	20	60,521	60,716
1995	4	2	4	61,938	61,948
1996				61,985	61,985
1997				35,644	35,644
1969–97	**1,396,325**	**520,850**	**508,521**	**355,888**	**2,781,584**

* Excluding MWA.

Source: Housing and Construction Statistics (various years)

	% of grants				
	Improvement	Intermediate	Repair	New system*	Total
1969	29.4	70.6	0.0	0.0	100.0
1970	36.6	63.4	0.0	0.0	100.0
1971	48.9	51.1	0.0	0.0	100.0
1972	63.3	36.7	0.0	0.0	100.0
1973	77.4	22.6	0.0	0.0	100.0
1974	85.5	14.5	0.0	0.0	100.0
1975	85.4	14.5	0.1	0.0	100.0
1976	84.1	15.8	0.1	0.0	100.0
1977	83.9	15.9	0.2	0.0	100.0
1978	85.9	13.8	0.4	0.0	100.0
1979	87.6	11.9	0.5	0.0	100.0
1980	88.4	10.9	0.7	0.0	100.0
1981	71.3	21.4	7.3	0.0	100.0
1982	52.6	19.8	27.6	0.0	100.0
1983	36.2	12.4	51.4	0.0	100.0
1984	36.6	12.7	50.7	0.0	100.0
1985	38.8	21.3	39.9	0.0	100.0
1986	41.5	21.7	36.8	0.0	100.0
1987	45.3	18.1	36.6	0.0	100.0
1988	45.8	16.2	38.0	0.0	100.0
1989	49.6	14.3	36.1	0.0	100.0
1990	56.7	14.1	28.2	1.0	100.0
1991	27.7	7.6	11.7	53.1	100.0
1992	4.5	1.2	1.4	92.9	100.0
1993	0.7	0.2	0.2	98.8	100.0
1994	0.2	0.1	0.0	99.7	100.0
1995	0.0	0.0	0.0	100.0	100.0
1996	0.0	0.0	0.0	100.0	100.0
1997	0.0	0.0	0.0	100.0	100.0
1969-97	**50.2**	**18.7**	**18.3**	**12.8**	**100.0**

Table A7.3: Grants by type, Wales (1969-97)

	Number of grants				
	Improvement	Intermediate	Repair	New system*	Total
1969	3,173	2,037	0		5,210
1970	3,698	2,179	0		5,877
1971	4,509	2,285	0		6,794
1972	10,082	2,850	0		12,932
1973	15,828	2,412	0		18,240
1974	22,363	2,365	0		24,728
1975	6,694	632	30		7,356
1976	5,954	528	75		6,557
1977	6,515	388	114		7,017
1978	5,373	414	144		5,931
1979	5,569	399	148		6,116
1980	6,789	412	147		7,348
1981	5,511	780	809		7,100
1982	5,050	1,236	4,703		10,989
1983	7,231	1,689	18,403		27,323
1984	8,337	2,640	19,001		29,978
1985	4,809	3,512	8,831		17,152
1986	3,984	3,584	11,003		18,571
1987	4,477	3,485	11,135		19,097
1989	5,144	3,100	11,943		20,187
1990	5,722	2,776	11,708		20,206
1991	6,498	2,385	16,229	58	25,170
1992	3,061	1,017	6,006	4,265	14,349
1993	416	287	516	10,454	11,673
1994	64	12	33	11,200	11,309
1995	101	16	38	9,970	10,125
1996	1	4	1	11,774	11,780
1997			7	12,404	12,411
1969-97	156,953	43,424	121,024	69,862	391,263

* Excluding MWA.

Source: Housing and Construction Statistics (various years)

	% of grants				
	Improvement	Intermediate	Repair	New system*	Total
1969	60.9	39.1	0.0	0.0	100.0
1970	62.9	37.1	0.0	0.0	100.0
1971	66.4	33.6	0.0	0.0	100.0
1972	78.0	22.0	0.0	0.0	100.0
1973	86.8	13.2	0.0	0.0	100.0
1974	90.4	9.6	0.0	0.0	100.0
1975	91.0	8.6	0.4	0.0	100.0
1976	90.8	8.1	1.1	0.0	100.0
1977	92.8	5.5	1.6	0.0	100.0
1978	90.6	7.0	2.4	0.0	100.0
1979	91.1	6.5	2.4	0.0	100.0
1980	92.4	5.6	2.0	0.0	100.0
1981	77.6	11.0	11.4	0.0	100.0
1982	46.0	11.2	42.8	0.0	100.0
1983	26.5	6.2	67.4	0.0	100.0
1984	27.8	8.8	63.4	0.0	100.0
1985	28.0	20.5	51.5	0.0	100.0
1986	21.5	19.3	59.2	0.0	100.0
1987	23.4	18.2	58.3	0.0	100.0
1989	25.5	15.4	59.2	0.0	100.0
1990	28.3	13.7	57.9	0.0	100.0
1991	25.8	9.5	64.5	0.2	100.0
1992	21.3	7.1	41.9	29.7	100.0
1993	3.6	2.5	4.4	89.6	100.0
1994	0.6	0.1	0.3	99.0	100.0
1995	1.0	0.2	0.4	98.5	100.0
1996	0.0	0.0	0.0	99.9	100.0
1997	0.0	0.0	0.1	99.9	100.0
1969-97	40.1	11.1	30.9	17.9	100.0

Table A7.4: Grants by type, Scotland (1969-97)

	Number of grants			
	Improvement	Intermediate	Repair	Total
1969		1,078	0	1,078
1970	48	1,272	0	1,320
1971	3,640	5,145	0	8,785
1972	6,964	9,183	0	16,147
1973	13,694	15,437	0	29,131
1974	26,736	1,977	0	28,713
1975	8,875	549	0	9,424
1976	6,694	511	1	7,206
1977	6,809	239	3	7,051
1978	6,625	206	9	6,840
1979	7,831	170	718	8,719
1980	10,353	173	2,894	13,420
1981	12,804	152	5,080	18,036
1982	15,376	313	8,268	23,957
1983	15,780	423	29,295	45,498
1984	18,179	1,185	41,297	60,661
1985	17,004	1,242	28,040	46,286
1986	11,289	738	19,426	31,453
1987	11,345	560	18,763	30,668
1988	10,999	363	20,150	31,512
1989	9,902	294	16,719	26,915
1990	9,054	358	14,174	23,586
1991	9,826	323	13,329	23,478
1992	9,812	308	14,778	24,898
1993	8,904	292	11,998	21,194
1994	8,828	316	10,552	19,696
1995	8,157	242	10,629	19,028
1996	7,571	217	8,012	15,800
1997	6,845	195	6,370	13,410
1969-97	265,598	11,346	280,505	613,910

Source: Housing and Construction Statistics (various years)

	% of grants			
	Improvement	Intermediate	Repair	Total
1969	0.0	100.0	0.0	100.0
1970	3.6	96.4	0.0	100.0
1971	41.4	58.6	0.0	100.0
1972	43.1	56.9	0.0	100.0
1973	47.0	53.0	0.0	100.0
1974	93.1	6.9	0.0	100.0
1975	94.2	5.8	0.0	100.0
1976	92.9	7.1	0.0	100.0
1977	96.6	3.4	0.0	100.0
1978	96.9	3.0	0.1	100.0
1979	89.8	1.9	8.2	100.0
1980	77.1	1.3	21.6	100.0
1981	71.0	0.8	28.2	100.0
1982	64.2	1.3	34.5	100.0
1983	34.7	0.9	64.4	100.0
1984	30.0	2.0	68.1	100.0
1985	36.7	2.7	60.6	100.0
1986	35.9	2.3	61.8	100.0
1987	37.0	1.8	61.2	100.0
1988	34.9	1.2	63.9	100.0
1989	36.8	1.1	62.1	100.0
1990	38.4	1.5	60.1	100.0
1991	41.9	1.4	56.8	100.0
1992	39.4	1.2	59.4	100.0
1993	42.0	1.4	56.6	100.0
1994	44.8	1.6	53.6	100.0
1995	42.9	1.3	55.9	100.0
1996	47.9	1.4	50.7	100.0
1997	51.0	1.5	47.5	100.0
1969–97	47.6	2.0	50.3	100.0

Table A7.5: Grants by type, Northern Ireland (1973-97)

	Number of grants				
	Improvement	Intermediate	Repair	New system*	Total
1973	1,293	1,053	0		2,346
1974	1,153	500	0		1,653
1975	1,106	434	0		1,540
1976	1,908	597	0		2,505
1977	1,853	334	12,943		15,130
1978	3,351	320	18,800		22,471
1979	4,219	288	22,700		27,207
1980	5,788	305	18,132		24,225
1981	4,999	322	18,290		23,611
1982	4,538	274	19,774		24,586
1983	4,308	247	19,828		24,383
1984	4,849	279	21,993		27,121
1985	4,936	248	18,690		23,874
1986	5,017	197	13,984		19,198
1987	4,415	174	7,296		11,885
1988	3,731	162	7,025		10,918
1989	3,111	139	4,594		7,844
1990	2,717	122	4,007		6,846
1991	2,672	92	3,780		6,544
1992	2,520	98	2,663		5,281
1993	2,454	96	2,271	1,137	5,958
1994	1,209	19	763	7,157	9,148
1995				9,612	9,612
1996				11,513	11,513
1997				8,188	8,188
1969-97	72,147	6,300	217,533	37,607	333,587

* Data for New system excluding MWA is for financial year.
Note: Data for 1973-76 is for approvals, supplied by NIHE.
Source: Housing and Construction Statistics (various years)

	% of grants				
	Improvement	Intermediate	Repair	New system*	Total
1973	55.1	44.9	0.0	0.0	100.0
1974	69.8	30.2	0.0	0.0	100.0
1975	71.8	28.2	0.0	0.0	100.0
1976	76.2	23.8	0.0	0.0	100.0
1977	12.2	2.2	85.5	0.0	100.0
1978	14.9	1.4	83.7	0.0	100.0
1979	15.5	1.1	83.4	0.0	100.0
1980	23.9	1.3	74.8	0.0	100.0
1981	21.2	1.4	77.5	0.0	100.0
1982	18.5	1.1	80.4	0.0	100.0
1983	17.7	1.0	81.3	0.0	100.0
1984	17.9	1.0	81.1	0.0	100.0
1985	20.7	1.0	78.3	0.0	100.0
1986	26.1	1.0	72.8	0.0	100.0
1987	37.1	1.5	61.4	0.0	100.0
1988	34.2	1.5	64.3	0.0	100.0
1989	39.7	1.8	58.6	0.0	100.0
1990	39.7	1.8	58.5	0.0	100.0
1991	40.8	1.4	57.8	0.0	100.0
1992	47.7	1.9	50.4	0.0	100.0
1993	41.2	1.6	38.1	19.1	100.0
1994	13.2	0.2	8.3	78.2	100.0
1995	0.0	0.0	0.0	100.0	100.0
1996	0.0	0.0	0.0	100.0	100.0
1997	0.0	0.0	0.0	100.0	100.0
1969–97	21.6	1.9	65.2	11.3	100.0

Table A7.6: Grants per 1,000 privately-owned dwellings, UK (1969-97)

	England	Northern Ireland	Wales	Scotland
1969	6.0		7.6	1.2
1970	6.2		8.6	1.5
1971	7.8		9.8	5.9
1972	10.5		18.4	10.6
1973	13.9	7.7	25.5	17.9
1974	16.0	5.4	34.2	33.2
1975	7.1	5.0	10.1	10.9
1976	5.6	8.2	8.9	8.2
1977	4.6	49.6	9.5	8.0
1978	4.6	73.7	7.9	7.6
1979	5.2	89.2	8.1	9.6
1980	5.8	79.4	9.7	14.5
1981	5.3	77.4	8.9	19.9
1982	7.8	79.3	13.4	25.8
1983	16.1	76.0	32.8	47.5
1984	17.1	82.2	36.2	61.7
1985	10.0	68.6	20.4	45.8
1986	8.2	53.3	21.8	30.3
1987	7.7	32.1	22.1	28.7
1988	7.3	28.8	22.9	28.4
1989	6.6	20.0	22.3	23.1
1990	6.0	16.9	27.5	19.4
1991	3.7	15.9	15.2	18.3
1992	3.6	12.5	12.3	18.7
1993	3.6	14.0	11.8	15.5
1994	3.9	21.9	10.4	13.9
1995	3.9	23.44	12.0	13.1
1996	3.8	27.35	12.5	10.7
1997	2.2	18.74	9.8	

Note: Includes improvement and conversion grants, repair grants, intermediate and standard grants, renovation grants, disabled facilities grants, common parts grants and HMO grants.
Source: Housing and Construction Statistics (various years)

Table A7.7: Grants under the old system by type (% of all grants)

	Improvement	Intermediate	Repair	All types
England	57.5	21.5	21.0	100.0
Northern Ireland	24.4	2.1	73.5	100.0
Wales	48.8	13.5	37.7	100.0
Scotland	49.2	3.2	47.6	100.0

Source: Housing and Construction Statistics (various years)

Table A7.8: Grants under the new system by type (1997) (% of all grants)

	Renovation		Disabled facilities		HMO	Common parts	
	Mandatory	Discretionary	Mandatory	Discretionary	All	All	MWA
England	47.3	12.2	33.6	0.8	4.6	1.6	23.1
Wales	71.2	–	24.6	1.0	2.6	0.6	19.5

Note: Northern Ireland has been omitted from the table as the information available does not cover disabled facilties grants.
Source: Housing and Construction Statistics (various years)

Table A7.9: Renovation grants under the new system, England

	Renovation		DFG		MWA	HMO	Common parts	All excl MWA	All inc MWA
	Mandatory	Discretionary	Mandatory	Discretionary					
Number of grants									
1990	259	255	360	13	6,667	5	4	896	7,563
1991	14,995	3,207	10,792	180	29,325	383	68	29,625	58,950
1992	29,166	5,123	15,453	285	28,153	839	162	51,028	79,181
1993	30,705	4,937	16,724	434	25,846	1,195	256	54,251	80,097
1994	32,866	4,739	20,409	501	30,522	1,584	422	60,521	91,043
1995	31,863	4,414	22,728	416	31,139	1,873	644	61,938	93,077
1996	30,900	4,495	23,024	605	33,245	2,206	755	61,985	95,230
1997	16,848	4,350	11,961	269	10,724	1,630	586	35,644	46,368
Value of grants (£000s)									
1990	1,144	309	656	37	3,541	29	16	2,191	5,732
1991	124,771	12,538	31,905	624	17,119	2,216	511	172,565	189,684
1992	289,640	21,027	57,723	1,321	18,014	7,022	983	377,716	395,730
1993	316,564	23,121	68,633	1,190	17,323	12,237	2,711	424,456	441,779
1994	340,094	22,706	85,507	1,104	21,306	14,592	2,805	466,808	488,114
1995	293,480	21,305	95,047	1,241	21,861	16,167	4,266	431,506	453,367
1996	265,089	27,419	97,436	1,548	23,976	16,300	3,898	411,690	435,666
1997	156,636	37,397	59,211	1,161	8,076	14,439	4,649	273,493	281,569
Value of grants (£000s, 1993/94 prices)									
1990	1,303	352	747	42	4,034	33	18	2,496	6,530
1991	133,728	13,438	34,195	669	18,348	2,375	548	184,953	203,301
1992	298,671	21,683	59,523	1,362	18,576	7,241	1,014	389,494	408,069
1993	316,564	23,121	68,633	1,190	17,323	12,237	2,711	424,456	441,779
1994	333,378	22,258	83,818	1,082	20,885	14,304	2,750	457,590	478,475
1995	278,557	20,222	90,214	1,178	20,749	15,345	4,049	409,565	430,314
1996	245,538	25,397	90,250	1,434	22,208	15,098	3,611	381,327	403,534
1997	141,810	33,857	53,606	1,051	7,312	13,072	4,209	247,606	254,917
Average grant (£)									
1990	4,417	1,212	1,822	2,846	531	5,800	4,000		
1991	8,321	3,910	2,956	3,467	584	5,786	7,515		
1992	9,931	4,104	3,735	4,635	640	8,369	6,068		
1993	10,310	4,683	4,104	2,742	670	10,240	10,590		
1994	10,348	4,791	4,190	2,204	698	9,212	6,647		
1995	9,211	4,827	4,182	2,983	702	8,632	6,624		
1996	8,579	6,100	4,232	2,559	721	7,389	5,163		
1997	9,297	8,597	4,950	4,316	753	8,858	7,933		
Average grant (£, 1993/94 prices)									
1990	5,032	1,380	2,076	3,242	605	6,607	4,557		
1991	8,918	4,190	3,169	3,716	626	6,201	8,054		
1992	10,240	4,232	3,852	4,780	660	8,630	6,257		
1993	10,310	4,683	4,104	2,742	670	10,240	10,590		
1994	10,144	4,697	4,107	2,160	684	9,030	6,516		
1995	8,742	4,581	3,969	2,831	666	8,193	6,287		
1996	7,946	5,650	3,920	2,370	668	6,844	4,782		
1997	8,417	7,783	4,482	3,907	682	8,020	7,183		

Source: Housing and Construction Statistics (various years)

Table A7.10: Renovation grants under the new system, Wales

	Renovation		DFG		MWA	HMO	Common parts	All excl MWA	All inc MWA
	Mandatory	Discretionary	Mandatory	Discretionary					
Number of grants									
1990	30	1	26	1	1,352	0	0	58	1,410
1991	2,609	419	1,124	42	6,744	69	6	4,269	11,013
1992	7,524	539	2,042	123	4,957	216	9	10,453	15,410
1993	7,892	380	2,331	310	4,768	249	28	11,190	15,958
1994	6,503	364	2,365	266	4,332	311	37	9,846	14,178
1995	8,160	179	2,791	307	5,537	307	30	11,774	17,311
1996	8,690	154	3,085	122	4,932	314	39	12,404	17,336
1997	6,934		2,393	101	2,363	255	54	9,737	12,100
Value of grants (£000s)									
1990	290	5	45	8	828	0	0	348	1,176
1991	36,535	3,192	4,322	154	4,992	827	38	45,068	50,060
1992	125,023	6,297	9,059	452	3,655	2,886	85	143,802	147,457
1993	140,395	7,706	10,942	1,262	4,015	3,416	133	163,854	167,869
1994	121,442	6,488	10,731	1,069	4,015	4,731	278	144,739	148,754
1995	135,914	3,744	13,595	1,207	5,001	3,803	258	158,521	163,522
1996	134,763	2,894	15,142	559	4,521	3,592	363	157,313	161,834
1997	112,171		12,678	973	2,095	3,131	809	129,762	131,857
Value of grants (£000s, 1993/94 prices)									
1990	330	6	51	9	943	0	0	396	1,340
1991	39,158	3,421	4,632	165	5,350	886	41	48,303	53,654
1992	128,921	6,493	9,341	466	3,769	2,976	88	148,286	152,055
1993	140,395	7,706	10,942	1,262	4,015	3,416	133	163,854	167,869
1994	119,044	6,360	10,519	1,048	3,936	4,638	273	141,881	145,816
1995	129,003	3,554	12,904	1,146	4,747	3,610	245	150,461	155,207
1996	124,824	2,681	14,025	518	4,188	3,327	336	145,711	149,898
1997	101,553	0	11,478	881	1,897	2,835	732	117,479	119,376
Average grant (£)									
1990	9,667	5,000	1,731	8,000	612				
1991	14,030	7,618	3,842	3,667	726	11,986	6,333		
1992	16,621	11,575	4,426	3,897	735	13,361	9,444		
1993	17,754	20,226	4,741	3,871	842	13,719	4,750		
1994	18,675	17,824	4,311	4,019	877	15,212	7,514		
1995	16,656	20,916	4,871	3,932	903	12,388	8,600		
1996	15,508	18,792	4,908	4,582	917	11,439	9,308		
1997	16,177	0	5,298	9,634	887	12,278	14,981		
Average grant (£, 1993/94 prices)									
1990	11,012	5,696	1,972	9,114	698				
1991	15,038	8,165	4,118	3,930	778	12,846	6,788		
1992	17,139	11,936	4,563	4,018	758	13,778	9,739		
1993	17,754	20,226	4,741	3,871	842	13,719	4,750		
1994	18,306	17,472	4,226	3,939	860	14,912	7,365		
1995	15,809	19,853	4,623	3,732	857	11,758	8,163		
1996	14,364	17,406	4,546	4,244	849	10,596	8,621		
1997	14,646	0	4,796	8,722	803	11,116	13,563		

Source: Housing and Construction Statistics (various years)

Table A7.11: Renovation grants under the new system, Northern Ireland (number of grants)

	Reno-vation	Replace-ment	DFG	Repairs	MWA	HMO	Common parts	All excl MWA	All inc MWA
1993	110	4	56	966	601	1	0	1,137	1,738
1994	1,210	61	395	5,470	1,422	21	0	7,157	8,579
1995	1,685	139	651	7,087	1,445	50	0	9,612	11,057
1996	1,386	131	621	9,335	1,647	40	0	11,513	13,160
1997	1,430	225	835	5,623	1,726	75	0	8,188	9,914

Source: NIHE (various years)

Table A7.12: Minor works assistance by type, England (1990–97)

	Thermal insulation		Patch and mend*		Staying put†		Elderly adaptation‡		Lead pipes§		All minor works	
Year	No	%	No	%	No	%	No	%	No	%	No	%
1990/91	5,512	35.9	1	0.0	9,454	61.5	407	2.6			15,374	100.0
1991/92	5,823	20.7	118	0.4	21,934	78.1	208	0.7			28,083	100.0
1992/93	5,309	19.3	21	0.1	21,749	79.2	384	1.4			27,463	100.0
1993/94	4,080	14.2	125	0.4	24,121	83.7	210	0.7	284	1.0	28,820	100.0
1994/95	3,364	11.2	37	0.1	25,899	86.4	406	1.4	273	0.9	29,979	100.0
1995/96	1,684	5.3	33	0.1	28,137	89.2	1,358	4.3	335	1.1	31,547	100.0
1996/97	2,632	8.3	6	0.0	28,479	89.3	574	1.8	196	0.6	31,887	100.0

* Grant for a temporary improvement to a property which is in a clearance area or will be within 12 months;
† Repairs, improvements or adaptations to properties owned or tenanted by a person aged 60 or more;
‡ Adaptations to property to enable an older person, not the owner or tenant, who is or who proposes to be resident in the property to be cared for by a friend or relative;
§ Replacement of lead water service pipes (introduced from September 1992).

Source: Housing and Construction Statistics (various years)

Table A7.13: Average value of improvement and mandatory renovation grants, UK (1979–94) (Average grant values, constant 1993/94 prices)

	Old system				New system		
	England	N Ireland	Wales	Scotland	England	Wales	N Ireland
1979	4,074	11,858	4,423	3,575			
1980	3,810	12,978	4,078	3,398			
1981	4,587	9,827	4,291	3,231			
1982	6,001	8,925	5,525	4,050			
1983	6,769	10,446	6,538	5,848			
1984	7,923	11,049	7,975	4,803			
1985	7,823	10,886	6,980	4,429			
1986	6,571	10,771	6,181	6,668			
1987	5,687	9,847	5,938	6,886			
1988	5,211	8,881	5,568	7,568			
1989	4,749	9,553	5,034	7,779			
1990	4,524	9,569	5,037	7,687	5,032	11,012	
1991	6,308	9,819	6,840	7,776	8,918	15,038	
1992	6,708	9,694	6,581	6,860	10,240	17,139	
1993	6,810		6,313	7,353	10,310	17,754	1,053
1994	9,396		3,834	6,596	10,144	18,306	13,131
1995	4,034		7,593	6,169	8,742	15,809	18,376
1996				6,642	7,946	14,364	13,775
1997				4,845	8,417	14,646	13,738

Notes: Average grant amounts for Northern Ireland under new system is estimated. Average renovation grant for Northern Ireland under the new system includes all renovation, mandatory and discretionary. Average amounts for 1985 Act grants not shown after 1992 for Northern Ireland.

Source: Housing and Construction Statistics (various years); NIHE (various years); Scottish Homes (various years)

Table A7.14: Declared renewal areas in England at end of June 1998

Area	Local authority	Declaration date	Dwellings in area
Castleton	Rochdale	14–Aug–90	1,575
Whitworth Road	Rochdale	14–Aug–90	1,366
Hyde	Tameside	11–Sep–90	3,102
Shelton	Stoke-on-Trent	22–Oct–90	2,229
Smawthorne	Wakefield	21–Nov–90	2,015
Daneshill	Leicester	29–Nov–90	534
Westcotes	Leicester	29–Nov–90	720
Monega	Newham	06–Dec–90	2,350
Sutton Village	St Helens	18–Dec–90	750
Easton	Bristol	01–Jan–91	2,630
North Saltley	Birmingham	14–Jan–91	1,920
South Saltley	Birmingham	14–Jan–91	1,673
Sparkbrook	Birmingham	14–Jan–91	1,166
Handsworth	Birmingham	14–Jan–91	2,800
Cape Hill	Sandwell	18–Jan–91	2,671
Rumworth	Bolton	30–Jan–91	2,654
Darnall	Sheffield	06–Feb–91	1,259
Trees	Rossendale	06–Feb–91	379
New Brighton South	Wirral	28–Feb–91	1,086
Rock Ferry West	Wirral	28–Feb–91	440
North Reddish	Stockport	13–Mar–91	4,535
Forest Town	Mansfield	01–Apr–91	340
Willow Green	Leicester	22–Apr–91	764
Seacombe	Wirral	21–May–91	1,388
East Accrington	Hyndburn	23–May–91	1,582
New Brighton North	Wirral	17–Jun–91	940
Rock Ferry East	Wirral	22–Jun–91	860
Brookhouse/Bastwell	Blackburn	01–Jul–91	3,250
Rugby	Rugby	30–Jul–91	1,360
Radcliffe	Bury	25–Sep–91	2,373
Haslingden No 1	Rossendale	13–Oct–91	1,282
Whitehaven	Copeland	22–Oct–91	1,050
Burngreave	Sheffield	30–Oct–91	1,656
Halliwell	Bolton	05–Nov–91	3,438
Hirst	Wansbeck	01–Dec–91	2,747
Sharrow	Sheffield	05–Feb–92	2,700
Southfield, Nelson	Pendle	04–Mar–92	1,388
Chesterton/Helena	Newham	17–Mar–92	620
Linacre	Sefton	24–Mar–92	1,200
Whitchurch	North Shropshire	30–Mar–92	1,162
Gorton	Manchester	15–Apr–92	2,177
Ermine Road	Chester	22–Apr–92	335
West Accrington/Scatcliffe	Hyndburn	24–Apr–92	1,558
The Measham	North West Leicester	28–Apr–92	492
All Saints	Wolverhampton	29–Apr–92	533
Poulton	Wirral	21–May–92	1,506
The Pear Tree	Derby	09–Jun–92	2,598
Central	Middlesbrough	01–Jul–92	440
Charterhouse	Coventry	08–Sep–92	1,395
Smawthorne Central/Glasshoughton	Wakefield	17–Sep–92	1,399
Western Road	Leicester	29–Oct–92	590
Alexandra	Chester	18–Nov–92	480
Stonebridge	Chester	18–Nov–92	358
Grasslot	Allerdale	27–Jan–93	336
Mossbay	Allerdale	27–Jan–93	361
Barton/Treadworth	Gloucester	23–Mar–93	2,876
Plashet	Newham	19–Apr–93	2,084
Ribblebank	Preston	21–Apr–93	733
Gorse Hill	Trafford	27–Apr–93	1,790

Table A7.14: Declared renewal areas in England at end of June 1998, continued

Area	Local authority	Declaration date	Dwellings in area
Willow Brook	Leicester	01-May-93	1,048
Murray Street	Hartlepool	01-May-93	835
Whitmore Reans	Wolverhampton	05-May-93	1,866
Caldmore/Palfrey	Walsall	12-May-93	2,228
Eccles	Salford	14-Jun-93	2,805
East Wigan and Ince	Wigan	30-Jun-93	1,193
Lye	Dudley	29-Jul-93	1,047
Central	Barrow	07-Sep-93	1,401
North Belgrave Phase 1	Leicester	30-Sep-93	920
Cobridge	Stoke-on-Trent	30-Sep-93	2,723
Westwood and Colhurst	Oldham	01-Oct-93	2,282
Morecambe West End	Lancaster	13-Oct-93	2,676
East Chorley	Chorley	02-Nov-93	827
Manningham	Bradford	16-Nov-93	2,000
Scotswood	Newcastle	01-Dec-93	791
Newgate Lane	Mansfield	15-Dec-93	821
West Bowling	Bradford	17-Jan-94	1,664
Newtown/Nichols' Town/Radcliffe	Southampton	19-Jan-94	1,567
Clerk Green	Kirklees	18-Mar-94	886
St Agnes/St Werburghs	Bristol	01-Apr-94	1,429
Boundary	Sefton	23-Jun-94	1,250
Shirebrook Model Village	Bolsover	06-Jul-94	817
Lawkholm	Bradford	26-Jul-94	1,300
St Marks	Derby	6-Sep-94	363
Bengeworth	Wychavon	01-Nov-94	841
Lightbowne	Manchester	21-Dec-94	492
Cobholm	Great Yarmouth	28-Mar-95	975
Burley Lodge	Leeds	27-Jun-95	688
Granby	Liverpool	01-Nov-95	710
West Central Halifax	Calderdale	23-Nov-95	674
Lower High Street	Cheltenham	29-Jan-96	578
Old Trafford	Trafford	30-Jan-96	910
Rugby No 2	Rugby	05-Mar-96	1,760
Sandfield	Rochdale	14-Mar-96	1,286
Crosby, Scunthorpe	North Lincolnshire	15-Apr-96	2,029
Claremont West	Blackpool	15-May-96	719
Bedford, Leigh	Wigan	26-Jun-96	837
Fairfield	Warrington	15-Jul-96	604
Harlesden	Brent	14-Aug-96	2,186
Highfields/Trinity St	Kirklees	02-Oct-96	476
Ibstock	North West Leicester	23-Oct-96	1,211
Ashton Renewal Area	Tameside	24-Oct-96	4,291
Deepdale	Preston	03-Jan-97	1,120
Dukesfield	Halton	10-Feb-97	338
Danehouse & Stoneyholme	Burnley	19-Feb-97	767
Ravensthorpe Dewsbury	Kirklees	17-Apr-97	700
Bellenden	Sothwark	16-Jul-97	3,324
Esaington Colliery	Easington	21-Jul-97	658
Clarendon	Middlesbrough	24-Sep-97	475
Fairfield 11	Warrington	15-Dec-97	1,036
Glodwick	Oldham	14-Jan-98	1,834
Blackburn Road	Rossendale	25-Jan-98	861
Southwater	Hastings	25-Mar-98	700
Hornsey Park	Haringey	26-Mar-98	1,020
Bank Top	Blackburn	07-Apr-98	982
Total dwellings			**159,816**
Average no of dwellings			**1,402**

Note: Where only the month of declaration is known, declaration is assumed to have taken place on the 1st of the month.

Table A7.15: Declared renewal areas in Wales at 1997

Area	Local authority	Declaration date	Dwellings in area
Renewal area			
Holyhead	Ynys Mon	Jul-91	1,685
South Riverside	Cardiff	Oct-91	2,314
West Rhyl	Rhuddlan	Mar-92	1,671
Coronation Road	Newport	Sep-92	857
Rhosllanerchrugog	Wrexham	Nov-92	1,371
Bethesda	Arfon	Mar-93	1,156
Colwyn Bay	Colwyn	Nov-93	1,380
Blaenau Ffestiniog	Meirionnydd	Sep-94	1,343
Penmaenmawr	Aberconwy	Nov-94	561
Smithfield	Wrexham	Dec-94	1,118
South Barry	Vale of Glamorgan	Mar-95	310
Ammanford	Dinefwr	Mar-95	1,000
South Llanelli	Llanelli	Mar-95	1,256
Valleys Action Programme Areas			
Trehafod	Rhonnda & Taff Ely	Dec-91	520
Oakdale	Islwn	Jan-92	620
Abertysswg	Rhymney Valley	Apr-92	556
Llanhileth	Blaenau Gwent	Jun-92	718
Tiryberth	Rhymney Valley	Nov-94	258
Rural Renewal Areas			
Llanfyllin	Montgomery	Nov-92	225
Amlwch	Ynys Mon	Nov-92	353
Trefor	Gwynedd	Mar-96	327
Total dwellings			19,599
Average number of dwellings			933

Source: Welsh Office

Table A7.16: Size distribution of declared renewal areas, England and Wales (number of renewal areas)

Number of dwellings	England	Wales
Up to 499	15	5
500-999	33	6
1,000-1,499	25	7
1,500-1,999	13	2
2,000-2,499	11	1
2,500-2,999	11	0
3,000-3,499	4	0
3,500 or more	2	0
Average	1,402	933

Table A7.17: Changing proportion of spending in renewal areas by programme (% of spending)

Year	Demolition	Grants	Group repair	Acquisition land/ buildings	Environ- ment	HA/ private rehabilitation	Enforcement action	New house building
1990/91	39.0	4.0	27.0	2.0	8.0	20.0	-	-
1991/92	11.0	23.0	10.0	42.0	6.0	7.0	-	-
1992/93	8.0	28.0	5.0	46.0	5.0	8.0	-	-
1993/94	13.0	29.0	10.0	38.0	5.0	4.0	-	-
1994/95	20.6	49.1	21.4	1.0	7.9	0.0	-	-
1995/96	8.7	52.2	29.8	1.7	7.7	0.0	-	-
1996/97	11.2	49.0	29.3	1.2	9.3	0.0	-	-
1997/98	8.3	36.3	23.9	0.8	16.0	0.0	0.1	14.5

Table A7.18: Housing action area improvements by source, Scotland (1979-97)

Period	Local authority	Housing association	Owner- occupier	Private landlord	Other	All improved
1979-92	9.5	47.8	24.9	14.7	3.2	34200
1992-95	0.9	25.9	52.7	20.0	0.6	3637
1995-97	11.1	38.1	35.7	10.8	4.4	1884
Total	**8.8**	**46.8**	**25.9**	**15.4**	**3.1**	**39721**

Table A7.19: Renovations to local authority stock (1969–96)

Year	England	Northern Ireland	Wales	Scotland
1969	26,560	na	2,809	11,067
1970	40,357	na	1,603	17,508
1971	59,144	na	1,994	27,756
1972	97,482	na	6,516	32,681
1973	110,053	237	7,874	70,147
1974	73,494	1,025	3,820	43,814
1975	36,163	835	943	24,734
1976	38,983	1,615	18	35,760
1977	37,551	1,363	2,000	56,402
1978	60,871	842	2,000	44,770
1979	75,967	1,064	2,000	34,805
1980	77,275	7,892	2,000	22,282
1981	52,931	59,609	2,000	26,065
1982	57,722	43,581	2,000	51,214
1983	85,461	14,008	2,000	41,583
1984	86,612	50,382	2,390	33,774
1985	96,482	17,496	1,728	53,093
1986	133,661	23,262	2,788	60,404
1987	148,362	40,282	5,886	81,530
1988	169,001	28,458	8,333	68,921
1989	194,928	14,163	8,444	52,549
1990	231,828	9,072	10,843	84,261
1991	184,762	9,542	10,513	70,361
1992	177,233	8,912	9,491	80,753
1993	248,722	6,928	23,264	90,519
1994	296,371	9,369	20,397	117,497
1995	308,058	4,054	16,665	75,845
1996	329,513	3,806	4,705	–

Notes: England: data for 1969-77 is for approvals; Scotland: all data is for approvals.
Sources: Housing and Construction Statistics (various years), Northern Ireland Annual Abstract of Statistics (various years)

Table A7.20: Average value of local authority renovation, housing association renovation and private sector grants, 1993/94 prices, England (1979–96)

	Local authority	Housing association	Private grants
1979	10,667	26,568	4,074
1980		26,254	3,810
1981		30,612	4,587
1982		28,291	6,001
1983	5,712	28,552	6,769
1984	7,702	25,944	7,923
1985	6,688	23,291	7,823
1986	5,937	23,111	6,571
1987	4,756	23,179	5,687
1988	4,498	24,882	5,211
1989	4,154	21,601	4,749
1990	3,749	23,747	4,524
1991	3,550	32,506	6,308
1992	3,021	32,368	6,708
1993	2,270	38,597	6,810
1994	2,227	28,079	9,396
1995	1,965		4,034
1996	1,879	22,149	

Note: Private sector grants arc all improvement, repair and intermediate grants 1979-89, and renovation grants 1990-94.

Source: Housing and Construction Statistics (various years)

Table A7.21: Renovations to housing association stock (1969–97)

Year	England	Northern Ireland	Wales	Scotland
1969	1,457		0	5
1970	2,684		17	46
1971	5,029		0	97
1972	4,198		2	165
1973	3,201		18	132
1974	3,952		21	159
1975	4,603		14	461
1976	13,388	6	0	156
1977	18,789	11	511	330
1978	13,056	36	237	1,447
1979	17,173	125	218	2,703
1980	14,832	155	252	2,787
1981	11,243	202	694	1,833
1982	17,362	276	1,009	3,422
1983	14,511	279	993	2,530
1984	18,453	329	760	1,424
1985	11,350	337	945	1,124
1986	12,712	442	907	1,414
1987	10,934	338	948	1,262
1988	11,235	191	867	1,225
1989	13,026	215	812	1,122
1990	10,657	366	399	816
1991	6,421	175	305	1,680
1992	7,531	269	322	1,785
1993	6,011	75	300	1,524
1994	6,881	206	287	1,229
1995	10,596	167	163	1,328
1996	9,005	285	147	
1997		133	131	

Note: England: data shows completions except 1969-77; Scotland: data shows approvals only; Northern Ireland: data not available 1969-75.

Source: Housing and Construction Statistics (various years); Northern Ireland Annual Abstract of Statistics (various years)

Table A7.22: Grants for people with disabilities, England

Year	Number of disabled grants	All grants excluding MWA	Disabled grants as % of all grants	Disabled grants £000s	All grants £000s	£ disabled grants as % all grants	Disabled grants £000 93/94 prices
1969	0	68,399	0.0	0	12,794	0.0	
1970	0	71,293	0.0	0	17,968	0.0	
1971	0	90,867	0.0	0	29,683	0.0	
1972	0	124,176	0.0	0	56,551	0.0	
1973	0	165,958	0.0	0	101,966	0.0	
1974	0	192,348	0.0	0	148,560	0.0	
1975	125	85,393	0.1	0	63,858	0.0	
1976	562	68,718	0.8	229	64,125	0.4	
1977	751	56,955	1.3	359	60,117	0.6	
1978	1,139	57,654	2.0	732	76,219	1.0	
1979	1,704	65,359	2.6	1,257	100,198	1.3	3,088
1980	2,515	74,465	3.4	2,273	127,303	1.8	4,717
1981	3,403	68,941	4.9	3,667	148,152	2.5	6,931
1982	6,216	104,028	6.0	9,917	282,159	3.5	17,526
1983	11,935	219,832	5.4	24,179	655,490	3.7	40,840
1984	15,226	229,107	6.6	35,717	839,383	4.3	57,411
1985	15,675	136,412	11.5	36,125	525,099	6.9	55,055
1986	19,176	113,328	16.9	38,924	394,922	9.9	57,576
1987	23,793	108,908	21.8	41,849	362,013	11.6	58,774
1988	26,836	105,303	25.5	50,473	347,074	14.5	66,420
1989	29,919	98,217	30.5	54,839	328,356	16.7	67,439
1990	32,588	89,973	36.2	68,265	314,019	21.7	77,769
1991	16,719	55,839	29.9	52,282	299,353	17.5	56,035
1992	16,452	54,907	30.0	61,788	398,895	15.5	63,715
1993	17,288	54,911	31.5	70,426	428,720	16.4	70,426
1994	20,926	60,716	34.5	86,712	468,358	18.5	85,000
1995	23,144	61,948	37.4	96,288	431,565	22.3	91,392
1996	23,629	61,985	38.1	98,984	411,690	24.0	89,615
1997	12,230	35,644	34.3	60,372	273,493	22.1	55,919

Source: Housing and Construction Statistics (various years)

Table A7.23: Grants for people with disabilities, Wales

Year	Number of disabled grants	All grants excluding MWA	Disabled grants as % of all grants	Disabled grants £000s	All grants £000s	£ disabled grants as % all grants	Disabled grants £000 93/94 prices
1969	0	5,210	0.0	0	1,307	0.0	
1970	0	5,877	0.0	0	1,784	0.0	
1971	0	6,794	0.0	0	2,849	0.0	
1972	0	12,932	0.0	0	7,879	0.0	
1973	0	18,240	0.0	0	14,312	0.0	
1974	0	24,728	0.0	0	22,784	0.0	
1975	6	7,356	0.1	0	7,666	0.0	
1976	16	6,557	0.2	14	7,635	0.2	
1977	68	7,017	1.0	30	8,089	0.4	
1978	92	5,931	1.6	57	8,331	0.7	
1979	168	6,116	2.7	119	10,398	1.1	292
1980	205	7,348	2.8	201	13,798	1.5	417
1981	267	7,100	3.8	291	14,514	2.0	550
1982	497	10,989	4.5	837	26,265	3.2	1,479
1983	887	27,323	3.2	1,784	74,373	2.4	3,013
1984	1,539	29,978	5.1	3,834	101,663	3.8	6,163
1985	1,755	17,152	10.2	4,003	57,221	7.0	6,101
1986	2,207	18,571	11.9	4,322	58,171	7.4	6,393
1987	2,325	19,097	12.2	4,763	59,491	8.0	6,689
1988	2,687	20,187	13.3	5,488	64,050	8.6	7,222
1989	2,993	20,206	14.8	6,879	65,844	10.4	8,460
1990	3,385	25,170	13.4	7,799	84,266	9.3	8,885
1991	558	14,349	12.0	6,626	93,801	7.1	7,102
1992	58	11,673	19.0	9,739	148,991	6.5	10,043
1993	2	11,309	23.3	12,205	164,405	7.4	12,205
1994	3	10,125	27.2	11,821	145,248	8.1	11,588
1995	0	11,778	26.3	14,802	158,538	9.3	14,049
1996	0	12,415	25.8	15,701	157,352	10.0	14,543
1997		9,737	25.6	13,651	129,762	10.5	12,359

Source: Housing and Construction Statistics (various years)

Table A8.1: Percentage shares of public spending on housing, England (1979–98)

Year	LA new build	LA renovation	LA grants to HAs	Private sector renovation	LA mortgages	Housing Corporation
1979/80	33	21	5	6	18	11
1980/81	30	20	5	8	18	15
1981/82	23	19	4	10	24	16
1982/83	18	24	3	14	20	19
1983/84	17	26	3	24	11	17
1984/85	18	30	3	20	9	16
1985/86	19	35	3	15	7	19
1986/87	16	40	4	14	5	19
1987/88	15	43	4	13	5	18
1988/89	18	43	3	10	7	18
1989/90	15	48	5	8	7	15
1990/91	12	39	4	11	4	24
1991/92	9	32	4	12	3	37
1992/93	4	30	6	10	3	46
1993/94	5	34	8	12	2	37
1994/95	3	40	7	12	2	32
1995/96	2	40	9	15	1	30
1996/97	2	39	9	17	1	29
1997/98	2	47	10	15	2	21

Source: Wilcox (1998)

Table A8.2: Percentage shares of public spending on housing, Wales (1981–97)

Year	LA new build	LA renovation	LA grants to HAs	Private sector renovation	LA mortgages	Housing Corporation
1981/82	35	19	0	14	4	25
1982/83	22	26	0	23	4	24
1983/84	18	19	0	43	3	16
1984/85	17	21	0	38	2	19
1985/86	15	28	0	31	1	23
1986/87	12	33	0	27	2	22
1987/88	14	33	0	24	1	22
1988/89	11	34	0	23	1	25
1989/90	8	39	3	19	1	24
1990/91	5	29	0	25	1	31
1991/92	3	23	0	35	0	36
1992/93	3	17	0	40	0	38
1993/94	2	20	0	41	0	33
1994/95	1	22	0	46	0	30
1995/96	3	22	0	43	0	26
1996/97	4	15	0	46	0	27

Source: Wilcox (1998)

Table A8.3: Percentage shares of public spending on housing, Northern Ireland (1985–98)

Year	NIHE new build	NIHE renovation	Private sector renovation	Voluntary housing
1985/86	33	29	22	15
1986/87	32	27	23	17
1987/88	28	33	19	18
1988/89	27	35	18	19
1989/90	27	35	17	18
1990/91	24	37	17	19
1991/92	26	34	17	21
1992/93	21	34	14	28
1993/94	22	38	15	23
1994/95	24	37	16	21
1995/96	26	32	19	22
1996/97	27	29	22	21
1997/98	24	29	22	25

Source: Wilcox (1998)

Table A8.4: Public expenditure on housing renovation, England (1979-98) (1993/94 prices)

	LA renovation	Private sector renovation	Housing association renovation	Total renovation spending
£million				
1979/80	1,776	558	456	2,790
1980/81	1,390	546	389	2,325
1981/82	1,172	607	344	2,122
1982/83	1,700	972	491	3,163
1983/84	1,939	1,757	414	4,110
1984/85	2,057	1,397	479	3,933
1985/86	2,004	885	264	3,154
1986/87	2,250	768	294	3,311
1987/88	2,447	751	253	3,451
1988/89	2,506	603	280	3,388
1989/90	3,631	601	281	4,514
1990/91	1,961	556	253	2,770
1991/92	1,589	584	209	2,382
1992/93	1,610	543	244	2,397
1993/94	1,710	594	232	2,536
1994/95	1,674	554	232	2,460
1995/96	1,471	551	206	2,229
1996/97	1,345	576	199	2,120
1997/98	1,351	435		1,785
% renovation spending				
1979/80	64	20	16	
1980/81	60	23	17	
1981/82	55	29	16	
1982/83	54	31	16	
1983/84	47	43	10	
1984/85	52	36	12	
1985/86	64	28	8	
1986/87	68	23	9	
1987/88	71	22	7	
1988/89	74	18	8	
1989/90	80	13	6	
1990/91	71	20	9	
1991/92	67	25	9	
1992/93	67	23	10	
1993/94	67	23	9	
1994/95	68	23	9	
1995/96	66	25	9	
1996/97	63	27	9	
1997/98	76	24	0	

Sources: Wilcox (1995); Housing and Construction Statistics (various)

Table A8.5: Public expenditure on housing renovation, Wales (1981–97) (1993/94 prices)

	LA renovation	Private sector renovation	Housing association renovation	Total renovation spending
£million				
1981/82	46	39	21	106
1982/83	84	77	29	190
1983/84	81	189	28	299
1984/85	71	138	20	229
1985/86	76	93	22	190
1986/87	116	111	21	248
1987/88	138	119	22	279
1988/89	131	112	22	264
1989/90	181	115	18	314
1990/91	121	137	9	267
1991/92	91	147	10	248
1992/93	81	197	10	288
1993/94	88	192	12	291
1994/95	89	189		
1995/96	85	186		
1996/97	51	170		
% renovation spending				
1981/82	43	37	20	
1982/83	44	41	15	
1983/84	27	63	9	
1984/85	31	60	9	
1985/86	40	49	12	
1986/87	47	45	8	
1987/88	49	43	8	
1988/89	50	42	8	
1989/90	58	37	6	
1990/91	45	51	4	
1991/92	37	59	4	
1992/93	28	68	4	
1993/94	30	66	4	

Sources: Wilcox (1995); Housing and Construction Statistics (various)

Table A8.6: Public expenditure on housing renovation, Northern Ireland (1984–98) (1993/94 prices)

	NIHE renovation	Private sector renovation	Housing association renovation	Total renovation spending
£million				
1985/86	120	91	8	220
1986/87	101	83	10	194
1987/88	112	63	8	183
1988/89	109	55	5	169
1989/90	93	44	5	142
1990/91	81	36	9	126
1991/92	71	34	6	111
1992/93	73	35	9	117
1993/94	79	32	5	116
1994/95	77	31	5	114
1995/96	69	42		
1996/97	59	45		
1997/98	57	43		
% renovation spending				
1984/85	55	42	4	
1985/86	52	43	5	
1986/87	61	34	4	
1987/88	65	33	3	
1988/89	66	31	3	
1989/90	64	29	7	
1990/91	64	31	5	
1991/92	63	30	7	
1992/93	68	28	4	
1993/94	68	27	5	

Sources: Wilcox (1995); Housing and Construction Statistics (various)

Table A9.1: Average weekly spending on repairs, maintenance and decoration by tenure (1986–97)

Tenure	1986	1987	1988	1989	1990	1991	1992	1993	1994 -95	1995 -96	1996 -97
£ per week											
All households	4.87	4.91	5.00	5.64	6.19	7.25	7.32	7.42	6.60	6.43	7.51
Owner-occupied owned outright	5.60	6.11	5.85	5.51	6.95	9.50	9.21	9.90	7.73	9.12	9.74
Owner-occupied with mortgage	8.12	8.03	7.92	8.36	9.38	10.45	10.91	10.25	9.74	8.88	10.59
Rented from local authority	1.25	1.02	1.11	1.07	1.57	1.40	1.29	1.44	1.47	1.64	1.47
Rented from housing association	–	0.89	1.05	0.67	1.52	1.90	2.01	1.19	0.78	1.33	1.31
Privately rented unfurnished	1.21	0.99	1.19	–	2.12	1.78	1.56	2.53	2.12	1.63	1.49
Privately rented furnished	0.73	0.74	1.07	0.91	1.33	0.39	0.74	1.41	0.60	0.85	1.38
Rent free	2.21	2.07	1.77	2.19	3.33	2.60	4.20	11.18	–	4.55	2.98
£ per annum											
All households	253	255	260	293	322	377	381	386	343	334	391
Owner-occupied owned outright	291	318	304	287	361	494	479	515	402	474	506
Owner-occupied with mortgage	422	418	412	435	488	543	567	533	506	462	551
Rented from local authority	65	53	58	56	82	73	67	75	76	85	76
Rented from housing association		46	55	35	79	99	105	62	41	69	68
Privately rented unfurnished	63	51	62		110	93	81	132	110	85	77
Privately rented furnished	38	38	56	47	69	20	38	73	31	44	72
Rent free	115	108	92	114	173	135	218	581	–	237	155
£ per annum (1993/94 prices)											
All households	375	359	342	361	367	404	393	386	336	317	354
Owner-occupied owned outright	431	446	400	352	412	529	494	515	394	450	459
Owner-occupied with mortgage	625	586	542	535	556	582	585	533	496	438	499
Rented from local authority	96	74	76	68	93	78	69	75	75	81	69
Rented from housing association	0	65	72	43	90	106	108	62	40	66	62
Privately rented unfurnished	93	72	81	0	126	99	84	132	108	80	70
Privately rented furnished	56	54	73	58	79	22	40	73	31	42	65
Rent free	170	151	121	140	197	145	225	581	–	225	140

Sources: CSO (1997)

Table A9.2: Average weekly spending on repairs, maintenance and decoration by age group (1997-98)

Age group, all tenures	£ per week	£ per annum
Under 30	3.70	192
30-49	8.60	447
50-64	10.50	546
65-74	5.90	307
75+	4.60	239

Table A9.3: Value of occupant work by tenure, England (1991)

Value of work	Owner-occupied	Privately rented	Rented from LA	Rented from HA	All tenures
No of households (000s)					
None	2,130	826	1,541	304	4,800
Under £500	2,686	443	922	156	4,207
£500-999	2,314	184	679	89	3,266
£1,000-2,499	2,630	156	583	93	3,462
£2,500-4,999	1,610	60	93	14	1,777
£5,000-9,999	992	30	48	6	1,076
£10,000-19,999	398	2	12	0	412
£20,000 or more	113	0	0	0	113
% of households by tenure					
None	16.5	48.6	39.7	45.9	25.1
Under £500	20.9	26.0	23.8	23.6	22.0
£500-999	18.0	10.8	17.5	13.5	17.1
£1,000-2,499	20.4	9.2	15.0	14.0	18.1
£2,500-4,999	12.5	3.5	2.4	2.1	9.3
£5,000-9,999	7.7	1.8	1.2	0.9	5.6
£10,000-19,999	3.1	0.1	0.3	0.0	2.2
£20,000 or more	0.9	0.0	0.0	0.0	0.6

Source: EHCS 1991: analysis of data

Table A9.4: Average value of work carried out by selected household characteristics, England (1991)

Characteristic		Average (£)	Number of cases (000s)
Household income	Under £4,000	695	3,606
	£4,000–7,999	964	4,651
	£8,000–11,999	1,577	3,049
	£12,000–15,999	1,959	2,745
	£16,000–19,999	2,883	2,170
	£20,000–23,999	2,445	1,128
	£24,000 or more	3,016	1,758
Age of household head	16–24	949	718
	25–34	2,007	3,126
	35–44	2,309	3,736
	45–54	2,206	3,093
	55–64	1,565	2,954
	65–74	1,026	3,031
	75–84	612	1,911
	85+	338	541
Household type	Lone adult	855	1,613
	Two adults	2,122	3,223
	Lone parent	957	782
	Small family	2,462	3,260
	Large family	2,492	2,025
	3+ adults	1,958	2,270
	Two pensioners	1,116	3,096
	One pensioner	547	2,842
Ethnic group of household head	White	1,665	18,281
	Black	1,016	263
	Asian	1,597	353
	Other	1,007	148
Length of residence	Under 1 year	1,498	1,420
	1–2 years	2,052	2,355
	3–4 years	1,953	2,514
	5–10 years	1,773	4,811
	11–15 years	1,756	2,227
	16–20 years	1,578	1,579
	21–30 years	1,363	2,200
	Over 30 years	847	2,006

Source: EHCS 1991

Table A9.5: Average value of work carried out by selected dwelling characteristics, England (1991)

Characteristic		Average (£)	Number of cases (000s)
General repair costs	None	1,841	4,005
	Under £1,000	1,550	8,801
	£1,000-2,499	1,676	3,682
	£2,500-4,999	1,633	1,748
	£5,000-9,999	1,812	655
	£10,000-14,999	1,269	162
	£15,000 or more	1,094	57
Dwelling age	Pre-1850	2,688	604
	1850-99	1,595	2,701
	1900-18	1,613	1,759
	1919-44	1,952	3,821
	1945-64	1,554	4,206
	1965-80	1,438	4,491
	Post-1980	1,485	1,527
Dwelling type	Terraced	1,547	5,613
	Semi-detached	1,660	5,948
	Detached	2,679	4,020
	Converted flat	719	1,120
	Purpose-built flat	544	2,353
Dwelling fitness	Fit	1,673	17,698
	Unfit	1,334	1,414
Dwelling value	Up to £40,000	990	5,257
	£40,001-£52,000	1,451	3,716
	£52,001-£68,000	1,652	4,237
	£68,001-£88,000	1,840	2,694
	£88,001-£120,000	2,148	1,720
	£120,001-£160,000	2,844	878
	£160,001-£320,000	4,312	569
	£320,001 or more	7,391	40

Source: EHCS 1991

Table A9.6: Building society lending by dwelling age/type, Great Britain (1973-97) (all purchasers)

Year	Pre-1919 terraced	Interwar semi- or detached	New	Pre-1919 converted flat	All pre-1919 stock
1973	10	12	28		18
1974	10	13	25		19
1975	10	15	19		19
1976	13	14	17		23
1977	13	15	17		24
1978	13	12	18		24
1979	14	12	17		24
1980	16	12	15		28
1981	17	11	12		28
1982	17	11	11		27
1983	15	11	12		26
1984	15	10	12		27
1985	16	10	11		28
1986	16	10	10	3	28
1987	15	9	10	3	26
1988	16	9	10	4	27
1989	17	8	11	3	27
1990	18	8	11	4	29
1991	15	8	12	4	27
1992	15	9	11	3	26
1993	12	9	11	3	24
1994	14	10	11	3	24
1995	16	16	13	4	24
1996	15	16	11	4	24
1997	15	17	10	5	24

Source: BSA/CML (various years)

Table A9.7: Building society lending by age of stock and type of purchaser, Great Britain (1974–98)

	% first-time buyers				% previous owners			
	Pre–1919	Interwar	Postwar	New	Pre–1919	Interwar	Postwar	New
1974	24	19	33	24	14	19	41	26
1975	25	18	39	19	14	20	46	20
1976	29	19	34	18	17	20	44	19
1977	30	19	36	16	18	21	44	18
1978	30	18	36	15	18	19	43	19
1979	31	18	35	15	18	20	43	19
1980	36	17	34	12	20	20	44	17
1981	36	16	38	10	21	20	46	14
1982	33	16	41	10	20	20	48	12
1983	31	16	43	11	20	20	48	13
1984	33	15	40	12	21	19	48	13
1985	35	15	40	10	21	19	48	13
1986	35	15	42	8	21	18	48	12
1987	32	15	45	8	21	17	49	13
1988	32	16	46	7	23	17	47	13
1989	31	14	47	8	25	16	45	14
1990	32	13	45	9	24	16	46	14
1991	32	14	45	10	23	15	49	13
1992	30	15	46	9	21	16	49	14
1993	28	15	48	9	21	15	50	14
1994	28	16	47	9	19	16	51	14
1995	27	16	48	9	21	16	47	16
1996	28	16	47	9	21	16	49	14
1997	28	15	50	7	21	16	50	13
1998	29	15	47	9	22	15	50	13

Source: BSA/CML (various years)

Table A9.8: Ratio of first-time buyers to existing owner purchasers by age of dwelling, Great Britain (1974-98)

	Pre-1919	Interwar	Postwar	New
1974	1.72	0.99	0.80	0.95
1975	1.71	0.91	0.84	0.94
1976	1.74	0.98	0.76	0.93
1977	1.68	0.91	0.81	0.88
1978	1.66	0.95	0.83	0.80
1979	1.71	0.92	0.81	0.82
1980	1.82	0.88	0.78	0.73
1981	1.77	0.82	0.82	0.72
1982	1.64	0.78	0.87	0.82
1983	1.55	0.81	0.89	0.85
1984	1.62	0.82	0.83	0.92
1985	1.65	0.82	0.84	0.79
1986	1.62	0.86	0.87	0.64
1987	1.51	0.90	0.91	0.62
1988	1.37	0.94	0.97	0.54
1989	1.23	0.87	1.04	0.58
1990	1.34	0.87	0.97	0.67
1991	1.39	0.90	0.92	0.74
1992	1.43	0.93	0.93	0.67
1993	1.36	0.99	0.95	0.64
1994	1.45	1.00	0.92	0.68
1995	1.29	1.00	1.02	0.56
1996	1.33	1.00	0.96	0.64
1997	1.33	0.94	1.00	0.54
1998	1.32	1.00	0.96	0.69

Source: BSA/CML (various years)

Table A9.9: Output on housing repair and maintenance, Great Britain (1985–97)

	Cash prices			Index	
	Public	Private	Total	Public	Private
1985	3,382	4,584	7,966	100	100
1986	3,585	5,077	8,662	106	111
1987	3,956	6,011	9,967	117	131
1988	4,446	7,084	11,530	131	155
1989	4,943	8,149	13,092	146	178
1990	5,384	8,455	13,839	159	184
1991	4,938	8,063	13,001	146	176
1992	4,991	7,595	12,586	148	166
1993	5,439	7,370	12,809	161	161
1994	5,963	7,804	13,767	176	170
1995	6,465	8,130	14,595	191	177
1996	6,637	8,398	15,035	196	183
1997	6,629	9,126	15,755	196	199

Source: Housing and Construction Statistics (various)

Table A9.10: Share of housing repair and maintenance output by size of firm, Great Britain (1990, 1992, 1994, 1996) (value of work done and % by number of employees)

	Q3 1990		Q3 1992		Q3 1994		Q3 1996	
No of employees	£m	%	£m	%	£m	%	£m	%
1	414.2	21.9	334.8	18.6	398.9	22.6	399.6	23.0
2–3	443.7	23.5	451.1	25.1	425.6	24.1	425.2	24.4
4–7	288.9	15.3	344.7	19.1	301.3	17.1	267.2	15.4
8–13	132.0	7.0	141.3	7.8	126.9	7.2	133.3	7.7
14–24	146.3	7.7	143.1	7.9	125.4	7.1	136.0	7.8
25–59	149.0	7.9	147.8	8.2	145.2	8.2	131.8	7.6
60–114	79.3	4.2	55.3	3.1	50.6	2.9	79.5	4.6
115–599	150.4	8.0	86.2	4.8	97.3	5.5	111.9	6.4
600 or more	87.2	4.6	96.2	5.3	94.6	5.4	55.3	3.2
Total	1,891.0		1,800.5		1,765.8		1,740.0	

Source: Housing and Construction Statistics (various)

Appendix B: Key data on housing conditions and renovation activity by local authority

Per 1,000 private dwellings

LA	% private dwellings 1997	Unfit 1998	Demolitions 1973–98	Grants 1978–94	Renovation grants 1990–96	DFGs 1990–96	MWAs 1990–96	LA renovation per 1,000 LA dwellings 1996/97	HA renovation per 1,000 private dwellings 1996/97	Average mandatory RG 1996/97	Average mandatory DFG 1996/97
Adur	86.15	8.88	0.27	41.64	4.59	6.24	21.96	800.04	0.04	3,822.00	4,486.00
Allerdale	77.47	22.29	24.49	245.69	13.77	3.94	21.08	889.87	32.57	21,213.33	4,816.00
Alnwick	75.91	0.55	4.83	184.53	10.86	2.58	2.30	431.75	7.30	11,382.67	9,905.33
Amber Valley	84.33	5.00	5.44	196.12	8.10	9.28	14.47	296.41	1.09	5,900.00	3,357.00
Arun	90.85	1.29	0.54	64.87	9.20	12.23	0.49	275.12	3.16	7,434.00	2,748.00
Ashfield	77.93	10.25	1.04	115.02	21.86	2.79	12.56	972.15	0.89	7,603.00	3,649.00
Ashford	80.97	1.15	1.47	79.64	4.94	4.13	18.28	484.20	0.50	6,249.00	5,871.00
Aylesbury Vale	82.93	2.90	1.86	83.19	4.96	12.23	2.56	908.77	0.89	6,664.00	3,714.00
Babergh	85.07	8.54	0.96	103.33	10.56	10.83	18.39	610.59	0.00	9,554.00	4,973.00
Barking and Dagenham	58.49	10.57	1.02	139.03	13.46	9.08	5.08	546.41	0.55	35,756.00	27,272.00
Barnet	84.19	3.42	0.24	52.58	5.94	3.33	10.88	1,258.87	7.29	5,819.00	8,606.00
Barnsley	70.57	14.79	13.04	146.76	18.44	15.29	15.08	859.73	8.03	4,799.00	2,618.00
Barrow-in-Furness	86.69	9.71	3.81	117.68	36.28	3.83	7.47	665.38	2.74	4,964.00	4,143.00
Basildon	72.58	5.64	0.79	18.76	1.83	5.84	3.78	1,230.61	0.00	4,928.00	6,941.00
Basingstoke and Dean	81.17	3.97	0.75	74.37	5.26	12.52	18.59	847.22	1.37	8,991.00	3,720.00
Bassetlaw	78.65	10.41	2.88	128.13	17.64	9.05	15.45	1,042.84	1.30	6,462.00	8,108.00
Bath and NE Somerset	82.36	8.28	4.69	141.56	14.18	11.89	22.79	5,828.57	5.00	11,278.00	3,718.00
Bedford	82.62	4.06	3.00	40.51	12.13	3.74	8.54	172.23	5.60	6,531.00	4,878.00
Berwick-upon-Tweed	77.74	–	3.18	96.93	8.30	3.72	4.20	1,035.07	1.15	9,281.00	2,179.00
Bexley	87.55	8.11	1.04	105.81	11.96	11.44	15.89	277.09	1.95	4,479.00	4,693.00
Birmingham	67.15	19.11	15.18	147.30	17.94	6.81	17.93	526.15	37.85	11,610.00	8,707.00
Blaby	90.89	5.15	1.39	50.95	15.23	4.78	15.18	1,088.52	0.75	7,301.00	5,939.00
Blackburn	75.55	41.06	163.77	269.50	24.22	9.34	58.58	454.09	11.80	10,270.00	3,259.00
Blackpool	88.97	7.02	2.65	52.60	4.95	7.13	10.97	708.06	2.89	10,712.00	3,370.00
Blaenau Gwent	67.38	10.90	40.44	509.23	79.93	13.80	67.58	945.53	0.44	19,558.51	6,294.12
Blyth Valley	68.11	14.99	7.06	69.56	13.88	4.41	14.95	1,182.70	11.82	9,804.00	2,852.00
Bolsover	76.67	10.26	27.27	267.41	22.64	9.42	2.58	1,707.03	2.01	6,474.00	6,307.00
Bolton	74.74	24.51	63.72	147.22	15.96	7.81	11.23	1,604.15	12.16	15,503.00	5,691.00
Boston	75.92	6.04	10.19	120.10	13.61	7.29	27.11	165.52	0.97	9,237.00	2,469.00
Bournemouth	89.47	2.80	0.63	37.31	2.54	3.85	35.36	1,990.10	0.50	7,813.00	3,553.00

Per 1,000 private dwellings

LA	% private dwellings 1997	Unfit 1998	Demolitions 1973-98	Grants 1978-94	Renovation grants 1990-96	DFGs 1990-96	MWAs 1990-96	LA renovation per 1,000 LA dwellings 1996/97	HA renovation 1,000 private dwellings 1996/97	Average mandatory RG 1996/97	Average mandatory DFG 1996/97
Bracknell	77.96	1.39	0.36	33.11	1.19	2.79	1.06	792.16	8.32	15,537.00	7,821.00
Bradford	80.70	8.53	17.56	126.91	18.65	6.32	7.84	137.55	7.38	11,345.00	6,578.00
Braintree	78.71	6.48	0.76	89.72	7.46	12.39	12.59	351.68	0.98	11,264.00	6,044.00
Breckland	83.83	7.88	2.02	110.65	10.18	8.85	3.29	122.34	3.45	8,158.00	2,447.00
Brent	74.22	16.02	1.85	66.57	7.26	1.68	3.94	234.96	59.22	13,534.67	15,228.00
Brentwood	85.55	8.30	0.94	41.37	5.24	4.53	11.14	1,378.98	0.47	10,223.00	4,852.00
Bridgend	82.12	7.20	9.33	247.07	43.22	9.15	35.91	35.93	1.86	14,158.62	7,282.05
Bridgnorth	82.37	6.95	2.73	113.04	12.81	4.73	25.22	169.30	0.17	15,826.00	4,782.00
Brighton	84.40	13.01	2.98	96.04	18.73	3.07	16.60	1,312.38	0.90	6,839.00	5,460.00
Bristol	74.88	13.50	5.70	81.28	8.08	4.63	15.43	2,479.38	16.49	5,280.00	4,728.00
Broadland	91.58	4.11	1.25	100.19	14.10	6.58	9.53	1,384.68	0.00	6,524.00	3,556.00
Bromley	85.65	4.56	1.30	94.88	7.98	4.77	18.23	117.18	21.67	6,744.00	6,060.00
Bromsgrove	88.15	1.00	1.45	54.13	0.97	14.55	0.00	835.10	0.94	14,809.00	3,667.00
Broxbourne	85.27	5.80	0.56	89.56	7.87	10.04	10.61	274.97	3.60	6,561.00	2,765.00
Broxtowe	85.94	3.76	1.20	99.14	5.92	2.09	2.92	707.99	1.39	10,924.00	5,592.00
Burnley	82.23	22.00	46.34	246.49	22.42	20.61	33.65	405.69	18.59	111,888.00	2,471.00
Bury	82.59	4.08	26.16	95.69	11.23	7.82	7.03	969.52	10.34	8,019.00	2,869.00
Caerphilly	76.38	6.00	13.72	694.77	82.14	42.52	56.11	1,085.56	0.21	8,597.19	2,577.14
Calderdale	80.22	6.93	13.96	199.54	19.80	20.43	2.72	206.13	8.65	13,194.00	2,054.00
Cambridge	74.04	4.19	1.06	105.41	9.20	6.22	7.08	1,329.24	7.17	12,518.00	13,634.0
Camden	58.79	15.68	1.57	99.09	2.33	0.87	1.35	209.75	58.44	6,638.67	9,372.00
Cannock Chase	77.60	6.45	8.19	30.38	7.96	9.75	2.17	767.73	12.05	4,744.00	4,043.00
Canterbury	85.23	0.99	0.42	64.46	6.57	5.20	5.72	623.79	1.87	5,477.00	5,565.00
Caradon	87.10	9.38	2.50	111.13	9.31	28.60	12.40	1,140.31	0.19	16,377.00	1,409.00
Cardiff	79.14	7.60	9.57	291.28	45.17	27.30	49.04	731.40	3.23	14,528.93	9,380.17
Carlisle	77.62	5.81	15.11	86.53	11.31	2.41	15.86	612.36	5.84	9,714.00	5,913.00
Carmarthenshire	81.64	8.70	7.35	998.94	48.86	12.74	36.30	297.24	3.23	15,621.92	4,022.06
Carrick	87.00	10.27	3.32	96.12	14.28	5.25	12.48	138.15	2.58	12,385.00	4,149.00
Castle Morpeth	77.69	5.90	0.36	198.47	16.95	2.18	0.56	334.91	0.42	10,024.00	4,589.33
Castle Point	94.05	5.59	0.66	36.61	1.02	2.59	0.00	175.40	0.12	3,712.00	9,864.00

Ceredigion	88.29	12.00	15.83	190.39	51.28	9.12	8.16	27.52	1.98	18,371.43	11,625.00
Charnwood	86.12	3.24	7.50	95.77	30.17	5.24	4.04	1,933.92	4.34	4,354.00	4,214.00
Chelmsford	84.71	2.92	1.23	39.47	2.77	4.29	10.44	244.44	1.09	5,288.00	3,820.00
Cheltenham	84.27	3.75	3.71	226.11	15.57	8.69	10.28	1,059.94	9.41	8,832.00	5,830.00
Cherwell	84.73	3.58	4.38	74.21	2.63	3.02	7.77	2,084.47	2.12	14,259.00	6,464.00
Chester	82.47	6.32	3.77	74.86	13.07	3.71	3.95	549.46	5.62	9,291.00	4,416.00
Chesterfield	70.54	7.86	18.04	138.40	23.05	5.25	29.15	552.73	8.35	11,494.00	5,884.00
Chester-le-Street	73.51	1.97	4.79	88.47	4.99	4.87	15.59	1,585.42	1.22	10,330.00	2,747.00
Chichester	83.17	7.31	0.60	61.92	8.29	13.28	5.32	114.97	0.53	6,276.00	2,672.00
Chiltern	84.75	2.74	1.29	49.99	3.81	4.68	6.02	301.69	0.20	4,369.00	2,901.00
Chorley	82.25	12.00	19.31	93.07	16.36	7.30	17.42	776.14	13.69	7,343.00	2,288.00
Christchurch	89.35	0.07	1.19	33.96	3.53	8.11	7.02	367.57	0.00	12,263.00	3,547.00
City of London	73.13	0.00	0.00	1.45	0.00	0.00	0.00	41,584.10	26.03	-	-
Colchester	78.00	4.27	0.37	81.84	24.05	5.75	19.02	1,087.80	0.74	8,405.00	5,180.00
Congleton	87.50	0.85	4.02	68.25	5.28	2.45	5.34	175.14	1.39	12,518.00	10,851.00
Conwy	87.84	5.20	2.51	324.10	29.02	10.78	39.88	553.05	0.85	15,351.56	8,581.40
Copeland	74.15	12.51	7.98	135.80	15.46	3.48	10.89	787.19	33.27	10,046.00	5,805.00
Corby	64.23	5.35	0.07	43.08	0.61	6.71	1.36	521.96	0.00	5,004.00	2,141.00
Cotswold	85.47	2.88	4.19	86.21	3.68	4.94	10.71	635.82	4.89	12,737.33	5,240.00
Coventry	78.66	9.09	1.38	118.59	25.11	2.86	5.63	453.70	23.49	6,095.00	9,525.00
Craven	89.88	5.36	1.25	96.27	7.55	2.26	0.14	391.69	0.67	10,875.00	3,175.00
Crawley	71.14	0.59	0.00	14.98	1.29	5.32	0.81	1,497.25	1.40	8,586.00	3,877.00
Crewe and Nantwich	82.46	2.64	17.99	100.56	11.16	4.18	15.18	322.23	6.05	4,496.00	5,750.00
Croydon	82.74	8.82	0.59	93.14	15.23	2.20	10.13	1,080.15	7.70	5,856.00	6,834.00
Dacorum	74.18	4.40	0.88	57.07	7.66	3.66	15.67	55.21	1.76	16,082.00	9,274.00
Darlington	79.48	4.07	1.63	85.76	14.57	5.23	10.52	477.07	8.31	6,964.00	2,229.00
Dartford	82.92	2.99	0.89	82.69	6.53	2.04	1.80	1,101.03	3.01	5,167.00	5,645.00
Daventry	82.81	3.01	0.98	117.44	6.27	7.51	14.76	502.74	1.33	9,754.00	4,290.00
Denbighshire	85.40	7.30	2.19	216.54	28.18	7.42	20.77	268.05	3.43	21,168.67	5,192.31
Derby	77.27	13.35	47.63	138.15	23.53	9.45	17.35	599.37	15.77	7,412.00	5,985.33
Derbyshire Dales	87.22	10.03	19.12	128.96	7.44	5.25	7.39	1,384.97	1.34	4,399.00	2,900.00
Derwentside	70.86	4.25	32.50	187.52	29.56	13.52	40.71	855.50	5.70	8,286.00	4,005.00
Doncaster	73.14	6.22	2.36	127.40	12.99	9.60	3.34	238.47	3.09	6,621.00	3,064.00
Dover	83.59	7.63	2.04	106.52	15.25	4.19	10.18	1,556.94	9.14	8,300.00	5,908.00
Dudley	73.34	5.56	6.01	29.33	9.76	4.66	3.35	521.33	7.09	10,728.00	6,863.00
Durham	72.56	5.20	5.51	71.89	6.50	4.00	1.97	562.64	6.93	5,551.00	2,744.00

Per 1,000 private dwellings

LA	% private dwellings 1997	Unfit 1998	Demolitions 1973-98	Grants 1978-94	Renovation grants 1990-96	DFGs 1990-96	MWAs 1990-96	LA renovation per 1,000 LA dwellings 1996/97	HA renovation per 1,000 private dwellings 1996/97	Average mandatory RG 1996/97	Average mandatory DFG 1996/97
East Cambridgeshire	83.50	7.49	0.79	113.65	12.93	8.26	19.70	144.85	0.60	8,738.00	4,139.00
Ealing	84.00	14.43	22.58	30.10	12.52	4.25	2.15	690.93	21.44	8,646.00	4,055.00
Easington	80.30	9.50	8.34	102.78	18.37	7.76	3.01	1,032.22	13.04	15,433.33	17,456.00
East Devon	62.89	3.92	0.27	45.38	6.05	4.11	13.02	157.69	4.89	11,817.00	3,513.00
East Dorset	88.65	6.38	0.24	22.49	7.03	4.89	10.43	355.38	0.92	5,080.00	3,855.00
East Hampshire	91.82	8.06	1.63	62.48	16.42	4.67	5.68	713.98	0.29	8,081.00	3,989.00
East Hertfordshire	87.04	5.99	0.99	111.33	6.36	3.10	2.19	887.76	0.07	8,792.00	4,200.00
East Lindsey	84.82	3.30	7.56	107.12	11.85	4.94	5.76	345.76	0.36	5,623.00	4,045.00
East Northamptonshire	88.20	2.97	6.07	66.33	6.75	6.27	23.24	222.03	1.12	6,277.33	3,429.33
East Riding of Yorkshire	88.26	2.50	3.44	82.45	4.47	3.05	6.55	685.84	2.37	12,169.00	4,849.00
East Staffordshire	83.55	6.30	11.68	220.91	12.89	10.35	23.13	266.81	4.33	8,853.00	6,335.00
Eastbourne	84.04	4.40	6.44	64.61	12.15	3.34	17.17	962.91	1.55	8,237.00	7,274.00
Eastleigh	87.85	1.52	0.57	97.24	6.52	7.32	11.28	907.99	2.53	9,184.00	4,357.33
Eden	90.01	7.31	5.80	133.04	11.54	4.67	7.38	339.84	1.46	18,068.00	3,407.00
Ellesmere Port	75.90	5.39	1.29	57.48	13.92	41.39	0.32	1,082.74	0.67	6,447.00	2,752.00
Elmbridge	88.23	1.29	1.13	44.38	5.24	2.56	5.78	3,936.59	0.22	6,143.00	5,283.00
Enfield	83.85	5.24	0.11	129.65	17.40	7.31	3.09	2,491.15	10.03	10,906.67	9,034.67
Epping Forest	82.17	11.50	1.31	67.27	3.44	2.77	12.25	55.91	0.72	8,688.00	3,172.00
Epsom and Ewell	89.99	-	0.74	17.12	3.90	2.22	6.12	183.09	1.20	6,997.00	7,583.00
Erewash	83.45	17.35	16.55	106.18	18.69	6.07	18.47	662.53	3.24	9,759.00	4,715.00
Exeter	79.34	8.67	0.56	107.49	16.59	16.54	37.43	173.25	1.70	4,803.00	5,623.00
Fareham	91.61	5.98	0.61	56.18	4.34	6.40	5.42	838.24	0.45	7,538.00	2,782.00
Fenland	84.36	9.16	14.96	126.34	10.41	12.70	10.51	1,658.38	1.10	11,606.00	4,541.00
Flintshire	82.10	4.90	3.69	133.22	25.00	15.07	13.07	172.81	0.77	64,465.00	24,645.16
Forest Heath	81.01	1.04	2.07	44.64	5.00	8.54	3.28	1,475.26	0.10	15,017.33	4,653.33
Forest of Dean	84.05	7.05	5.47	163.21	20.36	5.82	17.54	757.63	0.90	10,783.00	4,918.00
Fylde	91.98	-	-	75.23	8.12	5.24	14.71	418.87	0.92	8,354.00	3,890.00
Gateshead	62.38	9.55	32.75	211.57	17.05	3.66	23.87	1,397.41	16.10	5,917.00	4,569.00
Gedling	87.82	4.00	4.94	72.55	16.39	4.37	11.61	495.40	2.70	3,663.00	3,563.00
Gloucester	83.72	9.86	6.87	98.49	22.94	5.90	6.86	445.73	3.64	5,717.00	4,623.00

Gosport	75.51	9.79	1.43	95.54	12.55	5.56	6.01	64.26	1.23	7,044.00	6,288.00
Gravesham	80.12	7.69	1.07	84.36	9.92	2.87	8.39	545.40	3.33	7,739.00	4,943.00
Great Yarmouth	80.72	5.45	4.03	139.25	19.54	6.10	26.67	279.36	1.22	8,100.00	2,882.00
Greenwich	57.28	12.96	1.06	111.49	20.94	5.31	19.98	183.16	23.91	9,882.00	8,081.00
Guildford	84.31	4.79	0.69	77.67	5.93	3.82	5.32	184.50	1.77	10,288.00	6,125.33
Gwynedd	83.48	11.90	3.49	1,064.45	50.60	10.60	22.13	104.78	3.65	16,935.15	8,933.33
Hackney	39.14	17.03	15.87	145.52	13.36	3.27	22.11	197.50	92.98	55,456.00	30,236.00
Halton	66.92	3.04	17.34	137.97	0.00	0.00	0.00	286.20	4.73	–	–
Hambleton	82.72	1.23	0.75	98.46	4.73	2.86	2.72	466.32	1.75	6,665.00	4,513.00
Hammersmith and Fulham	64.86	15.74	1.59	198.33	13.28	3.38	11.71	104.41	77.01	12,062.00	7,221.00
Harborough	89.16	2.62	1.40	114.14	9.10	5.80	3.46	953.75	0.84	5,559.00	3,390.00
Haringey	69.82	21.30	1.73	173.31	7.00	2.11	9.65	591.35	48.96	14,410.00	10,946.00
Harlow	57.99	0.08	0.00	15.72	1.07	2.69	5.05	518.67	0.00	1,973.00	3,491.00
Harrogate	89.06	6.26	1.39	47.93	6.89	2.85	9.33	1,699.13	2.94	9,223.00	4,446.00
Harrow	89.33	6.43	0.15	62.81	12.42	1.48	1.51	332.71	9.08	7,413.00	12,588.00
Hart	88.99	0.17	1.23	47.85	2.00	2.95	13.31	529.27	0.56	6,502.67	9,477.33
Hartlepool	69.76	5.13	50.40	164.25	22.09	12.20	15.84	564.66	13.79	8,035.00	1,956.00
Hastings	84.33	16.56	2.27	255.75	28.27	3.61	25.94	453.24	3.11	11,206.00	9,831.00
Havant	79.49	5.20	1.81	26.88	7.62	14.45	3.93	128.91	0.76	5,157.00	3,248.00
Havering	84.46	3.99	0.35	53.44	5.31	1.71	0.71	670.24	1.43	2,972.00	6,631.00
Herefordshire	84.19	5.00	6.11	149.87	4.71	2.22	2.04	467.34	2.90	8,938.00	3,211.00
Hertsmere	80.98	4.14	0.00	38.25	0.99	1.31	2.64	329.58	0.00	–	–
High Peak	83.76	9.35	3.39	166.36	15.74	7.06	8.10	227.76	1.16	8,632.00	1,532.00
Hillingdon	80.12	6.24	0.14	5.14	10.29	8.67	5.03	15.63	0.09	10,253.33	9,412.00
Hinckley and Bosworth	87.93	15.99	3.97	49.68	7.09	1.94	13.11	268.25	1.28	8,129.00	4,314.00
Horsham	87.11	5.76	0.34	58.00	1.89	6.25	8.27	744.53	5.88	13,304.00	3,360.00
Hounslow	74.31	6.03	0.48	79.01	3.37	3.37	1.08	162.40	5.88	7,264.00	7,688.00
Huntingdon	83.52	2.76	1.94	82.67	1.71	1.92	2.00	1,134.54	1.88	8,836.00	4,742.00
Hyndburn	84.79	31.94	46.34	131.77	15.74	9.39	11.39	345.17	18.89	12,948.00	3,742.00
Ipswich	74.74	9.39	8.86	165.56	14.24	8.87	2.39	206.56	10.04	4,631.00	4,840.00
Isle of Anglesey	82.88	4.70	2.09	272.12	44.53	4.17	19.58	632.26	5.45	22,122.45	15,142.86
Islington	40.53	10.71	7.25	148.22	3.13	1.31	4.72	474.93	94.73	13,113.33	4,929.33
Kennet	74.33	0.51	0.29	86.65	5.19	7.28	1.58	702.61	6.71	7,054.00	5,465.00
Kensington and Chelsea	75.46	14.21	1.98	84.91	3.60	0.62	2.86	1,099.62	85.59	28,562.00	7,410.00
Kerrier	87.00	5.07	9.40	87.67	18.11	8.60	11.95	1,071.77	0.44	16,412.00	4,637.33
Kettering	83.90	5.21	4.02	157.91	4.26	3.54	6.70	487.69	9.57	5,508.00	3,494.00

Per 1,000 private dwellings

LA	% private dwellings 1997	Unfit 1998	Demolitions 1973–98	Grants 1978–94	Renovation grants 1990–96	DFGs 1990–96	MWAs 1990–96	LA renovation per 1,000 LA dwellings 1996/97	HA renovation per 1,000 private dwellings 1996/97	Average mandatory RG 1996/97	Average mandatory DFG 1996/97
Kings Lynn and West Norfolk	82.80	4.77	6.72	114.56	8.63	6.52	2.94	428.82	0.14	7,851.00	4,216.00
Kingston upon Thames	87.62	6.25	90.81	88.61	10.37	2.90	8.57	2,491.65	11.96	7,169.00	6,695.00
Kingston-upon-Hull	60.49	8.25	0.66	101.35	38.14	4.38	1.28	221.29	14.18	6,289.00	2,701.00
Kirklees	79.07	8.04	9.76	119.97	10.95	5.71	0.97	1,103.62	5.38	8,984.00	6,495.00
Knowsley	60.07	9.62	1.44	158.59	14.79	25.42	13.53	388.93	1.03	6,436.00	2,953.00
Lambeth	51.98	9.70	10.25	81.02	3.65	2.16	0.00	151.44	51.34	16,873.33	10,014.67
Lancaster	88.61	3.62	1.72	88.36	10.77	11.22	14.56	599.09	4.44	6,227.00	2,488.00
Leeds	70.62	13.84	31.44	69.15	15.61	16.53	7.84	80.70	16.64	10,184.00	448.00
Leicester	66.91	19.93	10.87	262.28	38.83	7.09	6.79	294.81	42.52	13,874.67	7,718.67
Leominster	–	–	–	169.21	37.32	7.17	18.20	–	–	9,221.00	2,490.00
Lewes	87.91	7.95	1.11	63.16	15.84	3.25	12.85	1,031.95	4.66	11,486.00	6,905.00
Lewisham	61.44	13.57	1.47	32.50	11.12	1.64	8.60	186.77	20.62	12,792.00	8,193.33
Lichfield	83.53	4.42	1.48	51.67	3.75	7.63	3.72	245.07	1.07	11,236.00	4,211.00
Lincoln	72.81	7.01	5.58	62.86	14.20	4.75	4.70	440.09	1.66	6,037.00	4,595.00
Liverpool	62.64	17.85	17.79	130.14	21.56	5.08	1.98	200.92	101.34	5,893.00	3,672.00
Luton	81.68	12.45	7.77	86.94	15.44	3.34	11.19	41.77	3.24	10,064.00	5,934.00
Macclesfield	84.85	5.20	3.45	70.45	8.15	4.24	2.76	985.95	4.97	6,816.00	2,941.00
Maidstone	84.23	6.23	1.20	71.26	12.00	2.03	29.10	1,325.78	3.32	4,507.00	6,621.00
Maldon	88.22	5.17	0.94	55.66	3.89	7.64	5.68	167.13	0.37	17,387.00	4,220.00
Malvern Hills	84.84	4.46	13.46	119.61	16.33	4.24	21.08	319.46	7.31	8,819.00	5,180.00
Manchester	55.69	9.50	17.51	146.88	17.55	15.96	32.46	389.16	76.66	9,365.00	4,357.00
Mansfield	76.34	10.48	9.38	140.66	11.98	12.34	15.73	1,392.42	11.10	9,902.00	4,153.00
Melton	85.79	0.69	17.96	147.02	12.31	12.49	10.51	351.87	0.00	11,746.00	2,210.00
Mendip	86.40	6.66	3.71	110.46	12.53	5.70	20.82	1,065.23	3.89	11,296.00	3,929.00
Merthyr Tydfil	70.72	13.30	41.98	420.35	42.01	4.62	59.45	335.29	1.14	18,458.65	10,590.91
Merton	84.64	12.51	5.41	73.25	13.41	2.39	5.82	1,708.42	8.04	4,613.00	4,834.00
Mid Bedfordshire	82.50	5.12	2.49	62.44	3.41	1.99	2.57	2,068.30	0.68	13,110.00	2,949.00
Mid Devon	83.94	6.91	1.87	118.05	8.58	8.04	35.26	154.97	4.47	13,887.00	5,623.00
Mid Suffolk	86.50	6.32	6.05	74.93	7.33	4.89	8.00	390.82	0.38	8,490.00	4,284.00
Mid Sussex	88.01	3.00	0.21	40.10	2.61	2.56	4.05	1,021.74	8.06	6,920.00	8,116.00

Local authority											
Middlesbrough	67.75	20.54	119.47	163.78	19.40	7.25	35.37	241.93	14.61	9,754.67	5,921.33
Milton Keynes	76.51	3.81	0.70	69.24	7.05	5.59	11.10	650.77	2.18	5,072.00	4,753.00
Mole Valley	85.48	4.04	3.24	80.05	2.13	4.69	4.35	845.60	6.87	12,548.00	12,241.33
Monmouthshire	84.17	9.30	2.47	278.35	16.96	6.93	27.92	217.74	6.74	10,878.05	3,774.19
North Lincolnshire	79.83	3.12	3.88	172.17	9.52	9.95	7.80	762.77	5.36	9,758.00	2,844.00
North Norfolk	86.08	7.87	4.29	130.21	10.13	4.50	20.66	254.69	1.64	7,043.00	3,508.00
North East Lincolnshire	82.62	-	11.63	217.70	21.26	9.92	38.95	2,460.84	5.87	7,382.00	3,168.00
Neath and Port Talbot	77.58	10.30	7.52	330.43	87.75	31.79	12.08	961.35	2.37	8,161.90	4,523.81
New Forest	89.22	4.03	1.63	63.62	8.68	8.47	2.03	420.40	0.21	9,813.00	4,597.00
Newark	81.15	6.97	1.96	128.72	11.36	18.73	13.37	137.48	3.88	16,108.00	5,969.33
Newbury	84.36	7.22	1.34	62.03	5.29	4.94	8.71	582.65	10.38	7,639.00	5,986.00
Newcastle upon Tyne	62.13	7.35	32.05	88.04	4.33	3.76	7.97	439.33	33.82	9,966.00	4,768.00
Newcastle under Lyme	77.97	8.21	15.02	66.61	4.22	3.54	11.06	611.59	3.74	7,930.00	4,418.00
Newham	61.92	15.00	15.35	49.58	1.15	0.09	0.75	37.27	24.37	-	-
Newport	74.30	8.00	14.88	145.38	27.82	7.86	44.40	225.42	0.51	24,675.00	5,375.00
North Cornwall	85.77	13.68	2.62	126.53	16.65	2.99	20.49	110.11	1.20	9,088.00	4,845.00
North Devon	87.93	5.00	1.48	108.79	15.45	8.88	14.54	91.85	5.10	10,021.00	3,076.00
North Dorset	83.41	1.74	2.78	64.30	3.12	2.04	0.95	456.73	6.74	5,606.00	4,521.00
North East Derbyshire	75.42	4.83	8.22	95.35	7.75	6.65	11.51	1,050.34	0.48	7,204.00	3,558.00
North Hertfordshire	75.64	7.11	1.37	43.04	6.32	4.71	8.94	758.29	1.90	5,854.67	5,113.33
North Kesteven	83.95	2.99	1.29	71.93	6.05	4.64	14.62	2,222.72	0.23	4,898.67	3,057.33
North Shropshire	83.54	5.19	4.67	147.73	16.83	4.86	14.63	198.26	0.31	11,526.00	3,988.00
North Somerset	88.06	1.73	1.48	35.28	4.45	4.39	7.06	2,061.03	1.05	4,728.00	3,664.00
North Tyneside	69.41	8.56	8.93	202.15	8.90	8.27	28.45	570.74	16.36	8,277.00	3,578.00
North Warwickshire	82.45	1.77	1.62	62.27	6.01	5.91	11.62	481.09	0.39	9,605.00	3,337.00
North West Leicestershire	81.02	7.35	2.64	179.70	22.92	9.25	22.12	406.48	7.28	7,043.00	3,618.00
North Wiltshire	83.25	2.00	2.22	108.42	6.01	3.25	9.40	248.25	0.07	11,137.33	5,096.00
Northampton	77.88	5.36	5.38	41.18	12.38	14.31	26.63	729.28	12.88	6,242.00	2,158.00
Norwich	57.89	6.47	2.89	141.63	32.06	18.62	10.01	426.61	11.47	7,464.00	3,018.00
Nottingham	62.10	16.23	35.70	177.81	16.72	6.14	0.22	153.31	43.19	7,350.00	7,093.00
Nuneaton and Bedworth	81.98	7.31	0.88	51.40	12.33	10.71	8.53	1,359.04	8.74	10,759.00	3,740.00
Oadby and Wigston	91.30	1.97	0.41	77.93	7.38	6.90	7.06	2,023.16	1.49	4,238.00	2,716.00
Oldham	73.07	14.40	60.37	174.03	13.21	4.83	14.20	729.64	21.10	17,403.00	4,517.00
Oswestry	81.08	7.78	14.35	78.30	9.11	4.58	0.00	62.44	2.23	-	2,155.00
Oxford	75.08	1.69	3.16	96.74	9.47	9.44	55.14	806.98	8.33	5,863.00	5,204.00
Pembrokeshire	83.43	11.10	4.15	478.92	47.78	21.03	49.16	857.08	11.35	21,335.40	5,543.21

Per 1,000 private dwellings

LA	% private dwellings 1997	Unfit 1998	Demolitions 1973–98	Grants 1978–94	Renovation grants 1990–96	DFGs 1990–96	MWAs 1990–96	LA renovation per 1,000 LA dwellings 1996/97	HA renovation per 1,000 private dwellings 1996/97	Average mandatory RG 1996/97	Average mandatory DFG 1996/97
Pendle	86.36	16.47	24.22	201.93	26.24	10.60	2.60	670.68	4.63	11,864.00	4,158.67
Penwith	87.44	8.67	5.78	108.50	14.84	7.81	19.42	232.16	0.36	5,828.00	1,604.00
Peterborough	74.35	20.68	2.68	150.57	14.02	4.29	23.82	94.61	5.50	14,488.00	11,096.00
Plymouth	75.21	5.86	1.58	100.75	7.93	4.88	28.21	1,082.99	13.93	13,983.00	6,076.00
Poole	88.30	4.82	1.43	57.46	7.01	3.45	4.20	1,611.42	0.52	7,304.00	6,963.00
Portsmouth	80.29	9.24	2.76	136.82	17.94	8.71	20.46	1,808.34	19.19	10,342.00	3,370.00
Powys	83.56	9.90	9.45	220.03	37.33	11.28	31.35	979.91	2.64	16,720.59	8,280.00
Preston	75.98	16.36	17.76	155.06	12.98	6.44	7.41	284.89	7.83	14,482.00	3,379.00
Purbeck	85.75	8.24	0.22	36.96	4.68	3.68	9.23	1,068.94	0.52	13,679.00	8,708.00
Reading	81.24	5.47	4.54	112.30	14.68	5.73	3.46	307.33	1.92	9,998.00	3,441.00
Redbridge	89.10	8.95	0.93	218.46	10.76	3.22	5.94	1,043.14	2.17	8,445.00	9,624.00
Redcar and Cleveland Langbaurgh	75.10	3.55	31.36	141.84	7.58	5.72	4.95	197.47	8.26	5,816.00	4,305.00
Redditch	70.20	6.89	6.25	43.96	10.36	5.41	13.45	1,232.35	0.05	7,985.33	4,378.67
Reigate and Banstead	86.07	6.94	0.34	44.75	3.71	2.04	4.51	698.52	0.62	3,861.00	4,503.00
Restormel	88.48	20.84	3.23	113.39	11.75	8.41	24.34	581.85	0.67	13,166.67	5,577.33
Rhondda Cynon Taff	81.60	11.90	13.26	507.25	79.94	13.62	52.36	546.73	0.75	10,720.29	4,379.12
Ribble Valley	90.72	6.33	0.93	109.49	4.91	4.36	25.64	1,979.66	1.39	16,727.00	5,313.00
Richmond upon Thames	86.58	5.17	0.30	83.29	9.59	5.33	5.32	1,053.65	11.48	5,318.00	5,935.00
Richmondshire	77.41	4.10	4.28	85.87	4.33	8.32	2.60	460.95	0.53	10,207.00	2,825.00
Rochdale	69.99	12.92	44.08	160.51	14.45	9.48	6.54	909.29	16.11	5,506.00	4,243.00
Rochford	90.56	7.71	1.68	37.32	2.90	3.45	5.40	520.25	0.00	5,568.00	4,066.00
Rossendale	79.42	29.48	33.99	207.82	13.91	8.85	25.51	591.82	19.95	10,545.00	3,432.00
Rother	89.57	8.25	0.49	59.23	24.56	3.50	3.63	2,329.72	3.44	7,104.00	11,102.00
Rotherham	68.84	11.81	37.83	187.95	12.41	45.05	13.81	290.46	8.31	5,492.00	2,222.00
Rugby	82.71	6.84	20.36	81.29	37.61	7.83	19.34	23.63	13.95	3,804.00	4,445.00
Runnymede	86.82	2.63	3.60	111.23	6.68	5.74	16.18	510.64	0.26	6,620.00	4,912.00
Rushcliffe	89.84	7.00	2.30	125.37	4.96	8.00	11.99	1,023.59	0.92	8,418.67	2,281.33
Rushmoor	76.64	2.76	6.88	87.45	2.85	10.89	5.39	1,292.67	2.06	7,199.00	6,539.00
Rutland	81.99	1.29	0.45	85.88	6.52	5.44	5.77	997.76	0.36	12,622.00	2,627.00

Authority											
Ryedale	87.27	10.74	1.44	67.98	11.30	12.65	17.16	232.53	20.07	15,299.00	5,409.00
South Cambridgeshire	83.49	3.54	1.23	27.83	3.17	6.16	4.19	352.87	7.03	7,429.00	2,914.00
South Northamptonshire	86.94	6.63	1.21	118.02	12.71	12.58	9.42	613.08	0.43	7,152.00	2,798.00
Salford	60.85	10.31	81.47	133.72	21.15	5.52	11.45	677.26	35.44	9,696.00	6,269.00
Salisbury	81.15	2.04	2.46	63.33	2.14	12.65	9.95	134.75	0.21	5,551.00	2,911.00
Sandwell	61.19	16.61	59.43	113.17	22.98	6.19	12.00	1,635.75	17.30	20,407.00	8,959.00
Scarborough	85.43	6.52	7.75	68.74	10.47	6.11	5.69	443.38	2.12	11,181.00	4,101.00
Sedgefield	66.63	4.29	6.55	97.61	6.42	5.16	12.38	440.65	9.74	5,278.00	5,133.00
Sedgemoor	85.46	4.89	3.11	81.69	1.86	9.30	6.19	407.97	0.40	14,649.00	3,985.00
Sefton	82.16	13.12	1.16	111.16	6.24	2.22	2.41	104.83	30.66	10,146.00	4,581.00
Selby	84.42	11.90	1.67	84.36	10.26	4.05	6.95	1,320.56	0.85	7,897.00	2,479.00
Sevenoaks	85.29	5.02	0.74	58.04	10.42	6.48	2.98	338.30	6.63	8,007.00	4,589.00
Sheffield	65.16	5.47	91.09	119.51	9.92	10.68	10.22	152.81	9.22	9,570.00	4,457.00
Shepway	86.60	0.81	2.83	89.57	7.28	3.03	10.34	2,100.18	5.35	5,668.00	3,022.00
Shrewsbury and Atcham	82.77	10.00	2.73	70.30	19.08	5.61	5.90	56.16	2.31	8,811.00	4,455.00
Slough	76.79	5.21	0.38	34.13	8.53	9.14	6.12	495.17	0.72	15,457.00	3,859.00
Solihull	81.72	0.22	0.67	31.13	8.50	7.19	3.24	4,585.75	0.50	2,434.00	3,468.00
South Bedfordshire	83.62	5.15	1.27	64.14	4.22	2.55	5.90	475.90	0.58	8,613.33	2,217.33
South Buckinghamshire	84.19	1.21	1.70	41.56	6.07	4.09	1.56	836.53	0.09	9,642.00	3,134.00
South Derbyshire	86.00	5.98	7.71	142.61	10.73	5.26	12.30	618.91	0.98	5,871.00	3,870.00
South Gloucestershire	88.40	2.77	2.04	104.09	6.55	5.46	9.20	1,201.66	0.82	7,872.00	3,132.00
South Hams	89.80	10.98	1.21	76.47	9.88	8.74	5.35	147.99	2.73	7,838.00	3,106.00
South Holland	84.23	7.04	6.00	77.91	5.39	3.16	10.57	244.92	1.20	11,373.00	4,478.00
South Kesteven	82.82	0.19	8.23	75.28	7.76	4.37	19.02	2,281.98	0.97	12,868.00	5,071.00
South Lakeland	89.53	5.89	2.07	60.87	3.95	2.15	3.90	338.50	1.29	58,662.67	4,698.67
South Norfolk	87.38	5.33	2.45	65.97	9.40	3.72	18.94	999.86	0.00	11,318.00	3,875.00
South Oxfordshire	84.57	3.58	0.92	56.17	6.24	4.61	7.18	106.35	6.01	26,434.00	13,620.00
South Ribble	87.96	4.96	1.59	109.50	4.82	9.20	28.38	705.58	1.14	17,480.00	4,669.33
South Shropshire	88.75	5.48	5.72	89.99	7.80	5.18	34.70	326.81	5.24	16,764.00	6,065.00
South Somerset	82.47	5.50	1.48	48.60	6.06	14.72	6.51	976.02	0.42	12,488.00	2,769.00
South Staffordshire	84.36	9.08	5.12	26.01	3.30	2.11	16.00	791.34	0.71	6,279.00	5,305.00
South Tyneside	58.27	4.25	50.32	126.72	10.45	6.31	21.76	641.62	31.43	13,985.00	3,968.00
Southampton	74.23	9.98	10.87	121.24	20.39	5.82	22.39	278.22	12.88	8,469.33	6,672.00
Southend-on-Sea	87.16	14.75	0.46	129.48	10.09	5.46	3.09	331.35	9.89	5,409.00	3,778.00
Southwark	41.46	7.32	44.14	120.59	9.63	2.47	1.15	54.20	24.60	17,446.67	8,161.33
Spelthorne	86.26	–	0.82	77.46	5.32	12.21	8.17	120.15	10.81	3,819.00	4,360.00

Per 1,000 private dwellings

LA	% private dwellings 1997	Unfit 1998	Demolitions 1973-98	Grants 1978-94	Renovation grants 1990-96	DFGs 1990-96	MWAs 1990-96	LA renovation per 1,000 LA dwellings 1996/97	HA renovation per 1,000 private dwellings 1996/97	Average mandatory RG 1996/97	Average mandatory DFG 1996/97
St Albans	84.63	8.29	0.56	52.17	8.69	3.52	11.42	1,980.50	0.45	8,581.00	4,141.00
St Edmundsbury	77.34	2.65	4.38	98.38	6.53	8.43	9.74	235.85	1.64	7,856.00	2,071.00
St Helens	72.39	22.12	56.58	142.49	19.19	7.67	36.95	833.57	35.92	14,824.00	5,818.00
Staff Moorlands	89.44	3.76	4.63	77.07	5.54	5.81	1.41	66.89	3.15	11,696.00	5,776.00
Stafford	80.98	–	3.23	45.31	8.46	7.93	1.44	2,714.64	1.43	12,505.33	7,744.00
Stevenage	63.99	0.66	0.00	25.66	2.53	5.29	4.89	737.00	5.84	2,222.00	3,327.00
Stockport	83.70	5.33	9.84	88.98	10.66	6.27	9.47	746.71	8.08	11,351.00	3,848.00
Stockton-on-Tees	75.36	5.35	5.96	93.78	24.28	23.45	7.39	573.54	10.30	4,125.00	2,703.00
Stoke-on-Trent	72.60	21.99	41.32	141.41	22.05	13.40	5.89	315.30	14.89	12,174.00	4,187.00
Stratford on Avon	85.01	3.16	10.59	54.60	2.19	1.94	6.62	1,760.52	0.12	2,717.00	2,474.00
Stroud	83.57	5.83	9.56	125.03	17.28	7.10	32.02	720.65	1.40	12,372.00	4,608.00
Suffolk Coastal	84.68	2.75	2.14	132.42	7.47	5.33	8.25	479.50	3.54	6,297.00	4,067.00
Sunderland	62.19	2.91	3.62	63.50	8.99	6.37	10.98	1,892.30	9.11	10,718.00	3,009.00
Surrey Heath	88.79	0.67	1.69	39.93	4.74	3.20	3.94	847.54	0.04	10,292.00	5,583.00
Sutton	82.41	2.02	0.57	71.25	8.05	3.18	15.53	387.48	23.00	4,531.00	5,707.00
Swale	84.32	18.48	3.35	199.99	33.15	15.13	50.94	325.46	0.25	7,248.00	4,766.00
Swansea	76.96	7.40	9.07	287.64	40.72	35.12	8.72	621.40	3.27	15,515.79	6,934.43
Tameside	72.39	15.94	36.85	98.58	11.06	4.69	9.24	466.67	5.24	8,636.00	6,047.00
Tamworth	74.76	4.64	4.27	163.31	10.40	4.51	8.17	238.41	20.49	19,382.67	4,845.33
Tandridge	87.94	0.08	0.18	46.87	3.28	7.60	9.67	88.03	0.57	4,123.00	2,727.00
Taunton Deane	80.03	5.91	2.92	90.05	0.66	2.96	0.00	1,180.93	0.00	3,587.00	6,673.00
Teesdale	84.84	1.36	7.87	85.67	17.46	9.05	11.16	1,324.36	2.26	8,896.00	3,288.00
Teignbridge	90.28	7.39	2.40	154.41	4.08	3.76	9.88	1,671.75	10.13	10,616.00	2,837.00
Telford and Wrekin	73.33	4.82	6.08	66.77	5.67	12.93	10.49	183.69	1.91	19,632.00	3,894.67
Tendring	91.27	3.43	2.39	67.87	11.83	9.48	11.58	311.96	0.31	8,989.00	3,622.00
Test Valley	82.66	2.48	2.77	76.34	13.80	6.61	0.00	945.88	0.59	5,961.00	3,344.00
Tewkesbury	84.90	7.40	3.35	70.44	8.76	3.62	8.27	1,251.52	3.47	10,118.00	3,993.00
Thamesdown (Swindon)	80.20	4.97	3.29	100.58	11.73	13.53	5.06	103.47	7.56	8,997.00	2,929.00
Thanet	86.49	3.49	1.32	90.00	7.58	2.43	10.60	1,786.14	1.11	14,396.00	7,643.00
The Medway Towns	92.77	16.60	1.96	203.37	12.23	7.24	13.54	754.24	2.72	7,998.00	7,159.00

The Vale of Glamorgan	85.51	7.30	1.49	179.19	38.61	27.33	1,169.52	16.62	1.90	11,775.00	4,573.53
Three Rivers	82.15	6.74	0.44	39.39	7.74	5.35	456.21	11.94	1.87	8,098.00	3,230.00
Thurrock	76.97	3.72	0.43	54.01	3.45	5.92	494.91	1.89	0.87	3,590.00	3,117.00
Tonbridge and Malling	81.79	8.87	2.58	81.45	8.16	11.12	780.04	12.77	0.75	8,712.00	4,495.00
Torbay	91.88	6.83	1.06	126.28	15.08	10.11	241.41	0.02	1.74	6,268.00	3,249.00
Torfaen	67.10	11.00	13.04	211.61	27.45	23.40	469.66	45.00	3.48	20,098.04	6,746.84
Torridge	89.26	7.50	0.35	151.86	11.50	5.21	97.92	21.42	3.26	9,136.00	4,168.00
Tower Hamlets	38.50	5.55	29.00	49.05	3.69	2.12	684.77	1.71	65.26	38,772.00	11,170.00
Trafford	80.72	4.01	11.06	66.90	21.43	9.12	151.55	5.68	7.25	4,241.00	4,052.00
Tunbridge Wells	83.53	5.76	1.05	84.63	20.50	3.05	238.65	4.34	1.30	8,159.00	4,148.00
Tynedale	82.62	5.64	1.06	104.35	4.48	3.41	77.62	4.40	0.73	11,824.00	5,917.00
Uttlesford	85.10	1.63	0.49	51.81	2.97	1.87	104.32	1.74	0.00	6,973.00	5,229.00
Vale of the White Horse	85.30	7.34	3.00	34.67	8.81	10.44	327.39	17.25	0.70	12,575.00	4,535.00
Vale Royal	81.60	2.49	4.23	87.60	4.88	3.07	268.95	2.04	0.05	7,914.00	4,524.00
Wakefield	67.59	10.20	14.12	114.35	18.79	7.16	446.35	5.94	3.73	9,412.00	6,962.67
Walsall	66.60	17.71	6.84	151.71	5.81	3.14	1,962.63	11.84	15.73	11,617.00	7,142.00
Waltham Forest	75.92	11.18	6.36	53.06	4.38	1.22	199.52	5.49	11.05	24,530.67	6,166.67
Wandsworth	74.80	2.21	1.59	228.18	16.28	2.18	1,745.38	7.74	46.71	9,805.00	6,105.00
Wansbeck	70.16	12.77	8.78	184.22	49.91	8.53	1,054.98	3.23	11.62	5,993.00	3,172.00
Warrington	79.07	8.02	9.73	91.09	12.48	5.70	389.33	22.71	3.83	9,063.00	5,314.00
Warwick	82.97	2.88	3.27	6.45	3.76	4.28	663.80	15.37	8.17	5,330.00	4,276.00
Watford	82.08	7.25	0.73	100.79	10.60	2.66	1,171.34	4.62	1.33	6,381.00	5,489.00
Waveney	84.56	2.78	9.95	254.27	20.43	27.37	459.49	3.98	4.82	3,984.00	3,126.00
Waverley	85.44	2.99	0.41	69.09	2.98	2.05	174.79	1.96	1.13	6,792.00	2,549.00
Wealden	91.85	2.52	0.66	67.39	16.04	3.37	734.50	34.67	0.37	9,603.00	7,625.00
Wear Valley	72.35	1.22	14.95	229.91	15.49	6.09	822.23	18.81	11.19	7,341.00	2,872.00
Wellingborough	77.75	3.87	8.53	123.15	14.98	11.66	780.12	5.24	2.31	4,023.00	2,163.00
Welwyn Hatfield	67.48	1.08	0.72	25.03	1.06	3.52	1,917.27	0.55	0.00	11,899.00	4,010.00
West Devon	90.41	9.49	1.39	133.00	3.99	2.46	62.37	7.93	1.35	6,129.00	–
West Dorset	86.88	9.60	2.88	85.81	12.46	8.02	230.37	21.51	4.54	6,406.00	2,693.00
West Lancashire	78.00	8.05	3.38	91.88	10.12	8.18	890.21	19.32	1.94	14,857.33	3,410.67
West Lindsey	84.56	6.84	2.18	141.69	10.46	4.84	593.67	35.10	1.43	6,435.00	2,489.00
West Oxfordshire	83.20	1.52	1.95	58.46	4.67	25.66	692.38	2.54	2.68	5,596.00	2,516.00
West Somerset	85.60	–	4.41	140.07	11.34	14.54	339.58	4.19	15.09	7,290.00	2,194.00
West Wiltshire	85.29	2.50	3.00	82.08	9.79	6.29	52.13	5.22	2.46	8,337.00	3,915.00
Westminster	74.98	9.25	8.25	83.04	2.27	1.06	438.28	8.70	65.98	7,429.00	5,851.00

Per 1,000 private dwellings

LA	% private dwellings 1997	Unfit 1998	Demolitions 1973-98	Grants 1978-94	Renovation grants 1990-96	DFGs 1990-96	MWAs 1990-96	LA renovation per 1,000 LA dwellings 1996/97	HA renovation per 1,000 private dwellings 1996/97	Average mandatory RG 1996/97	Average mandatory DFG 1996/97
Weymouth and Portland	84.29	1.60	1.28	126.08	10.86	6.86	11.11	536.60	10.01	5,447.00	2,045.00
Wigan	75.78	6.83	34.74	98.83	16.27	4.76	11.32	652.32	7.54	6,587.00	4,867.00
Winchester	79.94	2.13	2.61	95.44	6.57	3.80	18.34	220.15	52.48	16,889.33	4,048.00
Windsor and Maidenhead	84.88	3.53	0.35	63.86	4.73	4.29	5.77	334.82	9.50	6,722.00	6,453.00
Wirral	81.55	18.77	21.98	130.01	18.12	7.91	7.70	329.77	25.17	12,594.00	4,781.00
Woking	85.73	3.82	3.25	53.67	2.99	5.04	3.88	3,166.25	28.41	4,939.00	2,656.00
Wokingham	90.98	2.45	0.35	28.20	1.56	4.77	4.02	387.19	1.20	6,849.00	4,958.00
Wolverhampton	63.80	11.30	26.78	106.38	17.29	6.25	22.54	3,781.92	13.77	7,581.00	5,008.00
Worcester	81.71	2.70	2.66	105.75	6.90	3.65	21.13	538.91	5.28	9,184.00	4,906.00
Worthing	90.75	2.89	0.32	57.65	8.68	4.49	20.96	1,183.56	3.91	7,259.00	6,049.00
Wrexham	69.70	7.30	9.82	104.07	22.37	13.66	18.54	623.45	1.05	25,551.72	4,208.05
Wychavon	83.48	4.73	1.98	110.37	8.48	15.88	36.48	769.31	1.00	12,377.33	3,010.67
Wycombe	85.02	3.00	2.17	62.64	3.94	2.09	13.38	541.54	1.72	6,399.00	4,618.00
Wyre	92.44	6.41	1.97	30.64	11.74	11.72	7.21	444.16	2.39	7,936.00	3,397.00
Wyre Forest	81.74	6.41	10.14	86.95	6.48	5.73	20.96	1,448.96	1.48	14,949.00	5,633.00
York	82.03	6.14	0.87	134.81	5.22	2.30	15.49	1,294.13	5.29	13,623.00	6,235.00